Lecture Notes in Computer Science 16362

Founding Editors

Gerhard Goos
Juris Hartmanis

Editorial Board Members

Elisa Bertino, *Purdue University, West Lafayette, IN, USA*
Wen Gao, *Peking University, Beijing, China*
Bernhard Steffen, *TU Dortmund University, Dortmund, Germany*
Moti Yung, *Columbia University, New York, NY, USA*

The series Lecture Notes in Computer Science (LNCS), including its subseries Lecture Notes in Artificial Intelligence (LNAI) and Lecture Notes in Bioinformatics (LNBI), has established itself as a medium for the publication of new developments in computer science and information technology research, teaching, and education.

LNCS enjoys close cooperation with the computer science R & D community, the series counts many renowned academics among its volume editors and paper authors, and collaborates with prestigious societies. Its mission is to serve this international community by providing an invaluable service, mainly focused on the publication of conference and workshop proceedings and postproceedings. LNCS commenced publication in 1973.

Editors
Giuseppe Scanniello
University of Salerno
Fisciano, Italy

Simone Romano
University of Salerno
Fisciano, Italy

Rita Francese
University of Salerno
Fisciano, Italy

Valentina Lenarduzzi
University of Oulu
Oulu, Finland

Sira Vegas
Universidad Politécnica de Madrid
Madrid, Spain

ISSN 0302-9743   ISSN 1611-3349 (electronic)
Lecture Notes in Computer Science
ISBN 978-3-032-12091-5   ISBN 978-3-032-12092-2 (eBook)
https://doi.org/10.1007/978-3-032-12092-2

This Springer imprint is published by the registered company Springer Nature Switzerland AG
The registered company address is: Gewerbestrasse 11, 6330 Cham, Switzerland

If disposing of this product, please recycle the paper.

Giuseppe Scanniello · Valentina Lenarduzzi ·
Simone Romano · Sira Vegas · Rita Francese
Editors

Product-Focused Software Process Improvement

Industry, Doctoral-Symposium, Tutorial, and Workshop Papers

26th International Conference, PROFES 2025
Salerno, Italy, December 1–3, 2025
Proceedings

 Springer

Preface

On behalf of the PROFES Organizing Committee, we are delighted to present the proceedings of the 26th International Conference on Product-Focused Software Process Improvement (PROFES 2025). The conference took place during December, 1–3, 2025, in Salerno (Italy). Consistent with its long-standing tradition, PROFES 2025 centered on professional Software Process Improvement (SPI) motivated by product, process, and service quality needs. The technical program was curated by a committee of distinguished experts in software process improvement, software process modeling, and empirical software engineering.

This year, the conference received a total of 101 submissions, comprising 62 full research papers, 20 industry papers, and 19 short research papers. Following a rigorous evaluation process, 23 full research papers, nine industry papers (two of them initially submitted as full research papers), and 20 short research papers (seven of them initially submitted as full research papers) were accepted for inclusion in the program. Each submission underwent a single-blind review process conducted by at least three members of the PROFES 2025 Program Committee.

Alongside the main technical program, PROFES 2025 hosted a doctoral symposium, a tutorial, and three workshops. One paper was accepted for the doctoral symposium. The tutorial focused on quantum software engineering. The 1st International Workshop on Analytics for Software Product and Process Improvement (A-SPPI 20205) aimed to explore how software analytics can provide actionable insights for improving the quality of software products and processes. Six papers were selected for A-SPPI 2025. The 1st International Workshop on Promoting and Dealing with Advanced Technology in Healthcare (PATH 2025) aimed to explore the application of advanced technologies, such as artificial intelligence, in the healthcare sector, focusing on their potential to address key challenges related to clinical outcomes, while preserving data security, patient privacy, and system reliability. Eight papers were selected for PATH 2025. The 1st International Workshop on Quality Evaluation of ML-based Software Systems (QUEMALES 2025) aimed to bring together software-quality experts and practitioners to share experiences, new ideas, and solutions to face the challenges related to ML-based software quality evaluation. Five papers were selected for QUEMALES 2025.

We express our sincere gratitude for the privilege of serving as chairs for PROFES 2025. We extend our appreciation to the members of the Program Committee and additional reviewers for their rigorous and invaluable efforts in the evaluation of submitted papers. We are likewise indebted to all authors, presenters, keynote speakers, and session chairs for their contributions, which were essential to the success of PROFES 2025.

Finally, we acknowledge the guidance and support provided by the PROFES Steering Committee throughout the organizational process.

December 2025

Giuseppe Scanniello
Valentina Lenarduzzi
Simone Romano
Sira Vegas
Rita Francese

Organization

General Chairs

Giuseppe Scanniello	University of Salerno, Italy
Valentina Lenarduzzi	University of Oulu, Finland

Program Chairs

Simone Romano	University of Salerno, Italy
Sira Vegas	Universidad Politécnica de Madrid, Spain

Short-Paper Track Chairs

Marcela Fabiana Genero Bocco	University of Castilla-La Mancha, Spain
Miroslaw Staron	Chalmers University of Technology and University of Gothenburg, Sweden

Industry-Paper Track Chairs

Javier Gonzalez Huerta	Blekinge Institute of Technology, Sweden
Daniela Soares Cruzes	Norwegian University of Science and Technology, and Visma, Norway

Doctoral Symposium Chairs

Andreas Jedlitschka	Fraunhofer IESE, Germany
Emilia Mendes	Aarhus University, Denmark

Workshop and Tutorial Chair

Marco Torchiano	Politecnico di Torino, Italy

Publication Chair

Rita Francese   University of Salerno, Italy

Social Media Chair

Pietro Cassieri   University of Salerno, Italy

Web Chair

Sabato Nocera   University of Salerno, Italy

Local Organization Chair

Olimpia Perisano   Palazzo Innovazione, Italy

Program Committee - Full Research Papers

Sousuke Amasaki   Nanzan University, Japan
Hina Anwar   University of Tartu, Estonia
Beatriz Bernárdez   University of Seville, Spain
Stefan Biffl   Vienna University of Technology, Austria
Matteo Camilli   Politecnico di Milano, Italy
Panagiota Chatzipetrou   Örebro University, Sweden
Nelly Condori-Fernández   Universidad Santiago de Compostela, Spain
Anna Corazza   University of Naples "Federico II", Italy
Oscar Dieste   Universidad Politécnica de Madrid, Spain
Michal Dolezel   Prague University of Economics and Business,
                                  Czechia
Fabian Fagerholm   Aalto University, Finland
Anna Rita Fasolino   University of Naples "Federico II", Italy
Michael Felderer   German Aerospace Center (DLR) and University
                                  of Cologne, Germany
Julian Frattini   Chalmers University of Technology and
                                  University of Gothenburg, Sweden
Javier Gonzalez Huerta   Blekinge Institute of Technology, Sweden
Carmine Gravino   University of Salerno, Italy
Helena Holmström Olsson   Malmö University, Sweden

Emilio Insfran	Universitat Politècnica de València, Spain
Andrea Janes	Free University of Bozen-Bolzano, Italy
Slinger Jansen	Utrecht University, The Netherlands
Eriks Klotins	Blekinge Institute of Technology, Sweden
Jil Klünder	University of Applied Sciences and FHDW Hannover, Germany
Marco Kuhrmann	Reutlingen University, Germany
Patricia Lago	Vrije Universiteit Amsterdam, The Netherlands
Jingyue Li	Norwegian University of Science and Technology, Norway
Xiaozhou Li	Free University of Bozen-Bolzano, Italy
Alessandro Marchetto	University of Trento, Italy
Antonio Martini	University of Oslo, Norway
Shinsuke Matsumoto	Osaka University, Japan
Daniel Mendez	Blekinge Institute of Technology and fortiss, Sweden
Manoel Mendonça	Federal University of Bahia, Brazil
Tommi Mikkonen	University of Jyväskylä, Finland
Sandro Morasca	Università degli Studi dell'Insubria, Italy
Maurizio Morisio	Politecnico di Torino, Italy
Jürgen Münch	Reutlingen University, Germany
Marc Oriol Hilari	Universitat Politècnica de Catalunya, Spain
Dietmar Pfahl	University of Tartu, Estonia
Rudolf Ramler	Software Competence Center Hagenberg GmbH, Austria
Filippo Ricca	Università di Genova, Italy
Daniel Rodríguez	University of Alcalá, Spain
Pilar Rodríguez	Universidad Politécnica de Madrid, Spain
Iflaah Salman	Lappeenranta-Lahti University of Technology, Finland
Stefan Sauer	University of Paderborn, Germany
Kari Smolander	Lappeenranta-Lahti University of Technology, Finland
Martin Solari	Universidad ORT Uruguay, Uruguay
Kari Systä	Tampere University, Finland
Paolo Tell	IT University of Copenhagen, Denmark

Program Committee - Short Research Papers

Srijita Basu	Chalmers University of Technology and University of Gothenburg, Sweden

Luigi Buglione	DXC Technology, Italy
Priscila Cedillo	Universidad de Cuenca, Ecuador
Panagiota Chatzipetrou	Örebro University, Sweden
Maya Daneva	University of Twente, The Netherlands
Jakob Droste	Leibniz Universität Hannover, Germany
Jens Heidrich	Fraunhofer IESE, Germany
Emanuel Agustin Irrazábal	Universidad Nacional del Nordeste, Argentina
Sushant Kumar Pandey	University of Groningen, The Netherlands
Sandeep Kumar	Indian Institute of Technology, Roorkee, India
Emilia Mendes	Aarhus University, Denmark
Thamizhiniyan Natarajan	University of Limerick, Ireland
Nicolas Paez	Universidad Nacional de Tres de Febrero, Argentina
Francis Palma	University of New Brunswick, Canada
Dietmar Pfahl	University of Tartu, Estonia
Sheila Reinehr	Pontifícia Universidade Católica do Paraná, Brazil
Daniel Rodríguez	University of Alcalá, Spain
Gleison Santos	Universidade Federal do Estado do Rio de Janeiro, Brazil
Faiz Ali Shah	University of Tartu, Estonia
Damiano Torre	University of Washington Tacoma, USA
Ehsan Zabardast	Nordea and Blekinge Institute of Technology, Sweden

Program Committee - Industry Papers

Thomas Bach	SAP, Germany
Ricardo Britto	Ericsson and Blekinge Institute of Technology, Sweden
Lukas Fischer	Software Competence Center Hagenberg GmbH, Austria
Stephan Flake	S&N CQM Consulting & Services GmbH, Germany
Helena Holmström Olsson	Malmö University, Sweden
Eriks Klotins	Blekinge Institute of Technology, Sweden
Lukas Linsbauer	ABB Corporate Research, Germany
Stefan Marksteiner	AVL List GmbH and Mälardalen University, Austria
Fredrik Milani	University of Tartu, Estonia
Torvald Mårtensson	Saab AB, Sweden
Antonio Piccinno	University of Bari, Italy

Rudolf Ramler	Software Competence Center Hagenberg GmbH, Austria
Daniel Rodríguez	University of Alcalá, Spain
Dag Sjøberg	University of Oslo, Norway
Anders Sundelin	Ericsson Mobile Financial Services AB and Blekinge Institute of Technology, Sweden
Sahar Tahvili	Einride AB, Sweden
Jan Van den Bergh	Hasselt University and tUL and iMinds, Belgium
Andreas Wübbeke	South Westphalia University of Applied Sciences, Germany
Ehsan Zabardast	Nordea and Blekinge Institute of Technology, Sweden

Additional Reviewers

Maria Fernanda Granda	Universidad de Cuenca, Ecuador
Marius Irgens	University of Oslo, Norway
Karthik Shivashankar	University of Oslo, Norway

Contents

Doctoral Symposium Papers

Tutorial Papers

**1st International Workshop on Analytics for Software Product and
Process Improvement (A-SPPI 2025)**

1st International Workshop on Promoting and Dealing with Advanced Technology in Healthcare (PATH 2025)

**1st International Workshop on Quality Evaluation of ML-based
Software Systems (QUEMALES 2025)**

Industry Papers

Obtaining Test Data in the Estonian E-Government System: Challenges and Improvement Potential

Maj-Annika Tammisto[1]([envelope]) [iD], Rudolf Ramler[2] [iD], Faiz Ali Shah[1] [iD], and Dietmar Pfahl[1] [iD]

[1] University of Tartu, Narva mnt 18, 51009 Tartu, Estonia
{maj-annika.tammisto,faiz.ali.shah,dietmar.pfahl}@ut.ee
[2] Software Competence Center Hagenberg (SCCH) GmbH, Hagenberg, Austria
Rudolf.Ramler@scch.at

Abstract. The Estonian e-government system comprises close to 2000 interfaced information systems that exchange data on the X-tee interoperability layer. To test an information system that uses data received via X-tee as input, test data that resembles real-life data must be obtained. The goal of this study is to identify and describe the existing process of obtaining test data, the supporting factors and challenges that the users of the existing process face, and the impact of the identified challenges on testing. We pose three research questions and answer them with the help of expert knowledge gathered through introspection and an interview study. We found that (i) the current process for obtaining test data is manual and follows varying practices, (ii) the current process relies on humans who can be contacted to acquire test data, it has a range of challenges and the sole supporting factor in the current process is the expert knowledge of humans who create test data, and (iii) the long time and large effort required in the current process to gain even small sets of test data is the challenge that has the most negative effect on testing. We conclude that the current process needs improvement and suggest, in the first stage, the automation of identifying the scope of test data that can be obtained, in second stage, the automatic generation of synthetic test data on demand, and in the final stage, a Synthetic Data Digital Twin as an option to improve the current situation.

Keywords: Test data provisioning · Web service testing · E-government

1 Introduction and Motivation

Web services have been widely used for exchanging data between systems and applications since the early 2000s [1]. In addition to industrial organizations, the two most popular interaction styles, Simple Object Access Protocol (SOAP) and Representational State Transfer Protocol (REST) [2], have also been implemented for data exchange in e-government settings. In Estonia, X-Road technology is used for e-government to enable secure data exchange [18]. The Estonian

© The Author(s), under exclusive license to Springer Nature Switzerland AG 2026
G. Scanniello et al. (Eds.): PROFES 2025, LNCS 16362, pp. 3–18, 2026.
https://doi.org/10.1007/978-3-032-12092-2_1

implementation of the X-Road technology is called X-tee [3]. The implementation of one web service on the X-tee data exchange layer is a data service. Based on the X-tee fact sheet [10], the X-tee has almost 2000 interfaced information systems, more than 3500 data services, and approximately 52,000 organizations and institutions that indirectly benefit from the data services provided.

Organizations and institutions use Estonian e-government data received via data services as input to their business processes running in their systems. Whether it is their service provisioning, reporting, or another process that requires e-government data input from data services, the full functionality of the service may not work properly if the input data is missing, incomplete, or inconsistent. For example, if a bank requires the official income and tax liability data of its client from a data service provided by the tax authority to automatically evaluate the client's credit request and make an automatic decision, the automatic service process of the bank will not work if the data service fails to provide the required income and tax liability data. In such cases, one workaround would be to ask the client to provide the required data instead and do the credit request evaluation manually.

Now, consider a situation where the same automatic evaluation and decision process of a bank is still in the development phase and needs to be tested in a pre-production environment. Like in production, it needs the clients' income and tax liability data as input from a data service. Considering the sensitivity of such data and the General Data Protection Regulation (GDPR) [5], the usage of real-life raw data is not allowed for testing. Therefore, the data service must send synthetic test data instead. However, the synthetic test data must be as similar as possible to real-life data at least in terms of the data attributes that are directly used in the bank's automatic evaluation and decision process (e.g., realistic income ranges) and diverse (e.g., a variety of different age ranges) to ensure that it is possible to execute as many test cases as possible. The workaround of manually processing the credit request evaluation does not exist in this situation because it would mean that the functionality would not be tested.

Taking into account the large scale of the Estonian e-government ecosystem, there is a need for large amounts of test data to test changes made in already interfaced information systems, and the functionalities of the information systems that join X-tee. Obtaining test data can be challenging and may take more effort and resources than organizations and institutions are willing to invest.

The objective of this study is to identify and describe the existing process of obtaining test data for testing software systems and applications that use data services of the Estonian e-government system, the supporting factors and challenges that the users of the existing process face, and the effect of the identified challenges on testing.

The rest of this paper is structured as follows. Section 2 summarizes the specific background of our study. Section 3 provides our research questions and explains the methodology used in this study. The results of this study are presented in Sects. 4, 5, and 6. Section 7 includes the discussion of the results, limitations, and related work. The conclusion and possible future research directions are provided in Sect. 8.

2   Background

In the following, we describe the participants of the X-tee data exchange layer and an example of a software system to be tested with X-tee data services.

Participants of X-Tee. The X-tee data exchange layer is the backbone technology for the decentralized Estonian e-government system, where data is created and maintained in a distributed setting by several different government institutions. These government institutions (e.g., ministries and government boards) and authorized entities (e.g., telecoms and banks), are entitled to exchange data on X-tee and are called X-tee members. The information system of an X-tee member can have several parts that may function independently. For example, the X-tee member *Estonian Tax and Customs Board* owns the employment register TÖR that holds employment data as well as the sales tax register KMD, where the data are maintained to calculate the government sales tax. X-tee members must declare the different parts of their information systems as subsystems to use or provide X-tee services [6]. Every subsystem can provide and/or use several data services. For example, the subsystem *Estonian Tax and Customs Board - employment register* provides the data services *TOOTREG* and *TORIK* [8]. The information systems of Estonian government institutions, together with their subsystems, are listed in the database of the *Estonian Administration System for the State Information System (RIHA)* [7]. The *Estonian Information System Authority (RIA)* offers a public catalog that lists all subsystems of all X-tee members from all sectors with methods and data service descriptions [8].

Testing with X-Tee Data Services. Subsystems usually maintain one or several pre-production environments that contain a set of synthetic (i.e., different from real-life) test data to test their own features. At least one pre-production environment of a subsystem is likely configured to exchange test data in the X-tee pre-production layers ee-test and/or ee-dev for testing purposes. The X-tee pre-production layers allow a system under test (SUT), which is a new subsystem that is developed or an existing subsystem that is updated, to query test data from other external subsystems. No general Service Level Agreement (SLA) is in place to regulate the availability and quality of test data in the pre-production environments of subsystems. There is also no pre-production environment of every subsystem that is dedicated to test data exchange on X-tee and where the compatibility of test data with the test data of other subsystems is ensured.

Figure 1 illustrates a simplified example case of a credit request where the SUT requires data from three different subsystems. As shown in Fig. 1, the system will check three conditions related to a specific person who is the subject of the check. Each of these conditions may be true or false. When all three conditions are true, the system makes a positive decision and approves the credit request. When at least one of the three conditions is false, the system makes a negative decision and declines the request. Figure 1 shows the positive scenario where the evaluation of the data received from three different external subsystems allows the credit request to be approved. To cover all possible combinations of condition values in testing and to verify that the system will make a correct decision for every combination of condition values, the tester needs to run eight test cases. Therefore, the tester needs to obtain eight sets of test data for eight different test persons, where each set covers a unique combination of conditions in the pre-production environments of the three external subsystems. Note that this simplified example is very trivial, as the number of combinations to be covered and the complexity of the test data required is, in most cases, significantly more complex in real life.

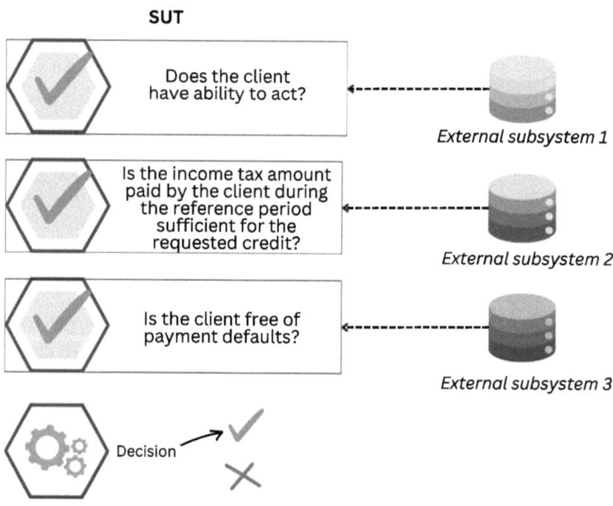

Fig. 1. Example case for testing with X-tee data services

3   Research Questions and Method

The objective of this study translates into the following research questions (RQs):

- RQ1: What is the current process of obtaining test data for an SUT that uses data services providing Estonian government data?
- RQ2: What supporting factors and challenges exist in the current process of obtaining test data?

– RQ3: What effects do the identified challenges have on the testing of the SUT?

When answering our RQs we distinguish two main cases. Case type A refers to situations where the SUT interacts and requests test data from only one external subsystem. Case type B refers to situations where the SUT interacts and requests test data from several external subsystems. In our context, it is not relevant if the SUT uses one or several data services provided by the same subsystem because the description of test data required from different data services of the same subsystem can be combined and obtained with one request of test data.

To answer the RQs, we develop an initial model of the typical process of obtaining test data for an SUT using data services. This initial model is based on the experience of the first author, who has been working as a quality engineer of subsystems that use and/or provide X-tee data services for several years. Then, we conduct a semi-structured interview study to validate and possibly enhance the initial model based on the experience of other specialists with a similar profile to the first author. The interview study follows the guidelines of the Empirical Standards for Software Engineering Research [9].

We select participants for the interview study based on the following criteria:

– The interviewee has practical experience in obtaining test data from one (Case type A) or several (Case type B) external subsystems.
– The interviewee is willing and able to share the experience and details about the process of obtaining test data.

Each semi-structured interview session consists of the following four parts:

– Part 0 (Purpose, Consent, Confidentiality): At the start, the interviewee is informed that the purpose of the interview is to collect information that will help answer RQs 1, 2, and 3. Moreover, the interviewees are asked to give consent for recording the session, informed that the recording will be kept confidential with the authors of this paper, that the interviewees are allowed to check and, if needed, correct the written interview report and that the recording is deleted after the written interview report is confirmed by the interviewee.
– Part 1: The first group of questions focuses on collecting information about the interviewee's profile, i.e., current position, previous positions (if any), and work experience in software testing and quality assurance.
– Part 2: The second group of questions focuses on collecting information about a typical case (of type A or type B) that the interviewee recalls. The interviewee is then asked about the field of the software development project, the data services involved, and the exact process followed to obtain test data. The answers to Part 2 questions will be used to answer RQ1.
– Part 3: The third group of questions identifies factors that either support or challenge the fast and easy acquisition of test data. In case challenges are mentioned, mitigation strategies for overcoming the challenges are collected. These answers address RQ2 and RQ3.

Up to one hour is planned for the duration of every interview session. After each interview, a written report is sent to every interviewee with the request to confirm it or make corrections, if necessary. Only data reviewed and approved by the interviewees is presented as the results of this study.

4   Data Collected in the Interview Study

In the following, we summarize how data was collected from the interviewees of our study. We approached eight specialists in our network with the request to assess their compliance with our interviewee selection criteria. Five of the eight specialists we approached were invited to the interview. All invited specialists agreed to participate. The interview duration was between 45 and 58 min. After each interview, we filtered and summarized the received information that was relevant to our study. The written reports were presented to the interviewees for correction (if needed) and approval. The full dataset created in this study is available in figshare[1].

5   Current State-of-Practice of Test Data Provisioning (RQ1)

Below, we present the initial model developed to describe the typical process of obtaining test data, as well as the variations of this model that were identified.

Three of the cases of this study are of Case type A, and two of Case type B. The domains covered in the study are social services, e-government services for employers, education, cross-border data exchange, and digital health services.

The model is shown in Fig. 2, and it includes both main case types, Case type A and Case type B, that are distinguished in our study.

The definitions of key terms used in the model are:

- SUT: the system under test.
- SUT representative: represents all persons and roles who are involved in the process of obtaining test data on the side of the SUT. It may be only one person (e.g. the software tester) or several people (e.g. software tester, test manager, team manager, etc.).
- External subsystem: the system or application that is not the SUT and that provides one or several data services that the SUT uses.
- External subsystem representative: represents all persons and roles who are involved in the process of obtaining test data on the side of the external subsystem. It may be only one person (e.g. the dedicated contact person for test data requests) or several people (e.g. dedicated contact person for test data requests, service desk specialist, etc.).

---

[1] **Data availability:** https://figshare.com/s/2c5cb4fe41ba685c95da.

5.1   Case Type A

The purpose of Case type A is to describe the situation where test data from precisely one subsystem are required for the SUT. In the following, we explain the pre-conditions, steps, and post-process activities that are typically followed.

Pre-conditions

- SUT needs test data 1 (TD1) from the external subsystem 1.
- SUT representative acquires the contacts of the external subsystem 1 representative.

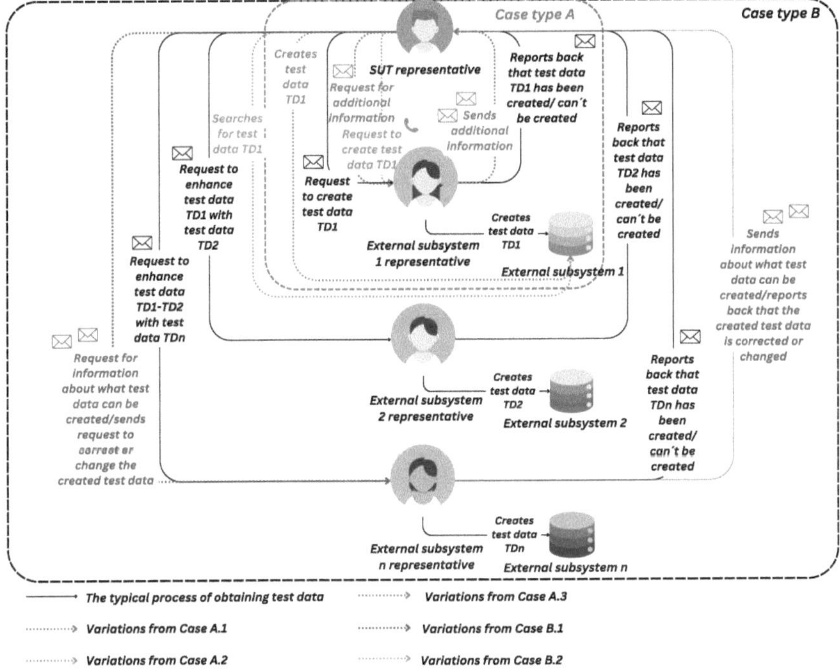

Fig. 2. The current process of obtaining test data for an SUT that uses data services providing Estonian government data

STEP 1: The SUT representative creates a free text description that specifies the exact requirements for TD1. These requirements are derived from the test cases that need to be executed. The SUT representative sends the free text description to the external subsystem 1 representative via e-mail.

STEP 2: The external subsystem 1 representative creates TD1 according to the requirements provided in the free text description.

1. If the requirements in the free text description are unclear to the external subsystem 1 representative, he/she contacts the SUT representative via e-mail and asks for more information.

2. If the requirements in the free text description can't be fulfilled when creating TD1, then the external subsystem 1 representative contacts the SUT representative via e-mail and reports that TD1 can't be created in the described way. The process ends here, or starts again with STEP 1.

STEP 3: The external subsystem 1 representative responds to the SUT representative via e-mail and reports that TD1 has been created according to the requirements in the free text description.

Post-process Activities:

- SUT representative runs the test case that uses TD1 as input.
- SUT sends a data service request for TD1 to the external subsystem 1.
- External subsystem 1 sends a data service response with TD1 to the SUT. If there are any misunderstandings in STEPS 1 to 3 due to which TD1 is not created according to the requirements in the free text description, the process starts again with STEP 1.

In the following, we describe all variations that were identified in the typical process for Case type A.

Variations in Pre-conditions

- Variation in Case A.3: The SUT representative has direct access to external subsystem 1, therefore, the contacts of the external subsystem 1 representative are not needed.

Variations in STEP 1

1. Variation in Case A.1: SUT representative sends a request for additional information after the typical process ends with STEP 2 because the content of the response from the external subsystem 1 representative is not unambiguous. The process ends with STEP 2 of the typical process after the external subsystem 1 representative reports clearly that TD1 cannot be created in the described way.
2. Variation in Case A.2: SUT representative reaches out to a personal contact in the organization of external subsystem 1 via phone after the external subsystem 1 representative responds with an automatic out-of-office message in the variation of STEP 2. The process continues with STEP 1 of the typical process.
3. Variation in Case A.3: SUT representative has direct access to external subsystem 1, and the SUT representative creates TD1 in external subsystem 1 without contacting the external subsystem 1 representative. Therefore, only the post-process steps of the typical process are needed.

Variations in STEP 2

1. Variation in Case A.2: The external subsystem 1 representative is not available at the time of receiving the request described in STEP 1 of the typical process, and responds with an automatic out-of-office message. Therefore, the process continues with a variation of STEP 1.

5.2   Case Type B

The purpose of Case type B is to describe the situation where test data from several subsystems are required for the SUT. In the following, we explain the pre-conditions, steps, and post-process activities that are typically followed.

Pre-conditions

- SUT needs test data 1-2-...-n (TD1-TD2-...-TDn), from n different subsystems.
- SUT representative acquires the contacts of the external subsystems 1, 2, ..., and n representatives.

STEP 1: The SUT representative creates free text descriptions that specify the exact requirements for TD1, the requirements for enhancing TD1 with TD2, and the requirements for enhancing TD1-TD2-... with TDn. These requirements are usually derived from the test cases of the SUT. The SUT representative sends the free text descriptions to the n external subsystem representatives via e-mail.
STEP 2: The n external subsystem representatives who were contacted by the SUT representative create TD1/TD2/.../TDn according to the free text descriptions they have received.

1. If the requirements in the free text description are not clear enough for an external subsystem representative, he/she contacts the SUT representative via e-mail and asks for clarification.
2. If the requirements in the free text description can't be fulfilled when creating TD1, TD2, ..., or TDn, then the external subsystem representative contacts the SUT representative via e-mail and reports that TD1, TD2, ..., or TDn can't be created in the described way.

STEP 2: The n external subsystem representatives respond to the SUT representative via e-mail and report that TD1/TD2/.../TDn has been created according to the requirements in the free text description.

Post-process Activities

- SUT representative runs the test case that uses TD1-TD2-...-TDn.
- The SUT sends a data service request for TD1 to the external subsystem 1, a data service request for TD2 to the external subsystem 2, and data service requests for ...-TDn to n external subsystems.
- External subsystem 1 sends a data service response with TD1, the external subsystem 2 sends a data service response with TD2, and n external subsystems send data service responses with ...-TDn to the SUT. If there are any misunderstandings in STEPS 1 to 3 due to which TD1-TD2-...-TDn is not created according to the requirements in the free text description, the process starts again with STEP 1.

In the following, we describe all variations that were identified in the typical process for Case type B.

Variations in STEP 1

1. Variation in case B.1: SUT representative contacts the n external subsystems to discuss how the necessary test data could be created before sending the requirements for TD1/TD2/.../TDn.
2. Variation in Case B.2: SUT representative uses data services provided by external subsystem 1 to search for TD1 in external subsystem 1 independently without contacting the external subsystem 1 representative.

Answer to RQ 1: The process of obtaining test data:

- **has a common pattern of a request-create-response cycle, but with variations (in one case, it was even completely bypassed)**
- **is not defined but follows established practices and individual preferences**
- **relies on direct personal communication**
- **uses free text descriptions that specify test data requirements.**

---

6 Test Data Provisioning Challenges and Impact (RQ2 and RQ3)

The Supporting Factors in the Current Process of Obtaining Test Data. In Part 3 of the interview session, we asked the interviewees for factors that either support or challenge the fast and easy acquisition of test data in the current process. As a supporting factor in the current process, the interviewees mentioned that the external subsystem representatives are helpful and knowledgeable of the business logic of their subsystems (A.2, B.1, B.2). The interviewees said that even if the current process is improved by creating realistic synthetic test data that is always available and covers the data services of all subsystems or if the SUT representative can, in the future, generate on-demand test data instead of asking the external subsystem representatives to do it, there should still remain the possibility to contact an external subsystem representative who is knowledgeable of the business logic of that system and can support the SUT representative if needed.

The Challenges in the Current Process of Obtaining Test Data. The interviewees mentioned ten challenges in total. We grouped the challenges into four groups (cf. Table 1). We also asked the interviewees to suggest possible solutions to overcome the current challenges or to improve the current process. The groups of challenges and the suggested solutions are summarized in this subsection.

Ch1 (Resources) was mentioned in the context of the manual work required from the SUT representative (A.1), the cost of time invested in the current

Table 1. Challenges of test data provisioning

ID and name	*Challenge description*	*Mentioned by*
Ch1: **Resources**	The current process requires a lot of resources (e.g., time, work)	A.1, A.2, B.2
Ch2: **Guidelines**	There is a lack of standardization in the current process	A.2, B.2
Ch3: **Scope**	There are no descriptions of all possible outputs that can be received from external subsystems	A.1, B.1
Ch4: **Support**	There is a lack of support in the current process for special cases	A.1, B.2

process even if the process runs smoothly (A.2) and the effect of the time invested in the current process on the efficiency of quality assurance (B.2). In A.1, the interviewee suggested improving the process by reducing the amount of manual work because, with the current process, their organization might not be able to cover the manual workload with the existing workforce should the number of test cases that require test data from external subsystems increase. The suggestion in A.2 was to create synthetic test datasets, possibly with the help of artificial intelligence (AI), that would be available for all data services of all subsystems. The interviewee in B.2 suggested that quality assurance is more efficient when the SUT representative can create test data instead of requesting it from the representatives of external subsystems.

Ch2 (Guidelines) refers to the fact that there are no general guidelines that would smoothly guide the SUT representative through the current process, e.g. the contact details of external subsystem representatives are mostly missing in the X-tee Self Service Portal [11] (A.2), there are no guidelines for verifying the test data received from the external subsystem (B.2) and the current process doesn't efficiently support change requests e.g. in case the test cases of the SUT are modified after the SUT representative has already sent the request for test data to an external subsystem representative (B.2). In A.2, the interviewee suggested a wider standardization of the on-demand test data creation process, including a list of dedicated contacts for every subsystem. The interviewee in B.2 presented an idea to have a dedicated channel, e.g. MS Teams, where the SUT representative could place and modify test data requests and follow the status of these requests.

Ch3 (Scope) combines the lack of information about what negative cases are possible in real life when it comes to data services sending faulty, incomplete, or missing data (A.1) and external subsystems often being a "black box" because the SUT representative doesn't know what exact data values can or cannot be created in an external subsystem (B.1). The interviewee in A.1 suggested that more information could be available about how test data is created in external subsystems to make test case design easier. In B.1, the interviewee suggested that there could be a web page or another central source where the data services of all subsystems would be described in a way that one could easily see what is the exact scope of test data values that the data services of an external subsystem can send. As an addition to this initial suggestion, the interviewee suggested that the SUT representative could create test data based on these descriptions instead of requesting test data from the representatives of external subsystems.

Ch4 (Support) is related to situations insufficiently supported by the current processes. There is a lack of support for the SUT representatives if the process ends with STEP 2 and no test data are created in the external subsystem (A.1). Guidelines are missing for situations where test data from external subsystems are required immediately, e.g. in case a critical incident occurs in the SUT (B.2). The interviewee in A.1 suggested process standardization and the documentation of solutions for a wider range of different situations to avoid "reinventing a bicycle". The interviewee in B.2 suggested that the SUT representative could either create test data instead of requesting it from the representatives of external subsystems, or there could be a dedicated channel where the SUT representative can place and modify ad hoc test data requests and follow the status of these requests.

The interviewees in A.1 and A.3 mentioned, as a supporting factor, that an in-house workaround they developed by themselves allowed the SUT representative not to use the current process of obtaining test data at all, e.g., when the process failed to provide the necessary test data (A.1). Although it was mentioned by the interviewees in a positive sense, we cannot accept it as a supporting factor in the current process of obtaining test data, therefore, we are presenting it among challenges. The answers of the interviewee in A.3 revealed that although they do not use the current process of test data at all and do not, therefore, have any challenges with it, they are unable to test their SUT according to Case type B because of test data inconsistencies between different external subsystems. As they do not contact any representatives of external subsystems to overcome those inconsistencies, they artificially convert Case type B to Case type A for their test cases. That requires a high amount of manual work and effort, as only one external subsystem at once is used for testing and test data that would normally be received from another external subsystem needs to be manually entered in the SUT. The interviewee in A.3. suggests that test data could be consistent between different subsystems.

Answer to RQ 2: The most important supporting factors are the external subsystem representatives. The challenges include the amount of resources that the current process requires, the lack of standardization of the process, the lack of descriptions of the test data that can be received from external subsystems, and the lack of support in case the current process fails.

The Effects of the Identified Challenges on Testing. The measurable effects of the challenges on testing are shown in Table 2. The first four columns show the case ID and the challenge IDs mentioned in every specific case. The fifth column shows the number of test data instances requested (req.) from one or several external subsystems and the number of test data instances received (rec.). The sixth column shows the number of days that were initially planned for the process, including post-process activities (pl.) and the actual number of days spent (used). When the interviewee did not provide a number for a certain field in the table, it is marked as "NA".

Table 2. Impact of the challenges

Case	Challenges and effects					
ID	*Ch1: Resources*	*Ch2: Guidelines*	*Ch3: Scope*	*Ch4: Support*	*#Output data (req.|rec.)*	*#Days (pl.|used)*
A.1	x		x	x	4|0	2|4
A.2	x	x			4|4	NA|3
A.3					NA|NA	NA|NA
B.1			x		1|1	7|21
B.2	x	x		x	9|9	3|14

Ch1 was mentioned by three of five interviewees, and the answers reveal that the effect of this challenge is significant. The cases A.1 and B.2 show a difference in days planned vs days used for testing, stating that significantly more time was required for the process as initially planned. A.2 did not provide the initially planned number of days, but the interviewee explained that they knowingly execute only a limited number of test cases in pre-production and put more effort in monitoring possible incidents in production, as their SUT is not providing critical services and testing with the current process is too expensive in their context.

> **Answer to RQ 3: The effect of the challenges on testing is severe as they cause:**
>
> - **considerably more time to be required for obtaining test data than planned (in most cases)**
> - **inability to obtain the required test data at all (in one case).**

7   Discussion and Limitations

The results of this study provide insight into the backstage of a large decentralized e-government system. The interviewees value the opportunity of contacting representatives of external subsystems because they know the external subsystems' business logic. Nevertheless, the amount of time and effort required for the current process (Ch1), combined with the SUT representative having no descriptions of all possible outputs that can be received from external subsystems (Ch3) is likely one of the root causes for the process often taking longer than initially planned. The difference in days planned for testing vs days used for testing is especially visible in cases B.1, and B.2, which means that the time required for testing increases exponentially when the number of external subsystems increases (see Table 2). Given that only a small fraction of SUT representatives who test with X-tee data services were included in this study, we can estimate that the working days lost due to the challenges of the current process add up to large volumes in the Estonian e-government. Furthermore, we assume that SUT testers working with X-Road technology outside of Estonia or in other decentralized e-government settings may encounter similar challenges.

Obtaining test data for e-government data services has, to our knowledge, previously received little attention from researchers. The existing literature explores e-government settings from other perspectives, such as interoperability infrastructure, e.g., [12,13], or recently also the possibilities of integrating new technologies such as large language models (LLM) and generative AI, e.g. [14] as part of e-government. There are also plenty of papers that suggest solutions for generating synthetic test data either specifically in e-government settings, e.g. [15], or for federated systems, e.g. [16], and API testing in general, e.g. [17]. Although existing research and synthetic test data generation solutions provide valuable information and inspiration for our future work, the related papers do not explain the existing process of obtaining test data in decentralized settings, nor do they state the challenges of the existing process and the effects of these challenges. We assume that the challenges identified in our study also occur in other decentralized systems. Thus, we believe that there is a wider target group outside the Estonian e-government settings that would benefit from solutions that mitigate the effects of the identified challenges.

A limitation of our study is that it covers only a fraction of X-tee subsystems. Nevertheless, in qualitative research, an effective sample size is less about numbers and more about the ability of data to provide a rich and nuanced account of the phenomenon studied [19]. After interviewing five specialists from different fields (social services, education, etc.), we see that the process of obtaining test data is always similar, with some small variations. Adding additional interviews would likely reveal some additional small variations in the process, but no significant new findings. Thus, we conclude that saturation has been reached.

In our study, we knowingly decided to accept the limitation of not assessing the quality and complexity of test cases designed by the SUT representatives. The measurable effects of the challenges presented as part of the answer to RQ3 don't therefore consider the possible variations in the complexity of the test data that was requested from external subsystems.

8   Conclusions and Future Work

The X-tee data exchange layer is used in the Estonian decentralized e-government settings. To identify and describe the existing process of obtaining test data for testing software systems and applications that use data services of the Estonian e-government system, we first developed an initial model of the typical process of obtaining test data for an SUT that uses X-tee data services. Thereafter, we conducted a semi-structured interview study to validate and possibly enhance the initial model, to establish a better understanding of the challenges that developers of SUT face when trying to obtain test data, and to assess how the identified challenges impact the testing process of SUT that uses data services on the X-tee data exchange layer. We found that the initial model has many variations. Four groups of challenges were identified, of which one has a significant negative effect on testing.

Our future work includes addressing the challenges identified in this study, particularly the ones where the negative effect on the efficiency of testing is most significant. We will also take into account the suggestions made by the interviewees and investigate the possibilities of using LLMs to create a tool that can be used to automatically identify the scope of data, including the possible value ranges that the data services provided by external subsystems can send to the SUT. Next, we plan to enhance this tool with the ability to consider frequency distributions and generate synthetic test data on demand. Our long-term vision is to create a Synthetic Data Digital Twin (SDDT) that contains synthetic test data that is consistent, covers the most frequently used X-tee data services, can be extended to cover additional X-tee data services, and where the synthetic test data evolves similarly to the real-life e-government data.

Acknowledgments. The research reported in this article has been partly funded by BMK, BMAW, and the State of Upper Austria in the frame of the SCCH competence center INTEGRATE (FFG grant no. 892418), part of the FFG COMET Competence Centers for Excellent Technologies Programme, as well as by grant PRG1226 of the Estonian Research Council.

Disclosure of Interests. The authors have no competing interests to declare that are relevant to the content of this article.

References

1. Baresi, L., Garriga, M.: Microservices: the evolution and extinction of web services? In: Microservices, pp. 3–28. Springer, Cham (2020). https://doi.org/10.1007/978-3-030-31646-4_1
2. Jesus Ekie, Y., Gueye, B., Niang, I.: A comparative analysis of SOAP and REST Web service composition based on performance in local and remote Cloud environments. In: Proceedings of the 4th Int. Conference on Networking, Information Systems and Security, KENITRA AA Morocco, pp. 1–8. ACM (2021). https://doi.org/10.1145/3454127.3457621

3. Data exchange layer X-tee | RIA. https://www.ria.ee/en/state-information-system/data-exchange-platforms/data-exchange-layer-x-tee. Accessed 11 Apr 2025

4. X-Road®– Security, X-Road®. https://x-road.global/security. Accessed 11 Apr 2025

5. Regulation - 2016/679 - EN - GDPR - EUR-Lex. https://eur-lex.europa.eu/eli/reg/2016/679/oj/eng. Accessed 11 Apr 2025

6. X-Road Terms and Abbreviations, X-Road. https://docs.x-road.global/terms_x-road_docs.html. Accessed 11 Apr 2025

7. Riigi infosüsteemi haldussüsteem RIHA. https://www.riha.ee/Avaleht. Accessed 11 Apr 2025

8. Catalogue of X-tee Subsystems and Methods. https://x-tee.ee/catalogue/EE. Accessed 11 Apr 2025

9. EmpiricalStandards/docs/standards/QualitativeSurveys.md at master acmsigsoft/EmpiricalStandards, GitHub. https://github.com/acmsigsoft. Accessed 11 Apr 2025

10. X-TEE FACTSHEET EE. https://x-tee.ee/factsheets/EE. Accessed 12 Apr 2025

11. X-tee iseteenindus. https://x-tee.ee/en/home. Accessed 12 Apr 2025

12. Bharosa, N., Lips, S., Draheim, D.: Making e-Government work: learning from the Netherlands and Estonia. In: Hofmann, S., et al. (eds.) ePart 2020. LNCS, vol. 12220, pp. 41–53. Springer, Cham (2020). https://doi.org/10.1007/978-3-030-58141-1_4

13. Not, E., et al.: Designing a digital environment to support the co-production of public services: balancing multiple requirements and governance concepts. Digit. Gov. Res. Pract. 5(3), 1–30 (2024). https://doi.org/10.1145/3664612

14. Alshahrani, A.: Adopting emerging technologies in digital government: a multi-case analysis of drivers, enablers, and challenges in Saudi Arabia. Digit. Gov. Res. Pract., 3719297 (2025). https://doi.org/10.1145/3719297

15. Tan, C., Behjati, R., Arisholm, E.: Enhancing synthetic test data generation with language models using a more expressive domain-specific language. In: Bonfanti, S., Gargantini, A., Salvaneschi, P. (eds.) Testing Software and Systems, pp. 21–39. Springer, Cham (2023). https://doi.org/10.1007/978-3-031-43240-8_2

16. Dankar, F.K., Madathil, N.: Using synthetic data to reduce model convergence time in federated learning. In: 2022 IEEE/ACM Int. Conference on Advances in Social Networks Analysis and Mining (ASONAM), Istanbul, Turkey, November 2022, pp. 293–297. IEEE (2022). https://doi.org/10.1109/ASONAM55673.2022.10068615

17. Kim, M., et al.: Enhancing REST API testing with NLP techniques. In: Proceedings of the 32nd ACM SIGSOFT Int. Symposium on Software Testing and Analysis, Seattle WA USA, July 2023, pp. 1232–1243. ACM (2023). https://doi.org/10.1145/3597926.3598131

18. Anthes, G.: Estonia: a model for e-government. Commun. ACM 58(6), 18–20 (2015). https://doi.org/10.1145/2754951

19. Hennink, M., Kaiser, B.N.: Sample sizes for saturation in qualitative research: a systematic review of empirical tests. Soc. Sci. Med. 292, 114523 (2022). https://doi.org/10.1016/j.socscimed.2021.114523

From C to Rust – How Feasible is it?

Ella Viirola[1], Johan Hummel[1], Emma Söderberg[1(✉)], Andreas Bexell[1,2],
Peter Kornevi[2], and Ulf Asklund[1]

[1] Lund University, Lund, Sweden
{emma.soderberg,andreas.bexell,ulf.asklund}@cs.lth.se
[2] Ericsson AB, Gothenburg, Sweden
{andreas.bexell,peter.kornevi}@ericsson.com

Abstract. The C programming language, while offering high performance and low-level control, is memory-unsafe. This makes it prone to programming errors that can result in serious software vulnerabilities and system instability. In this paper, we investigate the feasibility of transitioning a large code base from C to a memory-safe alternative, specifically Rust, in the context of a large company in telecommunications and networking. We explore technical challenges with translation, building on automatic translation with C2Rust, analyze performance impact, and survey developers' attitudes toward migration. We find that while C2Rust can generate correct code, significant manual effort is required in the translation process, especially to get the benefit of Rust's safety guarantees. In the internal environment, Rust integration is currently limited, in part by missing compiler support for code closely tied to hardware. Performance results from open-source projects relevant to the company indicate that Rust does not perform significantly worse than C, although further research is needed. Developer attitudes towards a switch were generally positive. Our conclusion is that full migration is currently unfeasible, but gradual adoption is possible. **Replication package**: https://zenodo.org/records/15754034.

Keywords: Software engineering · C2Rust · Programming language migration

1 Introduction

In February 2024, the White House released a report on cybersecurity and memory safety in software [2]. Errors in memory safety cause software vulnerabilities that can lead to unintended access, written, allocated, or deallocated memory. The report describes such memory safety issues as *"one of the most pervasive class of vulnerabilities that has plagued cyber defenders for decades"*. Two widely used programming languages, C and C++, are memory-unsafe, and previous industry analyses of security vulnerabilities at, e.g. Microsoft and Google (the Chromium project) found that up to 70% of security vulnerabilities in these languages are due to memory safety issues, despite preventive controls [18,19]. The

G. Scanniello et al. (Eds.): PROFES 2025, LNCS 16362, pp. 19–35, 2026.
https://doi.org/10.1007/978-3-032-12092-2_2

report states that the most effective way to eliminate these issues is to develop software using intrinsically memory safe languages, that is, languages that are designed to prevent memory safety vulnerabilities [2].

Rust is an example of a memory-safe language that has emerged as an alternative to C. The design of the language and its handling of memory bring appealing memory-safety properties, and the language has also been shown to have good performance characteristics which often are important in context where C is used. Although the White House report does not mandate a transition to memory-safe languages at this time, it encourages organizations to keep in mind the effect the choice of languages has on security. However, how should organizations with a large investment in C make plans in a potentially changing industry landscape that affects market shares?

In this paper, we investigate the overarching research question $\mathbf{RQ_1}$) *how feasible is it to migrate a large code base from C to Rust?* We focus on a large telecom company with a large C codebase. We conducted a mixed-method study in which we have analyzed a) the required technical steps for a translation on a selection of two internal modules and two open-source projects relevant to the company, b) the performance of translated Rust programs compared to the same program in C, and c) user input through interviews with professionals at the company.

Overall, we conclude that a full-scale migration from C to Rust is currently not feasible. However, with proper support, such as implementing Rust support in the compiler toolchain and investing in Rust training for developers, a gradual transition is possible. This transition should target well-encapsulated modules that expose narrow public interfaces, making them easier to translate without disrupting surrounding code. If advances are made in automatic translation, a broader migration may become feasible in the future. At such a point, it is important that the necessary toolchain and developer expertise is already in place.

The contributions of this paper are the following.

- A list of technical challenges related to compiler and environment support.
- An evaluation of the C2Rust tool for automatic translation of large and complex codebases, including observed limitations and suggestions for tool improvements.
- Performance comparisons between C, automatically translated Rust code, and manually refactored Rust code using real-world projects.
- Insights into professional developers' attitudes towards a language migration in a large-scale industrial project.

2   Background and Related Work

Here we provide background and related work on automatic translation from C to Rust, performance of translated code, and the Rust user experience.

2.1 Automatic Translation from C to Rust

The most commonly cited automatic translation method from C to Rust is C2Rust [12], which is a rule-based transpiler, with the primary goal of *"produc[ing] code that is functionally identical to the input C code"*. Generating safe Rust is not a goal of the translator, and the produced code is not memory-safe. In our study, we focus on the feasibility of applying C2Rust as-is in an industry codebase, but many papers have suggested tools that strive to improve the translation produced by C2Rust and get it closer to safe Rust (e.g., [5,6,16,20]), meaning the quality of C2Rust-translated code may improve in the future.

LAERTES [6] turns raw pointers to safe references through using the Rust borrow checker to derive lifetime information. With further improvements by Emre et al. [5], 21% of raw pointers can be translated. CROWN [20] uses static ownership analysis to reduce unsafe pointer uses, achieving a median reduction rate of 37.3% for raw pointers and 62.1% for raw pointer uses, outperforming LAERTES. CrustS [16] increases the ratio of "safe functions" (function declarations without the `unsafe` keyword) by pushing `unsafe` into the function body and minimizing `unsafe` blocks, although Emre et al. [5] point out that this does not necessarily lead to safer code, only less code that is marked unsafe.

In addition to C2Rust, large language model (LLM)-based transpiler tools have also been developed. Eniser et al. [7] present FLOURINE, which uses different LLMs to transpile C and Go programs to Rust. The best performing LLM produced translations of which 47.7% could be compiled. The translations were also less verbose and more idiomatic than those produced by C2Rust.

Emre et al. [5] discuss that a *"fully automated translation to completely safe Rust is difficult, if not impossible"*, and a more achievable goal is to instead aim to automatically translate as much of the C code into safe Rust as possible, and to provide information why the remaining code is unsafe, so it can be manually rewritten.

2.2 Performance of Rust Versus C

Comparing performance between C and Rust is not trivial, as it can heavily depend on the chosen benchmarks and implementation details of the compared program. Zhang et al. [21] find that Rust is in general slower than C, bringing on average a performance overhead of 1.77x compared to C. However, the benchmarks were chosen to minimize the implementation differences between the C and Rust programs, having similar code structures and using the same data structures, and may not be representative of most Rust programs. In contrast, a study by Li et al. [15] measured performance in Rust programs that were translated from C, where the requirement was instead that the program should have an equivalent external behavior to the C program, rather than similarity in the source code. For the Rust programs included in the study, which were most similar externally, the overhead was instead mostly within 1.2x, and many were even faster than the corresponding C programs. These results are corroborated by a study by Bugden et al. [3] that compared the performance of six programming languages, including C and Rust, running a bubble sort algorithm and a Monte Carlo π estimation algorithm. Rust had a lower CPU time than C for both algorithms, but conversely had a higher memory usage than C for both algorithms. In our study, we focus on the performance of code translated by C2Rust.

2.3   User Perspective on Rust

Fulton et al. [10] conducted an interview study, followed by a survey study, with developers about their experiences using Rust. The interviewees were mainly senior developers who had used Rust in their work and/or attempted to get their company to adopt Rust, and the survey participants in the study are selected from Rust forums. The study showed that developers find the major benefits of Rust to be its safety guarantees along with its performance. Their findings also indicate that a drawback of Rust is its steep learning curve, with Rust's programming paradigms and the borrow checker being particularly difficult for many to learn. Another drawback is that Rust lacks certain critical libraries and has a tendency to cause dependency bloat. Our study targets professional developers with a background primarily in C, regardless of prior Rust experience. This perspective allows us to investigate attitudes toward Rust from those who may not have used it yet but could potentially be affected by a transition in the future.

3   Method

To investigate our overarching research question ($\mathbf{RQ_1}$ *How feasible is it to migrate a large code base from C to Rust?*), we break out three secondary questions as follows:

- $\mathbf{RQ_{1.1}}$ *What are the technical challenges?* We investigate this question with a selection of cases of code modules/projects, from the internal code base of the company and from open-source projects relevant to the company. We also gather input from developers through interviews.
- $\mathbf{RQ_{1.2}}$ *Will the performance of the code be affected?* We investigate the effect on performance by measuring the execution time on translated C programs, with the original C program as a baseline.
- $\mathbf{RQ_{1.3}}$ *What is the developers' perspective?* We gather input from developers at the company by conducting interviews.

Study Context. The company is a Swedish networking- and telecommunications company with roughly 93 000 employees, around 13 000 of which are employed in Sweden [8]. The company has a large codebase developed over many years. The company's portfolio includes several custom-designed application-specific integrated circuits (ASICs), which implement proprietary instruction set architectures (ISAs), which means they do not conform to any publicly documented

Table 1. Summary description of the projects used in the evaluation.

Project	Files	Description
`Internal-Small`	15	Internal utility library, few external dependencies.
`Internal-Larger`	166	Part of baseband implementation, with outgoing and incoming dependencies.
`OSS-Small`	2	C-FFT [13]: Three implementations of Fourier transforms: naïve, Cooley-Tukey and Good-Thomas.
`OSS-Larger`	64	XCM [9]: Interprocess communication service implemented by the company. Optimised for C.

instruction set. The ASIC runs a custom operating system developed by the company. As a result, no open-source compiler targets this architecture out of the box. The company has its own C dialect, compiled with a custom compiler frontend derived from Clang, with an LLVM-based backend. The frontend compiles the C dialect into LLVM intermediate representation and on to target-specific assembly code. The compiler does not support Rust code.

The work presented in this paper is based on work carried out in a MSc thesis project at the company [11].

3.1 Technical Challenges ($RQ_{1.1}$)

To investigate the technical challenges of migrating from C to Rust, we used a combination of automatic and manual translation on a selection of C code from the internal code base and from open-source software (OSS), see Table 1. In the selection of internal modules, we searched for largely self-contained modules of limited size and varying complexity. In the selection of open-source projects, we searched for projects relevant to the company with limited size and varying complexity. We focus our investigation on the correctness of the translated code, that is, whether it compiles and passes tests, and not readability, but where relevant, we include reflections from our experience reading the translated code.

We performed translation of the C code (`Original`) in two steps: first, an automatic translation using C2Rust, minimally modified to compile (`MinMod`), and second, refactoring the code manually to more idiomatic Rust (`RustLike`), by i) minimizing unsafe code by replacing unsafe operations and types, ii) replacing calls to external functions with safe Rust variants or calls to other translated files when possible, iii) removing `allow` keywords added by C2Rust (except `allow`s for naming conventions), and iv) accepting Clippy suggestions. Clippy [1] is the Rust linter, that gives suggestions on how to make more idiomatic Rust code, e.g. restricting unsafe code into unsafe blocks as well as correcting C-style code. See Fig. 1.

For the proprietary code, we had to disqualify files with custom keywords that were not recognized by C2Rust. Manual work was often required to resolve missing declarations and type or `struct` definitions. Due to time constraints, for

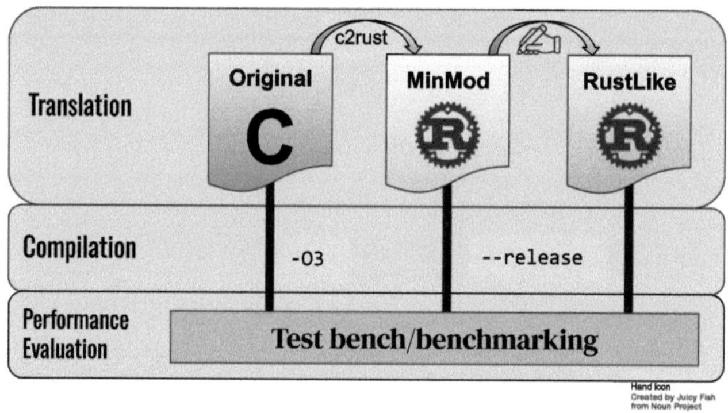

Fig. 1. Translation and performance testing procedure.

OSS-Larger we only translated a subset of files consisting of the main file xcm.c and its import chain, excluding free-standing header files. The refactoring was also limited; we accepted Clippy suggestions and linked Rust files, but limited manual rewrites to i) files with thread handling, rewritten to use native Rust threads (2 files), and ii) functions that included a goto statement in Original, as they are not supported in Rust (7 functions in 4 files).

3.2　Performance Analysis ($RQ_{1.2}$)

We analyzed performance (execution time) for the OSS projects for the C programs (Original), compiled with -O3 when possible, and for the automatically created Rust (MinMod) and the refactored Rust files (RustLike), compiled with the --release flag. We do not analyze performance for Internal-Small and Internal-Larger, as the percentage of translated code was too low to give meaningful results.

For OSS-Small, we used an existing benchmarking file in the project. We benchmarked the three methods in the library by iterating them $75,000$ times each in one run, over a total of 50 runs, of which the 10 first were warm-up runs. The benchmarks were repeated for all variants.

For OSS-Larger, each of the 165 test cases (excluding a set of 30 test cases in Python, which took significantly longer to run) was individually timed. A benchmark ran 4 runs of 20 iterations, of which the 4 first were warm-ups. The tests could fail due to data races in the tests themselves [9], as the tests were run in parallel, which means that some tests could have less than 16 values for a test. We normalized the data to one array of 16 values per test-variant combination, which was an average of the 4 runs. This was repeated for all variants. We performed a Kruskal-Wallis test [17] for each method to find if there were statistical differences ($p < 0.05$) in performance between variants. We also performed a Dunn's test [4], to see specifically which variant(s) differed significantly.

3.3   Developer Perspective (RQ$_{1.3}$)

We recruited participants through our connections at the company, looking for participants who work or have worked with C and/or know the concept of memory safety. We aimed to find participants from different teams as they might encounter different issues in their day-to-day work. We ended up with six participants, all male, with a range of backgrounds and roles within the company, and a varied familiarity with both C and Rust, see Table 2.

Table 2. Overview of interview participants.

Participant	Experience Company	Experience C	Experience Rust
P1	Software Developer, at company 15+ years	Primary language (10+ years)	Basic - tutorials, experimentation
P2	Software Developer, at company 20+ years, with some years as project manager	Primary language	No experience
P3	Software Developer, at company for 5+ years, software developer 15+ years	Primary language	No experience
P4	Operational Product Owner, at company 20+ years	Primary language	Familiar - seen examples online
P5	Senior Specialist (in-house C compiler), at company 10+ years	Primary language	Familiar - knows the rational, but no experience
P6	Senior Specialist (QA), at company 15+ years	Primary language (10+ years)	Experience - 2–3 years of development

The interviews were semi-structured [14], with 8 pre-prepared questions, included in the replication package, and were scheduled to take at most 45 min (average was 41 min). Before the interview, we obtained informed consent from the participants included in the replication package, and then we recoded the interviews. The second author asked questions, while the first author took notes and was free to ask follow-up questions. We asked general questions about the participant's role in the company, software development, C and Rust. The topic was successively narrowed down, as the participant was asked about benefits and challenges of C, suggestions for solutions, suggestions for memory-safe alternatives to C, experience of Rust and finally what benefits and challenges they would see with a switch from C to Rust. As an aid for participants who had not worked with Rust before, we showed a simple example program in both C and Rust, also included in the replication package. As all participants spoke Swedish, the interviews were conducted in Swedish.

We analyze the interview data collected through the following steps. 1) The first two authors separately read the interview notes and annotated interesting topics. 2) The first two authors discussed their annotations and categorized them into 11 codes. The interview notes were annotated with the codes and the results for each code were summarized. 3) The codes were reviewed and discussed with the remaining authors. 4) The first two authors then returned to listen to the interviews to extract quotes to support the findings under each code. The selected quotes were translated from Swedish to English.

4   Results

Here, we present the results organized after the secondary research questions.

4.1   Technical Challenges and Translation ($RQ_{1.1}$)

`Internal-Small`: This code could partially be translated; 11 of 15 C files contained uses of company-specific keywords not supported by C2Rust and were thus disqualified, leaving 4 files which were translated to Rust. For these files, 1 compiled successfully after transpilation, while the remaining 3 required manual intervention, adding necessary typedefs and declarations to create a "stand-alone" file, before successfully compiling. There was little need for manual intervention since these files are very small.

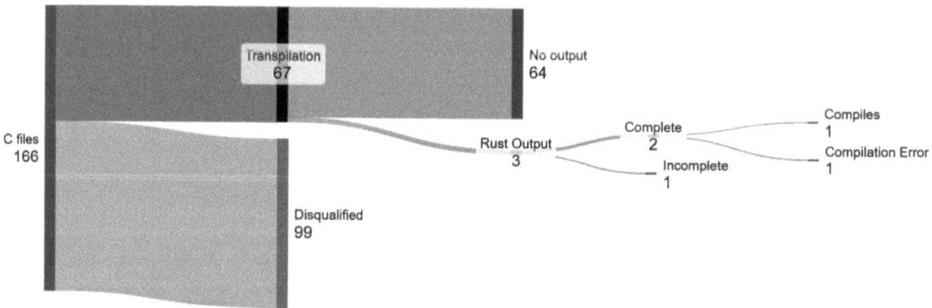

Fig. 2. Translation outcome for `Internal-Larger`.

`Internal-Larger`: This code could be partially translated, see Fig. 2; 99 of 166 C files were disqualified from translation due to the use of company-specific keywords unsupported by C2Rust, leaving 67 files for which we managed to generate Rust files in 3 cases. For these Rust files, 1 successfully compiled (after manual intervention), 1 compiled with compilation errors (several calls to functions not declared in the file – C2Rust failed to pull in these dependencies from the header file), and 1 was incomplete (used structs with bitfields and could therefore not be compiled, as the Rust version in the environment was too old). Due to the size and complexity of the files – many of which include numerous header files and deeply nested dependencies – resolving issues manually, by inlining missing declarations or definitions was not feasible. As a result, only one smaller file (191 LoC) was manually corrected and transpiled.

`OSS-Small`: This code could be fully translated using C2Rust. The generated Rust files were significantly larger, 330 LoC compared to 131 LoC, and mimicked the C code. That is, the Rust code used manual memory management, no native Rust types and methods, and kept pointers as-is, using `malloc` and `offset` to access. Consequently, all functions were marked `unsafe`. All functions defined in other files and libraries were imported via the `extern "C"` block, which pulls the definition from a C header file, even when the function is available in Rust. The generated code was generally hard to read, with many unnecessary casts, statements, and auto-generated variables. C2Rust also misinterprets certain code patterns, such as translating `for` loops to `while` loops when the iterators are declared beforehand. Linking generated Rust files was challenging. For each translated file, C2Rust creates duplicates of (i.e. redefines) all `structs` and types it needs from files the original C file imports, creating naming conflicts and requiring manual intervention. Still, C2Rust generated largely correct code. Excluding errors from the linking process, the translation resulted in 8 errors, all of which were missing `unsafe` keywords (6 from missing `unsafe` wrap around `no_mangle`, and 2 from missing `unsafe` before an `extern "C"` block). These errors are new for the Rust 2024 edition and could thus be resolved by switching Rust edition, or solved quickly manually. After these changes, the code compiled and produced correct test results. For the refactoring, it was easier to manually rewrite the code from scratch with the C code as reference in order to reach idiomatic Rust, rather than rework the `MinMod` code, as the project was small.

`OSS-Larger`: This code could be fully translated using C2Rust. The issues from `OSS-Small` were also found in `OSS-Larger`, but the scale of the project, as well as the Makefile-based build system, also lead to new problems. The duplication of `structs` and types was even more apparent with this project, as the import chains were longer; for example, the `xcm_socket` structure (and all the types and `structs` it in turn needs, resulting in almost 80 LoC) was defined in 14 out of 17 translated files. Library `structs` from `libc` were redefined, leading to a large amount of bloated code that could be replaced with a single import statement. This led to the translation being three times longer than the original; 11,813 LoC versus 3,808 LoC. Despite these issues, 11 out of 17 files only needed the additional `unsafe`s required by Rust 2024 to compile. However, building the project also resulted in some problems. Translated Rust files sometimes would not find functions imported from other C files through the `extern "C"` block, resulting in undefined reference errors, leading to additional files having to be translated and linked through Rust; 6 out of 17 files needed additional files. After these adjustments, the files compiled and the tests passed. Refactoring the files with `cargo fix` and `cargo clippy --fix` was effective; after at most two runs of the commands at most 7 warnings were left in any file (starting from as many as 353), and these warnings could be quickly resolved. Notably, Clippy gave incorrect suggestions twice, that would lead to the code not compiling if applied. During linking we encountered problems with circular dependencies, i.e., `struct` definitions depending on each other, which is not allowed in Rust. We resolved this by lifting out any circular definition to a separate crate.

4.2 Performance Results ($RQ_{1.2}$)

We performed a performance analysis on the selected open source projects.

`OSS-Small`: The performance results are presented in Fig. 3. The statistical analysis shows that `RustLike` outperforms both `MinMod` and `Original` in all Fourier methods, and `MinMod` outperforms `Original` in all methods.

`OSS-Larger`: The performance results are presented in Fig. 4. Averaged over 4 runs, 126 tests out of 165 had statistically significant differences between at least two of the median run times of the different variants. The tests were divided into several categories. Both Rust variants outperformed `Original` in the `xcm` test category (114 tests), and `MinMod` performed the best (fastest in 49 tests). However, the execution times, and thus the best performing variant, varied between runs in this category,

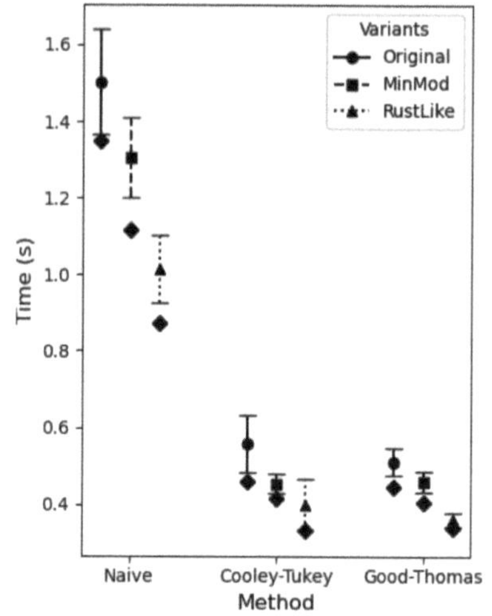

Fig. 3. Performance results for `OSS-Small`, which includes three methods for Fourier transformation. For each method, we show the results (confidence intervals, means, and medians) for each of the variants (`Original`, `MinMod`, `RustLike`).

which may be because it tested the communication aspect of the project – which can be subject to some latency – as well as the tests being run in parallel. On the other hand, `Original` consistently performed the best for the other five categories, being the fastest in 45 out of 50 tests, which contained much pointer handling. Overall, `MinMod` and `RustLike` also had very similar execution times, with statistical significance between the two in only 7 of all test cases, which may be due to the refactoring in `OSS-Larger` being limited.

4.3 Developer Perspective/Technical Challenges ($RQ_{1.3}$, $RQ_{1.1}$)

Attitude Towards C. The general attitude towards C was mixed among our interview participants. For example, P1 was more negative towards C expressing that for him as a developer he almost only sees downsides. P5, on the other hand, said *"[C] is the language I know best. I have read the specification and have a good understanding of the rules of the language, what pitfalls there are, etc. [...]. I like C quite a lot, but it does have its problems"*. P6 described his relationship with C as a love-hate one: C is fast and gets the job done, but it opens the door to many potential issues.

Still, all participants found **benefits with the C language**, primarily performance (mentioned by 4 of 6 participants), e.g., P4 said *"[C] is fast and efficient once you have learned how it works. It also has a close connection to assembler code which allows you to program rather close to the hardware."*

All participants also recognized that there are **downsides to the C language**. Five participants agree that C makes it easy to make mistakes, especially for less experienced C programmers. Although all participants mentioned problems related to memory safety as examples of downsides, some placed more emphasis on other aspects. P3 mentioned that C's lack of support for generic programming can lead to duplicated code. Two participants, P3 and P4, stated that while C is generally a fast language, there are cases where it is not fast enough and you thus need to resort to hand-tuned assembly code.

Most of the discussion around **how to mitigate the downsides of C** focused on memory-related issues. Three participants mentioned tests as a strategy. P4 also talked about code reviews and various tools for static and dynamic code analysis: *"[mitigating] is usually about reviewing the code and making sure that you test it and run it.*

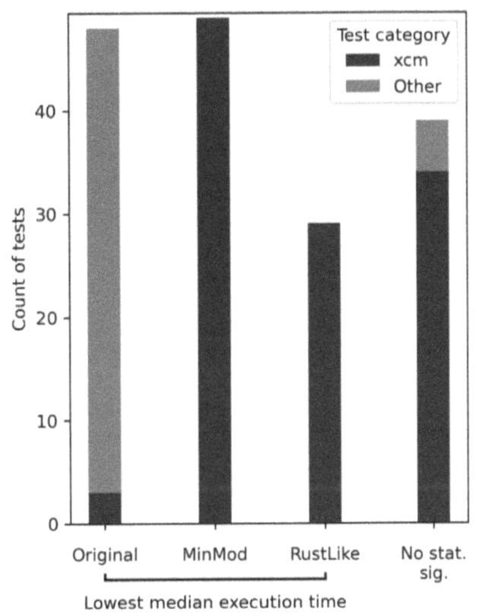

Fig. 4. Performance results for `OSS-Larger`, showing the count of tests where a variant (`Original`, `MinMod`, `RustLike`) had the lowest median execution time, if there was statistical significance between at least two medians for that test. The tests are divided according to their test category, `xcm` and Other for the five other categories.

[...] there are tools you can use, typically Valgrind." P3, P5 and P6 also talked about tools, but mentioned that some of the tools used for dynamic analysis come with performance/memory costs which often is unacceptable.

Attitude Towards Rust. With regard to **benefits of Rust**, P6 stated that *"Rust does everything right."* It is easy to make mistakes in C, such as not properly initializing a variable, but these would be prevented by Rust (as long as you do not use unsafe). It is especially useful for catching scenarios that are easy to miss or that you might not think about. Many can be found through static analysis, but Rust does the work for you and catches these at compile-time. P6 states that Rust cleans up all scenarios he sees are causing problems. *"It really holds the programmer's hand."* Even though the rest of the participants did not have any hands-on experience of Rust, all confirmed that the memory safety aspect would be very beneficial. P1 stated that *"it would be safer if I feel that I cannot do wrong."*

There were also **downsides with Rust** mentioned. P5 and P6 mentioned that the language itself might need some modifications because of the special hardware used at the company, which has a larger byte size and an explicit address space. P5 additionally said that the company has its own operating system and a language to handle parallelism; to use Rust's threading mechanism, it needs to be integrated with the current mechanisms. P6 also mentioned that most Rust libraries are developed by the community and *"everyone is using unsafe"*, leading to failure to achieve full memory safety due to propagation.

Attitude Towards a Migration from C to Rust. Regarding the overall attitude towards translation, several participants stated that switching languages would need to come with *"large benefits"*, as stated by P3. P4 said that the company *"has found a way to work with C that works relatively well. [...] There are surely benefits with having a language that is more strict [...] but even half-baked C-code can work if you test it and make sure it is in environments where everything is okay."* P3 further elaborated that the **translation needs to preserve or improve the quality** of the code, the tests, and the readability. Half of the participants also reiterate that performance cannot be affected as a requirement. In short, the switch would need to be planned carefully.

Despite this, all participants were positive towards switching from C to Rust, stating that **memory safety is important**. However, P5 also mentioned that he does not believe there is an immediate rush to transition due to external regulatory developments alone: *"Changes in legislation and regulations could come – it is good to be aware of and prepared for that. But I also think some people see this a bit too black-and-white. [...] I can't imagine that someone anytime soon will say 'now we're banning C.' There's just too much invested, the cost of replacing it is too high."*

Experience of Programming Language Migration. Three of the participants had previous experience of translating code to another language. P3 was part of a project rewriting C to C++, where it was **challenging to get people to really switch languages**; *"many of us here come from a C world, and learning to write good C++ code is not easy. Instead, you often write C++ with a C-syntax, and then take in some easier things in C++. [...] It's hard to relearn, unfortunately, when you know one language well."* P4 had translated Java to C with the experience that it was *"?moderately entertaining?"*. P5 had been part of switching out an old compiler framework; the backend was translated to LLVM and the frontend to Clang. He estimates that the human effort was 100 person-years, and there was **a lot of integration work**.

Challenges with Migration from C to Rust. All participants pointed out the **huge scale** of the company code base as a challenge of translating to Rust; translation would require a lot of work and would take a long time, especially if it must be done manually. P1 states that much work would fall on developers in the lower layers, as memory handling would need to be rewritten, and P4 theorized that they likely would not be able to use much OSS software to help either and would have to write much of the code in-house. And as P4 mentioned, all of this must happen in parallel as the company *"constantly has to add features and get products to come out [to customers]"*.

The **strict performance requirements**, especially at the lower layers of the stack, were lifted as a challenge by five participants. For example, P3 said *"we have some parts of the system that have extreme performance requirements, so that the code is written in Assembler. To move that over to Rust [...] I do not think that is possible right now."* Limited **Rust support in the toolchain** was also mentioned. P5 said that a new compiler frontend that can read Rust and interact with the existing compiler backend would be required. This would *"take a couple of years to do, to produce something of the same quality as the one that exists today"*. P4 mentioned potential problems with OSS transpilers *not working with company's C dialect*. He also suspects that transpilers produce *"a lot of junk code you have to go through manually anyway"*, and might result in more work than just translating the code by hand to begin with.

In addition to the technical challenges, the "mental challenges" of **learning a new language** were also mentioned, e.g., P6 said *"how do you retrain a whole organization that has written C for 30 years?"*. P4 reflected that Rust is further apart from C than for example C++, with a *"completely different set of rules you have to adapt to"*. P6 stated that Rust has a more challenging learning curve, mentioning the borrow checker and understanding ownership as examples. The compiler is very good at explaining when you have done something illegal, but *"it feels like a big paradigm shift, going from C to Rust."* The language is also relatively new, and P6 lifts a potential issue with consultants; the company employs many third-party consultants, and it might be hard to find many that know Rust.

Suggestions for How to Migrate from C to Rust. Many participants gave suggestions for how the translation could be approached. P3 and P5 suggested to start with a part that is not performance critical. P3 and P4 suggested translating a small module as a trial first, e.g., P4 said *"build up a small team that is good at Rust, and let them hack away at a small component that is not very central"*. P4 further suggested that a stepwise translation might be necessary first, with unsafe Rust as the first step, and then refactoring to safe Rust. Another approach, suggested by P2 and P4, would be to introduce Rust at an opportunity where *"you are going in and deep cleaning [the code] and making changes anyway"* (P4), like in the next technical evolution of the products, or in a context where translation is ongoing anyway. To handle the special requirements of company's hardware, P5 and P6 state that it might be necessary to create a company dialect of Rust.

5   Threats to Validity

The validity of this study is limited by the execution of the study as part of a master's thesis project by the first two authors, who carried out the study as a final step before they obtained their respective engineering degrees in computer science. Although they are familiar with Rust, they are not experienced Rust developers. However, one could argue that this level of experience may still be representative of what can be expected in an organization during the early stages of adoption, when developers are still becoming familiar with the language. Similarly, the first two authors have limited experience with the company (previous internships at the company). Some of the challenges faced in the internal environment could possibly have been avoided by a more experienced engineer at the company. However, the first two authors had a network in the company that connected them to senior engineers available to assist when needed.

The decision to conduct the performance analysis on open source projects was due to practical difficulties in performing the measurements within the company. Although this approach was not ideal, we believe the criteria used to select the OSS projects, such as size, testability, relevance to the company, and C-centric implementation, were fair and appropriate given the constraints. However, it does affect the generalizability of the results. Apart from not using the company-specific dialect of C and lacking integration with the broader company development environment and tool chain, other threats include the fact that the selected OSS projects are typically smaller, more modular, and better isolated than what appears to be the case for the typical internal code bases. This means that the translation process and performance results observed in OSS projects may not accurately reflect the challenges and characteristics present in tightly coupled large-scale industrial systems. Performance results are also likely affected by the machine that was used to run the code, and background processes or CPU load may have introduced noise into the measurement. For `OSS-Larger`, variability may also have been introduced from the tests running in parallel. We used several runs and statistical methods to mitigate this variability.

Finally, the interview participants were selected through recommendations from our network in the company. Our aim was to engage individuals with relevant experience in C, memory safety, and related concepts to ensure that the interviews would be meaningful. However, within the group of individuals that meet these criteria, there is a risk of selection bias. Since participants were identified through internal contacts, it is possible that those selected had stronger views on topics such as memory safety or language migration than the broader developer population. In addition, the sample size was relatively small (6 participants) and lacking certain forms of diversity; All participants were male, Swedish, and had worked within the organization for many years. This may limit generalization of the findings, as perspectives from more junior developers or individuals from more diverse backgrounds may not be adequately represented.

6   Conclusions

We investigated the feasibility of migrating a large code base from C to Rust through three perspectives: the technical challenges of translation, potential impact on performance, and the developers' perspective.

We found several technical challenges with translation on a large scale because the automatic translation via C2Rust is suboptimal. While the produced code (when attained) is correct, and C2Rust could thus facilitate translation of e.g. function signatures, most of the code is difficult to read, bloated, and unsafe. The challenges in the internal code base, with the company-specific C dialect and complex dependencies, imply that C2Rust is not suited for translating complex codebases, and is currently not feasible to use in an industry setting. Thus, most of the translation work would have to be performed manually, which was a concern developers expressed in their interviews. Despite this, the attitude towards a switch to Rust was overall positive, as long as it can preserve the quality of the current code.

From our performance analysis, we found inconclusive results. The results from **OSS-Small** show that Rust performs better, and that the compiler is good at aggressive optimizations. However, the C code was not optimised, and the results may therefore not be representative of an industry codebase. This is further strengthened by the results from **OSS-Larger**, which is stated to be an optimised C project. The two Rust variants did outperform **Original** in the **xcm** category, but with some variance between runs, and the **Original** variant consistently outperformed both Rust variants in pointer handling. This is not a surprising result, as C2Rust handles e.g. pointer addition by calling functions, in comparison to C where it is handled with simple arithmetic addition, which likely incurs less overhead. While it is not impossible for Rust to outperform C, as the Rust code still had much room for improvement, larger rewrites may be necessary to achieve performance comparable to C; i.e. a C-style direct translation is unlikely to preserve the performance of the original code. It should be noted that because of the challenges translating the code, we did not manage to translate a sufficient amount of code to draw definite conclusions from our performance analysis. However, from our results we observe that there is no indication that Rust performs significantly worse than C.

Overall, we conclude that a full-scale migration from C to Rust is not currently feasible. However, with proper support, such as implementing Rust support in the compiler toolchain and investing in Rust training for developers, a gradual transition is possible. This transition should target well-encapsulated modules that expose narrow public interfaces, making them easier to translate without disrupting surrounding code. If advances in automatic translation are made, via C2Rust or LLM-based transpilers, a broader migration may become feasible in the future. At that point, it is likely that the necessary toolchain and developer expertise will already be in place, thanks to incremental adoption efforts started earlier.

Acknowledgments. This work was partially supported by the Wallenberg AI, Autonomous Systems and Software Program (WASP) funded by the Knut and Alice Wallenberg Foundation, and the Competence Centre NextG2Com funded by the VINNOVA program for Advanced Digitalisation with grant number 2023-00541.

References

1. Clippy Documentation. https://doc.rust-lang.org/clippy/
2. Back to the Building Blocks: A Path Toward Secure and Measurable Software. Technical report, The White House (2024). https://upload.wikimedia.org/wikipedia/commons/e/e6/Back_to_the_Building_Blocks_-_A_Path_Toward_Secure_and_Measurable_Software.pdf
3. Bugden, W., Alahmar, A.: The safety and performance of prominent programming languages. Int. J. Software Eng. Knowl. Eng. **32**(05), 713–744 (2022)
4. Dinno, A.: Nonparametric pairwise multiple comparisons in independent groups using Dunn's test. Stand Genomic Sci. **15**(1), 292–300 (2015)
5. Emre, M., Boyland, P., Parekh, A., Schroeder, R., Dewey, K., Hardekopf, B.: Aliasing limits on translating C to safe rust **7**(OOPSLA1) (2023)
6. Emre, M., Schroeder, R., Dewey, K., Hardekopf, B.: Translating C to safer Rust. Proc. ACM Program. Lang. **5**(OOPSLA) (2021)
7. Eniser, H.F., et al.: Towards translating real-world code with LLMs: a study of translating to rust (2024). https://arxiv.org/abs/2405.11514
8. Ericsson: Company facts. https://www.ericsson.com/en/about-us/company-facts
9. Ericsson: Extensible Connection-oriented Messaging (XCM). https://github.com/Ericsson/xcm
10. Fulton, K.R., Chan, A., Votipka, D., Hicks, M., Mazurek, M.L.: Benefits and drawbacks of adopting a secure programming language: rust as a case study. In: USENIX Association Seventeenth Symposium on Usable Privacy and Security (2021)
11. Hummel, J., Viirola, E.: From C 2 Rust: Evaluating the Feasibility of Translating C to a Memory-Safe Programming Language at Ericsson (2025). Student Paper, LU-CS-EX: 2025-23
12. Immunant: C2Rust Manual. https://c2rust.com/manual/
13. jtfell: c-fft. https://github.com/jtfell/c-fft
14. Knott, E., Hamid Rao, A., Summers, K., Teeger, C.: Interviews in the social sciences. Nature Reviews Methods Primers (2022)
15. Li, R., Wang, B., Saxena, P., Kundu, A.: Translating C to rust: lessons from a user study. In: 32nd Annual Network and Distributed System Security Symposium (NDSS 2025) (2025)
16. Ling, M., Yu, Y., Wu, H., Wang, Y., Cordy, J.R., Hassan, A.E.: In rust we trust: a transpiler from unsafe C to safer rust. In: Proceedings of the ACM/IEEE 44th International Conference on Software Engineering: Companion Proceedings, ICSE 2022, pp. 354–355. ACM (2022)
17. McKight, P.E., Najab, J.: Kruskal-Wallis test. In: The Corsini Encyclopedia of Psychology, p. 1 (2010)
18. Microsoft: A proactive approach to more secure code. https://msrc.microsoft.com/blog/2019/07/a-proactive-approach-to-more-secure-code/
19. T.C. Project: Memory Safety. https://www.chromium.org/Home/chromium-security/memory-safety/

20. Zhang, H., David, C., Yu, Y., Wang, M.: Ownership guided c to rust translation (2023). https://arxiv.org/abs/2303.10515
21. Zhang, Y., Zhang, Y., Portokalidis, G., Xu, J.: Towards understanding the runtime performance of rust. In: Proceedings of the 37th IEEE/ACM International Conference on Automated Software Engineering, ASE 2022. Association for Computing Machinery, New York (2023)

Cross-Domain Evaluation of Transformer-Based Vulnerability Detection on Open and Industry Data

Moritz Mock[1]([✉]) [iD], Thomas Forrer[2], and Barbara Russo[1] [iD]

[1] Faculty of Engineering, Free University of Bozen-Bolzano, Bolzano, Italy
{momock,brusso}@unibz.it
[2] R&D Department, Würth Phoenix, Bolzano, Italy
thomas.forrer@wuerth-phoenix.net

Abstract. Deep learning solutions for vulnerability detection proposed in academic research are not always accessible to developers, and their applicability in industrial settings is rarely addressed. Transferring such technologies from academia to industry presents challenges related to trustworthiness, legacy systems, limited digital literacy, and the gap between academic and industrial expertise. For deep learning in particular, performance and integration into existing workflows are additional concerns. In this work, we first evaluate the performance of CodeBERT for detecting vulnerable functions in industrial and open-source software. We analyse its cross-domain generalisation when fine-tuned on open-source data and tested on industrial data, and vice versa, also exploring strategies for handling class imbalance. Based on these results, we develop AI-DO (*A*utomating vulnerability detection *I*ntegration for *D*evelopers *O*perations), a Continuous IntegrationContinuous Deployment (CI/CD)-integrated recommender system that uses fine-tuned CodeBERT to detect and localise vulnerabilities during code review without disrupting workflows. Finally, we assess the tools perceived usefulness through a survey with the companys IT professionals. Our results show that models trained on industrial data detect vulnerabilities accurately within the same domain but lose performance on open-source code, while a deep learner fine-tuned on open data, with appropriate undersampling techniques, improves the detection of vulnerabilities.

Keywords: Vulnerability Detection · Deep Learner · PHP · Cross-Domain Technology Evaluation · Data Balancing

1 Introduction

The role of security experts in software development is of paramount importance. Their major task is to review developers' code pushed into a development pipeline and report back security weaknesses. Often, their work is performed manually as the last task before code delivery. They frequently rely on publicly available open-source information and, at times, use black-box static analysers

©The Author(s) 2026
G. Scanniello et al. (Eds.): PROFES 2025, LNCS 16362, pp. 36–52, 2026.
https://doi.org/10.1007/978-3-032-12092-2_3

that are not always integrated into the companys development pipeline, creating custom rules to make the security scanner work for a specific application [34].

In this work, we aim to investigate whether a deep learner can be leveraged to enhance the automatic detection of vulnerable functions in industrial software and how it can be integrated into a company's DevOps environment. To this end, we first evaluated the performance of CodeBERT, a deep learner pre-trained on source code on the detection of vulnerable functions in both industrial and open-source software. Then, we examined whether this capability is retained when the model is fine-tuned on open-source data and then tested on industrial data. We further developed a tool (AI-DO) to automate the detection of vulnerable functions in an industrial DevOps environment embedding a deep learner, it is designed to allow to exchange the deep learner for future adjustments. AI-DO has been developed as a recommender system running over the Continuous Integration - Continuous Deployment (CI/CD) pipeline with a deep learner pre-trained on open source. It leverages multi-channel monitoring data to automatically detect and localise security weaknesses in code and present them to reviewers in their native environment. Finally, we gathered feedback from the companys IT professionals regarding the tool. To guide the analysis for our case study, we have defined two research questions:

RQ1. *Can CodeBERT be employed for vulnerability detection in industry source code?* This research question aims to explore how a deep learning model can be leveraged for the detection of vulnerabilities in industry. Our approach is therefore twofold: first, we compare the performance of a pre-trained model fine-tuned and tested with different balancing strategies on industrial data and open source data. Then, we develop AI-DO, embed it into the industrial DevOps of a company and ask the opinion of the company's IT professionals.

RQ2. *How well does CodeBERT fine-tuned on open source vulnerability data generalise to industrial technology-specific data?* This research question investigates the performance of fine-tuned models trained on open data and tested against industry data and vice versa. Furthermore, we explored various strategies for fine-tuning to mitigate data imbalance.

Overall, the contribution can be summarized with the following:

- We performed a cross-domain performance evaluation on between datasets collected in industry and open data and made them available.
- We implemented AI-DO, which supports reviewers in detecting vulnerabilities during the review process; furthermore, we have surveyed developer's about the a tool, *e.g.,* AI-DO, can support the review process.

The paper is structured as follows: Sect. 2 contains the related work, followed by the methodology in Sect. 3. Section 4 presents the case study, going over to the Sects. 5 and 6 which discuss the threats to validity and conclusion.

2   Related Work

We have reviewed the existing literature according to two dimensions: (i) AI models for vulnerability detection, and (ii) cross-domain evaluation of datasets collected in open-source and industry contexts.

2.1   AI Models for Vulnerability Detection

Vaswani *et al.* [37] introduced the transformer architecture, enabling efficient learning across diverse tasks. Typically, transformer models are pre-trained on general tasks and subsequently fine-tuned for specific applications, such as vulnerability detection in source code. BERT [4], trained on an English corpus, was later extended by RoBERTa [2], which modified the training data, objectives, and parameters, while still focusing on the English language. Building on previous developments, CodeBERT [7] leverages multiple programming languages into its pre-training, using the CodeSearchNet dataset [13]. This domain-specific training improves performance on code-related tasks compared to general-purpose models such as RoBERTa. Fu *et al.* [9] proposed LineVul, a model designed to detect vulnerabilities using the Big-Vul dataset [6], which is derived from CVE-referenced commits. Their approach initially focused on function-level vulnerability detection and was later extended to perform detections at the line level. In their work, Fu *et al.* employed CodeBERT as the underlying model and processed source code at the function level, treating it as plain text without incorporating any structural or positional information, later their approach was refined for line-level detection. Hin *et al.* [12] introduced LineVD, a deep learning framework, leveraging CodeBERT, that reframes statement-level vulnerability detection as a node classification task over program dependency graphs. By combining graph neural networkscapable of capturing control- and data-dependency structureswith to process raw source tokens, LineVD significantly outperforms prior techniques, achieving over a 105% improvement in F1-score on Big-Vul, a real-world C/C++ vulnerability dataset.

2.2   Cross-Domain Performance Evaluation of Datasets

Evaluating the performance of a novel approach is often limited to a single dataset, which may have been specifically created for that particular approach. However, assessing a tool's performance is resource- and time-consuming and using different benchmarks can unveil a lack of robustness in the approach. A comparison of different Static Application Security Testing (SAST) tools, focusing on their performance in detecting vulnerabilities in Java projects indicating that the combination of multiple SAST tools increases the accuracy of detecting vulnerabilities [17]; however, it is not considered to solely relay on them. In contrast, when evaluating different deep learning approaches on a new created dataset, trained and tested, resulted into a performance drop of up to 91% [1], indicating that a shift in the dataset makes highly specialized deep learning techniques impractical.

Despite the growing need to protect industry code from vulnerabilities [5,25], to the best of our knowledge, no cross-domain evaluation has been performed between open data, which are widely used in academia, and industry data. Therefore, the evaluation conducted in this work represents a critical first step in bridging the gap between academic research and industry practices. In contrast to the existing work, we do not focus solely on open data but investigate the performance of the a deep learner, in our case CodeBERT [7], trained on open data and applied on industry data. For the particular use case of the company, as an integration within the review process of source code.

3 Methodology

This section illustrates our methodology, starting with the creation of the dataset, going over to the multiple fine-tuning strategies of CodeBERT and cross-validation, concluding with the implementation details.

3.1 Dataset Creation and Annotation

To the best of our knowledge, there are no publicly available datasets of PHP functions annotated for vulnerability using a consistent methodology for both open and industrial code. As such, in this section, we present our technique to create and fuse three datasets: one from industry data, *i.e.*, *Industry Dataset* (ID) and the other two from open source data, the former from popular technology-agnostic open source projects, *i.e.*, *Generic Open-source Dataset* (GOD), and the latter from open source data originated from the same type of technology of the industrial data, *i.e.*, *Technology-similar Open-source Dataset* (TOD).

For each of the datasets, we applied the same annotation process as illustrated in Fig. 1.

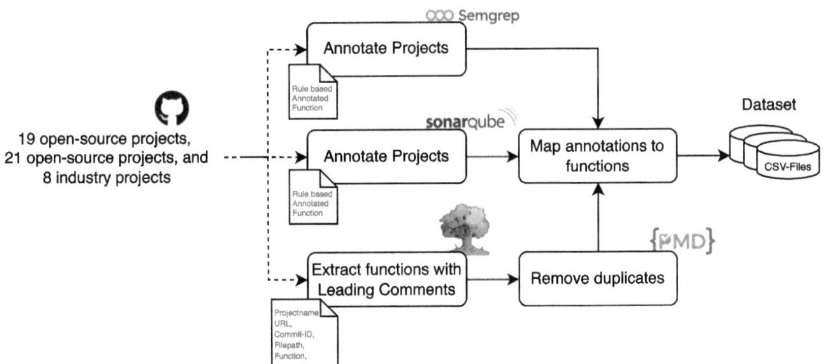

Fig. 1. Creation of an annotated dataset by data fusion of two annotation types from static analysers for 40 open source and 8 industry projects.

To extract the PHP functions, we leveraged TreeSitter [36], which was already employed successfully in recent mining studies [22,23]. After extracting the functions from each project, we removed duplicates. We used PMD-CPD [26], which detects duplicated code using a sliding-window approach and 99% Jaccard index threshold [32]. Following Mock *et al.* [23], we set the window size to 30, to balance coverage and computational cost.

Combining annotations from different tools helps detect a greater number of vulnerabilities in source code [24], we performed function-level annotations at the project level and mapped the output to the extracted functions. We leveraged two state-of-the-art static analysersSemGrep [28] and SonarQube [33]which are widely used and accepted in both industry and academia [14,16]. We reviewed the resulting function annotations and decided not to leverage the labels Info or Minor from SemGrep, and Warning from SonarQube, as indicators of vulnerabilities. The annotation is counted uniquely, *i.e.,* a function might have multiple vulnerabilities; however it is counted once. The schema of the datasets consists of two main parts. The first part contains the information that helps to extract a function, *i.e.,* the url, commit-id, filename, and position of the function in the original file. The second part contains the annotation per severity level. The data is provided in three distinct CSV files, one for each of the datasets.

The datasets were created to meet the quality standards defined by the framework proposed by Croft *et al.* [3], which specifies five attributes: accuracy, uniqueness, consistency, completeness, and currentness. *Accuracy* refers to the extent to which the data correctly represents the true value of the intended property. In our context, this means whether each function is accurately labelled as vulnerable or not. We employed Semgrep and SonarQube, two state-of-the-art SAST tools, for the automatic labelling of the functions. *Uniqueness* is the degree to which there is no duplication in records. In our context, this means whether each function has been unique in the dataset. We leveraged PMD-CPD [26] with 30-token sliding window to detect duplicate code snippets across functions. To remove ducplicates, we also compute the Jaccard similarity of each function pair and removed functions of 99% or higher similarity. *Consistency* is the degree to which data has attributes that are free from contradiction and are coherent with other data. In our context, this means whether each function have been annotated in a consistent manner with the different analysers over the different types of datasets. For this we leveraged the two SAST tools in the same version and setting across annotation of the three datasets. *Completeness* refers to the extent to which the data associated with an entity contains values for all expected attributes and related instances. In our context, this means that (1) the dataset must include sufficient information for each function to be uniquely identified within the source code and (2) the output of the static analysers can be used to clearly identify a function as vulnerable or not. For this, we include the Url, commit-ID, file path, and start/end-position of each functions using TreeSitter [36], a light-weighted code parser, such that the function can be traced back to the original location[1]. The output of the SAST tools is

---

[1] Due to company restrictions, the Url and commit ID are omitted for the dataset ID.

mapped automatically to the associated functions and stored by severity level; the scripts are available in the replication package [21]. *Currentness* is the degree to which data has attributes that are of the right age. In our context, this means that the data of the open source datasets pertain to the same period of time of industrial dataset. All datasets were created simultaneously leveraging the same SAST tools and configurations, ensuring temporal alignment of vulnerabilities.

3.2 CodeBERT Fine-Tuning

CodeBERT is a pre-trained deep learner on six programming languages developed by Microsoft Research [7]. It is designed specifically to work with both natural and programming language inputs. CodeBERT has been trained on the dataset CodeSearchNet [13]. CodeSearchNet covers six programming languages (Python, Java, JavaScript, PHP, Ruby, and Go) and provides general code understanding but lacks vulnerability information. CodeBERT has better performance than other pre-trained models, *e.g.*, UniXcoder [11], also in different software engineering settings [20].

Fine-tuning refers to the process of further training a pre-trained model on a specific downstream task, allowing it to adapt to task-specific data and improve performance. During this process, the weights of the models are changed so that the model can perform the desired task [4]. In our case, we performed fine-tuning on the pre-trained model CodeBERT [7]. We have fine-tuned CodeBERT on each of the three datasets for which we set the block size, batch size, and learning rate as 512, 16 and 2e-5 respectively, as suggested in the recent literature [9,30]. We fine-tuned each model for 10 epochs and performed a manual early stopping [27] if the F1 increases more than 0.001 within five epochs. We randomly split each dataset in 80%/10%/10%, for training, validation, and testing respectively. Furthermore, we trained and validated the model using four different data balancing techniques: (NB) no balancing, *i.e.*, the natural distribution of the dataset is taken; (USC) undersampling with the size of the smallest class across all datasets [15], *i.e.*, in our case, the vulnerable instances of ID constitute the smallest class with 4,934 instances, and all other classes have been balanced accordingly; (URSC) undersampling with the size of the relatively smallest class per dataset [9], *i.e.*, in each dataset, the smaller class (the vulnerable class) determines the sample size for the non-vulnerable class; and (WLF) weighted loss function with inverse class frequency [30], *i.e.*, the natural distribution of the dataset is maintained, but during training, the importance of the two classes is differentiated by adjusting the loss functions weights. The loss function quantifies the discrepancy between the model's detections and the actual values during training, serving as a metric to guide optimization by penalizing inaccurate detections [20]. No balancing was applied to the validation and testing set, *i.e.*, the natural distribution of the datasets were maintained.

Table 1. Development team' role and IT experience

Role		# Years working in industry
Software Developer	6	1–3 years
Software Engineer	2	12, 15 years
Software Engineer in R&D	1	2 years
Security Software Engineer	1	4 years
Software Architect	2	5, 11 years
DevOps	2	5 years
Team Leader	1	15 years

3.3 Cross-Domain Evaluation

We used precision, recall, and the F1 score to evaluate the performance of Code-BERT in vulnerability detection in the testing portion of the three data sets. We repeat the analysis for each of the balancing techniques. Performance measures are computed as follows:

$$P = \frac{TP}{TP+FP}, \ R = \frac{TP}{TP+FN}, \ F1 = 2 \cdot \frac{P \cdot R}{P+R}. \tag{1}$$

The goal of cross-domain analysis in our context is to evaluate the performance of CodeBERT on industry data after it has been fine-tuned on open source data. This analysis helps answer questions such as: **RQ1.**and **RQ2.** To investigate these problems, we fine-tune CodeBERT on the two datasets GOD and TOD and analyse its performance on the testing portion of the ID dataset. We then compared CodeBERT's performance on ID with its performance on the same dataset on which it has been fine-tuned, also using different balancing strategies.

4 Case Study

The case study was performed at Würth Phoenix, an Italian software company. We selected an ERP project written in PHP as it is representative of the company's business. The project has over 2.2 million lines of code, spanning over 74 thousand commits written in a period of up to 20 years. The development team consists of 15 members with the roles and IT experience reported in Table 1.

The company's internal CI/CD pipeline runs on a self-hosted and maintained instance of OpenShift [29]. Before the release of every new feature of the project, a five-step workflow is sequentially followed in the pipeline: low-level code design, development, code review, security review, and staging. *Low-level code design.* When a new feature is requested by a customer or internally, a low-level code design is performed [10,19]. Multiple developers internally discuss the new feature, including how it can be implemented, where best to place it in the

Table 2. Summary of annotations categorised by severity levels and tools.

Dataset	# fns	# vulnerable fns	Sonarqube			Semgrep
			Major	Critical	Blocker	Error
GOD	206,647	48,797	38,249	16,084	2,061	647
TOD	238,161	21,579	16,210	10,195	2,361	122
ID	64,333	6,149	3,337	4,094	322	0
Total	509,141	76,525	57,796	30,373	4,744	769

architecture of the current source code, and, if the current code needs to be modified, how to do this with minimal impact while still maintaining high reusability for the future. If needed, the feature is broken down into multiple tasks so that it is easier to handle them within a sprint [31]. The security expert participates in Sprint meetings to anticipate potential security risks and ensure security by design. *Development.* Based on the JIRA issues, developers implement the requested feature. A single task can be a feature or part of a larger feature. At this stage, no reviewers (code or security) are involved. *Code Review.* In this stage, newly added, changed, or removed code is inspected regarding architectural consequences, maintainability, and general quality of the code. Developers, architects, and software engineers are typically involved. *Security Review.* In the security review, newly added, changed, or removed source code is inspected for potential vulnerabilities, following the same schema as the code review by the security expert. *Deployment.* Issues' resolutions follow a pre-defined deployment schedule if they are general features. However, if they are vulnerability patches, they are deployed directly without respecting the general schedule.

4.1   Data Collection

The dataset GOD contains 209,532 functions of 21 open-source PHP projects selected based on their popularity. The dataset TOD contains 240,876 functions of the top 19 GitHub Enterprise Resource Planning tools (*ERP*) written in PHP (forks have been excluded). The dataset ID consists of 65,385 functions of eight ERP projects of the partner company. For each project, we collected all the functions included in the most recent version of project's repository. We then applied our approach and successfully removed 6,136 duplicated functions (1,052 in ID, 2,885 in GOD, and 2,229 in TOD), which were consistently duplicated with the two SAST tools. 76,181 were marked as vulnerable by SonarQube, and an additional 769 by SemGrep, resulting in a combined total of 76,525 vulnerable functions. It should be noted that the sum does not add up due to partial overlaps of the different severity levels. Table 2 illustrates the resulting datasets, with further insights into the severity levels from each SAST tool.

4.2   Cross-Domain Performance Evaluation

Plots in Fig. 2 illustrate Precision, Recall, and the F1 score of CodeBERT in each of the configurations of this study: the colour of the bars represents the type

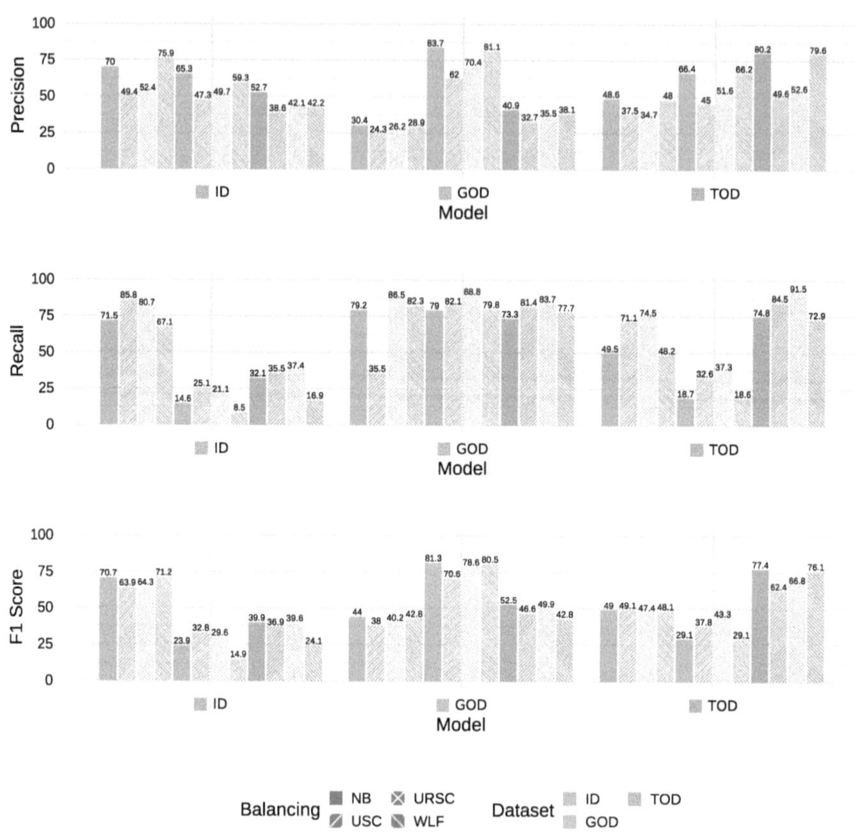

Fig. 2. Testing performance of CodeBERT fine-tuned on different datasets and with different balancing strategies.

of dataset chosen for testing. For example, green means that the performance of CodeBERT has been tested on ID. The pattern of the bars represents the balancing strategy. For instance, no pattern means that fine-tuning has been performed without balancing. On the x-axis, the labels indicate the datasets which have been used to fine-tune CodeBERT, *i.e.,* trained and validated on the vulnerability task. Thus, the first green bar in Fig. 2 refers to the F1 score (70.7) of CodeBERT that has been fine-tuned without balancing and tested on ID.

In vulnerability detection, the primary objective is to minimize false negatives (FN), since even a single undetected vulnerable function can lead to significant damage if exploited [18]. Therefore, in the following analysis, we prioritize recall over precision, as capturing all potential vulnerabilities is considered more critical than avoiding false alarms. To guide our analysis, we applied a three-fold approach: (1) analyse the most effective balancing strategy, (2) analyse how fine-tuning on different datasets affects the performance of CodeBERT on unseen data, and (3) restrict our analysis to the performance of CodeBERT on industrial unseen data.

To analyse the most effective balancing strategy, we analyse the plots in terms of the four balancing strategies described in Sect. 3.2.

- When both fine-tuning and testing are performed with the same dataset, we observe higher F1 score and precision with NB or WLF, whereas any type of *undersampling* is generally preferred to reduce FNs (increased recall).
- When fine-tuning is performed with ID and TOD and testing with GOD, we observe higher F1 score and recall with any type of *undersampling* techniques, whereas NB or WLF are better choices to increase precision.
- When fine-tuning is performed with ID and GOD and testing with TOD, we observe higher F1 score and precision without balancing (NB), whereas any type of *undersampling* techniques is preferred to increase recall.
- When fine-tuning is performed on TOD and GOD and testing is computed on ID, we observe higher F1 score and precision with NB and WLF, whereas any type of *undersampling* techniques is preferred to increase recall.

In summary, when maximizing recall is the primary objective, we recommend applying undersampling techniques. Conversely, for optimizing overall performance as measured by the F1-score, either no balancing or the use of a weighted loss function is more appropriate.

We then study how fine-tuning on different datasets affects the performance of CodeBERT on unseen data.

- When CodeBERT has been fine-tuned with TOD, we observe the best performance for all measures is testing with the same dataset. In addition, recall is better when testing with ID than with the dataset GOD.
- When CodeBERT has been fine-tuned with GOD, we observe the best performance for Precision and F1 score when testing with GOD, whereas testing with ID produces similar - sometimes even better - recall.
- When CodeBERT has been fine-tuned with ID, we observe the best performance for all measures when testing with ID itself. Testing with open source data produce a poor recall.

Generally speaking, testing on the same dataset on which CodeBERT has been fine-tuned yields better performance. However, in terms of FNs, we can observe that (1) Fine-tuning on open-source data and testing on industrial databoth from the same technologyresults in fewer FNs compared to testing on general open-source data. Technology-related open source data does not generalize well to general open source data. (2) Fine-tuning on industrial data and testing on open-source data leads to a significant increase of FNs. (3) Fine-tuning on technology-agnostic open source data is worth to detect vulnerabilities of industrial code (similar or better recall). Motivated by the last result, we pose the following question. Thus, when we further restrict our analysis to the performance of CodeBERT on industrial unseen data we notice that:

- precision and F1 score decrease if CodeBERT has been fine-tuned with any open-source data;

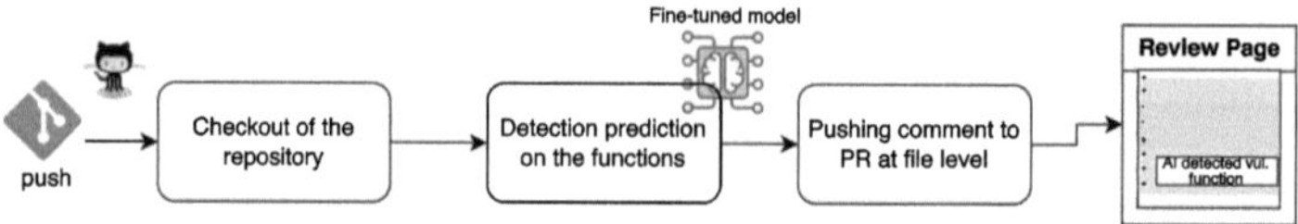

Fig. 3. Flow of the pipeline integrated into a GitHub Action.

– fine-tuning with GOD combined with undersampling within the same dataset (URSC) yields higher recall than fine-tuning with ID or TOD using any balancing techniques. In addition, CodeBERT achieves higher recall if fine-tuned on the GOD dataset rather than on the ID dataset, whether using NB or WLF techniques.

In summary, using technology-agnostic open-source data to detect unseen industrial vulnerabilities can result in better control of FNs than using industrial data from the same system. However, FPs are an issue.

4.3 AI-DO

In the previous section, we showed that CodeBERT successfully detects vulnerabilities in industrial software. We also observed that CodeBERT can be fine-tuned on technology-agnostic open source data for this task. Thus, we developed AI-DO that leverages an instance of CodeBERT fine-tuned on GOD on the DevOps pipeline of the company illustrated in Sect. 4. AI-DO is integrated within a GitHub Action; furthermore, it leverages git [35] and TreeSitter [36] for the automatic extraction of functions changed or newly added within a pull request. Figure 3 illustrates the process of pushing to the repository, triggering the pipeline, detecting the vulnerabilities, and commenting on the pull request (PR). The first step is divided into five sub-steps critical to the vulnerability detection process. First, git diff identifies the affected file paths and the corresponding modified lines. The repository is checked out with both the **destination** and **source** branches. The files impacted by the pull request are extracted using git diff, along with the modified line ranges. Functions from these files are parsed using TreeSitter [36] and filtered based on their overlap with the modified lines to ensure relevance. The fine-tuned instance of Code-BERT is applied to the relevant functions. Functions detected as vulnerable are automatically tagged to support reviewer decision-making. An example setup and the source code are available in the replication package [21]. Finally, we presented AI-DO to the IT professionals of the company and collected their opinions with a brief survey.

AI-DO hosts a deep learner that is fine-tuned offline, ensuring complete non-intrusiveness in the development process. This model can be periodically updated offline with new data to improve accuracy, if necessary. Furthermore, AI-DO is designed to allow the fine-tuned model to be replaced, enhancing its usability and applicability beyond the scope of our work.

Developers' Perspective We administered a brief questionnaire about AI-DO[2] to 13 of the 15 IT professionals at the company (two developers were absent). The questionnaire collects information about their review process, their opinion on a line-level vulnerability detection tool like AI-DO, and their demographic. The questionnaire alternates closed and open questions.

We review their answers by their role as illustrate in Table 1. The security expert has been conducting code reviews focused on security for four years, multiple times per week, identifying vulnerabilities several times each month. However, he is only moderately enthusiastic about the tool. This is a typical reaction among specialized professionals, who often believe that new tools might eventually put at danger their role in the organization [8]. The two DevOps experts have different levels of experience with vulnerability detection during the review process. Both review code weekly to identify bugs; however, the expert who encounters vulnerabilities more frequentlyapproximately one per monthexpressed greater appreciation for the tool, stating: This tool is really useful to speed up and improve the development process! It could help to spot issues before they go to production. Conversely, the expert who rarely encounters vulnerabilities is the most negative among all participants and suggests that the tool should be enhanced with a more extensive set of detection rules. The three software engineers, although they do not normally find many vulnerabilities during their review tasks, greatly appreciate the tool. Two of them have extensive experience in IT and code review. The third is a junior engineer whose work focuses more on process quality than on code, as she rarely performs code reviews. The four developers are junior professionals who perform code reviews frequentlymultiple times a weekas it is one of their primary tasks. All are moderately satisfied with the tool, although they acknowledge lacking sufficient experience in vulnerability detection. The two software architects, who review code as frequently as the developers, are more enthusiastic about the tool. They both recommend enhancing it to provide more detailed information on the type of vulnerability and to explain the reasoning behind AI-DOs output (*i.e.*, the vulnerable lines of code). The team leader is an experienced professional who performs code reviews sporadically, approximately once per month, also with the specific aim of detecting vulnerabilities. He moderately appreciate the tool, considering it insufficiently precise, as vulnerabilities often span multiple lines and classes.

In summary, professionals enthusiasm for security tools largely depends on their experience with vulnerability detection and how well the tool supports their specific needs. While experts who frequently find vulnerabilities see clear benefits, those with less exposure or more specialized roles tend to be more cautious or critical, often concerned about the tools limitations or its potential impact on their expertise.

Implementation Details and Replication Package. The implementation details can be found in the replication package [21].

---

[2] Available in the replication package [21].

4.4   Answers to the Research Questions

RQ1. Yes, CodeBERT fine-tuned on data of the company performs comparatively well on industrial unseen data with at most a 10% decrease of the F1 score with respect to CodeBERT fine-tuned and tested on open source unseen data. Using a weighted loss function in fine tuning this gaps further reduces. However, when the focus is on reducing FNs, undersampling techniques can be more efficacious. After introducing AI-DO, which implements our approach in the companys DevOps PHP environment, we observed that professionals enthusiasm for the tool depends on their experience with vulnerability detection and the extent to which it addresses their specific needs. Experts who frequently detect vulnerabilities recognize clear benefits, whereas those with less exposure or highly specialized roles are more cautious as they may see its potential to diminish the value of their expertise.

> CodeBERT is suitable for vulnerability detection in the industrial domain, achieving performance comparable to its detection capabilities in the open-source domain. Undersampling techniques can help decrease the number of FNs in both domain. Automating vulnerability detection in an industrial DevOps environment characterized by clearly defined roles eventually needs to address the resistance of highly specialized professionals who may perceive their roles as being at risk.

RQ2. We conducted a cross-domain evaluation by fine-tuning CodeBERT on technology-specific and technology-agnostic open-source data (resp. TOD and GOD) and testing it on unseen industrial data (ID). We found that fine-tuning with URSC undersampling on a technology-agnostic open-source dataset can provide better control of false negatives in detecting unseen industrial vulnerabilities than fine-tuning industrial data from the same system with any balancing techniques. This may be due to the greater heterogeneity of vulnerability types and coding styles present in the open-source dataset that can improve the models ability to identify real vulnerabilities in industrial systems, reducing false negatives that could otherwise leave security flaws unaddressed. However, this detection capability comes at the cost of increased false positives, which can burden development teams with unnecessary investigations and potentially reduce trust in AI-DO.

> Fine-tuning CodeBERT with technology-agnostic open-source vulnerability data using appropriate undersampling improves the detection of industrial vulnerabilities. However, this may increase professional' workload and affect trust in a detection tool.

5   Threats to Validity

Construct Validity: Threats to construct validity refer to the extent to which the experimental setting actually reflects the construct under study. We study the portability of a fine-tuned pre-trained deep learner for vulnerability detection between open and industry data. Three datasets were collected using the same; differences in sample size and vulnerability count were addressed by balancing and weighting strategies. The deep learner was created in the same way for all the datasets; enabling fair same-domain and cross-domain performance comparison.
Internal Validity: Threats in this category are related to internal factors that could have influenced the results. Threats including duplicate code in the datasets, which we mitigated by PMD-CPD, and possible shared code between open and industry datasets from sources like Stack Overflow, which could not be identified.
External Validity: Threats in this category concern the generalizability of the results. Results may be specific to our datasets. A domain shift was found to reduce the generalizability, as intended in our study design. Results from the survey might be biased in favour of the work, as the first author had prior contact with the participants; a replication of the survey would strengthen the findings. PHP was selected as target programming language due to the need of the company for it, which might limit broader generalizability.
Conclusion Validity: This aspect regards the relationship between treatment and outcome, *i.e.*, if we can ascertain, with a given significance, that the outcome was a consequence of the treatment. We applied standard metrics to evaluate model performance to assess the performance of the deep learner.

6   Conclusion and Further Work

We evaluated a fine-tuned deep learning model for vulnerability detection in an industrial setting. The insights we collected led to the development of AI-DO, which we later evaluated by surveying developers from 13 companies to assess its value. To examine cross-domain applicability, we created three datasets annotated under the same policy: one company projects, and two from open-source projectsone domain-related and one general. Fine-tuning CodeBERT on the three datasets individually, and further assessing different balancing strategies, enabled us to study learning transfer. Results show the approach is feasible and valuable for companies aiming to shift left vulnerability detection, *i.e.*, detecting vulnerable code as early in the development process as possible. Developers were open-minded regarding the tool, AI-DO, but concerns arose regarding trust and localisation of the solution. Models trained on industrial data performed well in-domain but poorly on general open-source code, likely due to differences in vulnerability types and coding standards. Training on technology-agnostic open data with undersampling increases the detection of vulnerabilities in the industrial dataset. Future work includes extending to multiple programming languages, transformer models, and annotation types, leveraging our new multi-annotation dataset [23].

Acknowledgement. Funded by the European Union- Next Generation EU, Mission 4 Component 1 CUP I52B23000570003. The work has been funded by the project CyberSecurity Laboratory no. EFRE1039 under the 2023 EFRE/FESR program. We acknowledge ISCRA for awarding this project access to the LEONARDO supercomputer, owned by the EuroHPC Joint Undertaking, hosted by CINECA (Italy). We thank Würth Phoenix for hosting the first author and providing the data for this work. This work was supported by the Open Access Publishing Fund of the Free University of Bozen-Bolzano.

References

1. Chakraborty, P., Arumugam, K.K., Alfadel, M., Nagappan, M., McIntosh, S.: Revisiting the performance of deep learning-based vulnerability detection on realistic datasets. IEEE Trans. Software Eng. **50**(8), 2163–2177 (2024). https://doi.org/10.1109/TSE.2024.3423712
2. Chen, T., et al.: The lottery ticket hypothesis for pre-trained BERT networks. In: Advances in Neural Information Processing Systems, vol. 33. Curran Associates, Inc. (2020)
3. Croft, R., Babar, M.A., Kholoosi, M.M.: Data quality for software vulnerability datasets. In: 2023 IEEE/ACM 45th International Conference on Software Engineering (ICSE), pp. 121–133 (2023). https://doi.org/10.1109/ICSE48619.2023.00022
4. Devlin, J., Chang, M.W., Lee, K., Toutanova, K.: BERT: pre-training of deep bidirectional transformers for language understanding (2019). https://arxiv.org/abs/1810.04805
5. Dong, C., Li, S., Yang, S., Xiao, Y., Wang, Y., Li, H., Li, Z., Sun, L.: LibvDiff: library version difference guided OSS version identification in binaries. In: Proceedings of the IEEE/ACM 46th International Conference on Software Engineering. ICSE '24, Association for Computing Machinery, New York, NY, USA (2024)
6. Fan, J., Li, Y., Wang, S., Nguyen, T.N.: A C/C++ code vulnerability dataset with code changes and CVE summaries. In: 2020 IEEE/ACM 17th International Conference on Mining Software Repositories (MSR), pp. 508–512 (2020)
7. Feng, Z., et al.: CodeBERT: a pre-trained model for programming and natural languages. arXiv preprint arXiv:2002.08155 (2020)
8. Fitzgerald, B., Kesan, J.P., Russo, B., Shaikh, M., Succi, G.: Adopting Open Source Software: A Practical Guide. The MIT Press (2011)
9. Fu, M., Tantithamthavorn, C.: LineVul: a transformer-based line-level vulnerability prediction. In: Proceedings of the 19th International Conference on Mining Software Repositories, pp. 608–620 (2022)
10. Gamma, E.: Design patterns: elements of reusable object-oriented software. Person Education Inc (1995)
11. Guo, D., Lu, S., Duan, N., Wang, Y., Zhou, M., Yin, J.: UniXcoder: unified cross-modal pre-training for code representation (2022). https://arxiv.org/abs/2203.03850, published in ACL 2022
12. Hin, D., Kan, A., Chen, H., Babar, M.A.: LineVD: statement-level vulnerability detection using graph neural networks. In: Proceedings of the 19th International Conference on Mining Software Repositories, pp. 596–607. MSR '22, Association for Computing Machinery, New York, NY, USA (2022)

13. Husain, H., Wu, H.H., Gazit, T., Allamanis, M., Brockschmidt, M.: CodeSearch-Net challenge: evaluating the state of semantic code search. arXiv preprint arXiv:1909.09436 (2019)
14. Improta, C., Tufano, R., Liguori, P., Cotroneo, D., Bavota, G.: Quality in, quality out: investigating training data's role in AI code generation. In: 2025 IEEE/ACM 33rd International Conference on Program Comprehension (ICPC) (2025)
15. Le, T.H.M., Ali Babar, M.: Mitigating data imbalance for software vulnerability assessment: does data augmentation help? In: Proceedings of the 18th ACM/IEEE International Symposium on Empirical Software Engineering and Measurement, pp. 119–130. ESEM '24, Association for Computing Machinery, New York, NY, USA (2024). https://doi.org/10.1145/3674805.3686674
16. Lenarduzzi, V., Lomio, F., Huttunen, H., Taibi, D.: Are SonarQube rules inducing bugs? In: 2020 IEEE 27th International Conference on Software Analysis, Evolution and Reengineering (SANER), pp. 501–511 (2020)
17. Li, K., et al.: Comparison and evaluation on static application security testing (SAST) tools for java. In: Proceedings of the 31st ACM Joint European Software Engineering Conference and Symposium on the Foundations of Software Engineering, pp. 921–933. ESEC/FSE 2023, Association for Computing Machinery, New York, NY, USA (2023)
18. Li, Z., et al.: VulDeePecker: a deep learning-based system for vulnerability detection. arXiv preprint arXiv:1801.01681 (2018)
19. McConnell, S.: Code complete. Pearson Education (2004)
20. Mock, M., Borsani, T., Di Fatta, G., Russo, B.: Optimizing deep learning models to address class imbalance in code comment classification. In: 2025 IEEE/ACM International Workshop on Natural Language-Based Software Engineering (NLBSE), pp. 45–48 (2025). https://doi.org/10.1109/NLBSE66842.2025.00016
21. Mock, M., Forrer, T., Russo, B.: Cross-evaluation of transformer-based vulnerability detection on open and proprietary data (2025). https://github.com/CybersecurityLab-unibz/cross_domain_evaluation
22. Mock, M., Forrer, T., Russo, B.: Where do developers admit their security-related concerns? In: Agile Processes in Software Engineering and Extreme Programming – Workshops, pp. 189–195. Springer Nature Switzerland, Cham (2025)
23. Mock, M., Melegati, J., Kretschmann, M., Diaz Ferreyra, N.E., Russo, B.: MADE-WIC: Multiple annotated datasets for exploring weaknesses in code. In: Proceedings of the 39th IEEE/ACM International Conference on Automated Software Engineering, pp. 2346–2349. ASE '24, Association for Computing Machinery (2024)
24. Nguyen-Duc, A., Do, M.V., Luong Hong, Q., Nguyen Khac, K., Nguyen Quang, A.: On the adoption of static analysis for software security assessment–a case study of an open-source e-government project. Comput. Secur. **111**, 102470 (2021)
25. Pan, S., Bao, L., Zhou, J., Hu, X., Xia, X., Li, S.: Unveil the mystery of critical software vulnerabilities. In: Companion Proceedings of the 32nd ACM International Conference on the Foundations of Software Engineering, pp. 138–149. FSE 2024, Association for Computing Machinery, New York, NY, USA (2024)
26. PMD-CPD (2024). https://pmd.github.io/pmd/pmd_userdocs_cpd.html
27. Prechelt, L.: Early stopping-but when? In: Neural Networks: Tricks of the trade, pp. 55–69. Springer (2002)
28. r2c: Semgrep (2024). https://semgrep.dev, version 0.73.0
29. Red Hat, I.: OpenShift: Kubernetes Platform for Developing and Running Applications (2011). https://www.openshift.com/. Accessed 16 Jun 2025

30. Russo, B., Melegati, J., Mock, M.: Leveraging multi-task learning to improve the detection of SATD and vulnerability. In: 2025 IEEE/ACM 33rd International Conference on Program Comprehension (ICPC), pp. 01–12 (2025)
31. Schwaber, K., Sutherland, J.: The scrum guide. Scrum Alliance **21**(1), 1–38 (2011)
32. Sneath, P.: The application of computers to taxonomy. Microbiology **17**(1) (1957)
33. SonarSource S.A: Sonarqube (2024). https://www.sonarqube.org, version 9.4
34. Thomas, T.W., Tabassum, M., Chu, B., Lipford, H.: Security during application development: an application security expert perspective. In: Proceedings of the 2018 CHI Conference on Human Factors in Computing Systems, pp. 1–12 (2018)
35. Torvalds, L., Hamano, J.C.: Git: Distributed Version Control System (2005). https://git-scm.com/. Accessed 16 Jun 2025
36. Tree-sitter Project: Tree-sitter: an incremental parsing system for programming tools (2018). https://tree-sitter.github.io/tree-sitter/. accessed 16 Jun 2025
37. Vaswani, A., et al.: Attention is all you need. In: Advances in Neural Information Processing Systems (2017)

Software Testing Education and Industry Needs - Report from the ENACTEST EU Project

Mehrdad Saadatmand[1]([✉]) [iD], Abbas Khan[1] [iD], Beatriz Marin[2] [iD],
Ana C. R. Paiva[3] [iD], Nele Van Asch[4], Graham Moran[5], Felix Cammaerts[6] [iD],
Monique Snoeck[6] [iD], and Alexandra Mendes[3] [iD]

[1] RISE Research Institutes of Sweden, Västerås, Sweden
{mehrdad.saadatmand,abbas.khan}@ri.se
[2] Universitat Politècnica de València, València, Spain
bmarin@dsic.upv.es
[3] INESC TEC, Faculty of Engineering, University of Porto, Porto, Portugal
{apaiva,afmendes}@fe.up.pt
[4] AE nv, Leuven, Belgium
nele.vanasch@ae.be
[5] NEXO QA, Barcelona, Spain
graham.moran@nexoqa.com
[6] LIRIS, KU Leuven, Leuven, Belgium
{felix.cammaerts,monique.snoeck}@kuleuven.be

Abstract. The evolving landscape of software development demands that software testers continuously adapt to new tools, practices, and acquire new skills. This study investigates software testing competency needs in industry, identifies knowledge gaps in current testing education, and highlights competencies and gaps not addressed in academic literature. This is done by conducting two focus group sessions and interviews with professionals across diverse domains, including railway industry, healthcare, and software consulting and performing a curated small-scale scoping review. The study instrument, co-designed by members of the ENACTEST project consortium, was developed collaboratively and refined through multiple iterations to ensure comprehensive coverage of industry needs and educational gaps. In particular, by performing a thematic qualitative analysis, we report our findings and observations regarding: professional training methods, challenges in offering training in industry, different ways of evaluating the quality of training, identified knowledge gaps with respect to academic education and industry needs, future needs and trends in testing education, and knowledge transfer methods within companies. Finally, the scoping review results confirm knowledge gaps in areas such as AI testing, security testing and soft skills.

Keywords: software testing · education · industry needs · knowledge transfer

G. Scanniello et al. (Eds.): PROFES 2025, LNCS 16362, pp. 53–68, 2026.
https://doi.org/10.1007/978-3-032-12092-2_4

1   Introduction

Given the growing role of software systems and digital services in daily life and industry, coupled with the rapid advancement of technologies and the increasing complexity of software systems, there is a continuous demand for the improvement or development of new, more effective and adaptive software testing techniques and strategies.

Although there is no doubt that effective software testing is crucial, sometimes it is neglected, which results in flawed and unreliable software applications. The cause is originated from a skills mismatch between what is needed in industry, the learning needs of students and the way testing is currently being taught at Higher Education (HE) and Vocational Education and Training (VET).

The increasing complexity of software systems (e.g., driven by the proliferation of Internet-of-Things (IoT), adoption of Artificial Intelligence (AI), persistent security vulnerabilities, increasing product variability, and evolving development practices) demands updated software testing courseware that addresses technical challenges, automation needs, security concerns, regulatory compliance, and essential soft skills.

Therefore, to identify and develop software testing teaching materials aligned with industry needs, we need to foster a collaborative environment where HEs, VETs and companies can share knowledge and develop new approaches to software testing education, considering a broader socioeconomic context. This will improve students' learning performance and their software testing skills, given that software testing is increasingly important in digital job profiles across the labor market. In the long term, this will improve the quality of the software on which our digitalized society depends.

In this scenario, with all these current and evolving challenges, there is an urgent need for the adaptation of educational programs.

This paper presents a study performed in the scope of the ENACTEST European project[1] [10,11] that, by working directly with industry, aims to identify the competences needed by practitioners in their daily jobs and, from there, identify the adaptations needed to be implemented in software testing educational programs. In this regard, the paper particularly focuses on answering the following research questions (RQs).

> **Research Questions**
>
> **RQ1:** *What are the perceived competence needs for testers in industry?*
> **RQ2:** *What are the knowledge gaps in the current testing education?*
> **RQ3:** *Which of the identified industrial competence needs and knowledge*
> ...   *gaps are not covered in the literature?*

Firstly, RQ1 focuses on the collection of data on various trainings and educational sessions provided to testers in professional settings, with the aim of highlighting the needed competences. RQ1 also focuses on how this knowledge

---

[1] https://enactest-project.eu/.

is transferred within the company. Secondly, RQ2 aims to identify the gaps in software testing training and education that need to be addressed. Thirdly, RQ3 focuses on highlighting the unique industrial competence needs that are not covered by existing literature, and in turn, validates the findings of RQ1 and RQ2.

This study investigates industry expectations regarding software testing education in academia, and identifies existing gaps as well as emerging trends. The identified gaps are useful for enhancing academic curricula and practical training, fostering the alignment with real-world needs. Overall, this work equips the industry with valuable guidance to promote continuous learning in a rapidly evolving body of knowledge.

This paper is structured as follows. Section 2 provides a brief description of the European research project, ENACTEST, in which this work is being performed. Section 3 describes the method used to collect qualitative data about software testing industrial needs. Section 4 describes the results and observations of the study performed. Section 5 presents the threats to validity, and Sect. 6 concludes and points to future work.

2   ENACTEST Project

ENACTEST [10] is an ERASMUS+ EU project (2022–2025) which addresses the challenges in software testing education from three interconnected perspectives within computer science education: students, industry, and academia. The ENACTEST project aims to create educational materials, known as capsules, which are designed to be concise and easy to incorporate into existing courses without adding extra workload for educators. The capsules introduce innovative teaching techniques in higher education (universities and vocational centers) tailored to students' learning needs and aligned with industry requirements in order to enhance students' competencies and, consequently, their skills as future professionals in the software testing processes.

The project consortium comprises a diverse group of beneficiaries to ensure the outcomes benefit the entire socioeconomic landscape. The active involvement of industry is crucial for the success and relevance of the ENACTEST results. In response to the rapidly evolving demands of the software sector, the inclusion of small businesses and applied research centers within the ENACTEST consortium plays a key role in ensuring that the educational capsules developed are aligned with current professional practices and industry expectations. Concretely, the ENACTEST consortium includes four universities, one vocational training center, and four small businesses: Universitat Politècnica de València (UPV) - Spain, Katholieke Universiteit Leuven (KU Leuven) - Belgium, Universidade do Porto (UP) - Portugal, Università degli Studi di Napoli Federico II (UNINA) - Italy, RISE Research Institutes of Sweden (RISE) - Sweden, Centro Superior de Formacion Europa-Sur (CESUR) - Spain, NEXO QA - Spain, INOVA+ - Portugal, and CTG - Belgium.

The capsules undergo a continuous process of refinement and validation [11]. Along with the materials and resources developed, the latest version of each capsule is published on the ENACTEST project website. This enables the broader community to access and utilize them for educational and professional purposes [4].

Moreover, considering the dynamic nature of industry, and the flexibility and adaptability required in research projects [12], the ENACTEST team decided to first identify the industry needs directly through relevant industry stakeholders, in order to obtain first-hand information that reflects the most recent demands. After that, the ENACTEST team decided to contrast these needs with the existing literature in order to validate them broadly.

3   Study Design

In this section, we describe the method used to collect qualitative data about the industrial needs of software testing.

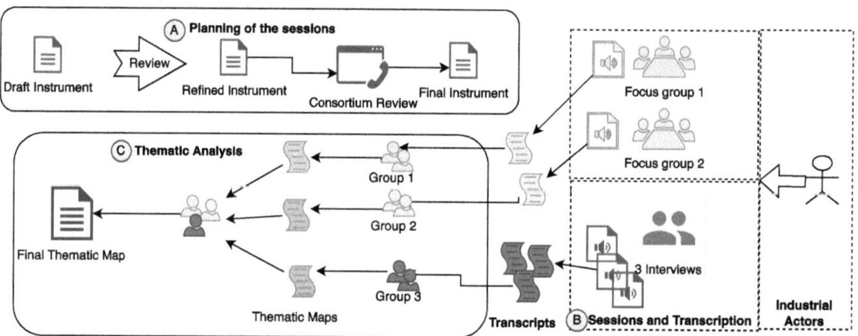

Fig. 1. Mixed-method study design to collect qualitative data about industrial needs

Figure 1 illustrates the study design and procedure, which began with planning the sessions and interviews (A). During the planning phase, a series of meetings were conducted to draft an instrument for the study. Then, the instrument was reviewed by the relevant part of the project consortium, and a final version was produced for use in conducting the studies with key actors. This was followed by the session and transcription (B), and thematic analysis (C). Next, we provide a brief overview of the procedure used to obtain and analyze the results.

A. Planning of the sessions: As mentioned, an initial instrument was drafted by the ENACTEST partners. Four experts from the consortium (two from industry and two from a research institute) contributed to the development of the initial draft of the instrument. To divide the work better, the instrument was split into three parts, covering data collection for testing, training, knowledge gaps, and knowledge transfer. The creation of the instrument was guided by the standard terminologies used in the field of software testing. The produced initial instrument was reviewed, refined, and reordered by all four members of the consortium. Finally, the entire ENACTEST consortium was invited to review and refine the instrument, resulting in a final three-part instrument. Below, we briefly summarize the topics covered in the three-part instrument that has been produced.

Part 1: Software Testing Training
Demographics of software testing training at the participant's company
- Type (internal or external), and Topic
  The mode of Delivery of the training that is given at the participant's company

- Delivery mode (virtual, on-site), Evaluation method (Exercises, questionnaire, example cases), training material used (slides, case studies, software)

Adequacy of the training to current needs

- Theory vs practice, Interaction, learning evaluation, things missing from the training

Part 2: Knowledge Gaps and Void

- Gaps in software testing education, training, business knowledge, tooling, and current practices
- Needed skills from a five-year perspective
- Ways to fill the gaps

Part 3: Knowledge Transfer
Knowledge transfer process at the participant's company

- Mode and direction of transfer (formal or informal), Budget assignment

Mediums of knowledge transfer

- Types of sessions, Tools used, and material used for facilitating knowledge transfer

---

In parallel, while drafting the initial instrument, a diverse set of industrial actors was identified, working in a total of six domains. The key industrial actors were informed about the study and asked to provide a list of potential participants that would be relevant to the study. Based on convenience sampling, a total of 12 participants were reached who participated in the two focus group sessions and the interviews performed. We refer readers to Sect. 3-A for more details about the background of the participants.

Three working groups were formed within the ENACTEST consortium to conduct the sessions and transcribe the recordings. The working groups were also responsible for analyzing the collected data and reviewing the reported results of the other groups. After the final instrument was drafted (step A) and participants were sampled from the industry (left part of Fig. 1), the three working groups organized three sessions based on the availability of all the participants. The selected participants who agreed to participate in the sessions were briefed in advance about the ENACTEST project and the session in an email. Two sessions were planned and executed as focus groups, following the guidelines [2]. In addition, the third working group used interviews as a research method to collect data from three interviews. All the sessions used the same study instrument that was produced as output of step (A) of Fig. 1. In the actual sessions (step B of Fig. 1), consent for recording was obtained from the participants, and the sessions were recorded. The sessions lasted from one to two hours and included a brief introduction to the project's objectives and the activity itself.

The recorded audio files of the session were transcribed and anonymized to omit any confidential information. The transcription of three interviews and two focus groups resulted in a total of 70 pages of Word documents that were again subjected to anonymization of confidential information. The resultant documents were analysed following the guidelines for the commonly used analysis method for qualitative data, thematic analysis [1].

C. Thematic Analysis Qualitative data can be analyzed in several different ways. In our case, we use the commonly applied thematic analysis approach following the guidelines proposed by Braun and Clarke [1]. We introduce some important background concepts related to thematic analysis as follows.

- *Theme* is an abstraction of a commonly occurring pattern within qualitative data.
- *Sub-Theme* is an abstraction of a sub-pattern within a theme.
- *Codes* act as labels assigned to chunks of qualitative data (such as sentences) for indexing.
- *Thematic Map* is a visual or tabular representation of the extracted themes, sub-themes, and codes.

As mentioned, three working groups were formed by the ENACTEST team that took each session's transcript for analysis. Following the cited guidelines, each transcript was independently coded by each group. The codes were directly extrapolated from the transcripts by identifying keywords that were mentioned during the focus group sessions. For example, the code'security testing' was identified from the comment "security testing is a necessary skill that modern testers should have". The coded transcripts were then analysed for recurring themes and subthemes. As a result, three thematic maps were derived from the two focus group sessions and the interviews. Members of the working groups reviewed each other's coded transcripts and thematic maps. Then, three working groups collected all the extracted themes and sub-themes in a final collective thematic map where the themes are ranked based on the frequency of occurrence in the transcripts. The resultant thematic map comprises more than 60 themes and sub-themes, each with its corresponding frequency. In the following sections, we present the results in a traceable manner where the themes are linked to sub-themes and codes and are supported by additional evidence (quotes) from the actual transcripts. Note that the quotes from the transcript (in italics) are rewritten for better readability, and context is added in [squared brackets] when needed.

Participants

Focus group 1: The first set of participants for the first focus group were selected based on convenience. To enable diversity in data collected, the domain chosen for the first target group was the safety-critical transportation domain of the railway industry. A company in Sweden was approached to participate in the study and was briefed about the ENACTEST project. We managed to recruit five participants from the railway industry working in two different teams. We ensured diversity among the selected participants in their roles, experiences, and gender. Nevertheless, every participant worked (directly or indirectly) in software testing, verification, and safety compliance in their daily work, with experience ranging from 1 to 15 years.

Focus group 2: The second set of participants—for a second focus group—were recruited from the web/mobile application development domain. For this set of participants, we recruited experienced developers and testers based on convenience, with experience ranging from 8 to 15 years. Below, we provide a brief summary of the participants' background.

- Participant 1: 15 years of experience in testing within various sectors, performing manual testing, test automation, quality control for certification, and external and internal audits.
- Participant 2: 10+ years of QA experience within various sectors, focusing on manual testing, test automation for web and mobile applications.
- Participant 3: 8 years of QA experience, mainly working with testing automation for web and other applications.
- Participant 4: 10 years of QA experience, focusing on both manual and automated testing for web, mobile, and backend applications.

Interviews: Interviewees 1 and 2: Both representing Partena Professional, brought a combined view from both a technical and operational standpoint. Their experiences added depth to the discussions, especially in terms of integrating technical expertise with business objectives. They currently focus primarily on optimization and standardization within company projects.

Interviewee 3, from Robovision, provided a unique viewpoint based on their role in overseeing software testing processes. Their contributions shed light on the managerial and strategic aspects of software testing and training. Interviewee 2 has over 20 years of experience in Test Management and Test Automation. As Test Program manager, Interviewee 2 coordinated several programs where multiple agile test teams were working together (in parallel) to deliver a program in the same release.

Interviewee 4, Representing Daedalus, provided insights from their experience in software development and testing. Their perspective was particularly valuable in understanding the practical applications of testing methodologies within a corporate setting. With more than 15 years of experience in the healthcare industry, they gave insights into how testing is done in their company.

4   Industry Needs: Thematic Analysis and Observations

In this study, we have consciously deviated from the traditional approach of initiating our research with a literature study. Instead, we began with an industry-driven exploration, positioning real-world practice and current challenges as the foundation for identifying training needs in software testing. The goal was to start from the perspective of what students will need in the work field.

Therefore, we designed and conducted two focus group sessions and a series of in-depth interviews with industrial actors. These participants came from sectors such as the railway industry, software consulting and healthcare. The study instrument was co-developed by different partners and refined collaboratively across the consortium. It focused on gathering data about training types, challenges, knowledge gaps, transfer mechanisms, and future needs. This allowed creating a grounded picture of how testing knowledge is developed and shared in industry settings.

Professional Training (RQ1). Across the various interviews and focus groups, it became clear that most companies rely on informal, hands-on approaches to training. Mentoring and learning through real project work stood out as the preferred form of skill development, especially for junior testers. While internal sessions and workshops are common (1), formal external training is used more selectively (2), often as a follow-up after employees have settled into their roles. Pre-recorded online courses (e.g., via Coursera or LinkedIn Learning) are available in some organizations, but participants often found them less engaging and disconnected from their day-to-day work. This can be distilled from the following quote from focus group 2: *"So, the learning platforms that we use the most are Coursera, Udemy, LinkedIn Learning, this is like the three business licences that the company has."* One company lets their employees spend a lot of training on how to use Azure DevOPs and make a test plan in it (3).

Challenges. Several challenges were identified from the focus groups. (1) It's difficult to get all trainings standardized as people have varying degrees of experience. This feedback was received from our interviews: *"It can take up to 6 months to get people up and running on the technical side of testing and the business side of testing. Where of course the functional part is the most difficult."* (2) The current training frameworks are not unified and structured enough to standardize skill levels across teams. (3) Balancing the technical aspects of software testing with an understanding of business processes and objectives remains a challenge as well.

Evaluation of the Training. Participants across interviews and focus groups highlighted differing approaches to training evaluation and ongoing support. Focus Group 1 participants described an informal evaluation process, where the effectiveness of training was observed through project performance and feedback from mentors or line managers. In contrast, in Focus Group 2, participants noted that formal evaluations of training in day-to-day testing activities were lacking. They expressed a need for a centralized training portal that would provide continuous access to materials, allow for regular knowledge assessments, and enable timely support from trainers. One participant suggested, *"I would say it could be really useful to have like a space where questions can be asked and at some point during a short period of time you will be answered"*. Interview findings echoed this diversity, noting that practices vary across companies. While the presence of a mentor providing ongoing feedback and suggestions was seen as a central component of continuous learning, one participant also emphasized the importance of formal certification, stating that obtaining the ISTQB Foundation certification serves as an objective within the company and adds value to the learning process.

Together, these perspectives indicate a need for more structured, consistent approaches to both the evaluation and support of training in practice.

Knowledge Gaps (RQ2). A number of knowledge gaps were identified too, both for new graduates and in more experienced testers. Key areas that are identified are AI in testing, security testing, and the use of automated tools. Participants and interviewees noted that while theory is sometimes covered in education, practical applications are often forgotten and therefore not developed as a skill. There is also a strong demand for testers to better understand quality standards, domain-specific tools, and how to think like a tester rather than a developer. This is evidenced by following quote from focus group 2, *"Because if you work both as a programmer and as a tester in courses, then you don't really want to find faults in your code."*. In several cases, the lack of experience with real-life testing cases was seen as a critical shortcoming in existing training programs. Given the popularity of Agile Software Development, specific gaps on Agile testing, Test-driven Development and Behaviour-Driven Development were mentioned frequently.

Future Needs and Trends. Looking ahead, several trends are shaping how training needs are evolving. Security testing is becoming a must-have skill (1). The growing importance of AI and automation was also mentioned frequently (2); not just in terms of testing AI systems, but also in using AI to support test generation, review, and fault detection. This was also mentioned by a participant from focus group 2: *"AI is developing so fast in the technology sector, and we need to keep growing in parallel with it"*. Beyond technical skills, there's increasing awareness that testers need a well-rounded profile: communication skills, business understanding, and product knowledge are all seen as essential to succeed in today's teams (3).

Knowledge Transfer. When it comes to transferring knowledge within teams, most companies blend formal and informal methods. Some teams organize regular sessions–such as weekly QA meetings or monthly deep-dives on specific topics–to keep knowledge flowing and shared across teams (1). This is a direct answer from a participant in focus group 1: *"The best way to transfer knowledge is direct communication in one-to-one sessions."* One-on-one mentoring is especially important, often supported by documentation, internal wikis, or collaborative tools like Confluence (2). Formal handovers (3) are also used in some organizations when project responsibilities shift.

As described in Sect. 3, to identify and extract the patterns and commonalities specific to training needs, gaps, and knowledge transfer, we classified the gathered industrial inputs by analzying the transcripts from the focus group studies and interviews using different codes and sub-codes. This process helps to represent and highlight specific topics and subtopics discussed within the focus groups and interviews. Considering the appearance frequency of each code topic in the transcripts of the studies, the information is visualized in Fig. 2. A detailed analysis of this information is provided in Deliverable 3.1 of the ENACTEST project[2].

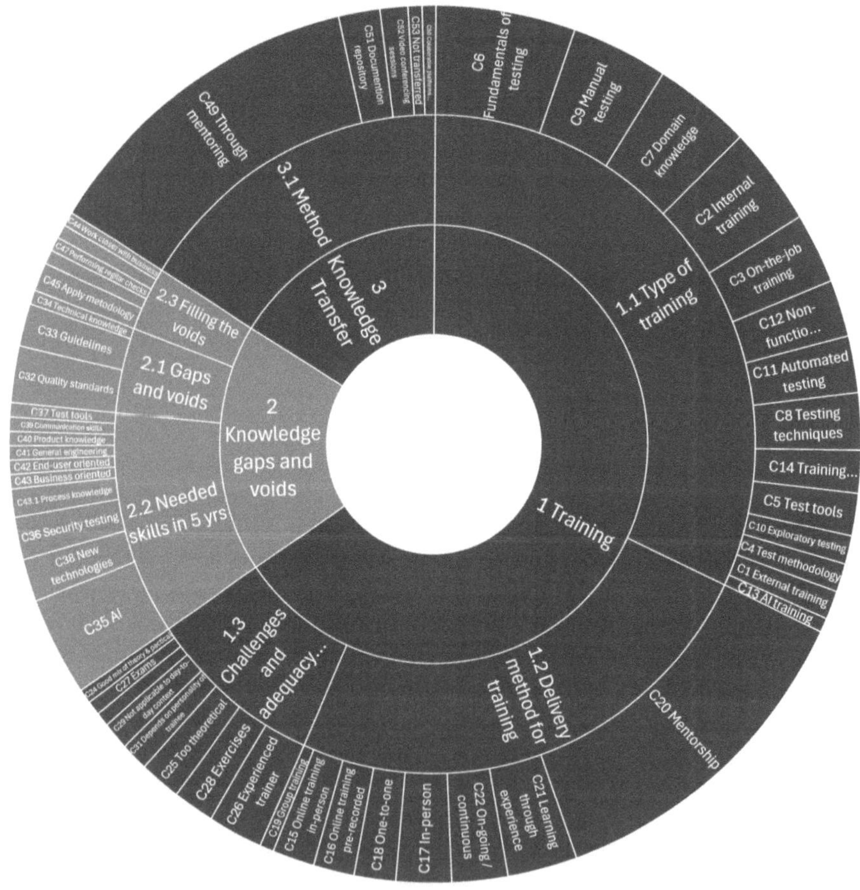

Fig. 2. Classification of training needs and practices - themes and codes represented based on frequency

---

[2] https://enactest-project.eu/resources/project-results/.

4.1 Discussion and Reflections

In this section, we discuss the most prominent themes and observations across the studies with respect to the demographics of training in industry in the light of the identified needs, and also present a summary of the testing needs, trends and knowledge transfer methods.

Our analysis across the sessions with key industrial actors shows that the onboarding process of these companies often includes sharing of training materials with new employees, briefing them about the way of working, standards and processes. This is very well in line with the training needs we identified about processes and standards. The collected data shows a trend that most new employees again have to learn new processes and standards when employed at a new company. This shows the lack of training and education on standard ways of working (for example, the gated process followed in safety-critical systems or test-driven development). The analysis further indicates that trainings are then requested as the employees go forward in their roles. Trainings are also often internal; nevertheless, a limited number of external trainings are also used to train the employees in a specific problem area or tooling. A very prominent and effective model of training was found to be the application of mentorship supplemented with learning through experience. Many of the actors use a senior developer or tester to train junior employees in real-world projects. This seems to be effective, as new employees get their hands on real projects and still have a learning environment created by a senior mentor. In general, the following testing training categories were identified: i) training during on-boarding, ii) training based on special requests, iii), internal vs external, and online vs on-site training, and iv) mentorship and learning through experience.

Certain challenges regarding software testing training were also identified in our analysis. In particular, our analysis shows that non-interactive online trainings (often pre-recorded) lack the human touch and is often not as effective. In addition, at times, employers expect employees to find the time outside working hours to complete such training. In this regard, there is a need for more on-site and interactive software testing training to address the current need in the market. Another challenge we observed was the lack of balance between theory and practice, and the lack of material on new/emerging technologies for employees. It can also happen that the content of the training is often too disconnected from the daily work of the employees and does not specifically address their actual needs. Trainings can also often not be based on real cases for demonstration and training materials, making training less relevant to the daily needs of employees. Moreover, training materials could get outdated, and thus not account for new approaches and advances within software testing. This is also very well aligned with the identified needs, where, for instance, security testing, testing of AI-based systems, and the use of AI in testing were highlighted among the many identified needs in our industrial actors' inputs. In addition, prominent patterns in data from industrial actors also show the need for domain-specific knowledge, processes (agile and test-driven development) and knowledge about domain-specific standards.

With respect to knowledge transfer in industrial organizations, our study highlights the use of centralised repositories and recorded materials to transfer and disseminate knowledge within the organizations and testing teams. Furthermore, existing documentation and project history are also used to transfer knowledge in smaller teams (for example, specific project teams). Active knowledge is transferred either with formal handover sessions for knowledge transfer, one-to-one sessions, or collaborative workshops.

4.2 Validation

To validate these findings, we performed a curated small-scale scoping review [9]. In this scoping review, we aim to identify which industry needs have already been addressed in academic literature. After all, there is no guarantee that an identified need has never been addressed since academic research does not consistently get integrated into practice [7,8].

The search query constructed for our scoping review utilized the following logical combinations of keywords: (``software tester skills'' ∨ ``quality assurance skills'' ∨ ``QA skills'') ∧ (``future of software testing'' ∨ ``future skills software testing'').

We used this search query on several platforms: SCOPUS and Google Scholar for scientific literature, and industry-specific sources such as Capgemini, Practitest, and TestSigma for industrial reports. The search query yielded a total of 43 papers.

We filtered these 43 papers with a predefined set of inclusion and exclusion criteria to ensure the scientific rigor and relevance of the identified reports. Inclusion Criteria:

- Evidentiary Basis: Studies providing empirical evidence derived from previously peer-reviewed publications or recognized scientific reports.
- Methodological Rigor (Survey-Based Research): Primary research reports that utilized survey methodologies with a clearly defined and demonstrably representative sample of participants, ensuring generalizability of findings to the target population.

Exclusion Criteria:

- Temporal Relevance: Publications predating the last five years (i.e., prior to 2020), to ensure currency of findings in an evolving domain.
- Lack of Empirical or Methodological Foundation: Studies lacking a clear articulation of their methodology, empirical data, or theoretical framework (e.g. opinion papers), thus precluding an assessment of their validity or reliability.

Applying the inclusion and exclusion criteria left us with 30 papers that we considered relevant. We augmented this selection of 30 papers by performing backward snowballing: references from the selected papers were systematically checked for additional relevant publications (1-step backward snowballing) based on title. Each identified paper was rigorously assessed against the predefined keywords and the detailed inclusion and exclusion criteria described above to determine its qualification for inclusion in our review. Duplicates were removed.

After the comprehensive search and snowballing, a compiled list of 71 reports was established, comprising 43 reports from the initial search and an additional 28 papers identified through snowballing.[3]

We coded the information present in the papers concerning common trends and future skills required for software testing. More specifically, we aimed to gather following information: empirical validation, representative domain, identified needs, identified solutions for needs, identified knowledge transfer possibilities, identified tools for knowledge transfer, identified risks.

We then compared the identified codes of the scoping review with the prior identified codes of the focus groups and interviews (Sect. 4).

This yielded us following list of topics that were identified in the focus group, but not identified in our scoping review:

1. Training
   (a) Type of Training
       i. Manual testing: hands-on execution of test cases without automation
       ii. Automated testing: using scripts and tools to run test cases
       iii. Non-functional testing: testing for performance, security and usability
   (b) Delivery method of Training
       i. Online training pre-recorded: self-paced online courses
       ii. In-person: instructor-led virtual learning
       iii. One-to-one: individual coaching or training
       iv. On-going / continuous: continuous professional development
       v. Lunch sessions: informal learning discussions
   (c) Challenges and adequacy of training
       i. Too theoretical: training lacks real-world application
       ii. Exams: assessing knowledge through tests
       iii. Not applicable to day-to-day context: training does not match real work needs

2. Knowledge gaps and voids
   (a) Gaps and voids
       i. Quality standards: lack of clarity in quality benchmarks
       ii. Guidelines: absence of clear testing protocols
   (b) Needed skills in 5 years
       i. End-user oriented: focusing on user needs
   (c) Filling the voids
       i. Apply methodology

3. Knowledge Transfer

---

[3] All the identified papers can be found at https://anonymous.4open.science/r/IndustryNeeds-6C98/.

(a) Method
  i. Documentation repository: sharing knowledge via digital tools
  ii. Not transferred: knowledge retention issues

Consequently, our analysis of these 71 reports revealed that while current industry practices prioritize hands-on, practical training methods such as mentoring and on-the-job learning, there are still significant gaps not covered by research, especially in emerging areas like AI testing, security testing, and integrating new technologies. Soft skills, communication, and a stronger connection between testing practices and business goals also emerged as critical areas for development.

5   Validity Threats

While this study was carefully designed and executed to explore the training needs and knowledge gaps in software testing for industry needs, we analyze the threats to validity based on [14].

Internal Validity. The presence of researcher bias during the thematic analysis or in the interpretation of data cannot be excluded. However, to minimize it, we organized three independent working groups to conduct the coding of the data transcripts. Each group performed coding independently, after which cross-reviewing of coded transcripts and thematic maps were collected. This process helps ensure consistency and robustness in the final identified themes. Also, the instrument was carefully designed, with several people involved, to also reduce bias such as the Hawthorne effect.

Construct Validity of focus groups can be threatened by factors such as ambiguous construct definitions, where participants may interpret 'testing needs' differently; social desirability bias, where individuals adapt their answers to fit the group or please the moderator; and moderator influence, where leading questions can shape the discussion in unintended ways. To mitigate these risks, researchers have developed a protocol involving clear operational definitions of constructs, the use of neutral and well-piloted questions, moderator training to minimise bias and encourage diverse viewpoints, and triangulation with other data sources (e.g. individual interviews) to validate the accuracy of the group discussion in reflecting the intended construct.

External Validity. The relatively small and convenience-based sample of participants may not be representative of the broader software testing industry, limiting the generalizability of the findings. However, the sample includes participants with diverse roles and experience, and we validated our findings with the literature. This study was aimed to be qualitative, not quantitative, to obtain contextual insights into current industry practices. In addition, although most of the participants in Focus Group 2 were seniors, which could skew views toward more experienced perspectives, Focus Group 1 included less experienced participants, which adds some balance to the experiment.

6   Conclusion and Future Work

This paper has presented a study conducted within the European ENACTEST project, which aims to develop educational materials tailored to the evolving demands of software testing education.

The main goal of this study was to identify both current and emerging training needs in software testing, focusing on the perspective of what students will need in the real world. It was based on two focus group sessions, a series of interviews with professionals from different sectors and a curated literature review. By combining these research methods, it was possible to validate the findings, identify overlapping themes, pinpoint unique needs emerging from each approach, and identify major trends and common needs for future training.

This work revealed that while current industry practices prioritise hands-on, practical training methods such as mentoring and on-the-job learning, there are still significant gaps, especially in emerging areas like AI testing, security testing, and integrating new technologies. Soft skills, communication, and a stronger connection between testing practices and business goals also emerged as critical areas for development. These results are relevant for practitioners and researchers, who can use this information to provide students and novice practitioners with tailored training to help them acquire testing competence more quickly.

Moreover, the results obtained were instrumental for the design of educational materials that address identified educational gaps, respond to evolving industry requirements, and promote pedagogical effectiveness. More concretely, using these results we developed 17 diverse teaching capsules that support the industry needs and focus on different testing topics, such as GAMFLEW [13] that supports the industry need *Interactive sessions ensure real-time engagement and feedback*, ModelDefenders [3] which supports the industry need *Group training fosters collaborative problem-solving*, TSGame [6] that supports the industry need *Clear guidelines improve test planning and execution*, or GADGETS [5] that supports the industry need *Exploratory testing helps uncover hidden defects*.

The teaching capsules[4] developed in the ENACTEST project cover 79% of the needs identified in this work, demonstrating their relevance and identifying opportunities for future work, mainly addressing underrepresented areas. Nevertheless, it is important to note that there exist industry needs that can not be covered by using capsules of education as they must be experienced in live environments, for instance the lunch sessions for informal learning of exploratory testing.

Finally, we advocate that the results obtained equip the industry with guidance to promote continuous learning in a constantly evolving area. Future work considers to implement further capsules to support the remaining industry needs as well as a broader application of capsules at different companies, and higher education institutions.

---

[4] https://enactest-project.eu/capsules-repository/.

Acknowledgments. This work has been partially funded by ENACTEST (European innovation alliance for testing education) ERASMUS+ Project number 101055874, 2022–2025. The work is also supported by the Swedish Knowledge Foundation (KKS) through the ARRAY project. We would also like to thank the industry experts and professionals who participated in our studies and provided valuable inputs.

References

1. Braun, V., Clarke, V.: Using thematic analysis in psychology. Qual. Res. Psychol. **3**(2), 77–101 (2006)
2. Breen, R.L.: A practical guide to focus-group research. J. Geogr. High. Educ. **30**(3), 463–475 (2006)
3. Cammaerts, F., Snoeck, M.: ModelDefenders: a novel gamified mutation testing game for model-driven engineering. In: 16th IFIP WG 8.1 Working Conference on the Practice of Enterprise Modeling (POEM), vol. 3645. Springer (2024)
4. Doorn, N., Ricós, F.P., Marín, B., Vos, T.: Alianza europea de innovación para la educación del testing-proyecto enactest. In: Congresso Ibero-Americano em Engenharia de Software (CIbSE), pp. 367–370. SBC (2025)
5. Doorn, N., Vos, T.E., Marín, B.: Design of a serious game on exploratory software testing to improve student engagement, pp. 806–813 (2025)
6. Fasolino, A.R., Tramontana, P.: Test smells learning by a gamification approach. In: 3rd ACM International Workshop on Gamification in Software Development, Verification, and Validation, pp. 30–33 (2024)
7. Graham, I.D., et al.: Lost in knowledge translation: time for a map? J. Contin. Educ. Heal. Prof. **26**(1), 13–24 (2006)
8. Ioannidis, J.P.: Why most clinical research is not useful. PLoS Med. **13**(6), e1002049 (2016)
9. Levac, D., Colquhoun, H., O'brien, K.K.: Scoping studies: advancing the methodology. Implementation Sci. **5**, 1–9 (2010)
10. Marín, B., Vos, T.E., Paiva, A.C., Fasolino, A.R., Snoeck, M., et al.: ENACTEST-European innovation alliance for testing education. In: RCIS Workshops (2022)
11. Marín, B., Vos, T.E., Snoeck, M., Paiva, A.C., Fasolino, A.R.: ENACTEST project-European innovation alliance for testing education. In: CAiSE Research Projects Exhibition, pp. 91–96 (2023)
12. Pastor Ricós, F., Marín, B., Prasetya, I., Vos, T.E., Davidson, J., Hovorka, K.: An industrial experience leveraging the iv4XR framework for BDD testing of a 3D sandbox game. In: International Conference on Research Challenges in Information Science, pp. 393–409. Springer (2024)
13. Silva, M., Paiva, A.C., Mendes, A.: GAMFLEW: serious game to teach white-box testing. Software Qual. J. **33**(1), 5 (2025)
14. Wohlin, C., et al.: Experimentation in Software Engineering. Springer (2012)

Enhancing Regulation-Adherent Requirement Engineering with Contextual AI: An Industrial Study

Orhan Sirin[1], Malik Abdul Sami[1(✉)], Tuomas Granlund[1,2],
Jussi Rasku[1], Zheying Zhang[1], and Pekka Abrahamsson[1]

[1] Tampere University, Tampere, Finland
`azizorhansirin@gmail.com`,
`{malik.sami,jussi.rasku,zheying.zhang,pekka.abrahamsson}@tuni.fi`
[2] Solita Oy, Helsinki, Finland
`tuomas.granlund@solita.fi`

Abstract. Software projects in the medical device domain specify requirements at different abstraction levels (layers) to ensure traceability, compliance, and clarity. However, writing detailed lower-level requirements is time-consuming. Privacy and regulatory constraints often prohibit the use of external or public cloud services for processing sensitive requirement data. This restriction motivates the need for evaluating on-premise LLMs, which, to our knowledge, have not yet been studied in this context. This study investigates whether privacy-preserving, on-premise large language models (LLMs) can automate the decomposition of high-level requirements into system and software-level specifications while complying with data-protection regulations. Five open-weights instruction-tuned models ranging from 3 billion to 70 billion parameters are evaluated locally using the Ollama runtime. Four prompt strategies are tested: minimal, regulatory-context, example-driven, and retrieval-augmented generation (RAG), across two decomposition levels: user-to-system and system-to-software on real-world medical device requirements. The results indicate that (i) all on-premise models generate syntactically valid JSON and correctly structured requirements when prompted appropriately, (ii) example-driven prompts achieve the highest semantic similarity scores to the ground truth, (iii) larger models (R1 Distill Qwen 32B and LLaMA 3.3 70B) outperform smaller models, and (iv) RAG, which is used to fetch examples for few-shot prompting, shows no measurable benefit due to limited retrieval corpus. These findings demonstrate that local LLMs can effectively automate requirements decomposition while maintaining regulatory compliance. The Proposed approach has the potential to reduce the time used in requirements engineering while maintaining regulatory compliance.

Keywords: Requirements Engineering · Large Language Models · On-Premise LLM · Medical Device Software · Prompt Engineering · Regulatory Compliance

G. Scanniello et al. (Eds.): PROFES 2025, LNCS 16362, pp. 69–85, 2026.
https://doi.org/10.1007/978-3-032-12092-2_5

1   Introduction

Software development for medical devices follows strict regulations to ensure patient safety [6]. Under EU law, standalone software with an intended medical purpose is classified as a medical device and, as such, must comply with the same regulations as hardware medical devices. Compliance is often demonstrated by adhering to standards such as IEC 62304, which defines the software lifecycle processes necessary to ensure a device's safety and effectiveness.

Building on standards like IEC 62304, the regulatory framework places a strong emphasis on requirements engineering (RE) practices across multiple levels (layers) of abstraction. In particular, detailed and verified specifications are required from user requirements to system and software requirements. This process is time-consuming and laborious [1]. These challenges highlight the potential for artificial intelligence (AI) tools to accelerate requirement derivation and support faster iterative refinement cycles [2].

Recent advances in large language models (LLMs), trained on extensive text corpora, have demonstrated impressive performance across natural language processing (NLP) tasks [16]. Research explores their use in regulated domains such as banking, aviation, and healthcare [7,29]. Applications include legal document analysis [13] and requirement coverage assessment [19]. In software engineering, LLM applications range from requirement elicitation to code generation [14]. These studies indicate the feasibility of using LLMs to assist engineers in generating specifications and test cases from high-level descriptions.

However, using LLMs in safety-critical domains raises concerns, including their tendency to produce inaccurate information, known as "hallucination" [10], and data privacy risks associated with cloud-based models. Privacy-preserving, on-premise LLMs offer a solution to the latter challenge. Recent open-weights models such as Meta's LLaMA[1] and Mistral[2] demonstrate competitive NLP performance without commercial cloud infrastructure [13].

Despite this potential, research on using on-premise LLMs for generating lower-level requirements from higher-level requirements in medical device software development remains limited. Previous studies have primarily examined cloud-based LLM deployments, while the evaluation of locally executed models that operate under regulatory constraints has not yet been conducted in the context of medical device requirements engineering. Addressing this gap can reduce documentation efforts while ensuring data protection, privacy requirements, compliance with licensing conditions, and restrictions on third-party sharing of protected materials.

The objective of this study is to investigate the use of on-premise LLMs to automate the decomposition of high-level requirements into system and software-level specifications. It aims to answer the following research questions:

- **RQ1:** How effectively can on-premise LLMs generate lower-level requirements from higher-level requirements in a medical device context?

---

[1] https://huggingface.co/meta-llama/Llama-3.3-70B-Instruct.
[2] https://mistral.ai/news/mistral-small-3.

– **RQ2:** How do model size and prompt strategy affect the granularity and decomposition of requirements?

To address these questions, this study proposes a method where higher-level requirements serve as input to on-premise LLMs together with task specific prompting. The models generate lower-level requirements, subsequently reviewed by engineers as part of the development workflow. Four prompt strategies are evaluated across on-premise LLMs of different sizes. The use of on-premise LLMs ensures compliance by keeping sensitive and non-disclosable data on-site.

The contributions of this paper are:

– Implementation and evaluation of an on-premise LLM-based pipeline for decomposing high-level requirements into system and software-level specifications, using real-world data from a medical device company.
– Benchmarking of five open-weights instruction-tuned models and four prompt strategies across two requirement transformation layers, reporting results based on semantic similarity.

The paper is structured as follows. Section 2 reviews prior work on requirements decomposition and medical-device regulations. Section 3 presents system design, development, and evaluation procedures. Section 4 reports results. Section 5 discusses implications and limitations. Section 6 concludes the paper.

2   Background

This section outlines the regulatory context for medical device software, software requirements engineering practices, on-premise large language models, relevant text similarity methods, and existing research on LLM-assisted requirements engineering.

2.1   Medical Devices and Regulatory Context

A medical device includes any instrument, apparatus, software, implant, reagent, substance, or other item that the manufacturer intends for human use to support diagnosis, treatment, prevention, or monitoring of disease or injury [3]. Software, whether independently or as part of a larger system, is considered a medical device when used for such purposes. This classification is significant for requirement generation using language models.

Under the MDR, medical devices are categorized by their risk profiles, which include Class I (lowest), Class IIa, Class IIb, and Class III (highest). This classification significantly impacts the rigor of the design, development and maintenance processes related to these products. In compliance with the MDR classification rules, very few standalone software products are classified below Class IIa, which necessitates comprehensive certification processes to place products on the EU market [6].

Medical software development must comply with IEC 62304 and IEC 82304-1. These standards define life cycle processes, risk control, Information security, and verification requirements [26]. Creating compliant requirements is a complex task involving multiple stakeholders, evolving regulations, and extensive documentation [9]. Automating parts of this process using LLMs may support compliance efforts.

RE is the process of identifying, specifying, and validating stakeholder needs [18]. In regulated software, traceability is essential. Each requirement must be traceable to its source and to design and verification artifacts [5]. Traceability is mandated in standards such as IEC 62304, IEC 62366-1, and MDR [3].

Traceability supports quality assurance and patient safety. LLMs may support this process by reviewing requirements for coverage and consistency [19]. However, further empirical study is needed. Risk management is also central to medical software compliance. ISO 14971 and IEC 62304 require a documented risk management process covering risk identification, evaluation, control, and post-market monitoring [4,11]. Requirements traceability plays a key role in risk management by linking identified risks and the mitigation to corresponding requirements and related system artifacts.

2.2 Existing Approaches and Gaps

RE frequently involves natural language artifacts, making it suitable for natural language processing (NLP) methods. Traditional NLP techniques such as TF-IDF and classic classifiers have not led to significant improvements in RE tasks [17]. The emergence of large language models (LLMs) has renewed interest in automating RE activities, due to their advanced linguistic capabilities and contextual understanding [28].

Recent research applies LLMs to various RE tasks, including requirements classification, user story generation, and drafting of software requirements specifications (SRS). For instance, BERT-based models improve the accuracy of requirement classification [8]. LLMs such as GPT-4 have been used to generate user stories from stakeholder requests, showing measurable gains with improved prompt strategies [20]. Sami et al. introduced a GPT-based multi-agent system for automated user story generation and prioritization in an early study [23], and later extended this work with an evaluation in real-world agile projects using semantic similarity for user story assessment and Kendall's tau for prioritization [24]. These results support the use of LLMs for automating both elicitation and prioritization tasks in RE. Krishna et al. demonstrated that GPT-4 can generate SRS documents at a quality level comparable to junior engineers [12]. However, these studies generally use cloud-based models and do not address concerns such as data privacy or on-premise deployment.

The application of LLMs to safety-critical and regulated domains, such as medical device development, remains limited. In this context, requirements must be systematically decomposed from high-level user needs into detailed specifications, with strict adherence to regulatory standards. Errors or omissions during this process can have safety implications [27]. Studies examining LLM-based approaches for requirement coverage in the medical domain highlight potential benefits, but typically rely on cloud-based models and do not address medical device regulation or privacy constraints [19].

Challenges for LLM adoption in medical device RE include compliance with regulatory frameworks, the need for domain-specific training, and strict data privacy requirements. The risk tolerance in safety-critical systems is low, and there is limited evidence on the reliability and completeness of LLM-generated requirements in these settings [15,30].

There is limited work on generating lower-level software requirements from high-level specifications in regulated domains. Prior research does not address requirements MDR conformance or on-premise deployment. Current approaches also require systematic verification for hallucinations, bias, and incomplete coverage. This work addresses these gaps by evaluating the use of on-premise LLMs for generating lower-level requirements in the context of medical device development. The focus is on data privacy, traceability, and alignment with relevant software development standards

3   Research Methodology

This study is framed as Design Science Research (DSR). The problem addressed is the generation of lower-level requirements for medical device software under regulatory constraints. The designed artifact is an on-premise LLM-based requirement decomposition pipeline. Its development covered design of prompt strategies and model configurations, while the artifact output was evaluated through semantic similarity metrics. Accordingly, this section is structured into two parts: design and development, and evaluation.

3.1   Design and Development

This phase involves designing and implementing a method that applies on-premise LLMs to derive system and software requirements from user requirements in compliance with medical device standards (IEC 82304-1, IEC 62304). These standards mandate traceability across three layers: user, system, and software requirements.

Prompting Pipeline and Execution. The experiment involved two decomposition layers: user-to-system and system-to-software. Each transformation was tested using four prompt strategies:

- **Minimal Prompting:** Basic task instruction, no examples.
- **Regulatory Context Prompting:** Role-based prompting with references and excerpts of relevant IEC 82304-1 and IEC 62304 clauses.
- **Example-Driven Prompting:** Few-shot role-based prompting using 11 manually curated requirement pairs for each level.
- **Retrieval-Augmented Generation (RAG):** As with Example-Driven Prompting but with two examples selected with RAG from the third product data using SBERT-based *All Mpnet Base V2* embedding model.

Each prompt template was applied per transformation layer with adjusted instruction (e.g., 23 system requirements per user requirement; 34 software requirements per system requirement). Prompts were reviewed and refined with domain experts. The pretraining corpora of the selected models are not publicly disclosed in sufficient detail to verify whether international standards such as IEC 62304, IEC 82304-1, ISO 14971, or regulatory requirements from MDR were included. To avoid assuming that the models inherently contain such knowledge, four prompt techniques were designed: minimal prompts with no regulatory context, example-driven prompts with requirement pairs, regulatory-context prompts embedding regulatory excerpts, and RAG prompts combining examples with retrieval.

The execution flow for each promptmodellayer combination involved five steps: the input was first formatted and injected into a selected prompt template, then sent to the model via the Ollama API with conversation history preserved. The output syntax was validated against a structured JSON schema using Pydantic. Any malformed responses, or hallucinated outputs that referenced out-of-batch content, were identified and logged. Finally, all valid results, metadata, and chat histories were saved for evaluation and reproducibility. Refer to Fig. 1 for details.

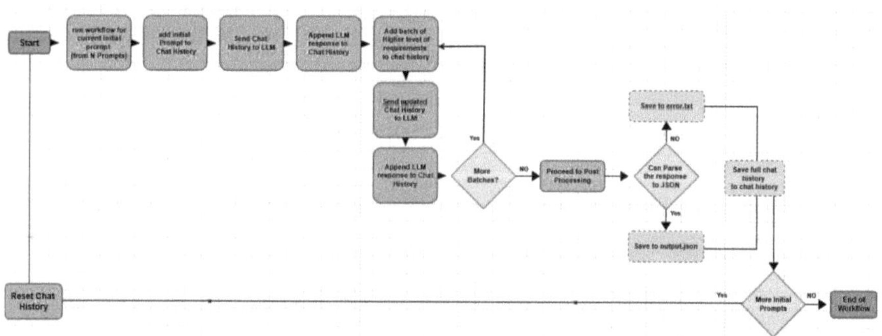

Fig. 1. LLM-based requirement generation pipeline.

To support long prompts with examples, the context window was increased to 40,000 tokens. The context grew due to appended history, requiring an extended buffer for model response. Outputs not matching schema or referencing previous batches were excluded from similarity scoring and logged for auditability. Across all runs, the system generated a total of 7,576 low-level requirements, including both system and software requirements. Valid outputs were collected for evaluation. Error cases and full chat histories were also saved.

Table 1 summarizes the prompt strategies and their characteristics. It also illustrates the prompting approaches by showing selected details from the minimal, regulatory, and example-based prompts for both transformation layers.

Table 1. Prompt types and key characteristics for requirement decomposition

Prompt	Layer	Key Prompt Content
Minimal	User → System	*"I need low-level system requirements for high-level user requirements of a medical device... You may generate around 2-3 system requirements for each user requirement"*
	System → Software	*"I need low-level software requirements for high-level system requirements... You may generate around 4 software requirements for each system requirement"*
Regulatory Context	User → System	*"You are a requirements engineer who is proficient in the medical device domain... Consider following the related standards... IEC 82304-1 4.2, IEC 82304-1 4.5, IEC 62304 5.2.2, and IEC 62304 5.2.6"*
	System → Software	*"You are a requirements engineer... Consider following related standards... IEC 82304-1 4.2, IEC 82304-1 4.5, IEC 62304 5.2.2, and IEC 62304 5.2.6"*
Example-Driven	User → System	*"You are a requirements engineer... Consider following similar approach with given user and system requirement pairs... cDSI REQ-1: As a specialist, I want to select a patient... System Requirements: 1: The system shall allow listing patients..."* (10+ examples provided)
	System → Software	*"Consider following similar approach with given system and software requirement pairs... cDSI REQ-12: The system shall allow listing patients... Software Requirements: 1: The unit shall provide an API..."* (10+ examples provided)
RAG	Both layers	As with Example-Driven but using Retrieval Augmented Generation with examples from third set of requirements

Model Runtime and Infrastructure: Five instruction-tuned models, ranging from 3B to 70B parameters, based on quantization support and deployment feasibility were selected (see Table 2).

Model selection followed two principles: (i) feasibility of local execution within the available infrastructure, and (ii) coverage of diverse model families and parameter scales to enable comparative evaluation. Five instruction-tuned open-weight models were chosen, ranging from 3B to 70B parameters, drawn from different architectures (Meta LLaMA, Alibaba Qwen, Mistral, and DeepSeek). Smaller models enabled testing within constrained GPU resources, while larger models reflected expected scaling gains [13]. The use of open-weight instruction-tuned models ensured compliance with regulatory requirements, since cloud or proprietary models could not be used due to model licensing, data and document licensing terms, and data protection constraints. [7].

Initial tests used LM Studio (RTX 4070 GPU, 12GB). Full-scale runs were conducted on CSC Puhti (V100, 32GB VRAM) using the Ollama runtime and SLURM scripts. The Ollama context length was set to 40,000 tokens to support full promptresponse chains.

Table 2. Instruction-tuned LLMs used in the evaluation

Model	Size	Organization
LLaMA 3.2	3B	Meta
Qwen 2.5	14B	Alibaba
Mistral	24B	MistralAI
R1 Distill Qwen	32B	DeepSeek
LLaMA 3.3	70B	Meta

Data Acquisition: This study used requirement documentation of three legacy products that had gone through a full regulatory review. Each product included requirements specified at user, system, and software abstraction levels. Two of the three products were used for model evaluation, comprising a total of 27 user, 110 system, and 451 software requirements. The third product was used to construct example-based prompts. Requirements were extracted from DOCX files and converted to structured JSON outlined below via a preprocessing script.

label

```
"User Req-1": {
  "URS_Description": "User Requirement Description Here
    ",
  "SRS_Data": {
    "System Req-1": {
      "SRS_Title": "System Requirement Title Here",
      "SRS_Description": "System Requirement
        Description Here",
      "IRS_Data": {
        "Software Req-1": "Software Requirement Here"
      }
} } }
```

3.2   Evaluation Procedure

Four prompting strategies were evaluated per model for both decomposition layer (usertosystem and systemtosoftware). Text similarity metrics were used to evaluate LLM-generated requirements against ground truth.

Traditional text similarity approaches, such as term frequencyinverse document frequency (TF-IDF) and cosine similarity, represent documents as sparse vectors and compare their orientation in vector space [22]. However, these methods do not capture semantic meaning.

To address this limitation, Sentence-BERT (SBERT) [21], which encodes sentences into semantic embeddings, was applied. For each higher-level requirement, the cosine similarity between SBERT embeddings of the LLM-generated lower-level requirements and their corresponding human-written ground truth requirements was computed. When the two sets differed in size, a greedy one-to-one matching algorithm was used: at each step, the unmatched generated and human requirements with the highest similarity were paired and removed from further consideration. The mean similarity of these matched pairs was used as the similarity score for each higher-level requirement. These scores were then averaged across all requirements, models, prompt strategies, and both decomposition layers (user-to-system and system-to-software).

4   Results

The experiment produced 7,576 generated requirements in total using five LLMs, four prompting strategies, and two decomposition layers (user-to-system and system-to-software). Each subsection below is aligned with a specific research question. Furthermore, one example of the requirements generation task and generated requirements is provided below. With user level requirement:

> User REQ–1: As a customer, I want to access patient records from my office computer, so that I don't need special equipment to perform my tasks.

generated system level requirements were (Example Driven - Llama 3.3 70B):

> SYSREQ–1.1: The system shall be accessible through a standard web browser.
> SYSREQ–1.2: The system shall not require any special hardware or software to access patient records.

RQ1: Effectiveness of On-Premise LLMs to the Task: To assess generation effectiveness, a comparison between LLM-generated requirements to human-written ground truth was made using SBERT-based cosine similarity. Two layers were evaluated: The user-to-system layer consisted of 27 user requirements across two products, and the system-to-software layer had 110 system requirements across the same two products. For each promptmodellayer combination, the average similarity score was computed using the SBERT-based greedy matching approach, as described in Sect. 3.2. Averaging over higher level requirements helps smooth out the stochasticity of the experimental setup.

The results in Table 3a and Fig. 2a show varying performance across models and prompting strategies for the user-to-system layer. R1 Distill Qwen 32B achieves the highest score with minimal prompting (0.523), whereas LLaMA 3.3 70B performs best with RAG prompting (0.536, the highest score in this task).

Table 3. Similarity scores for both layers.

(a) User-to-System layer

Prompt\Model	Llama 3.2 3B	Llama 3.3 70B	Mistral 24B	Qwen 14B	R1 Distill Qwen 32B
Minimal	0.513	0.494	0.517	0.467	**0.523**
Regulatory Context	0.479	**0.509**	0.490	0.487	0.507
Example Driven	0.446	0.506	**0.514**	0.470	0.474
RAG	0.483	**0.536**	0.514	0.528	0.510

(b) System-to-Software layer

Prompt\Model	Llama 3.2 3B	Llama 3.3 70B	Mistral 24B	Qwen 14B	R1 Distill Qwen 32B
Minimal	0.519	0.530	**0.565**	0.536	0.551
Regulatory Context	0.502	**0.540**	0.539	0.480	0.516
Example Driven	0.532	0.626	0.621	0.602	**0.632**
RAG	0.537	0.570	0.559	**0.572**	0.571

Bold = Best per row;   = Best per column

Smaller models like LLaMA 3.2 3B show inconsistent responses with complex prompting, with regulatory and RAG strategies producing lower scores than with minimal prompting.

Table 3b and Fig. 2b shows results of system-to-software layer, which demonstrates clearer patterns. Example-driven prompting produces the best results across most models, with reasoning model R1 Distill Qwen 32B achieving the highest score (0.632). All models show substantial improvement with example-driven prompts compared to minimal prompting. LLaMA 3.3 70B, Mistral 24B, and Qwen 14B all achieve their best performance with example-driven strategies.

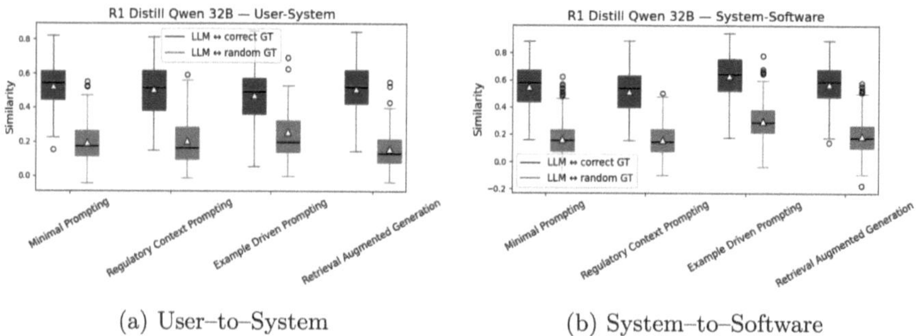

(a) User–to–System   (b) System–to–Software

Fig. 2. Average similarity scores across models and prompt types.

The similarity distributions across models and prompts (Fig. 2) showed consistent scores around 0.5 to 0.6. In both decomposition layers, larger models (R1 Distill Qwen 32B, LLaMA 3.3 70B) yielded higher similarity scores,

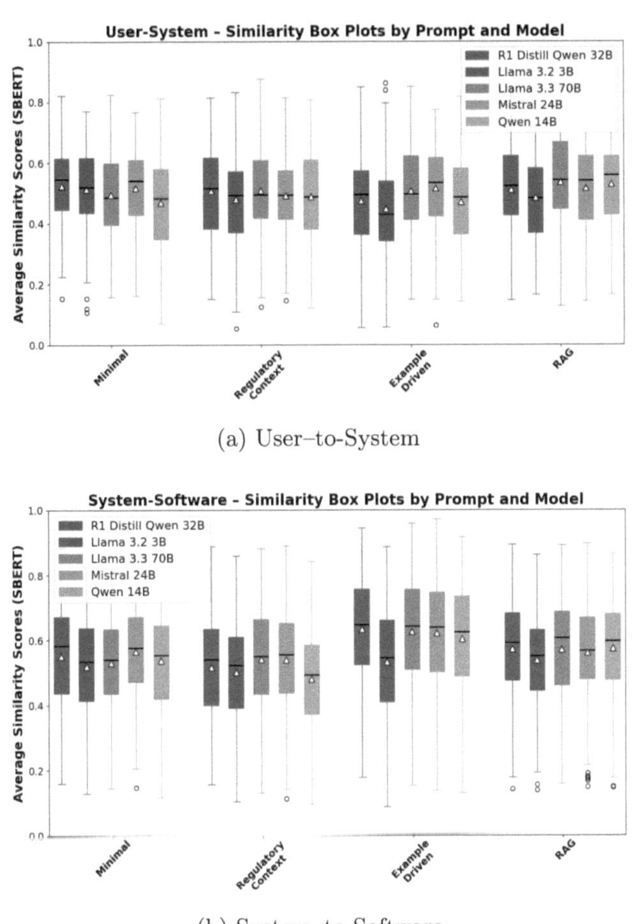

(a) User–to-System

(b) System–to-Software

Fig. 3. R1 Distill Qwen 32B: correct vs. random ground truth similarity

with minimal to moderate variation across prompt types. Minimal prompting had consistently lower average similarity, except for R1 Distill Qwen 32B at the User-to-System layer, where minimal prompting achieved the highest score (0.523). Retrieval Augmented Generation (RAG) presented competitive results but exhibited greater variability, suggesting potential issues with retrieval effectiveness. Baseline comparisons (Fig. 3) reinforced these findings by showing substantial and consistent improvement over random matching, validating the semantic relevance of the generated requirements.

For both layers example-driven prompts outperformed minimal prompts across all models. Regulatory prompts benefited larger models, particularly in user-to-system decomposition. RAG showed mixed results due to potential context overflow. Larger models combined with targeted prompts achieved more human-like decomposition granularity.

RQ2: Granularity Impact of Model Size and Prompting: The analysis in Table 4a shows the granularity comparison for system-to-software decomposition across 110 system requirements. R1 Distill Qwen 32B demonstrates good performance with RAG prompting, generating more requirements than humans in 58% (64 cases out of 110) while producing fewer in only 26% (29) of the cases. This model, along with others, also excels with minimal prompting, producing more requirements in 57% and less in 26% of the cases. Similarly, Qwen 14B shows very strong performance with RAG prompting, producing more requrements than humans in 72% of the cases. The smaller LLaMA 3.2 3B model struggles with producing enough detailed lower-level requirements particularly with example-driven prompts, producing more requirements than humans in only 6% (7/110) cases indicating significant undergranulation.

Table 4. Granularity in Requirements Decomposition over Prompting Strategies

(a) System-to-Software layer

Model\count	Minimal		Regulatory		Example		RAG	
	LLM > Ref	Ref > LLM	LLM > Ref	Ref > LLM	LLM > Ref	Ref > LLM	LLM > Ref	Ref > LLM
R1 Distill Qwen 32B	57%	26%	20%	59%	40%	43%	58%	26%
Llama 3.2 3B	24%	46%	18%	61%	6%	73%	45%	35%
Llama 3.3 70B	57%	26%	20%	59%	20%	59%	57%	26%
Mistral 24B	57%	26%	20%	53%	16%	63%	53%	31%
Qwen 14B	57%	26%	20%	59%	6%	76%	72%	20%

(b) User-to-System layer

Model\count	Minimal		Regulatory		Example		RAG	
	LLMf > Ref	Reff > LLM	LLMf > Ref	Reff > LLM	LLMf > Ref	Reff > LLM	LLMf > Ref	Reff > LLM
R1 Distill Qwen 32B	41%	48%	22%	59%	7%	78%	26%	48%
Llama 3.2 3B	33%	48%	4%	70%	7%	67%	37%	48%
Llama 3.3 70B	41%	48%	22%	59%	22%	59%	41%	48%
Mistral 24B	41%	48%	19%	63%	19%	59%	22%	59%
Qwen 14B	22%	59%	7%	74%	11%	70%	41%	48%

Similarly, Table 4b presents the user-to-system layer results across 27 user requirements. The larger models (R1 Distill Qwen 32B, LLaMA 3.3 70B, and Mistral 24B) show similar performance patterns with minimal and RAG prompting, typically producing more requirements (typically in 41% of the cases) than humans. Again, LLaMA 3.2 3B performs poorly with regulatory prompting, generating more requirements than humans in only 1 case (4%) while producing fewer in 70% of the cases. The data reveals that models predominantly produce fewer requirements than humans across both tables in the user-to-system decomposition, indicating a tendency toward less granularity.

Overall, larger models combined with advanced prompting achieved more human-like decomposition granularity, often exceeding human detail level in system-to-software decomposition. Smaller models consistently underperformed, particularly with example-driven prompts, indicating limited capacity for fine-grained requirement generation.

5   Discussion

5.1   Summary of Findings

This study demonstrated that on-premise LLMs effectively generate lower-level requirements when provided clear high-level requirements and appropriate prompting is used. Model performance varied primarily based on model size and prompting strategy, with larger models consistently producing higher similarity to human-written requirements.

RQ1 concerned the effectiveness of on-premise LLMs for generating lower-level requirements in a medical device context. Here, LLM-generated requirements showed adequate semantic similarity to human-written versions. Larger models, R1 Distill Qwen 32B and LLaMA 3.3 70B, consistently achieved high similarity scores, with the R1 Distill model showing similar performance to the larger LLaMA model. This indicates that a reasoning fine-tune might be useful for such requirements decomposition tasks. Example-driven prompts led to the closest similarity with human-authored requirements. Perhaps surprisingly, prompts providing regulatory context to the LLMs yielded only marginal gains, mostly with large models. RAG results were mixed, likely due to a limited retrieval corpus.

Regarding RQ2, decomposition granularity is clearly influenced by both model size and prompt strategy. In the system-to-software decomposition, larger models tended to produce more fine-grained outputs than the reference, especially when paired with RAG or even minimal prompts. However, in the user-to-system layer, models struggled to match the human-written reference abstraction level.

These results are consistent with prior studies that demonstrated the effectiveness of LLMs in requirements engineering, primarily using cloud-based solutions [12,19]. While Krishna et al. and Preda et al. showed the potential of LLMs for drafting and assessing requirements in both general and medical software domains using cloud-based models, our study evaluates on-premise LLMs in regulated medical device development, with an emphasis on data privacy and compliance. To our knowledge, this is the first empirical evaluation of on-premise LLMs for requirement decomposition in this setting.

5.2   Implications for Practitioners and Researchers

For practitioners in the medical device industry, our experiments indicate that on-premise LLMs are a feasible tool for accelerating the drafting of initial product-specific requirements. However, their use must be embedded within a robust quality management system that includes rigorous human-in-the-loop oversight and the formal verification processes mandated by standards such as IEC 62304.

Given the consistent semantic relevance observed from the larger models (e.g., R1 Distill Qwen 32B or LLaMA 3.3 70B), engineering teams can leverage them to generate requirement statements that more closely align with human-authored precision. Nevertheless, the observed variability in output granularity highlights the necessity to explicitly define requirement decomposition rules in prompts and implement rigorous review workflows to ensure the resulting specifications are verifiable, complete, traceable, and suitable for inclusion in regulatory submission documents. This aligns with the concept of Symbiotic AI (SAI) systems, where humans and AI are conceived as entities that learn and evolve together over time, with AI supporting rather than replacing human actors [25]. Our results demonstrate such symbiosis by embedding on-premise LLMs within quality management processes, ensuring that human oversight remains central while AI accelerates requirement drafting and decomposition. This disciplined, framework-based approach for leveraging LLMs is not limited to medical devices; it provides a transferable model for other safety-critical and regulated sectors, such as aerospace and automotive, where rigorous requirement traceability and validation are paramount.

Researchers can benefit from insights related to the impact of model size and prompt techniques. Larger on-premise models consistently showed improved performance, particularly when combined with targeted prompt engineering approaches such as few-shot examples or retrieval augmented generation (RAG). However, researchers should remain aware of potential diminishing returns with increased complexity in prompts. Additionally, the variable success of RAG prompts emphasizes the need for further research into contextual integration techniques and context management to maximize utility.

5.3   Limitation and Future Work

This study was somewhat limited by computational resources not allowing the use of largest models. Furthermore, the dataset came from a single industrial source limiting its generalizability, human feedback was limited to one industry expert, and the empirical part was conducted by a single researcher.

Future research should address these limitations by incorporating diverse datasets, additional computational resources, and broader expert involvement. While a stratified sample of the generated requirements (0.5% of all, n=140) was manually reviewed to check for scope coverage and content validity, and no hallucinations referencing earlier batch content were observed, a more in-depth evaluation by several practitioners is needed to provide a qualitative assessment of LLM-generated lower-level requirements. Additionally, while averaging over the requirements set mitigates the effect of non-deterministic behavior of LLMs, the magnitude of the variance in generated requirements was not measured. In future research, we propose analyzing the effect of inherent stochasticity in the pipeline through repeated runs and reporting the variance in similarity scores. Furthermore, further investigations should consider additional evaluation metrics such as requirement coverage and traceability [31]. Such metrics would allow quantifying regulatory compliance of the human-produced and generated requirements Further exploration of enhanced RAG methods and domain-specific fine-tuning would also contribute to improving LLM-generated requirement quality.

6   Conclusions

In this study, on-premise LLMs were evaluated for their effectiveness for decomposing user and system requirements into system and software specifications in a medical-device context. A JSON-based generation pipeline was proposed, tested four prompting strategies, and compared five models ranging from 3 B to 70 B parameters. All models produced lower-level requirements in JSON. Larger and instruction-distilled models (Llama 3.3 70 B, R1 Distill Qwen 32 B) achieved higher semantic similarity with example-driven prompts; Llama 3.2 3 B scored lowest. Example-driven prompts with curated examples outperformed minimal and context-based prompts. Surprisingly, retrieval-augmented generation of examples provided no benefit. Manual review identified some omissions and out-of-scope outputs, underscoring the need for expert validation. It was also observed that models rigidly followed numeric cues, affecting requirement counts. The results demonstrate on-premise requirement generation is technically feasible but the results were limited by one dataset, expert, and GPU-constrained models.

Acknowledgments. The authors would like to thank Business Finland and the members of the PROFIT consortium for supporting this work, Combinostics Oy for providing the data, and CSC IT Center for Science, for providing computational resources through the Puhti supercomputer.

References

1. Alsaadi, M., Lisitsa, A., Qasaimeh, M.: Minimizing the ambiguities in medical devices regulations based on software requirement engineering techniques. In: Proceedings of the Second International Conference on Data Science, e-Learning and Information Systems, pp. 1–5 (2019)
2. Arora, C., Grundy, J., Abdelrazek, M.: Advancing requirements engineering through generative AI: assessing the role of llms. In: Generative AI for Effective Software Development, pp. 129–148. Springer, Heidelberg (2024). https://doi.org/10.1007/978-3-031-55642-5_6
3. European Parliament and Council of the European Union: Regulation (EU) 2017/745 of the European Parliament and of the Council of 5 April 2017 on medical devices (2017). https://eur-lex.europa.eu/eli/reg/2017/745/oj/eng
4. Flood, D., McCaffery, F., Casey, V., McKeever, R., Rust, P.: A roadmap to iso 14971 implementation. J. Softw. Evol. Process **27**(5), 319–336 (2015)
5. Gotel, O., Finkelstein, A.: Extended requirements traceability: results of an industrial case study. In: Proceedings of ISRE '97: 3rd IEEE International Symposium on Requirements Engineering, pp. 169–178 (1997)
6. Granlund, T., Mikkonen, T., Stirbu, V.: On medical device software ce compliance and conformity assessment. In: 2020 IEEE International Conference on Software Architecture Companion (ICSA-C), pp. 185–191. IEEE (2020)
7. Hassani, S., Sabetzadeh, M., Amyot, D., Liao, J.: Rethinking legal compliance automation: opportunities with large language models. In: 2024 IEEE 32nd International Requirements Engineering Conference (RE), pp. 432–440. IEEE (2024)

8. Hey, T., Keim, J., Koziolek, A., Tichy, W.F.: Norbert: transfer learning for requirements classification. In: 2020 IEEE 28th International Requirements Engineering Conference (RE), pp. 169–179. IEEE (2020)

9. Hrgarek, N.: Certification and regulatory challenges in medical device software development. In: 2012 4th International Workshop on Software Engineering in Health Care (SEHC), pp. 40–43 (2012)

10. Huang, L., et al.: A survey on hallucination in large language models: principles, taxonomy, challenges, and open questions. ACM Trans. Inf. Syst. **43**(2), 1–55 (2025)

11. ISO, I.: 14971: 2019 medical devices–application of risk management to medical devices. ISO. Brussels: Medical Device Coordination Group (MDCG) (2019)

12. Krishna, M., Gaur, B., Verma, A., Jalote, P.: Using llms in software requirements specifications: an empirical evaluation. In: 2024 IEEE 32nd International Requirements Engineering Conference (RE), pp. 475–483. IEEE (2024)

13. Lai, J., Gan, W., Wu, J., Qi, Z., Yu, P.S.: Large language models in law: a survey. AI Open **5**, 181–196 (2024)

14. Marques, N., Silva, R.R., Bernardino, J.: Using chatgpt in software requirements engineering: a comprehensive review. Future Internet **16**(6), 180 (2024)

15. Meng, X., et al.: The application of large language models in medicine: a scoping review. Iscience **27**(5) (2024)

16. Naveed, H., et al.: A comprehensive overview of large language models. ACM Trans. Intell. Syst. Technol. **16**(5), 1–72 (2025)

17. Norheim, J.J., Rebentisch, E., Xiao, D., Draeger, L., Kerbrat, A., de Weck, O.L.: Challenges in applying large language models to requirements engineering tasks. Des. Sci. **10**, e16 (2024)

18. Nuseibeh, B., Easterbrook, S.: Requirements engineering. In: Proceedings of the Conference on the Future of Software Engineering, pp. 35–46 (2000)

19. Preda, A.R., Mayr-Dorn, C., Mashkoor, A., Egyed, A.: Supporting high-level to low-level requirements coverage reviewing with large language models. In: Proceedings of the 21st International Conference on Mining Software Repositories, pp. 242–253 (2024)

20. Rahman, T., Zhu, Y.: Automated user story generation with test case specification using large language model. arXiv preprint arXiv:2404.01558 (2024)

21. Reimers, N., Gurevych, I.: Sentence-bert: sentence embeddings using siamese bert-networks. In: Proceedings of the 2019 Conference on Empirical Methods in Natural Language Processing and the 9th International Joint Conference on Natural Language Processing, pp. 3982–3992. Association for Computational Linguistics (2019). https://doi.org/10.18653/v1/D19-1410

22. Salton, G., Buckley, C.: Term-weighting approaches in automatic text retrieval. Inf. Process. Manag. **24**(5), 513–523 (1988)

23. Sami, M.A., Waseem, M., Zhang, Z., Rasheed, Z., Systä, K., Abrahamsson, P.: Early results of an AI multiagent system for requirements elicitation and analysis. In: International Conference on Product-Focused Software Process Improvement, pp. 307–316. Springer, Heidelberg (2024). https://doi.org/10.1007/978-3-031-78386-9_20

24. Sami, M.A., et al.: A multi-agent llm system for automated requirements analysis: a study on user story generation and prioritization. In: Euromicro Conference on Software Engineering and Advanced Applications, pp. 178–187. Springer, Heidelberg (2025). https://doi.org/10.1007/978-3-032-04200-2_12

25. Shneiderman, B.: Human-centered artificial intelligence: reliable, safe & trustworthy. Int. J. Hum.-Comput. Interact. **36**(6), 495–504 (2020)

26. Stoppacher, S., Müllner, P.S.: Software as medical device in Europe. In: Reference Series in Biomedical Engineering, pp. 187–215 (2023)
27. Tsai, I.C., Wang, C.D., Chen, P.T.: Strategies for medical device development: user and stakeholder perceptions. J. Healthc. Eng. **2023**(1), 6724656 (2023)
28. Vogelsang, A., Fischbach, J.: Using large language models for natural language processing tasks in requirements engineering: a systematic guideline. In: Handbook on Natural Language Processing for Requirements Engineering, pp. 435–456. Springer, Heidelberg (2025). https://doi.org/10.1007/978-3-031-73143-3_16
29. Wang, H., Zhao, S., Qiang, Z., Xi, N., Qin, B., Liu, T.: Beyond direct diagnosis: LLM-based multi-specialist agent consultation for automatic diagnosis. arXiv preprint arXiv:2401.16107 (2024)
30. Weissman, G., Mankowitz, T., Kanter, G.: Large language model non-compliance with FDA guidance for Clinical Decision Support Devices (2024)
31. Whalen, M.W., Rajan, A., Heimdahl, M.P., Miller, S.P.: Coverage metrics for requirements-based testing. In: Proceedings of the 2006 International Symposium on Software Testing and Analysis, pp. 25–36 (2006)

A Small Dataset May Go a Long Way: Process Duration Prediction in Clinical Settings

Harald Störrle[(✉)] and Anastasia Hort

QAware GmbH, Munich, Germany
`harald.stoerrle@qaware.de,`
`anastasia.hort@qaware.de`
`https://www.qaware.de/`

Abstract. Context: Utilization of operating theaters is a major cost driver in hospitals. Optimizing this variable through optimized surgery schedules may significantly reduce costs and simultaneously improve medical outcomes. Previous studies proposed various complex models to predict the duration of procedures, the key ingredient to optimal schedules. They did so perusing large amounts of data.

Goals: We aspire to create an effective and efficient model to predict operation durations based on only a small amount of data. Ideally, our model is also simpler in structure, and thus easier to use.

Methods: Following a mixed-methods approach, we immerse ourselves in the application domain to leverage practitioners expertise, to make the best use of our limited supply of clinical data, and to conduct our data analysis in a theory-guided way. We perform a combined factor analysis and develop regression models to predict the duration of the perioperative process.

Findings: We found simple methods of central tendency to perform on a par with much more complex methods proposed in the literature. In fact, they sometimes outperform them. We conclude that combining expert knowledge with data analysis may improve both data quality and model performance, allowing for more accurate forecasts.

Conclusion: We yield better results than previous researchers by integrating conventional data science methods with qualitative studies of clinical settings and process structure. Thus, we are able to leverage even small datasets.

Keywords: Process Mining · Data Science · Factor Analysis · Machine Learning · Regression · Healthcare Analytics

1 Introduction

Conducting surgical procedures is one of the core processes of hospitals with a paramount impact on the economic balance sheet, accounting for an average of

40% of all expenses and generating approximately 60% of total revenue. The perioperative process stretches from the moment a procedure is decided upon to the moment a patient regains independence of medical supervision after a surgery [13, 29].

The perioperative process encompasses all activities before, during, and after a surgical procedure. They are critical from an economic point of view, because they take place in operating rooms, one of the most resource-intensive and strategically important areas of clinical infrastructure. The perioperative process may differ between hospitals, reflecting variations in management structure, clinical routines, and technical systems. In this study, we focus on three main sub-processes of the perioperative workflow at the LMU University Hospital (henceforth LMU), see Fig. 1. Because of their central role, we now describe them in greater detail.

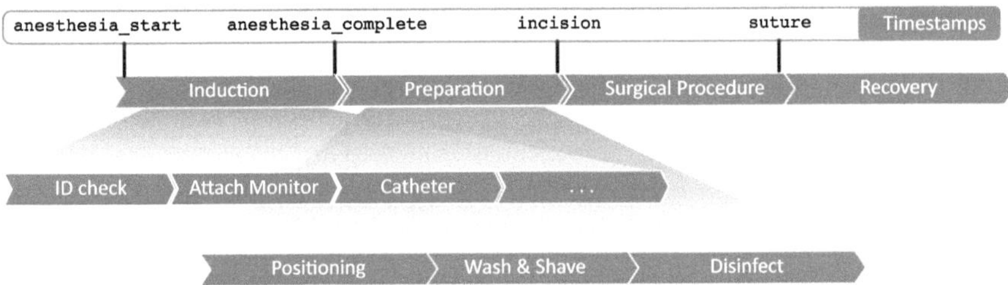

Fig. 1. The perioperative process is divided into the preoperative steps, commonly subsumed as induction, a surgical procedure, and recovery. Induction comprises the administration of anesthesia, positioning of the patient to facilitate access to body regions relevant to the surgical procedure, and further preparatory steps. From a process management point of view, the single largest independent variable is the precision of the duration estimation. Surgery duration is commonly measured as the incision-suture-time. The timestamps highlighted are important clinical KPIs.

During the *Induction*, the patient is being moved to the operating room, their identity is verified, monitoring devices for heart rate and respiration are attached, and catheters are emplaced. Most importantly, anesthesia is being administered. The duration of the induction phase is the time between start and completion of anesthesia. After induction, *Preparation* starts, where the patient is positioned according to procedural requirements, and the incision area is being prepared by washing, shaving, and disinfecting the skin, as appropriate. Often, a pause ensues while waiting for the surgeons. Then, the *Surgical Procedure* proper may start, marked by the *Incision* time. Surgery ends with the final suture. The duration of the surgical procedure is defined as the time between incision and the last suture. In the recovery phase, the anesthesiologist remains with the patient until they begin to breathe independently.

Surgical departments create daily or weekly operation schedules determining exactly when which operation is to take place, which medical staff and other resources need to be available at what time, and when patients are admitted to the wards for admission and examination. Creating optimal operation schedules is instrumental for hospitals: If schedules are too loose, the operating rooms are underutilized. On the other hand, if they are too tight, operations have to be deferred, which incurs costs that are unrecoverable from health insurers. Also, deferring operations may increase patient anxiety, while extending shifts may decrease staff satisfaction. So, optimizing operation schedules to improve the perioperative process offers significant reductions in healthcare costs, improved quality of medical services, and working conditions for medical staff [4,25,32].

However, surgical planning is an inherently complex process involving specialists from various departments, from surgeons and anesthesiologists across multiple specialties, via nursing staff to operating room coordinators and hospital administrators. All of these stakeholders must work in harmony to ensure a successful outcome. Additionally, emergency surgeries and unexpected patient reactions to medication may occur at any time, and take absolute precedence over any preconceived plan. Quick adaptation and restructuring of the surgery schedule occurs frequently at the LMU (though it might be less frequent in other hospitals). All in all, the planning process is highly dynamic and constantly evolving, requiring flexibility and a high degree of coordination [5,7]. From a process management point of view, this leaves us with two avenues of improvement. First, we may create optimal plans that, in the absence of any perturbations from emergencies, allow accurate and stable scheduling. Second, by creating such plans automatically, allowing for ad-hoc replanning, we may be able to mitigate or minimize the deleterious effects of emergencies. In this study, we show how both of these may be achieved by analyzing clinical processes and extracting high-quality predictive models from them.

2   Related Work

Recent studies have focused on using machine learning techniques to improve predictions of surgical durations. The goal is to schedule operating rooms more efficiently, reduce patient wait times, and make the best use of hospital resources. Even though the studies used datasets from different clinics, focused on various factors, and applied a range of modeling methods, they still reveal recurring patterns and consistent findings.

The analysis of existing research reveals that a critical step in all studies is the careful data preprocessing, which directly influences the accuracy of predictions. Kendale et al. [16] excluded stop words and applied term frequencyinverse document frequency (TF-IDF) to standardize procedure names, while Martinez et al. [18] used One-Hot and ordinal encoding. Yuniartha et al. [30] enhanced features with comorbidity and allergy information. The range of methods used in modeling varied from regression techniques to ensemble methods, with Random Forest and Gradient Boosting Machine (GBM) (especially XGBoost) repeatedly showing superiority [8,16,20,23,24], and Bagged Trees demonstrating high accuracy and efficiency [18]. Neural networks, though less commonly applied, as in the work of Jiao et al. [15] with a modular artificial neural network based on long short-term memory, were able to account for temporal structure and outperformed Bayesian models in real-time prediction. Adaptive solutions were also developed: the hybrid model by Soh et al. [27] used different regression algorithms for specific data subsets, taking into account the dynamic nature of the clinical environment, while Hosseini et al. [12] demonstrated the effectiveness of stepwise regression for certain surgical specialties, highlighting procedure codes as the main factor in prediction. Evaluation metrics were largely consistent in most studies, with mean absolute error (MAE) and root mean square error (RMSE) serving as standard benchmarks. Additional metrics such as r^2, mean absolute percentage error, and median absolute deviation were employed to capture different aspects of model accuracy and robustness.

Finally, the integration of domain knowledge was a distinguishing factor in the study by Strömblad et al. [28], who collaborated with clinical staff to identify over 300 relevant predictors. Although implementation details were not thoroughly reported, the inclusion of expert insights significantly contributed to improved scheduling outcomes.

Numerous studies aimed at improving the accuracy of surgical planning rely on the analysis of large datasets (typically 3–4 years' worth of data). In contrast, our dataset represents only one year of work (see Sect. 3.2 for details). The small sample size made it difficult to model data for individual departments. In response, we propose a new approach that involves modeling not only surgeries but also the entire perioperative process. By breaking the process into several stages and integrating knowledge about its specifics, we identified key factors affecting the duration of each step. This approach makes planning more flexible and adaptive to unforeseen situations.

3   Research Methods

Our approach follows a mixed methods approach, combining quantitative and qualitative methods as explained by the table below. The following two subsections describe the qualitative and quantitative research activities in detail, Table 1 presents a synopsis.

3.1   Qualitative Analysis

In the first stage of our research, we sought to understand the domain as such and build rapport with domain experts to ensure ecological validity of our work. We conducted semi-structured interviews with clinical staff involved in the perioperative process, such as anesthesiologists, surgeons, nurses, and administrators. We selected our interview partners through theoretical sampling [2,6,9,26]. Our insights are visualized in Fig. 1. To validate our findings and to further increase rapport with informants, we went on a field trip to the hospital, discussed preliminary results with our informants, and followed up with a survey. Finally, we

Table 1. In a first step, we established ecologic validity of our work through contextual understanding and building rapport with domain experts. This also informed our hypotheses, and the scope of the data we acquired. In a second stage, we analyzed these data, tested our hypotheses, and extract findings and evaluate the models. Finally, we presented both the qualitative and the quantitative results in a workshop at LMU.

Goal	Method	Outcome	This Article
Contextual understanding	Expert interviews, Field trip, Survey	Process model, Factorial model	Sect. 3.1, Figs. 1 and 2
Detailed analysis	Data analysis Hypothesis testing	Features pipeline, Model evaluation	Sect. 3.2 Sect. 4
Validation	Result presentation workshop	Confirmation	Sect. 6.2

derived a causal model about influence factors, likely causal relationships and potential outcomes, see Fig. 2. We used it to derive requirements for the data to be analyzed and define hypotheses to be tested.

These hypotheses formed the foundation of a causal model that not only reflects data-based dependencies but also structures and reveals the implicit knowledge embedded in clinical practice. The model was developed iteratively and validated in collaboration with clinical staff, with the goal of creating a realistic and practical representation of everyday operations–clear, transparent, and aligned with clinical routines.

We identified four relevant process variables: the durations of induction, preparation, the surgical procedure proper, and recovery, see Fig. 1. We focus on

- **Induction Duration**: the difference between timestamps `anesthesia_start` and `anesthesia_complete`.
- **Surgery**: the difference between timestamps `incision` and `suture`.

These four variables may be under the influence of three groups of factors. First, there are patient factors such as age, sex, and weight. Clearly, patient age affects many physiological and epidemiological variables, so that age affects almost all variables of the perioperative process. For instance, in old age, recovery from anesthesia takes longer. Also, there are many procedures that affect different age groups in a different way. For instance, hip replacements are very rare in younger patients.

Second, there are treatment factors, that is, factors pertaining to the medical practice. For instance, obviously, the surgical procedure performed has a major influence on the duration of the surgery. But this influence extends to the preoperative phase, for instance in that the positioning and induction depend on it as well. Observe that there are cross-dependencies, too, such as the correlations between sex and procedures (e. g., mastectomy affects women almost exclusively).

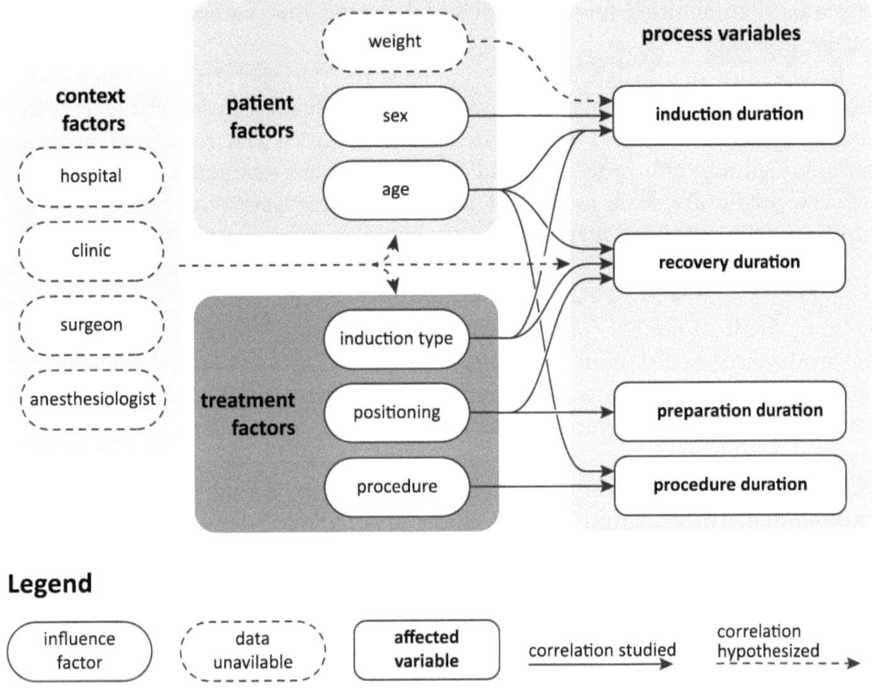

Fig. 2. Potential influencing factors: This figure illustrates the factors and their possible impact on the various steps of the perioperative process. All mentioned factors and their influence are based on insights gained through communication with clinical experts.

Third, there are context factors such as the hospital, the clinic within the hospital, and the individual surgeons in a given clinic. Our informants emphasized the influence of individual capabilities of a surgeon on surgery quality and duration. Also, the kind of procedures performed varies greatly with clinic. E. g., only a neurology clinic will perform brain surgery, which is much less standardized than, say, many orthopedic procedures.

3.2   Quantitative Analysis

In the quantitative part of our work, we processed these data and applied various statistical methods to test our hypotheses. Depending on the data properties, we applied the t-test, F-test, and the Kruskal–Wallis test to identify significant differences between groups and to explore potential causal relationships[1].

We also used the results to generate predictive models for procedure duration. Compared to similar studies, our dataset is relatively small in terms of both the number of documented surgeries and the number of features describing them.

---

[1] Background information on the applied statistical tests can be found in [21].

This posed difficulties for unsupervised learning due to sparsity and limited feature diversity.

Besides the qualitative study, we modeled the perioperative process based on the collected data. Using classical process mining tools from the *PM4PY* library, we reconstructed medical workflows from log data. The recovered workflows were divided into sub-processes, and for each one, we examined the relationship between predictors, such as patient positioning or anesthesia type, and process duration. This provided a structured basis for creating predictive models.

The staff at the LMU, one of the largest in Germany, documents and plan medical procedures using medical information systems. One of these is produced by Sqior Medical GmbH (henceforth Sqior, see https://www.sqior.de/), a leading producer of health care information systems. Data is entered manually and automatically. The data was anonymized and aggregated by Sqior and made available to us under a non-disclosure policy.

Data Acquisition: The data covered all operations taking place at the LMU between Jan. 18, 2024 and Jan. 23, 2025, and includes detailed documentation across ten specialty departments. The dataset consists of 427,959 events across 23,687 workflows, of which 17,358 include both `incision` and `suture` times. For the purpose of this study, only workflows containing both incision and suture timestamps were considered.

Preprocessing for the First Analysis: The raw data included up to 26 events per procedure. Based on the results of our qualitative analysis (see Sect. 3.1), we focused on three key sub-processes: *Induction, Preparation, Surgical Procedure.* Their durations were calculated as the time difference between the events `anesthesia_start`, `anesthesia_complete`, `incision`, and `suture`. Additionally, we considered planned durations for induction and surgery, the department, and patient characteristics (age and sex). We created separate datasets for each sub-process including the relevant duration and factors. Figure 3 illustrates the total number of workflows and their distribution across sub-processes. After that we applied the 1.5× interquartile range (IQR) [17] method to remove outliers.

Clustering: The dataset contains 11,296 unique procedure descriptions (16,576 records) and 2,081 unique induction descriptions (11,076 records). For normalization, we removed all non-alphanumeric characters. The resulting text data was converted to lower case. Induction data were normalized also using medical expertise and Sqior resources, standardizing synonyms and abbreviations. The text was vectorized using TF-IDF [22]. Clustering was performed with K-Means [10] for procedures and GMM [1,31] for induction, with the number of clusters determined using the mean Silhouette Coefficient. We thus combined algorithmic segmentation and clinical expertise to group interventions by complexity and structure in a clinically meaningful way.

Preprocessing for Regression: The dataset was split into training (80%) and test (20%) sets. One-Hot Encoding was applied for categorical variables such

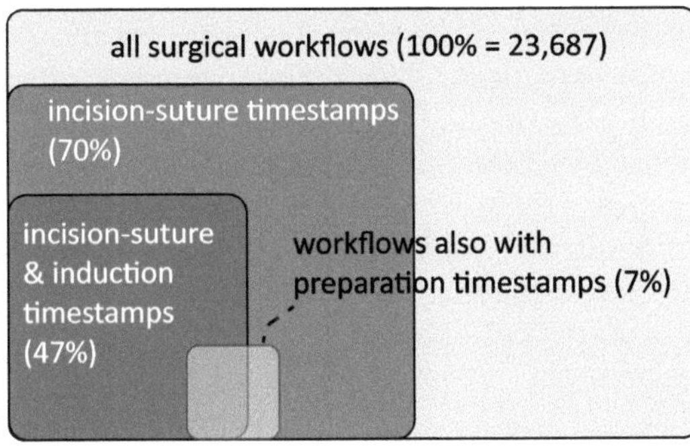

Fig. 3. Our base dataset contains all documented workflows recorded in the Sqior system from Jan. 18, 2024 till Jan. 23, 2025. Many records were incomplete and did not contain all timestamps necessary. Therefore, we created sub-sets for different analyses.

as sex, department, and Target Encoding (with smoothing parameter 40) for procedure clusters. To reduce the risk of overfitting, we implemented Smoothed Target Encoding based on Micci–Barreca's method [19]. The target value was computed based only on the training set and then assigned to the corresponding clusters in the test set to ensure that no information from the test set influenced the encoding process. In our analysis, we compared simple prediction methods (arithmetic mean) with regression models such as [14], Random Forest [3], and Gradient Boosting Machines (GBM) [11]. Hyper parameters were turned using grid search.

Evaluation of Models: Models were evaluated with different sets of predictors for each sub-process. The metrics were MAE, RMSE, r^2 and mean percentage deviation from plan. In addition, clinical practice considers a deviation of $\pm 20\%$ from the planned duration as acceptable, and this threshold was used as a reference point when interpreting the results.

4 Observations and Findings

At the beginning of our analysis, we focused on the most relevant metric in the dataset: the incision-to-suture time, which serves as a key indicator of actual surgical duration. Descriptive statistics revealed systematic over- and underestimation in manual planning. Surgeries planned for less than 15 min were almost always underestimated, as shown by box-plots where the entire deviation distribution 20 below zero. Overall, more than 60% of surgeries deviated by over 20% from their planned duration, with an average deviation of 68.43%. These results clearly show that current planning is often inaccurate and that there is a strong need for data-driven improvements.

To standardize and reduce variability in free-text fields efficiently, we simplified the language by reducing complex expressions and applying stemming.

Using TF-IDF vectorization and K-Means clustering, we grouped similar descriptions into meaningful categories. The optimal number of clusters was identified using the silhouette method. Anesthesia descriptions contained significantly more abbreviations than surgical ones. Here, Sqior's proprietary algorithms helped standardize terms, reducing the number of clusters from 135 to 15 without any loss in prediction quality. These 15 clusters are more interpretable and manageable in clinical practice.

We conducted a statistical analysis using t-tests, ANOVA, and Kruskal–Wallis tests to evaluate the influence of different factors on duration. While demographic variables such as age and gender were statistically significant, their practical effect was minimal. In contrast, the type of procedure, anesthesia method, and patient positioning were both statistically and practically relevant. Exploratory factor analysis confirmed that the most influential variables for surgical duration were the procedure description and department, while for anesthesia, the description of the method played the key role. Patient sex had no significant impact.

These findings were incorporated into regression models, ranging from simple averages to more advanced approaches such as linear regression, Random Forest, and GBM. We found that prediction accuracy remained relatively stable across different combinations of features and models. This aligned with the statistical findings, which showed that complex models offered only marginal improvements, while the simple mean already provided robust predictions (see Fig. 4). Given the high effort required to tune hyper parameters in complex models, the mean was chosen as a practical baseline solution.

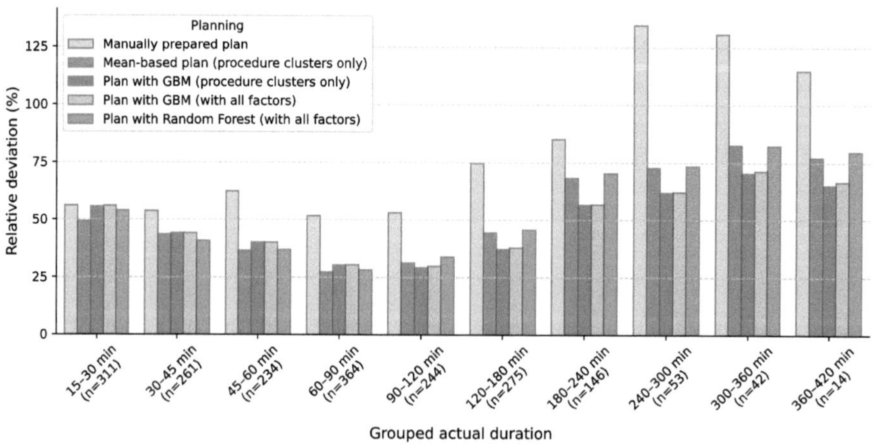

Fig. 4. Comparison of different planning approaches for predicting the duration of surgical procedures. Four strategies were evaluated: manual planning, calculation based on the arithmetic mean, Random Forest, and GBM. The relative percentage deviations were analyzed in relation to the actual durations of the surgeries. Both the arithmetic mean and GBM approaches used the surgical procedure description as input.

Unlike traditional methods that estimate procedure duration based on extracted procedure name or surgeon's subjective assessments, our approach leverages semantic clustering of over 11,000 unique free-text procedure descriptions. We grouped procedures based on semantic similarity rather than literal string matches. This allowed us to calculate stable average durations within clusters. This strategy is particularly valuable because, in real clinic practice, the same procedure can be described in many different ways depending on the surgeons' style or preferences. The traditional method of averaging by exact procedure name, like the Method of Taking Averages (MTA), does not account for this linguistic variability, resulting in inconsistent statistics and reduced reliability of estimates. In contrast, our approach creates a generalized and more robust model that handles lexical variation without sacrificing accuracy [16,27,28,30]. Moreover, this clustering technique provides the foundation for developing a new catalog of surgical procedures that better reflects the real-world diversity of medical documentation within the hospital. Such a catalog could significantly improve standardization, planning accuracy, and interoperability across departments and systems.

Furthermore, our study demonstrates that using a relatively small but carefully selected set of predictors such as induction type, patient positioning, and procedure type, together with simple models, led to a significant improvement in prediction accuracy compared to the original planned values. The reduction in average error was especially noticeable, with a decrease of 10.99% points for the induction phase and 25.61% points for the surgical phase.

Our analysis also carries practical implications. Automatic minimum duration recommendations, such as at least 20 min for induction, and buffer recommendations for high-variance clusters, can help improve planning accuracy. Early warning systems could identify bottlenecks when too many long procedures are scheduled in the same time window.

Nonetheless, there are limitations. The dataset lacks key contextual variables, such as the availability of personnel, nursing staff levels, or patient-specific risk factors like comorbidities or catheter-based imaging workflows. These gaps limit the explanatory power of the models. In addition, small cluster sizes (less than fifty cases) in sensitive areas reduced statistical reliability. Future work should integrate additional data sources and apply expert-based cluster validation to further enhance the precision and robustness of the models.

5   Interpretation

We observed that manually scheduled operations are typically estimated at durations that are multiples of 15 min, without the system enforcing such intervals (see Fig. 5). The true operation durations, however, are smoothly distributed over time. We strongly suspect that medical staff estimate operation durations based on intuition rather than data. It is likely that limited consideration is given to duration estimation.

We have shown that much more precise duration estimates can be generated automatically, yielding higher accuracy at lower planning cost. Clearly, more

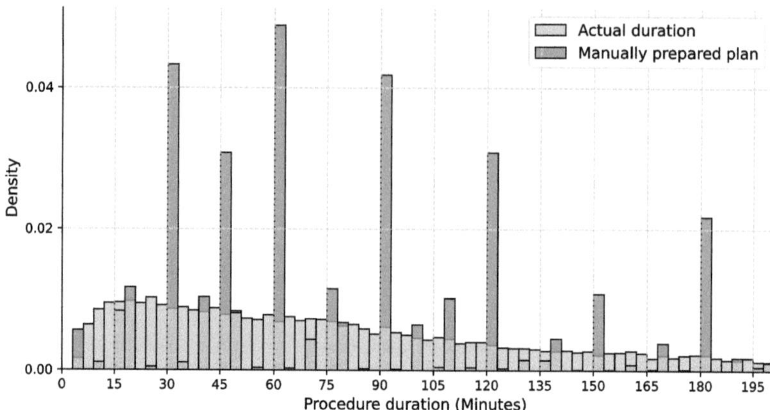

Fig. 5. Distribution of actual surgery duration and the manual plan (3-minute interval)

precise duration estimates are conducive to increased plan stability, and thus offer significant improvement of hospital economics and medical outcomes.

While previous studies have focused exclusively on the procedure incision-suture-time, our initial qualitative investigation in the medical workplace revealed that other parts of the perioperative process are also relevant, particularly, induction and patient positioning. Including them in the analysis yields a more comprehensive picture of the perioperative process, allowing for more precise duration estimations of the overall process. We conclude that a holistic view of medical processes is conducive to effective overall improvements.

Including medical expertise in the analysis process proved vital in another aspect, too: the knowledge gathered from hospital staff considerably improved normalization of prose comments on medical records and operation plans, leading to better clustering and in turn much better predictive models. The hybrid approach of combining data science with expert input not only enabled more effective grouping but also led to a meaningful breakdown of the process into finer steps that are operationally relevant.

In creating predictive models for operation duration, we identified a number of relevant factors such as type of positioning and induction, type of intervention, and patient characteristics such as age, sex, and weight. Regression analyses and hypothesis tests indicate, however, that patient characteristics have much less impact than other factors. Thus, practical predictions of operation durations do not require personal data, which potentially affect patient privacy rights. Good predictive performance can be achieved with just a few well-prepared features, which means that efficient models can be built in data-scarce environments, as well.

Nevertheless, we suggest that there are additional factors that likely influence procedure duration and should be included in future analyses. These include e. g., comorbidities, the general health of the patient, and medications currently being taken. Most clinical experts also believe that the surgeon can significantly influence the duration of the procedure.

We did not study second-order dependencies between patient and treatment factors, as they present redundant information only. Also, we did not study patient weight, as this information was not contained in our data set. However, this would make for interesting follow-up work, as we suspect that patient weight has a major influence on induction, e. g., by affecting the duration of positioning. Similarly, we did not study the influence of context factors, as our data only cover one hospital, and data on clinics and individual surgeons was not available to us. However, again, this would make for interesting follow-up work as it may uncover medical best practices that could be transferred from one hospital to another.

We believe that our findings are not restricted to the particular hospital we have studied. While other hospitals may have other profiles in terms of the procedures they perform, there are only two likely factors to explain major differences in average operation durations per procedure across hospitals: differences in execution or differences in individual capabilities. Both of these are interesting in their own right. When different hospitals do things differently and there are differences in medical outcome or cost, it is well worth studying such differences to spread best practices more quickly. When individual practitioners perform better than others, this should prompt us to improve staff training, or allocation. Either way, an analytical perspective based on medical practices holds significant improvements both in terms of economics, and medical outcomes.

6   Threats to Validity

Given the nature of our study, several of the widely known threats to validity simply do not apply. Take *internal validity* as an example. We have developed and analyzed a causal model for impact factors. While this model is plausible and straight-forward, and we believe in it, the model is not part of our conclusions. We only use it to create a predictive model, the effectiveness of which is undeniable. So, even if our model were wrong or incomplete, would this not affect our conclusions.

Similarly, *construct validity* is not a relevant category for our study: we measure only time durations such as incision-suture time or induction time that represent Key Performance Indicators well established in medical practice and research literature.

6.1   Conclusion Validity

From a data science perspective, 16,576 data records may appear to be a small data set, such that conclusions are in danger of introducing potential bias. From a medical perspective, however, this is a very large data set documenting the work of more than 5,000 medical professionals over more than a year. Recall that the conclusions we draw from our data analysis are mostly qualitative, indicating process improvement potential rather than changes to medical interventions. Thus, we believe our conclusions are well covered by the amount of data we have based them on.

Another potential weakness of data based studies is data quality.

It appears that some teams and clinics have a relaxed attitude towards documenting medical procedures. This change results in some events relevant to our analysis being missing from a significant number of workflows. For this reason, we treat each sub-process separately rather than modeling the perioperative process as a single continuous flow. Figure 3 illustrates these data gaps. Specifically, 69.98% of all workflows include both incision and suture events needed for modeling the procedure sub-process. 46.50% contain both the `anesthesia_start` and the `anesthesia_complete` timestamps and the associated attributes needed for modeling the induction step. Only 6.97% of workflows include events and information necessary for estimating the duration of the preparation phase.

We excluded 812 outliers that, according to medical professionals we consulted, were clearly flukes, such as when the induction timestamp is after the operation, or when operation timestamps indicated operation durations of several days. While the latter is not impossible, it is exceedingly rare and of no import to our conclusions. Again, we believe that our conclusions are not affected by poor data quality.

6.2   Ecologic Validity and Generalizability

Our study was conducted using real (historical) data, guaranteeing a high level of ecological validity. However, the site of our study is a university hospital that acts as a medical hub in a major metropolitan region. Therefore, the LMU University Hospital is faced with a very large diversity of medical cases as well as emergencies. This is a marked difference to many smaller hospitals, that care for far fewer complex and unusual medical situations. Thus, in smaller hospitals, creating a reliable operation schedule is typically an easier task. Conversely, however, smaller hospitals also have fewer staff and operating rooms, so there is a greater need for precise planning. In summary, we cannot know at this point, whether smaller hospitals will benefit from our approach in the same way and to the same degree that a major medical hub like LMU does. Observe, however, that our factor model (cf. Fig. 2) does document these potential influences, showing arrows from the context factors to the patient and treatment factor groups, respectively.

While average durations for standard procedures may vary between hospitals, each individual hospital can easily collect the data required to make predictive models that exceed manual estimates in quality. Even small hospitals can aggregate enough data to achieve significant plan stability improvements.

6.3   Ethical Considerations

Our study has not involved patients or their treatment, so our study did not require formal clearance from an Ethical Review Board or similar. We worked exclusively with anonymized, historical data that did not allow us to identify individuals, so our study does not affect privacy rights of patients either. Consequently, no consent of patients was required beyond the consent implied in undergoing medical treatment, as documented by the hospital. The data also did not contain personal information about medical staff, so no labor protection regulations were affected.

7   Contribution and Conclusion

High plan stability is a major goal of any hospital, as it affects economic as well as medical outcomes. Medical contingencies and ad hoc patient logistics aside, the only controllable factor for optimizing plan stability is the precision of effort estimations of procedures used to create the operation schedule.

We have studied medical data from a large and renowned university hospital with a high degree of digitalization, covering the work of more than 5,000 medical professionals for over a year. Yet, the estimates of operation duration are created manually, exhibiting artifacts and bearing little correlation to actual operation durations. Replacing manual estimates even by trivial estimation models like the arithmetic mean of historic durations of comparable procedures offers significant improvements of effort estimations. Our findings transfer to other settings, though the impact might differ depending on the profile of procedures executed at a given hospital.

By combining expert knowledge, data-driven hypothesis testing, statistical validation, process modeling, and clustering, we gained a deeper understanding of the perioperative workflow and significantly improved prediction accuracy and planning reliability.

From a data science perspective, we are working with a small data set. By integrating qualitative research methods to include human expertise from the medical professionals involved in the planning process, we were able to leverage this small data set to achieve major improvements. So, a small dataset *may* go a long way, sometimes.

Acknowledgements. The authors would like to thank sqior medical, Universitätsklinikum der LMU (Großhadern), and QAware for supporting our work, in particular Matthias Eimer, Nils Frielinghaus, Stephanie Grabow, Aline Karweik and PD Dr. Thomas Koperna.

References

1. Bai, J., Ng, S.: Determining the number of factors in approximate factor models. Econometrica **70**(1), 191–221 (2002). https://doi.org/10.1111/1468-0262.00273
2. Breckenridge, J., Jones, D.: Demystifying theoretical sampling in grounded theory research. Ground. Theory Rev. **08**(2) (2009)
3. Breiman, L.: Random forests. Mach. Learn. **45**(1), 5–32 (2001). https://doi.org/10.1023/A:1010933404324

4. Childers, C., Maggard-Gibbons, M.: Understanding costs of care in the operating room. JAMA Surg. **153**(4), e176233 (2018). https://doi.org/10.1001/jamasurg.2017.6233

5. Denton, B., Viapiano, J., Vogl, A.: Optimization of surgery sequencing and scheduling decisions under uncertainty. Health Care Manag. Sci. **10**, 13–24 (2007). https://doi.org/10.1007/s10729-006-9005-4

6. Denzin, N.K., Lincoln, Y.S. (eds.): The SAGE Handbook of Qualitative Research, 5th edn. SAGE, Thousand Oaks (2018)

7. Erdogan, S., Denton, B., Cochran, J.: Surgery planning and scheduling. In: Wiley Encyclopedia of Operations Research and Management Science. John Wiley & Sons, Ltd., Hoboken (2011). https://doi.org/10.1002/9780470400531.eorms0861

8. Gabriel, R., et al.: An ensemble learning approach to improving prediction of case duration for spine surgery: algorithm development and validation. JMIR Perioper. Med. **6**, e39650 (2023). https://doi.org/10.2196/39650

9. Glaser, B., Strauss, A.: Discovery of Grounded Theory. Sociology Press (1967)

10. Hartigan, J.A., Wong, M.A.: Algorithm as 136: a k-means clustering algorithm. J. R. Stat. Soc. Ser. C (Appl. Stat.) **28**(1), 100–108 (1979)

11. He, Z., Lin, D., Lau, T., Wu, M.: Gradient boosting machine: a survey (2019). https://arxiv.org/abs/1908.06951

12. Hosseini, N., Sir, M., Jankowski, C., Pasupathy, K.: Surgical duration estimation via data mining and predictive modeling: a case study. In: AMIA Annual Symposium Proceedings, pp. 640–648. American Medical Informatics Association (2015)

13. Hughes, S.J.: Oxford Handbook of Perioperative Practice. Oxford University Press, Cambridge (2022)

14. James, G., Witten, D., Hastie, T., Tibshirani, R., Taylor, J.: Linear Regression, pp. 69–134. Springer, Cham (2023). https://doi.org/10.1007/978-3-031-38747-0_3

15. Jiao, Y., et al.: Continuous real-time prediction of surgical case duration using a modular artificial neural network. Br. J. Anaesth. **128**(5), 829–837 (2022). https://doi.org/10.1016/j.bja.2022.01.017

16. Kendale, S., Bishara, A., Burns, M., Solomon, S., Corriere, M., Mathis, M.: Machine learning for the prediction of procedural case durations developed using a large multicenter database: algorithm development and validation study. JMIR AI **2**, e44909 (2023). https://doi.org/10.2196/44909

17. Levene, M., Harris, M.: Just Enough Data Science and Machine Learning: Essential Tools and Techniques, 1st edn. Addison-Wesley Professional, Hoboken (2025)

18. Martinez, O., Martinez, C., Parra, C., Rugeles, S., Suarez, D.: Machine learning for surgical time prediction. Comput. Methods Programs Biomed. **208**, 106220 (2021). https://doi.org/10.1016/j.cmpb.2021.106220

19. Micci-Barreca, D.: A preprocessing scheme for high-cardinality categorical attributes in classification and prediction problems. SIGKDD Explor. Newsl. **3**(1), 27–32 (2001). https://doi.org/10.1145/507533.507538

20. Miller, L., Goedicke, W., Crowson, M., Rathi, V., Naunheim, M., Agarwala, A.: Using machine learning to predict operating room case duration: a case study in otolaryngology. Otolaryngol. Head Neck Surg. **168**, 241–247 (2023). https://doi.org/10.1177/01945998221076480

21. Murphy, K., Myors, B.: Statistical Power Analysis, 5th edn. Routledge, Abingdon, Oxon; New York (2023). https://learning.oreilly.com/library/view/-/9781000843255/?ar

22. Papineni, K.: Why inverse document frequency? In: Proceedings of the Second Meeting of the North American Chapter of the Association for Computational Linguistics, pp. 1–8 (2001). https://aclanthology.org/N01-1004

23. Park, J., Roh, G., Kim, K., et al.: Development of predictive model of surgical case durations using machine learning approach. J. Med. Syst. **49**, 8 (2025). https://doi.org/10.1007/s10916-025-02141-y
24. Riahi, V., Hassanzadeh, H., Khanna, S., et al.: Improving preoperative prediction of surgery duration. BMC Health Serv. Res. **23**, 1343 (2023). https://doi.org/10.1186/s12913-023-10264-6
25. Rothstein, D., Raval, M.: Operating room efficiency. Semin. Pediatr. Surg. **27**(2), 79–85 (2018). https://doi.org/10.1053/j.sempedsurg.2018.02.004
26. Saldaña, J.: Fundamentals of Qualitative Research. Oxford University Press, Cambridge (2011)
27. Soh, K.W., Walker, C., O'Sullivan, M., Wallace, J.: An evaluation of the hybrid model for predicting surgery duration. J. Med. Syst. **44**(2), 1–16 (2020). https://doi.org/10.1007/s10916-019-1501-4
28. Strömblad, C., Baxter-King, R., Meisami, A., et al.: Effect of a predictive model on planned surgical duration accuracy, patient wait time, and use of presurgical resources: A randomized clinical trial. JAMA Surg. **156**(4), 315–321 (2021). https://doi.org/10.1001/jamasurg.2020.6361
29. Whitlock, J.: What does perioperative mean? (2025). www.verywellhealth.com/perioperative-defined-3157137. Accessed 2 Jan 2025
30. Yuniartha, D., Masruroh, N., Herliansyah, M.: An evaluation of a simple model for predicting surgery duration using a set of surgical procedure parameters. Inf. Med. Unlocked **25**, 100633 (2021). https://doi.org/10.1016/j.imu.2021.100633
31. Zhang, Y., Let al.: Gaussian mixture model clustering with incomplete data. ACM Trans. Multimedia Comput. Commun. Appl. **17**(1s) (2021). https://doi.org/10.1145/3408318
32. Zhu, S., Fan, W., Yang, S., Pei, J., Pardalos, P.M.: Operating room planning and surgical case scheduling: a review of literature. J. Comb. Optim. **37**(3), 757–805 (2018). https://doi.org/10.1007/s10878-018-0322-6

Developing an Agile Process for Quantum Annealing Applications: An Industrial Experience

Lodovica Marchesi[1(✉)] , Marco Di Francesco[2] , and Michele Marchesi[1,2]

[1] Department of Mathematics and Computer Science, University of Cagliari, Cagliari, Italy
lodovica.marchesi@unica.it
[2] Netservice S.p.A., Via Giovanni Antonelli, 50, Roma, Italy

Abstract. Quantum Annealing (QA) offers high potential for solving complex Quadratic Unconstrained Binary Optimization (QUBO) problems. However, developing practical QA applications remains challenging due to mathematical complexity, hardware constraints, and the absence of tailored software engineering methodologies. This paper introduces AQUA (Agile QUantum Annealing)–a novel agile process for QUBO/QA application development–created by an industry-academia collaboration between NetService SpA and the University of Cagliari. Designed using Design Science Research (DSR), AQUA adapts Scrum to address QUBO and QA specific requirements, structuring development into four phases: initial assessment including mathematical formulation, algorithm evaluation using prototypes, agile implementation, and deployment, including lifecycle maintenance management; the development is controlled by specific milestones. Validated on a real-world credit scoring proof-of-concept, AQUA demonstrates feasibility and provides the first explicit framework for systematic QA engineering. Contributions include: (1) a dedicated QA development methodology, (2) DSR application for process design, and (3) empirical validation.

Keywords: Quantum Annealing · Quantum Computing · QUBO · Software process · Agile Methods

1 Introduction

Quantum computing (QC) is a new computational paradigm that has been attracting increasing attention from both research and industry, achieving very high levels of interest. Its transformative potential across various industrial sectors is widely recognized [8,21]. This is evident also considering the substantial investments made by major tech companies such as IBM, Google, Amazon and Microsoft, who are actively working to offer QC as a service to address a new generation of highly complex computational challenges.

However, QC is still in the "Noisy intermediate-scale quantum era", or NISQ era, as defined by Preskill, meaning that the number of qubits of quantum processors is fewer than a few hundred, and they suffer from noise in quantum gates,

G. Scanniello et al. (Eds.): PROFES 2025, LNCS 16362, pp. 102–119, 2026.
https://doi.org/10.1007/978-3-032-12092-2_7

which limits the size of quantum circuits that can be executed reliably [18]. Consequently, we will have to wait many more years before the advent of QC systems and applications viable to solve real problems and to get the "quantum advantage", that is the demonstration that a programmable quantum computer can solve a problem in a time substantially shorter than using a classical computer.

A different quantum technology which is available today and which looks more mature than traditional QC is Quantum Annealing (QA). While QC is a general computation model – even proved to be Turing-complete – QA is aimed at solving the problem of finding the global minimum of a function with many local minima, with an approach derived from Simulated Annealing algorithm. In its present form, QA was first proposed by Kadowaki and Nishimori [10]. A Californian-Canadian company, D-Wave Quantum Inc., in 2011 announced the first commercial quantum annealer [9], followed by subsequent versions, the last of which is D-Wave Advantage2, released in 2025.

Unfortunately, creating QA applications remains a formidable task. Many steps must be performed to develop viable solutions to real problems. First, we need to assess if the problem to solve can be traced back to a quadratic unconstrained binary optimization (QUBO). If this is the case, the viability of a QA approach, possibly in synergy with the use of traditional optimization algorithms, must be determined, and whether this approach can provide better results than a purely classical approach. Once decided to use QA, depending on the size and type of the problem, further processing is needed to partition the problem and arrive at a solution in a guaranteed and cost-effective way. All these steps look like a process that should be managed using sound software engineering (SE) and operational research practices.

The Italian company NetService SpA, a software house and system integrator developing applications also in the field of discrete and binary optimization, and interested in being at the forefront of this new technology, decided to develop a life-cycle management process aimed at supporting QA application development. To this purpose, NetService won a grant from Italian National Centre for HPC, Big Data and Quantum Computing, as referenced in the Acknowledgment section below. This research work was performed in cooperation with the University of Cagliari.

The goal of the project, named "QUBO-HPC", was to produce a structured software engineering life-cycle approach to help in solving optimization problems using QA. Such an approach is considered more effective than relying on ad-hoc implementation strategies or the individual expertise of developers, which can lead to errors and increased maintenance costs. Employing agile practices, which emphasize team collaboration, rapid development cycles, and continuous delivery, can also provide significant benefits to the development of this kind of applications.

In this paper, we present Agile QUantum Annealing (AQUA), an agile yet formal approach to develop QA applications. The initial question we must address about AQUA is: why create a new methodology? Why not directly adopt an established approach like waterfall, iterative, or agile for developing

QA systems? The answer lies in recognizing that implementing QA for a particular problem goes far beyond a conventional software development project. Developing such a system has heavy mathematical and operating research activities, and typically includes exploratory steps, needed to properly set up the system. These unique requirements convinced us that a new software development methodology is necessary for QA development. In reality, AQUA is not completely novel – rather, it builds substantially upon traditional agile methods like Scrum [20].

To develop and validate our proposed approach, we adopted the Design Science Research (DSR) methodology, a framework focused on designing and rigorously assessing novel solutions [16].

The main contribution of our work is the proposal and description of AQUA method, the first explicit structured process to develop QA applications, based on sound software engineering practices, and in particular on Agile principles, developed using Design Science Research (DSR) approach.

The remainder of the paper is structured as follows. Section 2 reports the main related works on QC, QA, QUBO and Quantum Software Engineering (QSE); Sect. 3 briefly outlines DSR methodology; Sect. 4 describes how AQUA was designed and its features; Sect. 5 reports the proof-of-concept used and its evaluation; Sect. 6 reports the lessons learned and concludes the paper.

2   Background

2.1   Quantum Computing and Quantum Annealing

QC takes advantage of the fundamental principles of quantum mechanics, in particular "superposition" and "entanglement", to perform calculations far more efficiently than classical computers for specific types of problems. Unlike classical bits, which can only be in one of two states (0 or 1) at any given moment, quantum bits or "qubits" can exist in a superposition of states, allowing them to represent multiple values simultaneously. This technology enables quantum systems to perform many calculations in parallel, opening the door to significant computational speedups and holding the potential to revolutionize fields such as cryptography, optimization, materials science and artificial intelligence [18]. However, building practical, large-scale quantum computers remains a major scientific and engineering challenge, with numerous technical obstacles yet to be overcome.

Alongside gate-based QC, another quantum technology of interest is QA [10], specifically tailored for solving Quadratic Unconstrained Binary Optimization (QUBO) problems, that can be regarded as a relaxed form of the adiabatic model. QA functions as a heuristic, variational quantum algorithm that seeks to approximate the ground state of the Hamiltonian of an Ising or QUBO model [22], positioning it as a promising framework for tackling combinatorial optimization challenges.

The only available quantum computers featuring QA are those of D-Wave. The latest computer, Advantage 2, uses a quantum processing unit (QPU) containing 4,400+ superconducting qubits shielded to be protected from electromagnetic interference, able to efficiently implement the minimization of this Hamiltonian.

Another approach to solve optimization problems using QA is the use of the so-called "Digital Quantum Annealers" (DQAs), machines that reproduce the interactions between spins in the Ising model using CMOS or optical technology inspired by quantum phenomena, as described in a recent technical report [15].

To our knowledge, the only available guidelines covering the full spectrum of activities to solve a real problem using QA are those available on D-Wave website [2]. These guidelines cover the whole spectrum of system development, from assessing the business case, to mathematical formulation, to decision on which solver(s) to use. Many practical examples, written by D-Wave or contributed by users, are also available. However, D-Wave guidelines are not presented in a systematic way, and the practical examples are mainly focused on the mathematical aspects of the problem solution.

Besides QA, hybrid QAclassical algorithms have become a key strategy to solve real QUBO problems. In these approaches, classical routines handle problem decomposition, optimization orchestration, and post-processing, while the quantum annealer is used to solve smaller sub-problems or core components that benefit from quantum effects [22].

2.2   QUBO Optimization

The QUBO model is a core mathematical framework for minimizing or maximizing a quadratic function over binary variables. Its appeal lies in its ability to represent a broad class of Combinatorial Optimization (CO) problems within a unified formulation [5]. While traditional CO problems often require problem-specific algorithms, QUBO provides a standardized approach that facilitates consistent modeling and solution strategies across a wide range of applications in both classical and emerging computational environments.

From a more technical perspective, QUBO involves minimizing the following objective function:

$$f(\mathbf{x}) = a + \mathbf{b}^T\mathbf{x} + \mathbf{x}^T Q\mathbf{x}, \tag{1}$$

where:

- $\mathbf{x} = [x_1, x_2, \ldots, x_n]^T$ is a binary vector with $x_i \in \{0,1\}$ or $x_i \in \{-1,+1\}$ (spin/Ising form);
- a (constant), $\mathbf{b}$ (linear coefficients), and Q (quadratic matrix) are real-valued;
- No constraints are imposed on $f(\mathbf{x})$.

The binary form is preferred because the linear term $\mathbf{b}^T\mathbf{x}$ becomes quadratic, since $x_i^2 = x_i$:

$$\mathbf{b}^T\mathbf{x} = \sum_i b_i x_i = \sum_i b_i x_i^2$$
$$= \mathbf{x}^T \mathrm{Diag}(\mathbf{b})\mathbf{x} \tag{2}$$

Thus, minimization reduces to:

$$f(\mathbf{x}) = \mathbf{x}^T Q'\mathbf{x}, \quad \text{where } Q' = Q + \mathrm{Diag}(\mathbf{b}) \tag{3}$$

Since $x_i x_j = x_j x_i$, the matrix Q is symmetric.

While unconstrained QUBO has limited practical use, constrained optimization problems can often be reformulated as QUBO, typically using penalty methods, thus extending its applicability [5].

QUBO models belong to a class of problems known to be *NP-hard*. The practical significance of this fact is that exact solvers designed to find "optimal" solutions will most likely fail except for small problems. Using such methods, computations on realistically sized problems may require days and even weeks without producing quality solutions. Fortunately, notable successes are being achieved using modern metaheuristic methods designed to find high-quality, but not necessarily optimal, solutions in an acceptable computational time [23]. These approaches are also creating valuable opportunities to address these problems using quantum computing techniques [6].

2.3   Agile Approach and Quantum Software Engineering

Building on the evolution of traditional software engineering–which began with hardware-centric, hard-wired approaches in the 1950s and gradually matured into today's agile development practices, QSE is expected to follow a similar trajectory [17]. However, the unique nature of quantum programming, including QA, needs a reassessment of the practices that drive agility in conventional software development.

Quantum programming requires a fundamental shift in thinking, based on unfamiliar and non-intuitive quantum principles. For instance, programming involves manipulating the states of qubits and performing measurements on them. In such a scenario of uncertain requirements due to the paradigm shift and continuous technological innovation, these issues are typically addressed through agile and lean development practices, that have long been recognized for their practical benefits [3]. Unlike traditional models based on careful planning and complete collection of all requirements, agile emphasizes practices like active user engagement, incremental development, short development cycles, continuous releases, refactoring and many others.

Currently, QC and QA remain in an early stage. A recent, comprehensive paper by Murillo et al. [14], includes a deep discussion of QSE status and perspectives, almost entirely focused on classical QC. The Sect. 4.6 of this paper, "Software Development Processes", focuses on QC and makes no mention of QA.

Schereer et al. [19] propose a model for developing software systems using Variational Quantum Algorithms (VQAs), which target QUBO problems. Their model is iterative, and uses five phases (problem definition, quantum algorithm selection, implementation, fine-tuning and back-propagation). Though not explicitly agile and not targeted to QA, this is perhaps the only paper we found aiming to describe a structured process to develop quantum software for QUBO.

A recent paper by Khan et al. [11] investigates the causes of challenges that could hinder the adoption of traditional agile approaches in quantum software projects, and develops the AQSSPM model which could evaluate the success probability of agile-quantum projects, serving as a roadmap to industry practitioners for informed decision-making.

Anyway, adopting agile practices could significantly ease the complexities of QA software development [13]. As Piattini et al. suggest: *"it's essential to take an agile approach to developing QSE techniques–rather than waiting for quantum languages to fully mature"* [17].

Agile methodologies are particularly valuable for early bug detection and resolution, enabling timely and manageable fixes. Moreover, quantum software development already shares key characteristics with agile methodologies, including evolutionary feature development and use of trial-and-error algorithms.

Activity	Methodology	Output
1. Problem identification and motivation	• Literature search • Engagement with experts	• Investigation on existing solutions in literature • List of issues with existing solutions • Possible improvements using a more structured process

2. Definition of the objectives of a solution	• Engagement with experts
	• Hypothesis based proposal
		• Definition of key features of the proposed solution:
		  ○ A well-defined and documented software methodology
		  ○ A process that includes business case and exploratory moves
		  ○ Fase of introducing changes during the development
		  ○ Management of entire software lifecycle

3 Design and Development	• Use of principles of Agile Manifesto • Identification of roles, activities, deliverables, milestones using a top-down approach • Use of UML activity diagrams to document the process steps	• Definition of the roles of the methodology • Definition and documentation of the activities of the methodology • Definition of milestones
4. Demonstration.	• Proof-of-concept selection • Application of the methodology on the proof-of-concept	• Proof-of-concept analysis and definition of QUBO problem • Prototype running and validating the proof-of-concept implemented using the methodology
5. Evaluation	• Discussion of the solution • Evaluation by experts	• Assessment of the methodology • Proof-of-concept evaluation and validation of the methodology
6. Communication	• Dissemination of the study results	• This article

Fig. 1. Design Research outline: activities, methodologies and outputs.

3   Research Methodology

This study utilizes the Design Science Research (DSR) methodology, a research approach that emphasizes identifying practical problems and developing effective artifacts to address them. Specifically, we adopted the framework introduced by Peffers et al., who provided a detailed exploration of DSR methodologies and proposed a structured process tailored for research in information systems [16]. We also used the guidelines proposed by Hevner et al. [7].

The DSR process comprises six key steps. The initial step involves identifying the problem and establishing its significance, whereas step 2 is the definition of the objectives of a solution to this problem. It is typically performed with external experts, and produces a hypothesis based proposal. Step 3 of DSR methodology, in our case, is about designing and developing a prototype process. This activity starts from the detailed requirements defined in step 2, and proceeds to specific design and implementation activities.

Step 4 prescribes selecting a case study or, as in our case, a proof-of-concept validation, and applying the proposed process to it, gathering data about the validation. Step 5 evaluates the proof-of-concept validation with the help of experts, and verifies its viability and effectiveness. Step 6 communicates and disseminates the study results.

Figure 1 presents the research activities that we undertook to fulfill the objectives of our study. The structure and presentation of our work, as elaborated in the following sections, are aligned with this DSR framework.

4   Problem Definition and Solution Design

4.1   Problem Identification and Definition of the Objectives

Performing step 1 of DSR, we searched the scientific literature for methodologies aimed to manage the development of QA applications. We searched the "Scopus" database (title, abstract and keywords) using the string "quantum annealing", in AND with "software engineering", "software process" and "software development", finding 18 unique papers.

Among these papers, four deal with applying QUBO/QA to SE problems, such as test case minimization or finding clones. Six papers were about QA applications, two described software libraries, one was about reverse engineering of QA software, and one about the use of open source software in QC. We also considered 42 papers presented at the six Workshops on Q-SE held as workshops of ICSE conference from 2020 to 2025.

Almost all papers presented at Q-SE were about classical quantum circuit development. QA is sometimes quoted as a successful application of quantum principles, but no paper describes a SE method to develop QA applications. On the other hand several papers are about using agile principles for QC software development, as reported in Subsect. 2.3. In conclusion, we found no paper about the application of SE methods or practices to QA development.

The issues of present QA development, and the requirements of a QA development methodology were discussed with five researchers of Italian research centers managing High Performance Computing (HPC) facilities, who typically develop solutions to optimization problems using QC and QA. A project manager and a consultant, who work in the field, were also involved in the discussion. This group of five experts was also asked to provide suggestions for the proof-of-concept validation, and perform the evaluation of the methodology and its application.

The experts agreed on the lack of more formal methods for defining, designing and developing QA applications, and on the need to study and propose a software engineering method for this purpose. Everyone was familiar with the guidelines and steps proposed by D-Wave in their website, but everyone expressed interest in developing a more formally described methodology, capable of supporting other QA solutions, such as DQA, and not tied to a single vendor.

Together with the experts, and according to step 2 of DSR, we defined the objectives of our solution. In this context, the proposed methodology must provide a solution to the following issues:

1. Being able to adapt to various types of projects, that might have different types of objective functions to minimize, actors, duration, goals.
2. Ability to assess early the cost and viability of the project, and to decide whether to go on, or to drop it.
3. Explicit management of the mathematical formulation of the problem, and of the choice of specific algorithms and data transformations to get the solution.
4. Software development taking advantage of existing libraries, using an approach able to manage changes in the requirements and allowing to maximize the contribution of the members of the development group.
5. Ability to reduce the risk of side effects in case of software changes.
6. Management of the entire software life cycle, including evolutionary and corrective maintenance.

Taking advantage of the experts' opinions, and of our experience in studying and designing ad hoc methodologies for the development of specific software systems [12], starting from the quoted goals, we elaborated a new methodology for QA application development, that we called AQUA - Agile QUantum Annealing.

During the meetings with the experts, we also talked about possible proofs of concept to assess the methodology. As a proof-of-concept, they proposed the selection of the optimal feature to classify a set of samples, a general classification problem with many possible applications. In particular, the credit risk estimation was considered a good proof-of-concept, also for the availability of test datasets of various sizes.

4.2 Design and Development

Step 3 of DSR methodology was initially performed by gathering and analyzing the detailed requirements of the methodology to develop. After this step, a detailed design of the methodology was performed.

We started by discussing and describing the various roles of the professionals involved in the development, and we identified four major phases of the process, following also the ideas and suggestions that emerged from the discussions with the experts.

We identified nine professional roles needed to define, specify, design and implement a system able to solve an industrial QUBO problem using QUBO/QA approach. Four roles are typically found in every software development project:

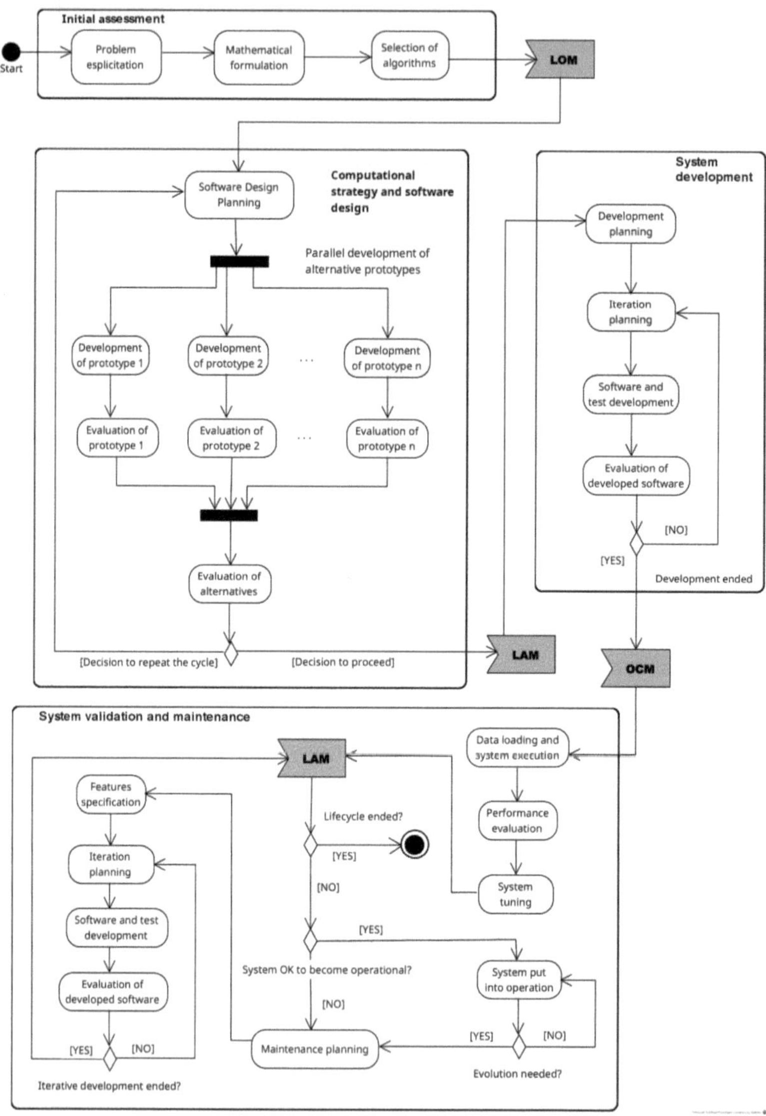

Fig. 2. The AQUA process, highlighting its four phases.

project manager, domain expert, programmer analyst and quality assurance expert. The "operations researcher" role is a mathematician expert in QUBO optimization models. The other four roles explicitly regard competences needed for large problems and their solution (software algorithm expert, HPC developer, data science expert), and of course quantum annealing (QA specialist).

These roles should be complemented with the typical roles of Scrum development. However, the project manager might act as a Scrum Master, if a specific professional is not available; the domain expert, who knows the problems from the client's perspective, can be the Product Owner; and of course all developers will be part of the Team.

Regarding the four phases, we detailed them by describing their goals, activities, deliverables and milestones, as reported in the followings.

The proposed process is summarized as a UML activity diagram in Fig. 2. It consists of four phases performed sequentially, which are detailed inside the frames in the figure. This figure also shows the major milestones of AQUA, using the "Accept Event Action" UML notation. The second phase allows for the possibility of developing demonstration prototypes in parallel, while the last two are incremental-iterative and follow an agile process, as it will be described in detail in the following sections.

At the end of each phase, except the last, it is checked whether the relevant milestone has been met, and it is possible to proceed to the next phase. Otherwise, the project can be aborted or the previous phase can be repeated. The final phase represents the system's commissioning and maintenance. Only if it is decided that its life cycle is complete the system will be decommissioned; otherwise, operations and maintenance activities continue to be performed following the same iterative-incremental approach.

Regarding the outputs of AQUA process, those of the first and second phases are documents describing the mathematical model, the specific algorithms to use (including hybrid approaches), a comparative analysis of the prototypes and the detailed specification of the chosen approach. We have no specific artifacts/documents in the design and development phase, but we adopted Scrum's ones.

Initial Assessment. This is the first phase of AQUA; in this phase, the optimization problem to be solved is verified to be expressible in QUBO form, and possible solutions are identified. This phase assumes that the large size of the problem and the difficulty of solving it with standard methods have already been established. It proceeds in sequential steps.

The first step is "Problem explicitation", involving the explanation of the problem and of its constraints, and the collection of historical data for better understanding the problem, and for testing the quality of the solution. This is followed by the "Mathematical formulation" step, when a rigorous formulation of the optimization problem and its constraints is made in mathematical form. In this step, also the transformation of categorical and numerical variables to binary ones must be described, if categorical and numerical variables are present.

The third step is the "Selection of algorithms" when the size, structure, and suitability of the problem for classical or quantum solvers are analyzed, and a selection of appropriate classical, quantum, and hybrid algorithms is made. It includes the evaluation of multiple alternatives, with analysis of related costs.

The phase is concluded with the "Lifecycle Objective Milestone" (LOM), named after the milestone concluding the "Inception Phase" of Rational Unified Process [1]. This is a major milestone, where a decision is made whether to continue the project, repeat the assessment by modifying the project objectives or evaluating other approaches, or abandon the project, providing reasons.

Computational Strategy and Software Design. This phase plans in detail the computational steps required to solve the problem, implementing and evaluating alternatives. After the initial design planning, the various possible alternatives for solving the QUBO problem are implemented at the prototype level and evaluated. The prototypes are developed in parallel.

Eventually, the alternatives are compared and the most promising one, or a mix of the approaches deemed best, is chosen. The phase ends with the "Algorithm Selection Milestone" (ASM), verifying if the following criteria are met:

- at least one prototype has been developed that demonstrates the ability to solve the problem in a reduced form;
- a review of the project objectives and risks has been performed;
- a rough plan for the overall project has been completed.

If the project does not pass this milestone, it may still be abandoned, or it will need to be revised, repeating this phase. The control flow of this phase is visualized in the center-left of Fig. 2.

System Development. In this phase, the final system is specified in detail and developed, following the Scrum agile method [20]. The first step is the planning of the development, performed by specifying the increments of the system to be implemented, called "Features", as prescribed by Scrum. The activity produces cards showing the increments that guide development and the specification of related acceptance tests. Their priority is given by the Product Owner (PO) on behalf of the customer who ordered the system, whereas the estimate of their complexity is made by the developers. If needed, the features can be supplemented with a more detailed mathematical description.

The first step of the iteration (Sprint) is the "Iteration planning". It produces the "Sprint backlog", that is the list of features that should be implemented in the iteration, and their breakdown into tasks. The features to be implemented in the iteration are chosen by the PO, the tasks are subscribed by the developers.

During the iteration, the team performs "Software and test development" step, according to a classical Scrum iteration. The PO is available to explain the features in detail, if necessary, with the help of the QA and QUBO experts. This step can be quite complex and can be broken down into various activities, covering all the technologies required for system development. The output of this step is of course the software for solving the QUBO problem, including data management, user interface, unit and acceptance tests.

At the end of the iteration, the "Evaluation of developed software" is a classical Scrum Sprint review, where the features developed in the iteration are evaluated to be accepted, or to be reworked in the subsequent iteration. When all the features are implemented, the "Operational Capability Milestone" (OCM) verifies if the developed system can be released for use in a real environment.

It is decided whether to proceed to Phase 4 or continue with further iterations of Phase 3. It may also be found that the system is not able to meet essential requirements and the project is canceled.

System Validation and Maintenance. In the last phase of AQUA, the developed system is deployed and put into operation on real data. Deployment is carried out through sequential steps for final system tuning. The first step is performed by loading real data and executing the system, to assess how the system behaves under a real load. In the second step, the accuracy and performance of the system are discussed, and possible ways to improve its functioning are proposed. The third step includes activities for performing minor changes and the tuning of the system, taking into account the performance evaluation.

Just before actual deployment, the "Lifecycle Assessment Milestone" (LAM) is evaluated. This milestone verifies whether the system can be actually useful as it is and can be put into operation, whether it needs corrections and/or upgrades, or whether it should be decommissioned. LAM milestone is verified not only at the end of the first deployment of the system, but also at the end of any further maintenance cycle.

Corrective and evolutionary maintenance is planned on the system, if necessary, to make it more accurate and effective. Next comes the maintenance phase itself, in which any major corrections and subsequent improvements requested by the customer are implemented in an agile manner, using the classic Scrum-like process. The control flow of the phase is visualized at the bottom of Fig. 2.

5   Experimental Validation

Experimental validation is a key step in DSR. Our proposal is not a specific information system or framework, to be validated building a prototype for one or more practical case studies, but a development methodology for QA. Finding a real case study, performing a complete development of a QA QUBO solver for such a case would be difficult and very time-consuming. For this reason, we opted for applying AQUA to a simple, yet relevant, synthetic, non-industrial case conducted in a controlled setting. It is a lab-based proof-of-concept validation carried out by experts and professionals, rather than an industrial case study. In the following, we describe the steps of the prototypical development performed, highlighting all the simplifications made.

5.1   The Proof-of-Concept

As a proof-of-concept, we chose the feature selection problem for credit risk assessment. Feature selection is an important problem in machine learning and classification systems, still with active research performed on it. Basically, it consists of analyzing a set of samples, each characterized by a number of features and belonging to a given class, to decide what features are irrelevant to classification, and can be discarded. In this way, it is possible to simplify the classifier, reducing its number of inputs, without compromising its effectiveness. This problem can be easily traced back to a QUBO problem where the variables correspond to the features, which are chosen if the corresponding variable is one, and ignored if it is zero. There are studies that support the effectiveness of QA compared to traditional methods, at least in some cases [4].

The proof-of-concept hypothesizes a scenario in which a bank requires a system able to classify credit requests into two categories: normal and risky. The system must learn from a dataset of past requests provided by the bank, in which each applicant is characterized by a set of personal, financial, and other data; the outcome of whether the loan was granted or not is also recorded. To enhance model performance, it's important to select only the most relevant features from the applicant dataset, removing redundant or unnecessary ones.

Applying AQUA to the Proof-of-Concept. The development served as a demonstration of the AQUA process and was carried out with acknowledged limitations. The authors assumed the various roles prescribed by the process and implemented the prototype accordingly. The deliverables and software produced by the various phases during the development (analysis of datasets, mathematical model, documentation of algorithms and related discussion, source code and results of the developed prototypes, system requirements, design and code, tests, report on the system execution on the large dataset) were collected and organized. These validation data were then discussed with the same experts who participated in the activity described in Sect. 4.1. In the following subsections, for the sake of brevity, we report only the essential information on how AQUA was applied to the use case.

Phases 1 and 2: Assessment and Design. We started with a literature search about the relevance of the credit classification problem, and about the datasets publicly available. We found some datasets usable for our problem. Among them, we used the German Credit Data (GCD), and the "Give Me Some Credit" Competition Data (GMS). GCD is a "classical' dataset, made available since 1997, and used in many studies about credit scoring. It consists of 1000 samples with 20 features regarding the decision to approve a loan, with 30% of samples whose application was rejected. GMS is a large dataset created for the classification competition "Give Me Some Credit" held in 2010. We used its 150,000 samples prepared for training, all endowed with 10 features and a target value.

We decided to use GCD as input data for the prototypes of Phase 2, a subset of 40,000 samples taken from GMS for assessing the system developed in Phase 3, and GMS as final, large dataset for the deployment in Phase 4.

We then proceeded to study and mathematically formulate the construction of the QUBO matrix, following the approach described in [4] as "QUBO-Correlation", with the computation of the Spearman correlation matrix among the dataset columns, and the correlation coefficients of each column with the target outputs.

We studied also the efficient computation of the correlation matrix for huge number of samples (up to billions of items) on highly parallel computers, to be able to run very large problems in reasonable times. Eventually, we studied various optimization algorithms able to solve our QUBO problem. Since the focus of AQUA is on quantum approaches, we decided to implement the algorithms QA, Hybrid QA and Quantum Approximate Optimization Algorithm (QAOA). At the end of Phase 1, we made the decision to continue the project and move on to Phase 2, considering the LOM milestone reached.

In phase 2 we developed the three prototypes. Since all prototypes share a common data preprocessing process, converting the data into numbers and calculating the QUBO matrix, we first wrote Python functions to read the dataset, convert all fields into numbers, normalize the columns, except the target, to a mean of zero and a standard deviation of one, and calculate the QUBO matrix.

Then, we started the development of the three prototypes in parallel, as shown in the center of Fig. 2. The first two prototypes were written to be run using D-Wave libraries and with access to D-Wave Advantage annealer. The QAOA prototype was written using Qiskit library, and run on a QC simulator.

The first two prototypes were coded quite smoothly, and were able to process the GCD dataset in a few seconds, yielding the same "optimal" results. QAOA, on the contrary, was not able to perform significant optimizations on the 20 binary variables of the QUBO problem, due to the constraints of the QC simulator.

During the discussion of the LOM milestone at the end of the phase, we dropped the QAOA approach. In the end, we choose "Hybrid QA" due to the ease of development and of interfacing with external system.

Phases 3 and 4: System Development and Release. This phase started with a planning session and with the specification of 16 key features, each provided also of a priority (High, Medium, Low), a forecast effort in "Feature Points" on a scale between 1 and 4, and a dependence graph. Each feature was also complemented with one or more acceptance test, made using the CMP dataset.

The software development of the proof-of-concept was done using four one-week iterations, implementing a subset of the features in each iteration. We followed a standard Scrum process, with Sprint planning meetings, development of features and tests, Sprint review meetings.

The QUBO problem, with the computation of the cross-correlation matrix, was built using a parallel computer. At the end of the development (last iteration) we developed a system that met all the objectives set.

The OCM milestone was verified by running the system on the GMS reduced dataset. 70% samples were used for computing the [Q] matrix, leaving the remaining 30% for testing the effectiveness of feature selection using a standard classifier (Logistic Regression). The dataset was ingested and pre-processed easily. The QUBO problem was then sent to the Quantum Annealer, finding an optimal solution using training data. The "best" solution included 4 out of 10 features, that were used to classify the test set, comparing the results with a classification using the whole set of features. The results were good, showing the same precision and a higher recall for the samples with target zero, and a higher precision but lower recall for the samples with target one. Overall, the accuracy of the classification increases from 0.75 to 0.83 using the reduced feature set.

According to the last phase of AQUA, the developed system was then put into operation on our largest dataset GMS of 150,000 samples. We used 120,000 samples for training and the remaining 30,000 for testing. In our demonstration system, there was not a specific "operation" system. The system was simply run and tested mimicking a release under operational conditions. As this was a test performance of AQUA process, to evaluate it and obtain feedback from the experts, we concluded the test and declared the LAM milestone reached.

Table 1. Evaluation according to DSR guidelines.

Guideline	Description
Design as an Artefact	The proposed process, AQUA, is well defined using phases, activities, roles, deliverables and milestones. A QA development team has all the needed documentation to take advantage of AQUA.
Problem Relevance	There is no specific development process for QA applications, but generic guidelines proposed by a vendor, in a scenario where the use of QUBO modeling and QA solutions to it is steadily increasing.
Design Evaluation	Our research involved an analysis of current approaches to tackle the identified problems. Additionally, we applied and validated AQUA on a proof-of-concept, evaluating its suitability and effectiveness.
Research Contributions	This research makes significant contributions through the creation of an innovative software development methodology that integrates Scrum with more sequential or parallel phases to assess the viability and to mathematically define the problem.
Research Rigor	The use of established tools like the Scrum methodology, user stories, and UML notation for describing AQUA's flow, ensures methodological rigor and aligns with best practices in the field of software engineering.
Design as a Search Process	This research began with an in-depth examination of industry practices and existing tools to identify critical gaps QA applications. Following this, a detailed analysis of business process requirements was carried out, guided by established industry standards and best practices.
Communication of Research	This study is designed to engage both technical and managerial audiences. While AQUA is described in technical terms, its primary goal is to solve challenges encountered by managers overseeing complex, cross-disciplinary systems involving QUBO problems and QA.

System Evaluation. The test application of AQUA to the proof-of-concept was evaluated against the requirements outlined in Sect. 4. This is step five of DSR.

A comprehensive assessment was conducted by the author of this research, together with four of the experts referred to in Sect. 4.1, to determine how effectively the AQUA process model addresses research challenges and drives the development of QA applications. The result reflects the suitability of AQUA to support the management and development of a QA optimization project. Here we do not have the room to report in detail the experts' assessment. However, the experts agreed that the six goals set in Sect. 4.1 were substantially achieved.

Regarding improvements, one expert suggested to explicitly provide the iterations with a retrospective activity, to improve not only system development practices, but also mathematical and optimization models. Another one suggested to define in deeper detail the testing strategies at the various stages of AQUA.

In summary, AQUA process has the potential to conceptualize and enhance the development practices in QA application development. It also looks very flexible and can manage different kinds of project types. This can improve project management performance and strengthen trust among multiple participants, if the development is very large. However, greater focus is needed on testing and verification of the developed solutions. Moreover, a solid methodology supporting the introduction of AQUA into an organization should be provided.

For evaluating the methodology used in this study, Hevner et al. [7] outlined seven guidelines for Design Science Research. Table 1 presents an assessment of this study's process in relation to these DSR guidelines, ensuring both rigor and relevance.

6 Lesson Learned and Conclusion

The research project that led to the creation of AQUA lifecycle was performed by professionals of NetService, with the cooperation of researchers of the University of Cagliari. The researchers proposed the use of DSR, which substantially helped to structure the research, providing a sound identification of its motivations and goals, and a roadmap for its definition, demonstration, and evaluation. DSR was unknown to NetService, but now it is another tool in our skill set.

At another level, the collaboration between our company, focused on software production, and university, which contributed QA expertise and research focus, was essential. However, at the beginning of the project we experienced cultural and communication challenges that we had to overcome.

Regarding the proof-of-concept on feature selection, it was relatively simple but allowed us to validate the entire process end-to-end, and to identify critical points (especially in QUBO formulation and QA hardware interfacing). It allowed to build confidence before tackling more complex, business-critical problems.

The creation of AQUA has some implications for the research community. We introduced a new research subfield, namely SE for QA, as a distinct area of study, similar to how SE for distributed systems or AI developed their own methodologies. This opens a line of research on process models, best practices, metrics, and empirical validation of QUBO/QA development methods. Moreover, AQUA provides a framework where theoretical advances in QA can be systematically tested and integrated, because it embeds mathematical formulation and optimization-specific decision points into the process. This fosters collaboration between researchers in algorithms, operations research, and SE.

For industry, AQUA lowers the entry barrier to QA by offering a structured, repeatable process that organizations can adopt without needing to invent their own development practices. Moreover, this clear lifecycle methodology helps organizations reduce the risks of investing in pilots that may otherwise fail due to lack of process rigor. By using agile practices familiar to software teams for QA development, AQUA facilitates training and risk management. Over time, methodologies such as AQUA can inform emerging standards and certifications, which are crucial for industrial adoption.

In conclusion, this research produced a structured, agile process suited to the emerging field of QA application development. Thanks to the use of DSR, AQUA was created in a systematic way, taking advantage of both academic research and industrial knowledge. It demonstrated itself to be an effective method for the selected proof-of-concept.

Though a validation on real world case studies is still lacking, due to the novelty of AQUA, we believe that it could be applied to guide the development of a notable number of systems aimed to solve QUBO problems. The positive results from the proof-of-concept suggest that using AQUA has the potential to shorten development time, improve solution quality, and enhance knowledge transfer among team members.

In the near future, we will extend the validation to the solution of real larger and more complex QUBO problems found in NetService's order portfolio. In this way, AQUA will be further validated, contributing also to improve productivity.

A further extension of AQUA we are presently working on involves endowing the process with tools for automated benchmarking and testing, including the definition of efficiency, productivity, and total cost metrics.

Acknowledgments. We acknowledge financial support under NRPP Call for tender by "National Centre for HPC, Big Data and Quantum Computing", Mission 4, Component 2, Spoke 1, No. 8145/2025 published on 22 December 2023, funded by the E.U.-NextGenerationEU, project title QUBO-HPC, CUP: 33C22001170001; and under CINECA ISCRA grant "Partitioning optimization problems for hybrid classical/quantum execution", IsCc2_QAHLOP.

References

1. Booch, G., Rumbaugh, J., Jacobson, I.: Unified Modeling Language User Guide, 2nd edn. Addison-Wesley Professional (2005)
2. D-Wave Inc.: Developing quantum applications. https://docs.dwavequantum.com/. Accessed 14 Aug 2025
3. Dybå, T., Dingsøyr, T.: Empirical studies of agile software development: a systematic review. Inf. Softw. Technol. **50**(9–10), 833–859 (2008)

4. Ferrari Dacrema, M., Moroni, F., Nembrini, R., Ferro, N., Faggioli, G., Cremonesi, P.: Towards feature selection for ranking and classification exploiting quantum annealers. In: Proceedings of the 45th International ACM SIGIR Conference on Research and Development in Information Retrieval, pp. 2814–2824 (2022)
5. Glover, F., Kochenberger, G., Hennig, R., Du, Y.: Quantum bridge analytics I: a tutorial on formulating and using QUBO models. Ann. Oper. Res. **314**(1), 141–183 (2022)
6. Glover, F., Kochenberger, G., Ma, M., Du, Y.: Quantum bridge analytics II: Quboplus, network optimization and combinatorial chaining for asset exchange. Ann. Oper. Res. **314**(1), 185–212 (2022)
7. Hevner, A.R., March, S.T., Park, J., Ram, S.: Design science in information systems research. MIS Quart. 75–105 (2004)
8. How, M.L., Cheah, S.M.: Business renaissance: opportunities and challenges at the dawn of the quantum computing era. Businesses **3**(4), 585–605 (2023)
9. Johnson, M.W., et al.: Quantum annealing with manufactured spins. Nature **473**(7346), 194–198 (2011)
10. Kadowaki, T., Nishimori, H.: Quantum annealing in the transverse ISING model. Phys. Rev. E **58**, 5355–5363 (1998)
11. Khan, A.A., et al.: Agile meets quantum: a novel genetic algorithm model for predicting the success of quantum software development project. Autom. Softw. Eng. **31**(1), 34 (2024)
12. Marchesi, L., Marchesi, M., Tonelli, R.: ABCDE–agile block chain DAPP engineering. Blockchain: Res. Appl. **1**(1) (2020)
13. Marchesi, L., Marchesi, M., Tonelli, R.: A survey on cryptoagility and agile practices in the light of quantum resistance. Inf. Softw. Technol. **178**, 107604 (2025)
14. Murillo, J.M., et al.: Quantum software engineering: roadmap and challenges ahead. ACM Trans. Softw. Eng. Methodol. **34**(5) (2025)
15. NOREA: Quantum annealing explained. Technical report, NOREA (2025). https://www.norea.nl/uploads/bfile/b2f8c1cd-f550-427e-90ac-535ee9e79af8. Accessed 14 Aug 2025
16. Peffers, K., Tuunanen, T., Rothenberger, M.A., Chatterjee, S.: A design science research methodology for information systems research. J. Manag. Inf. Syst. **24**(3), 45–77 (2007)
17. Piattini, M., Serrano, M., Perez-Castillo, R., Petersen, G., Hevia, J.L.: Toward a quantum software engineering. IT Professional **23**(1), 62–66 (2021)
18. Preskill, J.: Quantum computing in the NISQ era and beyond. Quantum **2**, 79 (2018)
19. Scheerer, M., Klamroth, J., Garhofer, S., Knäble, F., Denninger, O.: Experiences in quantum software engineering. In: 2023 IEEE International Parallel and Distributed Processing Symposium Workshops (IPDPSW), pp. 552–559. IEEE (2023)
20. Schwaber, K., Beedle, M.: Agile Software Development with Scrum. Pearson (2001)
21. Siddi Moreau, G., Pisani, L., Profir, M., Podda, C., Leoni, L., Cao, G.: Quantum artificial intelligence scalability in the NISQ era: pathways to quantum utility. Adv. Quantum Technol. 2400716 (2025)
22. Yarkoni, S., Raponi, E., Bäck, T., Schmitt, S.: Quantum annealing for industry applications: introduction and review. Rep. Prog. Phys. **85**(10), 104001 (2022)
23. Yulianti, L.P., Surendro, K.: Implementation of quantum annealing: a systematic review. Ieee Access **10**, 73156–73177 (2022)

Hindrances and Strengths in Software Delivery: Insights from a Developer Experience Study at the Swedish Transport Administration

Hannes Salin[1,2]($\boxtimes$) , Eriks Klotins[3] , and Ehsan Zabardast[3,4]

[1] Swedish Transport Administration (Trafikverket), Borlänge, Sweden
`hannes.salin@trafikverket.se`
[2] School of Information and Engineering, Dalarna University, Borlänge, Sweden
[3] Software Engineering Research Lab SERL, Blekinge Institute of Technology, Karlskrona, Sweden
`{eriks.klotins,ehsan.zabardast}@bth.se`
[4] Gaetir, Karlskrona, Sweden

Abstract. Developer Experience (DevEx) refers to the overall experience of software developers when interacting with tools, processes, and organizational environments. This paper reports on a DevEx survey conducted within the ICT division of the Swedish Transport Administration (STA), one of the largest software development organizations in the Swedish public sector. The survey, completed by 98 out of 122 invited software engineers, included both quantitative and qualitative data.

The initial results show strong (positive) scores in cultural factors, skills and competence, perceived responsibility and accountability, indicating a collaborative and supportive work environment. In contrast, the most frequently reported hindrances were meetings, context switching and inefficient work practices. Along with the analysis our study presents practitioner-oriented recommendations and lessons learned when conducting similar DevEx initiatives.

Keywords: Software Development · DevEx · Developer Experience · Public Sector

1 Introduction

To meet the growing demand for efficient, accessible, and accountable public services, government institutions are turning to digital transformation [13]. At its core, digital transformation uses technology to radically improve organizational performance and the way institutions interact with end-users and the environment [18]. Its success depends on how effectively software engineering aligns with organizational strategy to deliver solutions that support strategic goals.

Despite this ambition, public sector organizations operate under strict regulations to ensure predictable and transparent use of public funds [20,28]. In software engineering, these rules often translate into predominantly plan-driven

G. Scanniello et al. (Eds.): PROFES 2025, LNCS 16362, pp. 120–135, 2026.
https://doi.org/10.1007/978-3-032-12092-2_8

development models, with success measured by delivery schedules and budget adherence [3,16]. Such conditions can hinder the adoption of agile and lean practices, limit value delivery from software, and slow progress toward digital transformation. Borg et al. shows that the majority of software development in the Swedish public sector is *not* in-house, only 39% according to statistics from 2020 [7]. Furthermore, they show that public sector development faces similar challenges as in the private sector, e.g. legacy code, short-termed technical solutions; 47% of the agencies having in-house software development do indeed confirm the presence of a high degree of technical debt.

In recent years, initiatives such as the European Commission's Open Source Software Strategy have sought to modernize public sector software development by promoting code sharing and collaborative development across the EU [12]. These initiatives aim to improve public services while reducing costs. National strategies echo these goals. For instance, STA identifies digital services and data-driven decision support as core pillars in its roadmap to digitize the road transport system [5], a direction also observed elsewhere [13]. However, to make these modernization initiatives effective in practice, public sector organizations must adopt ways of working and technology that support continuous learning and incremental improvement.

A central practice in digital transformation is continuous improvement – making incremental changes guided by rapid feedback loops [6,17]. This approach combines objective metrics, such as DORA indicators [31], with engineers' insights into tools, processes, and workflows [10]. Together, these methods can identify trends and inform targeted improvements. This paper reports lessons learned from an initial survey of software engineers at the STA, designed to map potential improvement areas. The survey aims to establish continuous monitoring of the developer experience (DevEx) and to create a baseline for improving software development and delivery practices. While the questionnaire covered a wide range of topics, this study focuses on identifying the primary hindrances to engineering work. We analyze 98 responses from a sample of 122 engineers, representing a population of approximately 300 software engineers within the STA.

From the analysis, we identify the most significant hindrances perceived by the software developers as meetings, context switching and inefficient work practices. In addition, our results show that observability and telemetry are lacking, while the general satisfaction of tools and technology was high. The identified strengths were clusters of factors related to culture, skills, and competence, and responsibility and accountability, suggesting that the teams have a good foundation at the employee and team levels, but suffer from process-based factors in delivering software.

The remainder of this paper is structured as follows. Section 2 reviews the background on Developer Experience (DevEx) and its relevance to software delivery, particularly in the public sector. Section 3 describes the research methodology, including the case organization, data collection, and analysis approach. Section 4 presents the results of the survey, while Sect. 5 discusses the main hindrances and strengths identified, along with recommendations and lessons learned. Section 6 outlines threats to validity, and Sect. 7 concludes the paper with a summary of findings and directions for future work.

2   Background

Understanding Developer Experience (DevEx) is essential to improve software delivery performance, especially in complex and regulated environments such as the public sector. DevEx encompasses the full spectrum of a developer's interaction with tools, processes, and organizational structures, directly influencing productivity, quality, and job satisfaction. By framing delivery challenges through the lens of DevEx, organizations can identify and address hindrances such as slow feedback loops, high cognitive load, and disrupted flow. This section reviews key concepts, metrics, and prior research, establishing the foundation for our study within the STA's ICT division.

2.1   Developer Experience

DevEx refers to the holistic experience of software developers when interacting with tools, processes, and environments throughout the software development lifecycle. Hence, improving DevEx implies finding a good balance and mixture of tools, practices, processes, and social structures [14]. It is therefore more than DevOps tooling or organizational structures, and includes aspects such as cognitive load, tool affordances, workflow smoothness, collaboration, and communication support, and the ability to stay focused and engaged. DevEx is claimed to fundamentally influence large parts of the software development activities and overall productivity [11]. Moreover, recent research further strengthen the importance of DevEx and its relevance for improving software developer productivity in particular [27]. Not surprisingly, the effects of improving DevEx for productivity gains can be explained due to allowing the developers to get into the flow with minimal interruptions with improved focus, boosting creativity and having the necessary means for high-quality feedback in order to progress as efficiently as possible [14].

Concluding the importance of an organization's DevEx, it is not surprising that it can significantly impact the competitive advantage [21]. With highly motivated software developers being able to work efficiently and with minimal distractions, the overall organizational productivity is optimized. Therefore, we see an increase in the investment of dedicated DevEx teams [24] and technical DevEx platforms [4] in the industry.

2.2   Metrics

To assess the current state of a software development organization's DevEx, there is no single metric available. Instead, due to the complexity and nuances of how the developer environment is perceived, the key measurement is to focus on the developers and their lived experiences when delivering software [24], thus not necessarily hard, objective, and quantitative metrics. The natural way to approach these more qualitative measures is by carefully crafted surveys [14,22,24]. However, as pointed out by Noda et al., survey fatigue in the organization must be avoided [24]. The actual questions to include can differ depending on the organization, but common domains included in the surveys are related to feedback loops and cognitive load [24], and different code related measures such as git meta data (commit frequency, contribution statistics), and code ownership [8,32].

2.3   Challenges and DevEx Considerations

Industry and academic work increasingly frames software-delivery challenges through the lens of DevEx-the lived frictions developers face while shipping software. A practitioner framework distills DevEx into three cross-cutting dimensions–feedback loops, cognitive load, and flow state–which together explain many bottlenecks teams encounter in delivery [24]. Slow tool and human hand-offs (e.g., build and test latency, code-review wait time) lengthen feedback loops; sprawling code and documentation gaps inflate cognitive load; meetings and unplanned work erode flow–each directly impeding throughput and quality. The same work argues DevEx should be measured with perceptual (developer-reported) and workflow metrics, tied to "north-star" outcomes like perceived ease of delivery and productivity [24].

A recent systematic review consolidates 218 papers and identifies 33 DevEx factors and 41 practices that affect productivity, grouping them into ten themes (Dev-XP). Positively associated factors include availability of required resources, taskexpertise fit, and fewer interruptions; negatively associated ones include code complexity, heterogeneous task contexts (context switching), and non-adherence to standardization. The review highlights mitigation practices such as fragmenting large tasks, supporting mental models, timely technology evolution, and promoting developer ownership of artifacts–practices that map directly to reducing cognitive load, shortening feedback loops, and protecting focus [27]. At organizational scale, evidence from Google shows that what developers perceive about their environment causally affects self-rated productivity. Using panel analyses over repeated survey waves, code quality and technical debt emerge with particularly strong causal links to productivity, alongside infrastructure tools, support, team communication, clear goals and priorities, and organizational processes and their change. Notably, increases in perceived code quality tend to precede increases in perceived productivity, strengthening the case that managing internal quality is a first-order lever for delivery performance rather than a mere correlate [10].

Work on flow in software development adds granularity about day-to-day hindrances. A qualitative study of 405 developers reports the most prominent "flow barriers" as interruptions, overly easy, tedious, repetitive tasks, lack of opportunities to take on challenging work, insufficient and volatile requirements, tight timetables and deadlines, and problems with technology or software. These barriers align with the DevEx triad: interruptions and deadline pressure disrupt flow; poor requirements elongate feedback cycles and rework; tool and technology problems inflate cognitive load [29]. Introducing new delivery-enabling systems can itself be a source of friction when adoption overlooks DevEx. A case report on design-system rollout documents cultural resistance ("we don't need this to code UIs") and technical unfamiliarity as early blockers. Treating developers as primary users–conducting interviews to surface pain points, iterating artifacts (tokens, component library) and handoff processes, and fostering ownership–reduced friction and improved collaboration between UX and engineering, illustrating that change-management grounded in DevEx accelerates uptake and downstream delivery consistency [26].

Finally, work from a large public-sector technology organization with remote work context shows strong overall work engagement yet clear headroom on social, organizational factors, team communication quality, career-development discussions, and consistent feedback. Because these soft factors are repeatedly linked to satisfaction and perceived productivity, they represent practical levers for agencies operating under public-sector constraints to ease delivery hindrances without large tooling investments [9].

3 Research Methodology

The aim of this study is to gain preliminary understanding of what are the strengths and hindrances of software delivery at STA. We further guide our study with the following research questions:

- **RQ1:** What are the main hindrances to software delivery at STA?
- **RQ2:** What are the main strengths of software delivery at STA?

To collect the data, we survey the software engineers in STA. The survey is inspired by similar efforts at, e.g., Google [10] and Microsoft [14]. However, we design our own questionnaire based on the specific organizational context and interests of the management.

3.1 Case Organization

Our study was conducted at STA, a government agency responsible for Swedish road, railroad, maritime, and partly telecom infrastructures [1]. STA has almost 11.000 employees and contractors, while we focus our study on the ICT organization that consists of 250–300 software developers.

Typically, the engineering teams work in projects or in the PM3 governance model—developed in 2006—that has been adopted and further adjusted by several Swedish governmental agencies over the last decade [25]. The majority of the deliveries are within an agile context where Scrum or Kanban is adopted, sometimes mixed with more nonagile project management frameworks such as Excellence in Project Management [2]; however, there are no product owner roles implemented.

There is a considerable organizational isolation in STA ICT, that is, the department is divided into 5 units, and further each unit is divided into 2–5 sections. Each section has several teams working on their assigned products. Teams in different sections are rarely collaborating and there is no outspoken developer community.

3.2   Data Collection and Sampling

Our study addressed a subset of all teams in the software engineering departments of the ICT division of STA, $N = 122$ employees from one of the departments received the survey with 3 primary roles: software developers, test engineers, and operation engineers, since these are the roles included in the teams. The remaining 132 employees in that department who did not receive the survey were managers, architects, project managers, IT coordinators, and other administrative and/or strategic roles. The survey was created with an internal survey tool and sent out twice: initially 14th of April 2025, and the second time as a reminder, in mid Q2 2025. The survey was conducted in Swedish. All responses were anonymous.

The data was collected with an online questionnaire[1]. The questionnaire contained a total of 42 questions, of which 33 were 5-point Likert scale and the remaining were free-text questions. For the Likert scale questions, the answer options ranged $[-2..2]$. The answer options were formulated in a way that a higher score indicate more preferable answers. The middle, i.e., the zero, represents a neutral answer.

The wording of answer options was tweaked for each question, for instance "Very negative, .., Neutral, .., Very positive", "Not enough, .., fair, .., Too much", and "Never, .., Sometimes, .., Often".

Before launch, the survey was reviewed by all the authors, and additional feedback was collected from selected STA engineers. Based on this input the questionnaire forgo several review and improvement rounds.

3.3   Data Analysis

To analyze the responses, we perform qualitative analysis on the free text responses, followed by quantitative analysis of the Likert-scale answers.

We conduct qualitative analysis using thematic analysis with coding [19]. Each response was coded into one or several themes. Codes were extracted either explicitly, such as code MEETINGS from a response containing the word *"meetings"*, or implicitly, where the response describes the event of having a meeting. After the coding, a frequency analysis of each code was done, together with interpretative analysis supported by quotes from the responses.

For the quantitative analysis, we perform descriptive analysis and visualizations. We calculate the range, mode, and median of the answers. Further, we group the questions according to the median and mode of the provided answers

---

[1] Supplemental material: https://doi.org/10.5281/zenodo.16887068.

to identify potential strengths and hindrances. Given the relatively small organization, the number of responses, and concerns for participants privacy we leave stratified analysis outside this paper.

4   Results

This section presents the findings from the DevEx survey conducted within the ICT division of the STA. The results combine quantitative ratings across key areas–such as productivity, culture, skills, and autonomy–with qualitative insights from open-ended questions. Together, these data points provide a comprehensive view of the organization's strengths and the main hindrances affecting software delivery.

The survey was distributed to 122 of about 300 software engineers in the ICT division of STA. We received a total of 98 responses giving us 80% response rate. The survey questionnaire contained a mix of Likert-scale and free-text questions. We report them separately in the upcoming sections.

4.1   Quantitative Results

We structure the results by areas covered in the survey–productivity, team culture, skills and competence, developer experience, responsibility and accountability, and autonomy. Each area is covered by several questions, we present the results per area with violinplots, see Figs. 1, 2, 3, 4, 5 and 6. In the figures, we denote both the distribution, and the median value of the responses. We also denote the number of responses used in the analysis.

Looking at the areas, culture (see Fig. 3), responsibility and accountability (see Fig. 6), and skills and competence (see Fig. 4) are reported as positive and well above the neutral. Most negatively reported areas are developer experience (see Fig. 5) and productivity (see Fig. 1). This is due to low scores on questions about context switching and the use of telemetry.

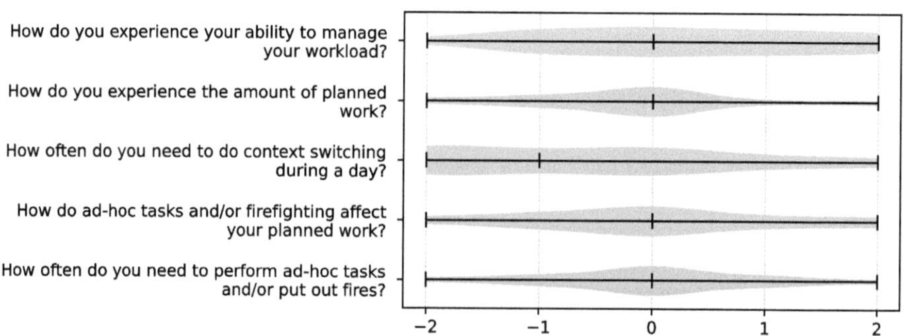

Fig. 1. Results from productivity-oriented questions (N = 63).

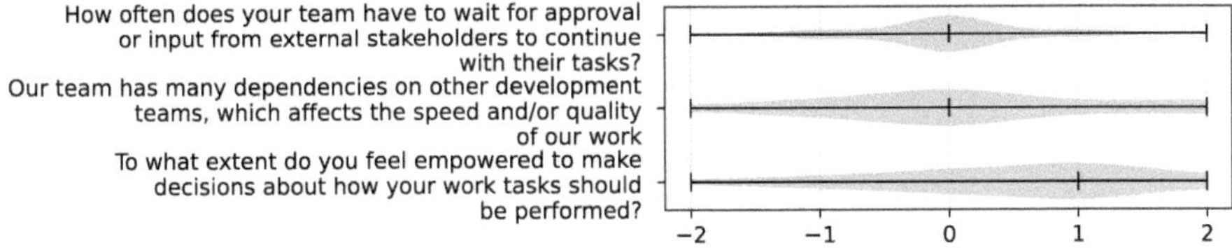

Fig. 2. Results from autonomy-oriented questions (N=38). The answer distributions are centered around the neutral and slightly positive options.

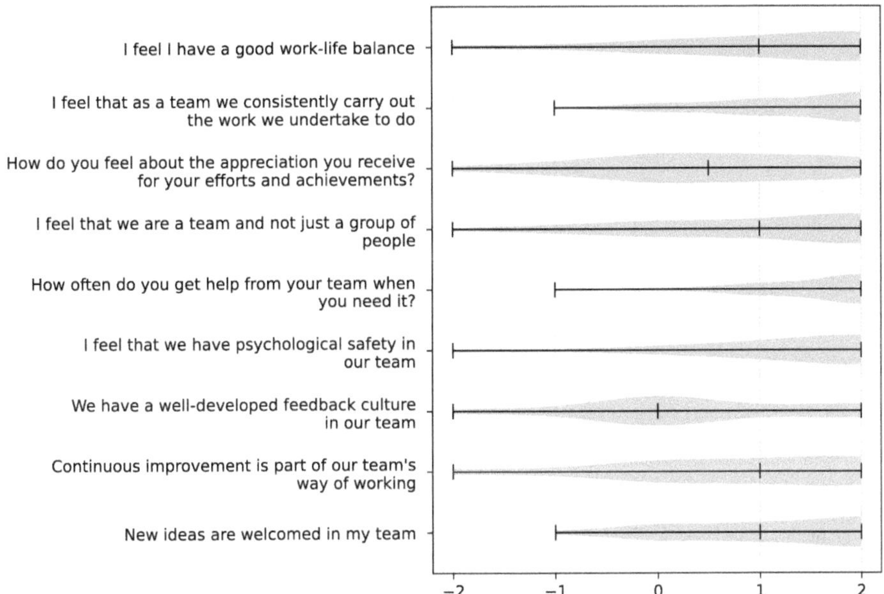

Fig. 3. The responses show a strong positive trend from culture-oriented questions (N = 38).

4.2   Qualitative Results

The survey included a free text question on what factors limit the productivity of the developers the most: *What are the largest impediments to your productivity?* A total of 49 responses were thematically coded (although 11 responses were part of partial responses of the whole survey). The frequency of the codes are summarized in Fig. 7, showing that meetings, context switching, and work practices are the top three factors impacting their potential software delivery capacity, framed as a non-defined term "productivity" in the survey.

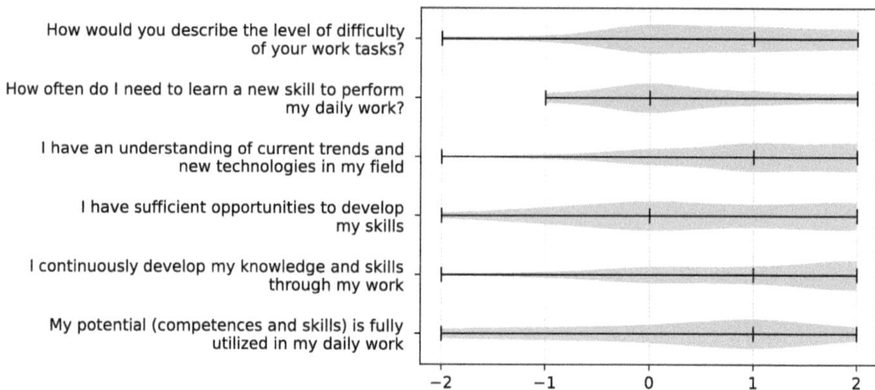

Fig. 4. Results from skills- and competence-oriented questions (N = 55). The responses show a strong positive trend.

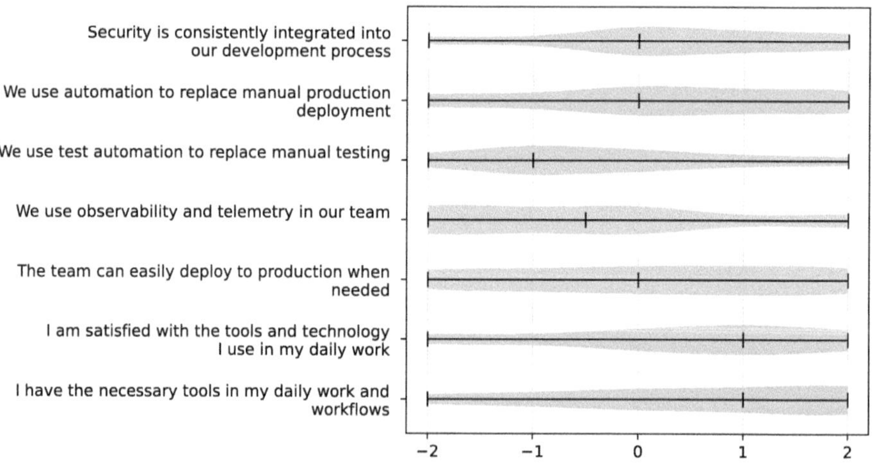

Fig. 5. Results from developer-experience-oriented questions (N = 56). The responses highlight shortcomings in test automation and observability.

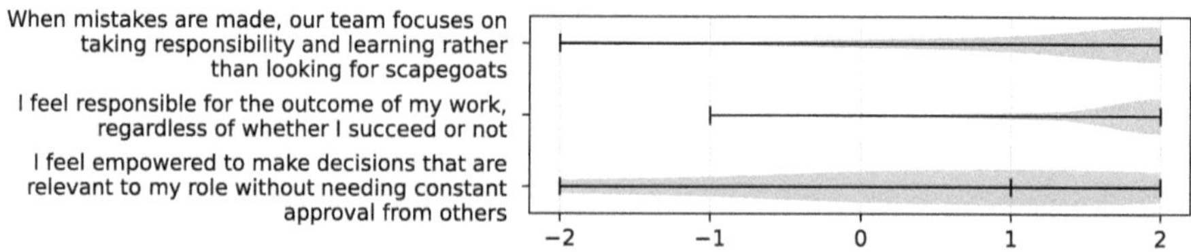

Fig. 6. Results from responsibility- and accountability-oriented questions (N = 54). The responses show a strong positive trend.

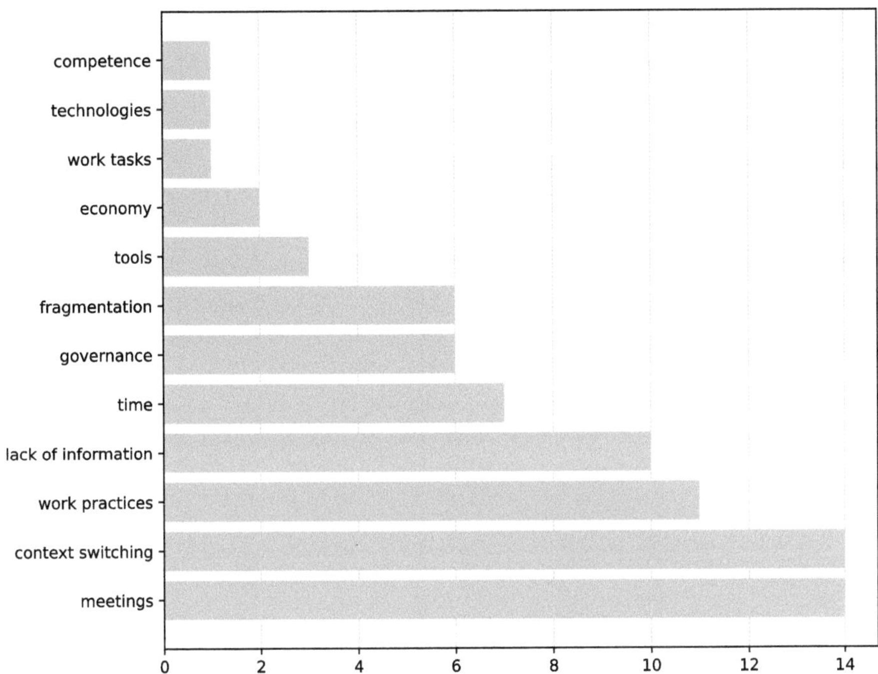

Fig. 7. Frequency of reported factors from survey free text question on what is the perceived largest hindrance for productivity. A total of 76 codes were extracted from 49 respondents, where each code's frequency is shown.

Meetings. A total of 14 of 49 respondents (29%), with 14 out of 76 total registered codes (18%), reported meetings as a hindrance factor. Most responses had explicit statements such as *"too many meetings"*, *"a lot of meetings"*, *"meetings"* and *"planned activities, e.g., meetings"*. Only a few responses included type or reason for the meetings: *"meetings with no agenda"* and *"...meetings with project team where maybe the developers do not need to participate."* 2 respondents expressed that there were no hindrance at all.

Context Switching. In total 4 respondents stated that meetings directly lead to context switching, as a negative perception, whereas 14 respondents in overall mentioned this code (28%). For example, explicit statements such as *"Meetings! Which often leads to context switch deluxe"* but also some ambiguous responses such as *"Meetings and context-switch."* (not clear wether these are separated factors or bounded). Overall 14 "context switching" codes (18%) were extracted, thus same percentage as for meetings. Most likely there are several root causes, although not many (except meetings) were explicitly stated.

Work Practices. As the third most commonly frequent code, work practice-based factors were mentioned; in total 11 codes (14%) from 11 respondents (22%). Statements such as *"unclear best practices," "Lack of established work flows for how one should work with the container platform and releases,"* and *"...all parts of the ICT division is not onboard that is decided that we work in teams."* The most frequent code combination with *work practices* was *governance* (occurrence 5 of 10 responses), highlighting bureaucracy and unclear directives from management.

5   Discussion

This section interprets the survey findings, examining how the identified strengths and hindrances influence software delivery within the STA's ICT division. By linking the results to existing research and practical considerations, we highlight underlying causes, explore their organizational implications, and outline recommendations for addressing key challenges and leveraging existing advantages.

5.1   What are the Main Hindrances to Software Delivery at STA?

The qualitative data clearly show that the three most significant hindrance factors for software development delivery are meetings, context switching, and inefficient work practices. Although the quantitative data indicates that several areas such as tool satisfaction, empowerment, appreciation, work-life balance, and psychological safety are high (4.0 out of 5.0), 12 different hindrance factors were expressed where meetings and context changing the top two. We suspect that these are more bounded together than was expressed in the responses. However, future investigations need to explore these topics in particular to understand the root causes. Moreover, as seen in Fig. 1, context switching is indeed perceived as a barrier.

Context switching in itself may have many different root causes, although this study shows preliminary results that meetings—as expected—is one major driver. Although there are some attempts to automatically measure actual context switching for developers [23, 30], having fully automatic metrics fed into a DevEx aggregated evaluation is still open for investigation. Instead, finding the root cause and managing it seems to be potentially more fruitful than setting up specific metrics for context switching. Moreover, if the root cause is related to other people driving the amount of meetings and other dependencies that are unnecessary for the developer teams, e.g., project managers who use team members due to the lack of technical skills when discussing/explaining matters with stakeholders, the problem is then a managerial matter. Removing, educating, or coaching might be concrete actions in such a case, where a project manager needs to shift towards shielding the developer team rather than exploiting it. The data in this study also highlight that meetings in particular are indeed the most frequent barrier for developers to be productive, thus investigating if the root cause can be bound to other roles in the organization would be of highest importance.

Interestingly, there is also a strong perception that there is no observability and telemetry as shown in Fig. 5. However, this hindrance was not expressed in free text responses, suggesting that while developers are aware of certain technical capability gaps, these are not (yet) perceived as the worst hindrances in their day-to-day work compared to meetings and work practice-related frictions. This hypothesis is also supported by the higher (positive) score of perceived satisfaction with tools and technology shown in Fig. 5.

5.2   What are the Main Strengths of Software Delivery at STA?

The strongest areas of perceived strengths according to the data is primarily culture, skills and competence, and responsibility areas. Given the high scoring in Fig. 3 it suggests that people feel safe, help each other and have a high degree of work ethic. For skills and competence, a continuous skill development is noted for the majority. For the responsibility area, all factors were perceived as strongly positive: feeling responsible for the outcome, feeling empowered to make decisions, and having a good environment in which mistakes are not punished. All these factors combined points towards a healthy environment where collaboration and engagement in the work is present.

Although the data are not sufficient to reveal too strong conclusions, it seems that human-centered factors, including culture, are in place. However, there is no indication in the data on why or how these factors have developed into the current state. It is noteworthy that, from a managerial perspective, nothing in the data indicates leadership issues, but we are careful in drawing too strong conclusions that good leadership is part of the root cause; this has yet to be further investigated.

5.3   Recommendations to Practitioners

To summarize the findings and the observed managerial approach in planning and running the initial steps towards a DevEx initiative, we propose a set of practical recommendations to other practitioners. Without any order of significance:

– To get a good understanding of the drivers behind certain hindrance factors for the teams, include or make separate investigations for project managers, engineering managers, or other roles that are tightly coupled and influence the developer teams; a DevEx survey can give much data, but in a highly bureaucratic organization such as STA, complementary analysis is needed outside the developer perspective. This recommendation is based on the hypothesis that there are other drivers (roles) except software developers that are the root cause of flooding teams with perceived, unnecessary, and wasteful meetings. This is derived from the fact that the root causes of hindrances were not described in detail and could not be linked to external influences given the asked questions.

- Include leadership and/or organizational components in the survey to better understand how (if) those are factors that influence the overall developer experience. For example, questions on team leadership but also upper management—is there a clear vision, goal, or communication?. These data points could be of interest when correlated with the other areas. This recommendation is based on the insight that the deployed survey could be complemented with above mentioned areas to better cross-check other responses to potentially find root causes.
- Formalize a DevEx program or initiative within which the survey can be framed to give a better understanding *why* that the survey is needed. In the department studied at STA this part was only initiated and not fully developed. Based on a post survey discussion with the management team of the department, they hypothesizes that a stronger and more extended communication with the developer community about why the DevEx survey was launched could have contributed an even better response percentage.

5.4   Lessons Learned from Deploying the DevEx Survey

The survey was deployed in a time frame in which the organization as a whole was facing several different surveys in a short period of time (agile maturity, learning behavior, skill mapping). Although the risk of survey exhaustion was high, the number of responses was good enough. However, in the follow-up survey, the communication effort will be improved; it will be launched primarily from the developer community itself rather than pushed from management, just as last time, but with a stronger framing of being part of a DevEx initiative (which was not formalized during the last survey deployment). Having iterations with reminders is needed; almost a third of the responses were registered after the reminder.

Regarding the content of the survey, only 38 respondents identified their primary team and several of those who answered did not understand the question. Given this and the fact that there were clusters of questions that were not answered, it suggests that additional explanations are needed in the next survey, preferably with example answer texts.

Future work includes adjusting the upcoming surveys with the proposed changes, i.e., including leadership-related questions, supporting help text to the questions, and investigating what potential overlaps there are with concurrent survey initiatives in the organization. Moreover, the DevEx survey is planned to run continuously two times annually, and hence longitudinal data collection will be conducted to track the impact of targeted interventions and organizational changes on both strengths and hindrances over time.

6   Threats to Validity

We acknowledge the study's limitation of generalization of the findings due to the nature of being a case study. With the target company's specific environment, culture and organizational structure it is difficult to compare all findings to other companies in general, however, following the principle of generalization by similarity [15] we may find some results transferable for organizations with similar structure add context. In particular, the Swedish public sector could be a domain with many shared characteristics.

The data set is based on many software developers from different teams, where each team may work independently on a product, isolated from other teams and other organizational units. This implies that there should be some local environmental and cultural differences among the teams, although not necessarily significant as per the registered responses. In any case, participant bias might be occurring where respondents answer what they assume management expects. On the other hand, having a broad response span in the data set from the many teams represented in the organization, we argue that such bias should be less significant in the overall analysis.

7   Conclusion

This study provides an initial baseline for the developer experience in the ICT division within STA, identifying both the hindrances and the strengths associated with the organization's software delivery. Although not fully representable for the broader Swedish public sector, STA has one of the largest software development organizations among Swedish government agencies, thus giving some indications on public sector DevEx factors. Although cultural aspects, skills, perceived responsibilities, and accountability were consistently rated high in the DevEx survey, the most reported hindrances were meetings, context change, and inefficient work practices. The proposed recommendations for practitioners include investigating the influence from other roles outside the teams and incorporating leadership-related questions for future DevEx surveys.

References

1. Bransch – Trafikverket. https://bransch.trafikverket.se. Accessed 04 Jul 2025
2. XLPM Online. https://xlpm-online.com. Accessed 04 Jul 2025
3. Al-Aini, R.A.H.: Cost management of it development projects: case study of a Swedish public sector company (2025)
4. Aune, A.A.W.: Towards enhanced developer experience: an empirical study on successful adoption of internal developer platforms. Master's thesis, NTNU (2024)
5. Bårdén, S., Ernfors, M.: Färdplan–digitaliserat vägtransportsystem, version 2024 (2024)
6. Birk, A., Rombach, D.: A practical approach to continuous improvement in software engineering. In: Wieczorek, M., Meyerhoff, D. (eds.) Software Quality, pp. 34–45. Springer, Heidelberg (2001). https://doi.org/10.1007/978-3-642-56529-8_3
7. Borg, M., Wernberg, J., Olsson, T., Franke, U., Andersson, M.: Illuminating a blind spot in digitalization software development in Sweden's private and public sector. In: Proceedings of the IEEE/ACM 42nd International Conference on Software Engineering Workshops, pp. 299–302 (2020)

8. Brasil-Silva, R., Siqueira, F.L.: Metrics to quantify software developer experience: a systematic mapping. In: Proceedings of the 37th ACM/SIGAPP Symposium on Applied Computing, pp. 1562–1569 (2022)

9. Cerqueira, L., et al.: Assessing software practitioners' work engagement and job satisfaction in a large software company-what we have learned. SN Comput. Sci. **6**(3), 273 (2025)

10. Cheng, L., et al.: What improves developer productivity at google? Code quality. In: Proceedings of the 30th ACM Joint European Software Engineering Conference and Symposium on the Foundations of Software Engineering, pp. 1302–1313 (2022)

11. Combemale, B.: Towards a science of developer experience (devex). arXiv preprint arXiv:2506.23715 (2025)

12. European Commission, DG Digital Services: Open source software strategy 2020–2023 (2020). https://commission.europa.eu/about/departments-and-executive-agencies/digital-services/open-source-software-strategy_en. Accessed 04 Jul 2025

13. Ferreira, A., Santos, C.: Digital transformation in public sector: systematic literature review. In: Enhancing Public Sector Accountability and Services Through Digital Innovation, pp. 265–288 (2025)

14. Forsgren, N., Kalliamvakou, E., Noda, A., Greiler, M., Houck, B., Storey, M.A.: Devex in action. Commun. ACM **67**(6), 42–51 (2024)

15. Ghaisas, S., Rose, P., Daneva, M., Sikkel, K., Wieringa, R.J.: Generalizing by similarity: lessons learnt from industrial case studies. In: 2013 1st International Workshop on Conducting Empirical Studies in Industry (CESI), pp. 37–42 (2013). https://doi.org/10.1109/CESI.2013.6618468

16. Heiling, J.: Digital transformation and the accounting for intangible assets in the public sector. J. Public Budgeting Account. Financ. Manag. (2025)

17. Klotins, E., Gorschek, T., Sundelin, K., Falk, E.: Towards cost-benefit evaluation for continuous software engineering activities. Empir. Softw. Eng. **27**(6), 157 (2022)

18. Kraus, S., Jones, P., Kailer, N., Weinmann, A., Chaparro-Banegas, N., Roig-Tierno, N.: Digital transformation: An overview of the current state of the art of research. SAGE Open **11**(3), 21582440211047576 (2021)

19. Krippendorff, K.: Content Analysis: An Introduction to its Methodology. Sage Publications (2018)

20. Lappi, T., Aaltonen, K.: Project governance in public sector agile software projects. Int. J. Manag. Proj. Bus. **10**(2), 263–294 (2017)

21. Leander, K.: Developer experience as a competitive advantage. In: Developer Experience Unleashed, pp. 21–41. Springer. Berkeley (2025). https://doi.org/10.1007/979-8-8688-0242-3_2

22. Leander, K.R.: Measuring Developer Experience, pp. 183–221. Apress, Berkeley (2025). https://doi.org/10.1007/979-8-8688-0242-3_8

23. Meyer, A.N.: Detecting developers' task switches and types. IEEE Trans. Software Eng. **48**(1), 225–240 (2020)

24. Noda, A., Storey, M.A., Forsgren, N., Greiler, M.: Devex: what actually drives productivity: the developer-centric approach to measuring and improving productivity. Queue **21**(2), 35–53 (2023)

25. Nordström, M.: Pm3 evolutionen: En innovationsberättelse från systemförvaltning till IT-governance. Linköping University Electronic Press (2014)

26. Palomino, P., et al.: Enhancing developer experience (DEVEX) for successful design system implementation. Int. J. Hum.–Comput. Interact. **41**(1), 807–819 (2025)

27. Razzaq, A., Buckley, J., Lai, Q., Yu, T., Botterweck, G.: A systematic literature review on the influence of enhanced developer experience on developers' productivity: factors, practices, and recommendations. ACM Comput. Surv. **57**(1), 1–46 (2024)
28. Ribeiro, A., Domingues, L.: Acceptance of an agile methodology in the public sector. Procedia Comput. Sci. **138**, 621–629 (2018)
29. Ritonummi, S., Siitonen, V., Salo, M., Pirkkalainen, H.: Flow barriers: what prevents software developers from experiencing flow in their work. In: Socio-Technical Perspective in Information Systems Development, pp. 247–264. CEUR Workshop Proceedings (2022)
30. Silva, L., Barreto, C., Lima, M., Madeira, H.: Enhancing task in-progress time predictions through affective and personality factors. ACM Trans. Software Eng. Methodol. (2025)
31. Wilkes, B., Milani, A.M.P., Storey, M.A.: A framework for automating the measurement of devops research and assessment (dora) metrics. In: 2023 IEEE International Conference on Software Maintenance and Evolution (ICSME), pp. 62–72. IEEE (2023)
32. Zabardast, E., Gonzalez-Huerta, J., Tanveer, B.: Ownership vs contribution: Investigating the alignment between ownership and contribution. In: 2022 IEEE 19th International Conference on Software Architecture Companion (ICSA-C), pp. 30–34. IEEE (2022)

STRIPID: Simulation Test Ranking and Interactive Performance Inspection for PID Controllers

Alejandra Duque-Torres[(✉)], Claus Klammer[ID], and Stefan Fischer[ID]

Software Competence Center Hagenberg (SCCH) GmbH, Hagenberg, Austria
{alejandra.duque-torres,claus.klammer,stefan.fischer}@scch.at

Abstract. Evaluating Proportional-Integral-Derivative (PID) controller performance across a wide range of parameter configurations is a complex and time-consuming task, particularly in industrial settings with diverse machine variants and strict control requirements. Engineers must analyse large volumes of simulation data to assess metrics such as rising time, overshoot, and energy consumption-often relying on manual inspection or ad hoc scripts that are error-prone and difficult to scale.

In collaboration with an industrial partner, we developed a Python-based analysis and ranking tool to automate this process. STRIPID (Simulation Test Ranking and Interactive Performance Inspection for PID controllers) extracts domain-relevant metrics, applies reference-based normalisation and customisable scoring functions, and enables interactive exploration of simulation results. It supports dynamic adjustment of evaluation thresholds and incorporates expert-informed penalties to refine ranking outcomes.

This paper presents STRIPID's architecture and scoring approach, and shares insights from its development in a real industrial testing context. STRIPID significantly reduces manual effort and enhances the consistency and traceability of PID parameter evaluation, offering a practical solution for tuning support and robustness analysis in control systems engineering.

Keywords: PID Controller Tuning · Parameter Evaluation · Test Run Evaluation · Ranking System

1 Introduction

Proportional-Integral-Derivative (PID) controllers are essential components in a wide range of applications, from industrial automation to robotics and aerospace systems [4,5,9,21]. Their simplicity and effectiveness make them the most widely adopted control strategy for dynamic systems [4]. However, tuning PID controllers to achieve optimal performance is a complex task, requiring extensive simulations to evaluate system behaviour under varying conditions [6]. As the number of test cases grows, engineers face significant challenges in evaluating

G. Scanniello et al. (Eds.): PROFES 2025, LNCS 16362, pp. 136–150, 2026.
https://doi.org/10.1007/978-3-032-12092-2_9

system responses across multiple performance dimensions-such as energy efficiency, rising time, and stability-often relying on manual inspection or trial-and-error strategies. This process is not only time-consuming but also prone to inconsistency, especially when working with diverse machine configurations or non-standard evaluation criteria.

Evaluating PID controller performance across a large number of parameter configurations requires analysing simulation results in detail. This involves computing key performance metrics such as energy efficiency, response times, and stability indicators to identify well-performing setups. However, manual analysis across hundreds or thousands of test runs is not only time-consuming but also prone to inconsistencies and subjective interpretation. Moreover, existing tools often lack the flexibility to handle diverse configurations or apply customizable ranking criteria, limiting their usefulness for in-depth performance evaluations.

Each configuration must be assessed across several dimensions-rising time, overshoot, energy consumption, stability-and many of these evaluations are still performed manually or through static scripts. This makes the process not only time-consuming and error-prone but also difficult to scale, automate, or explain to stakeholders. The complexity is further amplified when multiple machine variants must be supported simultaneously, and tuning decisions must remain traceable and justifiable.

To address the practical challenge of evaluating large-scale PID simulation results in configurable industrial systems, we present STRIPID (Simulation Test Ranking and Interactive Performance Inspection for PID controllers), an interactive Python-based tool developed in collaboration with an industrial partner. STRIPID automates the extraction of domain-relevant metrics, applies customizable scoring transformations that reflect engineering priorities (*e.g.*, penalising overshoot or long rising times), and enables dynamic exploration of test outcomes through an intuitive visual interface. It supports threshold tuning, score weighting, and reference-based normalisation, offering a flexible and reproducible approach to PID evaluation. Integrated into real-world workflows, STRIPID helps engineers identify robust parameter configurations efficiently and enables traceable, data-driven decision-making in controller validation.

The main contributions of this work are:

- A lightweight, Python-based tool that enables systematic scoring and ranking of PID simulation results across multiple machine configurations.
- Integration of domain-specific performance metrics-such as overshoot, rising time, and energy-with configurable scoring functions and ranking strategies.
- An interactive dashboard that allows practitioners to explore trade-offs, adjust thresholds, and visually inspect control responses.
- Validation through a real industrial collaboration, demonstrating practical relevance in highly configurable mechatronic systems.
- A structured dataset to support further research in PID tuning, robustness evaluation, and learning-based performance modelling.

The remainder of this paper is structured as follows: Sect. 2 reviews core concepts related to PID control, testing practices, existing analysis tools, and relevant datasets. Section 3 outlines the industrial context that motivated this work. Section 4 describes the architecture and implementation of the proposed analysis and ranking tool. Section 5 presents the key lessons learned, industrial relevance, and research opportunities derived from this work. Finally, Sect. 6 concludes the paper and outlines future directions.

2   Background

This section introduces the key concepts and tools relevant to our work: the role of PID controllers in industrial systems (Sect. 2.1), common testing methods and challenges (Sect. 2.2), existing tools for analysing simulation results (Sect. 2.3), and related datasets (Sect. 2.4).

2.1   PID Controllers in Control Systems

PID controllers are essential components in control systems, valued for their simplicity and effectiveness in maintaining system stability and performance across a wide range of industrial applications [6]. These controllers work by continuously adjusting control inputs based on the proportional (K_p), integral (K_i), and derivative (K_d) components of the error between a desired set-point and the actual process variable [13]. The combined action of these terms enables PID controllers to mitigate errors, reject disturbances, and achieve precise control.

However, ensuring that a PID controller performs optimally requires rigorous testing and evaluation. Poorly tuned parameters can result in significant performance issues, including overshoot, instability, and slow response [5]. Overshoot refers to the excessive deviation from the target set-point, which can lead to inefficiency or instability. Instability manifests as sustained oscillations or divergence in the system output, preventing it from settling at the desired set-point. Slow response describes prolonged settling times that delay the system in reaching its target value, reducing overall efficiency.

2.2   Testing PID Controllers

Testing PID controllers is a systematic process aimed at assessing their performance under various conditions to identify the most effective parameter configurations. This process ensures that controllers meet critical performance requirements, such as minimizing overshoot, reducing settling time, and maintaining system stability, even in the presence of disturbances or uncertainties [15]. Simulation-based testing plays an important role in this process. It allows researchers and practitioners to evaluate the behaviour of PID controllers in a controlled and cost-effective virtual environment [12]. By modelling system dynamics, simulations enable the exploration of a wide range of scenarios, including varying operating conditions and external disturbances, without the risks associated with physical systems. This approach also facilitates iterative refinement of parameters, as multiple configurations can be tested efficiently to optimize controller performance before deployment.

The most widely used approaches for tuning and testing PID controllers fall into several categories. For instance, classical tuning and testing methods rely on empirical and analytical approaches that provide straightforward guidelines for parameter selection [1]. Techniques such as the Ziegler-Nichols [16] and Cohen-Coon methods [25] are commonly used to estimate PID parameters based on system responses to step changes. These methods simplify the tuning process by offering predefined rules. Data-driven approaches [10] have gained prominence in recent years, as they optimise parameters using data collected from simulations or operational systems. Methods such as Virtual Reference Feedback Tuning (VRFT) [7] and Fictitious Reference Iterative Tuning (FRIT) [22] exemplify this category. By leveraging operational or simulated data, these techniques minimise dependence on explicit system models, making them particularly effective for non-linear or time-varying systems. Both methods, however, require iterative testing and involve observing key performance indicators to validate the effectiveness of the tuned parameters [17].

Optimisation-based tuning methods utilise algorithms to explore the parameter space and identify optimal configurations. Techniques such as Genetic Algorithms and Particle Swarm Optimisation evaluate multiple configurations by minimising performance indices, including Integral Absolute Error (IAE) and Integral Time Absolute Error (ITAE). Although computationally intensive, these methods provide robust solutions for determining optimal parameters in complex systems. Testing within these approaches often focuses on analysing the performance of selected parameters against predefined benchmarks.

Across all these methods, a common challenge arises: the need to evaluate how well the selected parameters perform across multiple test runs. This critical step, which ensures the robustness and reliability of the controller, is still predominantly performed manually by experts. The evaluation process often relies on visual comparisons of system responses or iterative fine-tuning.

2.3 Existing Tools for Analysing Simulation Test Results

In iterative testing and simulation processes, analysing and comparing results across multiple test runs is a critical step for evaluating and refining PID controller performance. This involves not only verifying key metrics such as overshoot, settling time, and stability but also performing deeper analyses to understand system behaviour under diverse scenarios. While simulation tools generate raw data, effective analysis requires specialised tools or frameworks to manage the volume and complexity of results, enabling meaningful comparisons and actionable insights.

Among these tools, MATLAB Simulink [11] stands out as one of the most widely used platforms for modelling and simulating dynamic systems, including PID controllers. Its capabilities are particularly valuable for iterative testing, offering pre-built blocks for PID tuning and optimisation-based parameter adjustment. With additional toolboxes, such as the Optimisation Toolbox and Simulink Test, users can automate simulations and compare results against predefined benchmarks. However, despite its comprehensive features, MAT-LAB Simulink presents challenges when dealing with large-scale iterative test runs. Analysing and comparing numerous results often becomes a manual, time-consuming process, requiring advanced expertise to interpret the data effectively. Furthermore, while its visualisation tools are powerful, the lack of built-in ranking or clustering capabilities limits its efficiency for deeper analysis. Additionally, MATLAB's licensing fees can be prohibitively expensive for many researchers and small organisations, potentially restricting access to its advanced features.

In contrast, Python-based ecosystems, including libraries such as Pandas, Matplotlib, and SciPy, offer a flexible and open-ended approach for analysing test results. These libraries enable users to design workflows for aggregating, filtering, and visualising data from simulation outputs. This flexibility is particularly advantageous for researchers needing to adapt their analysis methods to specific challenges.

2.4 Existing Datasets

Datasets focused on control systems, particularly PID controllers, are relatively scarce. Below, we describe some of the most notable datasets in this area:

- *ICS Security Dataset* [23]: This dataset provides operational data from industrial control systems, focusing on normal operations and various cybersecurity attack scenarios. While primarily designed for anomaly detection and robustness testing in security contexts, it has been used in studies evaluating intrusion detection systems [8] and anomaly detection algorithms [14,24].
- *HAI Security Dataset* [18,19]: This dataset replicates industrial processes such as power generation and hydropower. It includes both normal operations and attack scenarios, providing a robust dataset for cybersecurity and anomaly detection research in the context of control system. The dataset has been utilized in publications such as "HAI 1.0: HIL-based Augmented ICS Security Dataset" [18], which introduced the dataset, and "Two ICS Security Datasets and Anomaly Detection Contest", [20] which described its use in benchmarking anomaly detection algorithms during the HAICon 2020 competition [18].
- *Industrial PID Loop Data Repository* [3]: This repository offers time-series data from Single Input Single Output (SISO) PID control loops, collected from various industrial processes. It has been instrumental in research on fault detection and diagnosis, as well as control performance monitoring. Bauer et al. [2] evaluated and compared multiple fault detection methods using this repository, providing insights into their comparative effectiveness. Additionally, in [3], the authors emphasised the repository's role in advancing Control Performance Monitoring (CPM), highlighting the significance of sharing real-world data for industrial control research. While this repository is invaluable for fault detection, its limited configurational diversity restricts its use for exploring PID parameter tuning or system performance optimisation.

These datasets demonstrate the importance of operational and simulation-based data in advancing control systems research. While they provide valuable resources for cybersecurity and fault detection, they may not fully address the needs of researchers focusing on PID tuning and performance evaluation.

3 Industrial Context

This work has been carried out in collaboration with a long-term industry partner in the field of machinery and plant engineering. The company develops highly configurable machines capable of producing and handling a wide range of products across different domains, depending on customer needs. Each machine can be tailored through a large number of configuration options, including size, power, features, and operational flexibility.

This collaboration is part of a broader effort to address the challenges associated with tuning PID controllers in complex and flexible industrial systems. These machines are designed to support diverse production scenarios and must adapt to varying operating conditions. However, their precise application contexts are often unknown at the time of manufacturing. As a result, customers are typically responsible for configuring and optimising the machines-including tuning the PID controller settings-to meet their specific operational requirements.

At the core of this flexibility lies a mechatronic architecture that integrates mechanical, electronic, and software components. A critical part of this control stack is the PID controller, which regulates key variables such as the pressure and speed of hydraulic components. Ensuring robust and optimal performance across a wide range of machine configurations is a non-trivial task: tuning the controller for one setup must not compromise performance in others. Moreover, evaluating the behaviour of different parameter combinations across many test runs is both time-consuming and highly reliant on expert judgment, making the process difficult to scale or standardise.

Motivated by these challenges, we collaborated with our industry partner to explore automated ranking mechanisms for PID simulation test runs. The goal was to develop a lightweight tool capable of systematically evaluating and comparing large sets of test results using configurable performance metrics-while maintaining transparency and domain interpretability. This close collaboration ensured that STRIPID was grounded in practical needs and usable within existing engineering workflows.

4 STRIPID Overview and Architecture

To address the complexity of evaluating PID controller performance across large parameter spaces and machine configurations, we developed STRIPID, an interactive Python-based tool that automates the analysis, scoring, and ranking of simulation test results. STRIPID was designed to reduce manual effort, improve consistency, and support domain-specific decision-making during PID tuning.

STRIPID ingests simulation test results, extracts control performance metrics, applies customisable scoring transformations, and provides interactive visualisations that help practitioners explore and compare test outcomes. It operates through the following seven-stage pipeline:

1. **Data Loading:** Simulation test runs are provided as JSON files containing raw pressure and speed signal responses, time arrays, and PID parameters.
2. **Feature Extraction:** Performance metrics such as rising time, pressure ratio (overshoot), and energy consumption are computed from the time-series data.
3. **Normalisation:** Extracted metrics are normalised with respect to reference test runs (typically the best-performing configuration in each group).
4. **Threshold Adaptation:** Practitioners can interactively set overshoot limits and energy clipping thresholds to suit different operational requirements.
5. **Scoring:** Metrics are transformed into scores between 0 and 1 using domain-informed, non-linear scoring functions.
6. **Ranking:** A composite score is calculated by applying user-defined weights to the individual metric scores. Test runs are then ranked within groups and across the full dataset.
7. **Visualisation:** An interactive dashboard enables users to sort, filter, and visually compare test cases through tables and signal plots.

Below, we describe in detail the stages from *feature extraction* to *visualisation*.

4.1   Feature Extraction

Each simulation test case includes the following input data:

- **PID Parameters:**
    - K_r (Normalised Gain): The base gain applied to the error signal.
    - T_n (Reset Time): Also called the integral time, it defines the duration over which past errors are accumulated.
    - T_v (Rate Time): Also known as the derivative time, it determines the anticipation window for predicting future error trends.
- **Controller Output Signals:** For this specific industrial case, the PID controller regulates:
    - The actual pressure signal over time.
    - The actual speed signal over time.
    - The reference target signal for pressure (P_{Ref}).
    - The reference target signal for speed (S_{Ref}).

From these inputs, STRIPID computes:

- **Rising Time (RT):** Time taken for pressure to increase from 10% to 90% of the target.
- **Pressure Ratio (PR):** Ratio between the peak measured pressure and the target pressure, used to quantify overshoot.

$$PR = \frac{P_{peak}}{P_{target}}$$

- **Energy Metrics:** Total energy of pressure and speed signals computed using:

$$E = \int (derivative)^2 \, dt$$

These metrics were selected based on their relevance to common control objectives, including response speed, stability, and energy efficiency.

4.2   Normalisation and Scoring

To enable fair comparison across configurations, metrics are normalised using reference test cases. For energy metrics, values are scaled relative to a designated reference run (e.g., t0). Overshoot and rising time metrics are transformed via scoring functions:

- **Pressure Ratio Scoring** (PR_{score})
  A quadratic scoring function is applied to penalise overshoot deviations:

$$PR_{score} = \begin{cases} -20 \cdot (PR - 1)^2 + 1 & \text{if } PR \geq 1 \\ \cdot (PR - 1)^2 + 0.95 & \text{if } PR < 1 \end{cases}$$

  This function can be dynamically recalculated if the overshoot allowance is adjusted.
- **Rising Time Scoring** (RT_{score})
  A reference-based formula compares each RT to the minimum observed value plus a configurable offset:

$$RT_{score} = \frac{RT_{ref}}{RT - RT_{min} + RT_{ref}}$$

This formulation ensures:

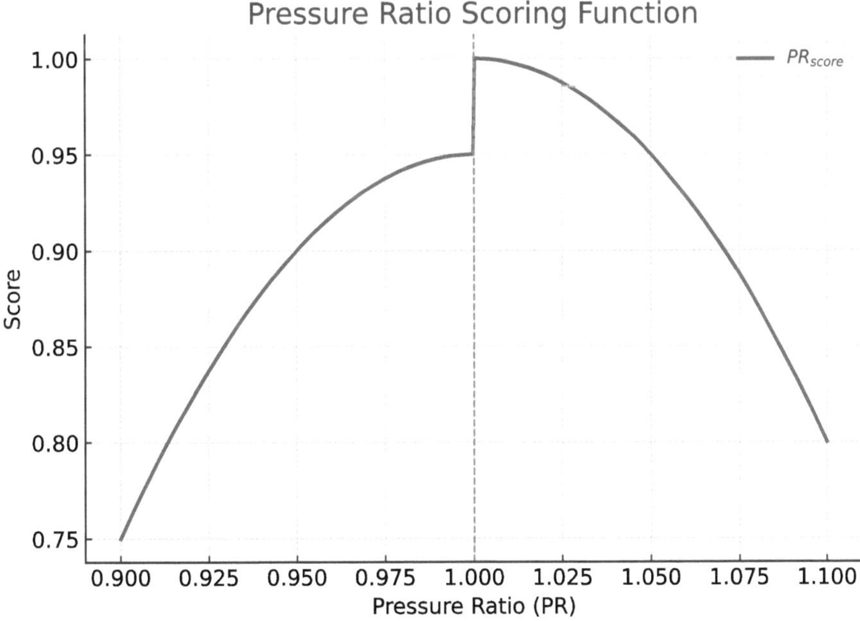

Fig. 1. Quadratic scoring function applied to Pressure Ratio (PR). The function penalises deviations from the ideal PR = 1, applying sharper penalties for overshoots above the target and softer penalties below 1.

- When $RT = RT_{min}$, the score is maximal (equal to 1).
- When the deviation $(RT - RT_{min})$ equals RT_{ref}, the score is 0.5.
- As the rising time increases beyond $RT_{min} + RT_{ref}$, the score smoothly decays toward zero.

By adjusting RT_{ref}, the sensitivity of the scoring function can be adapted to different scenarios and test case distributions, making the function highly flexible for diverse simulation sets.

- **Energy Normalisation and Combination:** To ensure fair comparison across test cases within the same configuration group, the energy metrics are first normalised using a baseline reference run-typically the test case t0. For each group, the pressure and speed energies are normalised as follows (Fig. 1):

$$P\text{-}Eng_{\text{norm}} = \frac{P\text{-}Eng}{P\text{-}Eng_{\text{ref}}}, \quad S\text{-}Eng_{\text{norm}} = \frac{S\text{-}Eng}{S\text{-}Eng_{\text{ref}}}$$

Next, a clipping function is applied to mitigate the impact of outliers and allow tuning of energy sensitivity. User-defined thresholds θ_p and θ_s are used to cap the energy values before min-max scaling:

$$\text{norm}_{Eng_p} = 1 - \text{minmax}_{\text{scale}}\left(\min(P\text{-}Eng_{\text{norm}}, \theta_p)\right)$$

$$\text{norm}_{Eng_s} = 1 - \text{minmax}_{\text{scale}}\left(\min(S\text{-}Eng_{\text{norm}}, \theta_s)\right)$$

Finally, the normalised pressure and speed energy values are combined into a single metric using a user-defined balance parameter $w \in [0, 1]$, which deter-

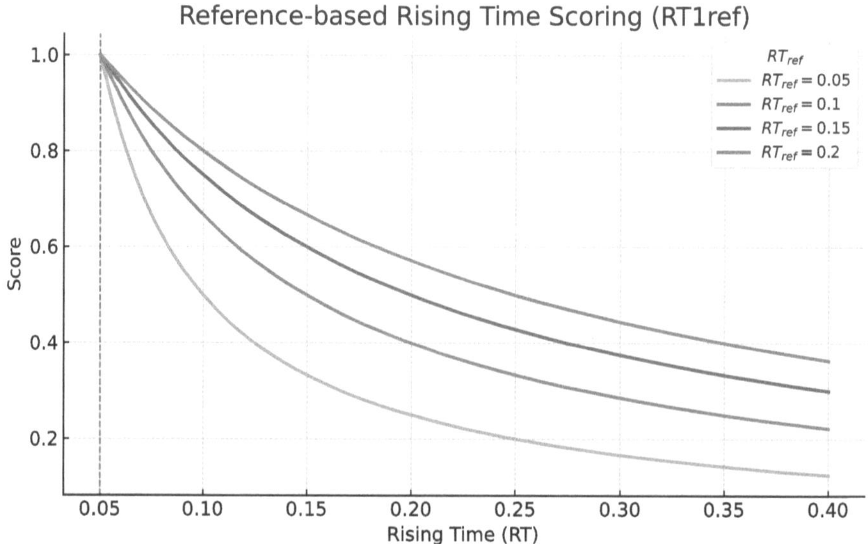

Fig. 2. Reference-based scoring function for RT. The function favours values closer to the minimum observed RT, with a decaying score as RT increases beyond the reference baseline.

mines their relative contribution:

$$\text{norm}_{Eng_{\text{combined}}} = (1 - w) \cdot \text{norm}_{Eng_p} + w \cdot \text{norm}_{Eng_s}$$

Here, w is specified via the `Eng_balance` parameter and can be adjusted interactively during analysis to reflect the importance of speed versus pressure in a given tuning scenario (Fig. 2).

These transformations convert raw metrics into interpretable scores between 0 and 1, enabling multi-objective evaluation and ranking.

4.3   Ranking Strategy

Each test run receives a composite score calculated as a weighted sum:

$$\text{score} = w_{PR} \cdot \text{PR}_{\text{score}} + w_{RT} \cdot \text{RT}_{\text{score}} + w_{Eng} \cdot \text{norm}_{Eng_{\text{combined}}}$$

Users can interactively adjust the weights w_{PR}, w_{RT}, and w_{Eng} to prioritise different aspects of control performance. STRIPID supports both:

- **Group Ranking (GR):** Comparison of test runs within a single configuration group.
- **Overall Ranking (OR):** Ranking across all test cases in the dataset.

Relative scores are also computed for visualisation purposes, helping users interpret how each test run performs relative to others.

4.4   Visualisation Layer

STRIPID provides an interactive dashboard that includes:

- A sortable table displaying test cases, rankings, and individual metric scores.
- Signal plots for visualising pressure and speed response curves.
- Sliders and controls to adjust metric weights and thresholds.
- Real-time updates to scores and rankings as parameters are changed.

This visual interface allows engineers to explore alternative scoring strategies, detect outliers, and identify robust configurations without relying on manual inspection. A demo is available in our GitHub Repository[1]

5   Discussion

This section reflects on the practical insights gained during the development and application of the PID simulation analysis and ranking tool, highlighting its impact, limitations, and opportunities for further development.

---

[1] https://github.com/aduquet/PROFES2025-IndustryTrack.

5.1 Lessons Learned

STRIPID proved particularly useful for identifying optimal PID configurations in a systematic and reproducible manner. By making key performance metrics explicit and comparable, it reduced reliance on manual interpretation of plots and personal heuristics. This was especially valuable when evaluating controller behaviour across multiple machine variants, where the performance landscape is too large and inconsistent for visual inspection alone.

We found that allowing dynamic re-weighting of scoring components (e.g., rising time vs. energy) was critical. Different tuning contexts demanded different trade-offs, and practitioners were able to adapt the ranking criteria on the fly to match their objectives (*e.g.,* minimising overshoot in one case, maximising speed in another).

5.2 Industrial Relevance

In collaboration with our industry partner, STRIPID supported real-world evaluation workflows in the machinery and plant engineering domain. Engineers used the interactive visualisation interface to rapidly explore configuration alternatives, identify outliers, and prioritise robust parameter sets for further testing. The scoring and ranking system enabled clearer communication of tuning decisions within the team and improved traceability for later debugging or refinement.

5.3 Research Opportunities

The dataset produced in this work offers a structured foundation for exploring advanced testing and tuning strategies in control systems. It spans multiple machine configurations and includes performance-relevant metrics, enabling systematic analysis of PID behaviour under diverse operational conditions. In addition to supporting data-driven parameter tuning, the dataset facilitates research in clustering controller responses, predicting system behaviour from parameter inputs, and anomaly detection in control signals. It also provides a reproducible environment for identifying edge cases and validating control software updates without exhaustive manual simulations. Furthermore, the dataset enables exploration of higher-level testing techniques such as simulation-based test selection, surrogate modelling of control performance, and metamorphic testing. These approaches can help reduce test effort, detect robustness issues, and enhance confidence in control logic, especially in configurable or safety-critical systems.

5.4 Ethics and Data Protection

The dataset was developed in collaboration with an industrial partner, following ethical guidelines and respecting data protection protocols. Although it is based on simulated outputs, care was taken to exclude proprietary or sensitive information related to the partner's systems. Specific details of internal controller implementations and exact machine configurations have been omitted to comply with confidentiality agreements.

Nevertheless, the dataset includes all relevant simulation parameters, control signals, and performance metrics necessary for reproducibility and research. It is intended exclusively for research and educational purposes. Access to the dataset can be granted upon request and is subject to responsible research use and appropriate citation of this work.

5.5   Limitations and Challenges

While effective, STRIPID has certain limitations. The scoring functions, although configurable, still require careful interpretation and domain knowledge to calibrate effectively. For example, the choice of thresholds or the definition of a "good" rising time remains context-specific and subjective.

Additionally, STRIPID currently assumes a batch evaluation mode, where all test results are available up front. It does not yet support real-time signal ingestion or incremental updates, which may be desirable for online tuning or closed-loop testing environments.

5.6   Opportunities for Extension

STRIPID has significant potential for future development to address its current limitations and expand its functionality. One promising enhancement could involve the automation of parameter tuning and ranking through the incorporation of machine learning algorithms. This approach would minimise manual intervention, improving both usability and efficiency.

Broadening STRIPID's compatibility with other simulation platforms, such as Simulink or Modelica, could significantly increase its versatility, making it more accessible to a wider range of industrial users. Enhancing visualisation capabilities, such as incorporating multi-pane views or automated report generation, would further improve its usability and make it more suitable for presentations and analysis. Cloud deployment is another potential extension, as it could address scalability concerns by allowing users to leverage distributed computing resources for handling large datasets. Finally, releasing STRIPID under an open-source license would foster collaboration within the research and industrial communities.

5.7   Threats to Validity - Dataset

The dataset, while offering valuable insights into PID controller behaviour, is subject to certain threats to validity that researchers should consider when interpreting results and generalising findings.

Internal Validity

Despite the versatility and utility of the analysis tool for computing metrics, visualising responses, and ranking PID controller simulation test runs, several limitations reveal opportunities for future enhancement. The dataset used is generated entirely from simulations that-although carefully tuned to approximate real-world machine dynamics-may not fully capture the complexities of physical systems. Moreover, confidentiality constraints with our industrial partner necessitated omitting detailed PID tuning parameters and machine-specific configurations, potentially hindering exact reproducibility.

External Validity

The dataset's scope is limited to six machine configurations. While these configurations reflect meaningful industrial scenarios, they may not generalise to broader applications or more complex systems. Furthermore, the dataset focuses exclusively on pressure and speed control, which restricts its applicability to control systems where other parameters, such as temperature or flow rate, are critical.

Construct Validity

Metrics such as rise time, energy, and oscillation amplitudes are derived using Python libraries, which may differ from methods employed in other studies or industrial standards. These variations could limit the direct comparability of findings across datasets or research contexts. However, since these metrics are derived directly from the raw pressure and speed signals provided in the dataset, they can be easily recalculated using alternative methods or definitions to suit specific research requirements.

6   Conclusion

This paper presented a lightweight, interactive tool for analysing and ranking PID controller simulation test results. Developed in collaboration with an industrial partner, STRIPID addresses the challenges of evaluating large parameter sweeps across multiple machine configurations, providing a reproducible and configurable framework for tuning and testing. By combining domain-informed scoring functions with interactive visualisations, STRIPID enables practitioners to explore trade-offs between control objectives, detect unstable configurations, and prioritise parameter sets for deployment. Its modular design and open implementation support adaptation to diverse industrial contexts.

In addition to STRIPID, a structured dataset was generated to support further research in control system validation. It enables exploration of learning-based tuning, robustness analysis, and testing techniques such as surrogate modelling and metamorphic testing. Future work will focus on extending STRIPID's capabilities toward real-time analysis, adaptive ranking strategies, and broader support for other controller architectures. We hope this contribution encourages further collaboration between academia and industry in the development of reliable, interpretable, and efficient control validation tools.

Acknowledgement. The research reported in this paper has been funded by the Federal Ministry for Innovation, Mobility and Infrastructure (BMIMI), the Federal Ministry for Economy, Energy and Tourism (BMWET), and the State of Upper Austria in the frame of the SCCH competence center INTEGRATE [(FFG grant no. 892418)] in the COMET - Competence Centers for Excellent Technologies Program managed by Austrian Research Promotion Agency FFG.

References

1. Altinoz, O.T., Erdem, H.: Particle swarm optimisation-based PID controller tuning for static power converters. Int. J. Power Electron. **7**(1-2) (2015)
2. Bauer, M., Auret, L., Bacci di Capaci, R., Horch, A., Thornhill, N.F.: Industrial PID control loop data repository and comparison of fault detection methods. Ind. Eng. Chem. Res. **58**(26), 11430–11439 (2019)
3. Bauer, M., Auret, L., le Roux, D., Aharonson, V.: An industrial PID data repository for control loop performance monitoring (CPM). IFAC-PapersOnLine **51**(4), 823–828 (2018). ISSN 2405-8963
4. Benotsmane, R., Kovács, G.: Optimization of energy consumption of industrial robots using classical PID and MPC controllers. Energies **16**(8) (2023). ISSN 1996-1073
5. Blevins, T.L.: PID advances in industrial control. IFAC Proc. Vol. **45**(3), 23–28 (2012)
6. Borase, R.P., Maghade, D.K., Sondkar, S.Y., Pawar, S.N.: A review of PID control, tuning methods and applications. Int. J. Dyn. Control **9**(2) (2021). ISSN 2195-2698
7. Campi, M., Savaresi, S.: Direct nonlinear control design: the virtual reference feedback tuning (VRFT) approach. IEEE Trans. Autom. Control **51**(1), 14–27 (2006). https://doi.org/10.1109/TAC.2005.861689
8. Catillo, M., Pecchia, A., Villano, U.: CPS-guard: intrusion detection for cyber-physical systems and IoT devices using outlier-aware deep autoencoders. Comput. Secur. **129**, 103210 (2023). ISSN 0167-4048
9. Coskun, M.Y., İtik, M.: Intelligent PID control of an industrial electro-hydraulic system. ISA Trans. **139**, 484–498 (2023). ISSN 0019-057. https://doi.org/10.1016/j.isatra.2023.04.005. https://www.sciencedirect.com/science/article/pii/S0019057823001751
10. Formentin, S., van Heusden, K., Karimi, A.: A comparison of model-based and data-driven controller tuning. Int. J. Adaptive Control Signal Process. **28**(10) (2014)
11. MathWorks Inc.: Optimization toolbox version: 9.4 (r2022b) (2022). https://www.mathworks.com
12. Kapinski, J., Deshmukh, J.V., Jin, X., Ito, H., Butts, K.: Simulation-based approaches for verification of embedded control systems: an overview of traditional and advanced modeling, testing, and verification techniques. IEEE Control Syst. Mag. **36**(6), 45–64 (2016)

13. Knospe, C.: PID control. IEEE Control Syst. Mag. **26**(1), 30–31 (2006). https://doi.org/10.1109/MCS.2006.1580151
14. Kumar, A., Choi, B.J.: Benchmarking machine learning based detection of cyber attacks for critical infrastructure. In: 2022 International Conference on Information Networking (ICOIN), pp. 24–29 (2022). https://doi.org/10.1109/ICOIN53446.2022.9687293
15. Li, Y., Ang, K.H., Chong, G.: PID control system analysis and design. IEEE Control Syst. Mag. **26**(1) (2006). https://doi.org/10.1109/MCS.2006.1580152
16. Meshram, P.M., Kanojiya, R.G.: Tuning of PID controller using Ziegler-Nichols method for speed control of DC motor. In: IEEE-International Conference on Advances in Engineering, Science and Management (ICAESM 2012), pp. 117–122 (2012)
17. Munaro, C.J., Pimentel, M.R., Bacci di Capaci, R., Campestrini, L.: Data driven performance monitoring and retuning using PID controllers. Comput. Chem. Eng. **178** (2023). ISSN 0098-1354
18. Shin, H.K., Lee, W., Choi, S., Yun, J.H., Min, B.G.: Hai security datasets (2023). Accessed 07 Nov 2024
19. Shin, H.K., Lee, W., Yun, J.H., Kim, H.: HAI 1.0: HIL-Based Augmented ICS Security Dataset. USA (2020)
20. Shin, H.K., Lee, W., Yun, J.H., Min, B.G.: Two ICS security datasets and anomaly detection contest on the HIL-based augmented ICS testbed. In: Cyber Security Experimentation and Test Workshop, CSET 2021, pp. 36–40. Association for Computing Machinery, New York (2021). ISBN 9781450390651
21. Singcuna, S., Kittisupakorn, P., Banjerdpongchai, D., Dawkrajai, J., Daskalov, P., Georgieva, T.: Implementing PID control on plc benchmark to enhance industrial automation skills towards asean factori 4.0. In: 2023 Joint International Conference on Digital Arts, Media and Technology with ECTI Northern Section Conference on Electrical, Electronics, Computer and Telecommunications Engineering (ECTI DAMT & NCON), pp. 409–414 (2023)
22. Soma, S., Kaneko, O., Fujii, T.: A new method of controller parameter tuning based on input-output data – fictitious reference iterative tuning (frit). IFAC Proc. Vol. **37**(12), 789–794 (2004). ISSN 1474-6670
23. Team, I.D.: ICS security dataset (2020). https://www.kaggle.com/icsdataset. Accessed 07 Nov 2024
24. Tushkanova, O., Levshun, D., Branitskiy, A., Fedorchenko, E., Novikova, E., Kotenko, I.: Detection of cyberattacks and anomalies in cyber-physical systems: approaches, data sources, evaluation. Algorithms **16**(2) (2023). ISSN 1999-489https://doi.org/10.3390/a16020085. https://www.mdpi.com/1999-4893/16/2/85
25. Utami, A., Yuniar, R., Giyantara, A., Saputra, A.: Cohen-coon PID tuning method for self-balancing robot. In: 2022 International Symposium on Electronics and Smart Devices (ISESD), pp. 1–5 (2022). https://doi.org/10.1109/ISESD56103.2022.9980830

Doctoral Symposium Papers

Development of a Model-Driven DevOps Solution Based on Context-Engineered LLM Code Generation: PROFES Doctoral Symposium

Uldis Karlovs-Karlovskis$^{(\boxtimes)}$ (ID)

Riga Technical University, Riga, Latvia
`uldis.karlovs-karlovskis@rtu.lv`

Abstract. DevOps practices have been widely studied since 2009, nonetheless automated generation of Continuous Integration and Continuous Delivery (CI/CD) pipelines from high-level software architecture models remain underexplored. This paper addresses that gap through Model-Driven DevOps with AI (MDDOAI), a model-to-code approach that automates pipeline synthesis from architectural intent and enriches the output with context engineering method. The solution combines ATL based model transformations with Acceleo-driven code generation to produce deployable CI/CD configurations. For Quality Evaluation the approach includes runtime as validation and unsupervised code regeneration to ensure LLM produced pipelines meet functional requirements. A working prototype demonstrates the feasibility of scalable, model-driven pipeline automation, improving maintainability in modern DevOps environments.

Keywords: DevOps · CI/CD automation · Model-Driven Engineering · Model transformation · Pipeline generation · Large Language Models

1 Introduction

Originating around 2009 to bridge the gap between development and operations teams, DevOps has since evolved into a key practice enabling automation, collaboration, and continuous delivery across the software lifecycle [1]. While DevOps practices are widely adopted, CI/CD pipeline configuration remains a persistent bottleneck in the delivery process.

This research area falls within the field of Information Technology, more specifically it focuses on the area of improving software engineering practices. As systems scale and diversify due to modular architectures, heterogeneous stacks, or organizational growth, pipeline definitions become fragmented across teams. This fragmentation

The original version of the chapter has been revised. Missing acknowledgments section has been added. A correction to this chapter can be found at
https://doi.org/10.1007/978-3-032-12092-2_31

reduces visibility, increases the risk of misalignment, and slows feedback loops, even when the software itself is ready for deployment. In many cases, the pipeline becomes the bottleneck between completed code and delivery. According to SlashData [2] approximately 83% of software developers worldwide engage in DevOps-related activities such as continuous integration, automated testing, or deployment. With an estimated global developer population of 26.9 million [3] this means over 22 million engineers regularly interact with CI/CD tooling, underscoring the critical role of pipeline automation across diverse IT projects.

Although CI/CD practices are nearly universal and software architecture continues to evolve, the manual effort needed to build and maintain pipelines remains a significant barrier. This not only wastes valuable engineering resources but also delays deployment, breaks feedback loops, and slows release timeline. What is lacking is a generalizable, scalable method for defining pipelines in an abstract yet adaptable form, one that enables consistent automation across projects. Addressing this gap is critical for reducing DevOps overhead and improving efficiency and agility across the software industry. Generalizability and abstraction could be resolved by applying Model-Driven Engineering (MDE) which is criticized for its scalability challenges. MDE, originating in the 1980s, is a paradigm that shifts the focus from code to models and can be applied across different software engineering methodologies, provides structure and traceability. The scalability challenges could be addressed with context-engineered LLM code generation. LLMs, which gained traction in the late 2010s through advances in transformer-based NLP models, contribute flexibility and generative capability.

To identify current state-of-the-art of combined technology, a related work analysis is conducted which answers the first research question:

RQ1: What are the current state-of-the-art approaches that combine Model-Driven Engineering, CI/CD automation, and LLM-based context engineering?

The results of the conducted related work analysis, and identified deficits in using software architecture models for input, lead to the **central hypothesis: Software architecture models can be systematically transformed into correct, reusable, and maintainable CI/CD pipelines across heterogeneous toolchains by applying MDE principles in combination with context-engineered LLMs.** The goal of the dissertation is to validate the hypothesis by developing a solution under the code name MDDOAI. The two remaining research questions (RQs) focus on novelty, quality evaluation, and field test validation:

RQ2: To what extent can the pipelines generated by the proposed non-deterministic MDDOAI approach be evaluated and trusted with respect to software quality, correctness, and maintainability?
RQ3: Does the developed solution validate the central hypothesis by demonstrating technical feasibility and potential for real-world adoption?

This study presents MDDOAI (Model-Driven DevOps with AI), a hybrid approach that combines Model-Driven Engineering (MDE) and Large Language Models (LLMs) to automate the generation of CI/CD pipelines from high-level software architecture models.

2 Related Work

Recent related work analysis conducted by the author [1, 4], have comprehensively mapped the current state of model-driven CI/CD research. These studies form the basis for the observations discussed in this section. These works identified recurring limitations in existing model-driven CI/CD approaches, which we further elaborate below.

Existing model-driven approaches to CI/CD pipeline generation show potential but fall short in practical applicability, automation depth, or toolchain coverage. Early efforts like García-Díaz [5] explored model-driven CI tooling but predate the DevOps paradigm and lack support for modern pipelines.

DevOpsML [6] proposed a megamodel-based framework using SPEM but remains largely theoretical, with limited tool support or real-world validation. Similarly, StalkCD [7] defines a Jenkins-specific metamodel with good coverage but lacks cross-platform applicability. The Two-Level Model-Driven Approach [8] identifies shared CI/CD concepts across tools like GitHub Actions, Jenkins, and CircleCI, yet fails to deliver full traceability or end-to-end generation from architecture to deployable code.

CI anti-pattern study [9] highlights recurring problems—manual errors, poor versioning, and fragmented tooling—but rarely consider model-driven solutions, suggesting limited adoption in practice.

While prior research has focused on generating initial project artifacts using MDE [10], less attention has been paid to automating operational aspects such as CI/CD pipeline generation. During this research, no identified work leverages context-engineering.

3 Research Approach and Methodology

3.1 Methodology

This research follows design science methodology aimed at evaluating the feasibility and effectiveness of model-driven DevOps automation with the aid of LLM transformation workflows. In the Problem Identification phase, we define the lack of scalable CI/CD pipeline automation; in Objective Definition, we aim to automate pipeline generation using MDE and LLMs; in Design & Development, we build the MDDOAI toolchain; in Demonstration, we apply it to two real-world systems and in Evaluation, we test the pipelines in live GitLab CI/CD environments. Three research questions guide the validation of the proposed approach, both in terms of novelty and practical impact.

Addressing RQ1. This question is addressed via a structured related work analysis in the previous chapter. By analyzing existing work, we determine whether any prior solution meets the criteria of full automation, platform independence, and real-world applicability. As per the analysis, there is currently no model-driven approach that enables full automation of CI/CD pipeline generation and context engineering from high-level architecture models while maintaining platform independence, traceability, and real-world applicability. Therefore, a hypothesis is drawn from the identified deficits and the MDDOAI as a solution is proposed to validate it.

3.2 MDDOAI Solution

The MDDOAI architecture is composed of two core phases: model transformations (M2M) and code generation (M2C). These transformations map a high-level software architecture metamodel to a Platform independent metamodel (PIM), and subsequently to a Platform specific metamodel (PSM), based on formal transformation rules. Finally, the CI/CD pipeline configuration is generated from the platform specific model with the assistance of context-engineered LLMs.

Transformations are executed using the ATL [11], where matched and lazy rules define how model elements are mapped between abstraction layers. This separation of transformations ensures clear progression from high-level architecture design to executable configuration. Each transformation layer introduces increasing specificity, with the final model fully aligned to the syntax and semantics of the target CI/CD platform.

In the final model-to-code phase, Acceleo is used to generate YAML configuration based on predefined templates mapped to PSM elements. However, to address limitations of static code templates, particularly in handling complex conditions, dynamic job definitions, or advanced GitLab features, a context-engineered large language model (LLM) is used to complement Acceleo. The LLM takes the PSM as input and generates additional configuration code that is outside the scope of the predefined Acceleo templates, effectively enhancing and completing the final *.gitlab-ci.yml* file. This hybrid generation approach improves coverage, adaptability, and robustness of the produced pipeline. The entire toolchain remains modular and extensible for other CI/CD platforms.

3.3 Solution Correctness

The correctness of the MDDOAI generated CI/CD pipelines is evaluated not through static validation alone, but by executing the generated configurations in a live GitLab CI/CD environment. The core idea is simple: if the pipeline runs successfully and produces the expected build, test, or deployment artifacts, then the output is correct. If it fails or deviates from the desired result, the LLM is informed that the outcome is incorrect and is prompted to regenerate the pipeline code.

This forms a feedback loop where the LLM iteratively refines its output based on the observed behavior of the pipeline. The process continues until the generated pipeline passes execution and meets predefined success criteria. At that point, the LLM is explicitly told that the result is correct—effectively reinforcing the learned pattern. While this isn't formal reinforcement learning in the algorithmic sense, it mimics its principles: the model is nudged toward correct behavior through guided iteration and feedback.

This pragmatic validation approach—using real CI/CD execution outcomes to confirm or reject generated output—ensures that correctness is defined not just by syntactic validity, but by actual runtime behavior. It also offers a natural safeguard against LLM hallucinations or partial completions: incorrect generations are caught early through system feedback, not developer guesswork.

Addressing RQ2. This question focuses on evaluating the reliability and determinism of LLM-assisted transformations. The assessment draws on practices from ML software quality evaluation, examining repeatability, traceability, and runtime correctness of the generated CI/CD configurations. The output of the MDDOAI approach can be trusted, not because the LLM is inherently reliable, but because every generated result is tested in a real environment and only accepted once it meets defined success conditions. This quality evaluation strategy ensures both correctness and traceability, making the generated pipelines dependable in practice.

3.4 Field Test Validation

To validate the approach a field test is conducted, where the MDDOAI solution is applied to two real-world software systems (both actively used in production environments): a CI pipeline for a proprietary chatbot framework and a deployment pipeline for PrestaShop-based e-commerce system. In both cases, minimal adaptation of the architecture model is required, and the generated configuration files (GitLab CI/CD YAML and deployment scripts) are successfully deployed and executed within live GitLab CI/CD environments. If the pipeline fails to execute or produces an unexpected output, the LLM is prompted to repeat the failed test and regenerate the configuration with revised context until the result is correct.

The pipelines are produced with little manual intervention beyond model instantiation, confirming that the combined model-driven approach can eliminate much of the low-level YAML authoring typically required. Because the transformation logic is decoupled from specific platforms by design, extending support to other CI/CD systems, such as GitHub Actions and Jenkins, requires only limited adjustments to the model-to-text generation layer.

Addressing RQ3. The hypothesis is evaluated through implementation in field tests of software development scenarios, scenario-based validation, and comparative analysis with manual pipeline authoring. The goal is to measure effort reduction and assess the adaptability of the platform-independent design. The MDDOAI approach is technically feasible, it has been demonstrated on production-grade projects and presents strong potential for practical adoption. Its architecture enables a scalable path forward for automating pipeline engineering through modeling and context-engineered LLMs.

4 Expected Contributions

This work contributes toward a more intelligent, accessible, and sustainable DevOps practice, lowering the entry barrier for small teams and improving efficiency for large organizations alike. While CI/CD pipeline code generation from models was performed decades ago, the results achieved in MDDOAI present the following contributions:

- A novel and more efficient method for developing CI/CD is developed.
- High-level software architecture models are used for transformation input.
- The MDE approach is enhanced with context-engineered LLMs.

Future iterations could implement unsupervised or semi-supervised reinforcement techniques, where failed build executions automatically generate training signals. Over time, this could enable the LLM to learn from its own mistakes, improving configuration accuracy and reducing the need for manual retries.

Additionally, scaling the approach to fully support multi-platform toolchains (e.g., Jenkins, GitHub Actions, Azure Pipelines) will require abstracting environment-specific quirks and adapting the model-to-text generation logic to new domains.

5   Conclusions and Future Work

This paper identifies a deficit in state-of-the-art solutions for CI/CD pipelines which leads to a hypothesis and the MDDOAI solution—a hybrid approach of Model-Driven Engineering and Large Language Models to automate the generation of CI/CD pipelines from high-level software architecture models. The solution significantly reduces manual effort, avoids redundant configuration, and improves engineering consistency.

Although the current prototype supports a limited subset of GitLab CI/CD features, extensibility is structurally embedded in the metamodel. The solution preserves traceability from architecture to deployment artifacts and aligns with established principles of automation, modularity, and reuse.

Ultimately, MDDOAI advances the state of DevOps automation by showing that intelligent, model-driven tooling can bridge the gap between design and deployment. It lays a scalable foundation for further research and practical adoption of AI-enhanced automation in software engineering.

Acknowledgements. The research leading to these results was supported by the EU Recovery and Resilience Facility within the Project No. 5.2.1.1.i.0/2/24/I/CFLA/003 "Implementation of consolidation and management changes at Riga Technical University, Liepaja University, Rezekne Academy of Technology, Latvian Maritime Academy and Liepaja Maritime College for the progress towards excellence in higher education, science and innovation" academic career PhD grant (ID 1017).

References

1. Karlovs-Karlovskis, U., Niķiforova, O., Pastor, O., Jansone, A., Vēveris, K.: From software architecture models to pipelines: A conceptual framework for model transformation in devOps. Frontiers in ITEMI (submitted for publication) (2025)
2. State of Continuous I & D, https://www.slashdata.co/post/state-of-continuous-integration-delivery-the-evolution-of-software-delivery-performance, last accessed 2025/07/22 (2025)
3. How Many Programmers are there in the World and in the US?, https://qubit-labs.com/how-many-programmers-in-the-world/, last accessed 2025/07/22 ((2025)
4. Karlovs-Karlovskis, U., Ņikiforova, O., Pastor, O., Vēveris, K.: MDDOAI: A model-driven devOps approach for CI/CD automation. IEEE 66th International Scientific Conference on Information Technology and Management Science (accepted for publication) (2025)
5. García-Díaz, V., Pelayo García-Bustelo, B.C., Cueva Lovelle, J.M.: MDCI: Model-driven continuous integration. J Ambient Intell Smart Environ **4**, 479–481. https://doi.org/10.3233/AIS-2012-0173 (2012)

6. Colantoni, A., Berardinelli, L., Wimmer, M.: DevOpsML: towards modeling DevOps processes and platforms. In: Proceedings of the 23rd ACM/IEEE International Conference on Model Driven Engineering Languages and Systems: Companion Proceedings. Association for Computing Machinery, New York, NY, USA (2020)

7. Düllmann, T.F., Kabierschke, O., Hoorn, A van.: StalkCD: A model-driven framework for interoperability and analysis of CI/CD pipelines. In: 2021 47th Euromicro Conference on Software Engineering and Advanced Applications (SEAA). pp 214–223 (2021)

8. Flores, A., Amaral, V., Gião, H., Cunha, J.: A two-level model-driven approach for reengineering CI/CD pipelines. Lisboa (2024)

9. Zampetti, F,, Vassallo, C., Panichella, S., et al.: An empirical characterization of bad practices in continuous integration. Empir Softw Eng **25**, 1095–1135. https://doi.org/10.1007/s10664-019-09785-8 (2020)

10. Nikiforova, O., Babris, K., Karlovs-Karlovskis, U., et al.: Model transformations used in IT project initial phases: Systematic literature review. Computers **14**, 40. https://doi.org/10.3390/COMPUTERS14020040 (2025)

11. ATL, https://wiki.eclipse.org/ATL/User_Guide_-_The_ATL_Language, l.a. 2025/07/22 (2025)

Tutorial Papers

Introduction to Quantum Software Engineering

Yoann Marquer$^{(\boxtimes)}$ and Domenico Bianculli

University of Luxembourg, Luxembourg, Luxembourg
`{yoann.marquer,domenico.bianculli}@uni.lu`

Abstract. Quantum computing allows for processing information exponentially faster than classical computing, which opens opportunities in many software applications. Nevertheless, the transition to this completely different programming paradigm, with counterintuitive quantum concepts, presents substantial difficulties for software engineers when developing quantum programs. In this tutorial, we present an introductory course on quantum computing and quantum software engineering frameworks and propose exercises on writing, executing, and analyzing quantum circuits.

Keywords: Quantum computing · Quantum software engineering

1 Introduction

Quantum computing (QC) uses quantum bits (qubits) instead of the bits used in classical computing, enabling massive parallel computation using quantum physics properties like superposition. This allows quantum computers to process information exponentially faster than any classical computer, with empirical evidence for quantum supremacy [2]. Thus, QC has an impact on many emerging technologies and industrial use-cases, especially regarding optimization problems [11]. For this reason, technology giants such as IBM, Google, and Microsoft have heavily invested in and committed to QC.

The availability of quantum computers with more and more qubits allows engineers to deploy more complex and diverse quantum programs at a larger scale. Engineering these programs is challenging, as they require expertise in various disciplines like physics and mathematics. Moreover, they involve unintuitive concepts like quantum superposition and entanglement, and are implemented in low-level, error-prone programming languages. Designing, implementing, testing, and maintaining such programs require the adoption of software engineering practices tailored to the specific domain (e.g., dealing with quantum-related bugs), leading to the establishment of *quantum software engineering* (QSE) as a discipline [17].

Furthermore, current quantum computers are called NISQ (noisy intermediate-scale quantum) computers, because they are larger than small-scale

G. Scanniello et al. (Eds.): PROFES 2025, LNCS 16362, pp. 163–168, 2026.
https://doi.org/10.1007/978-3-032-12092-2_11

prototypes with a few qubits, but not large enough so that quantum error correction can be applied [11]. Thus, current quantum executions are noisy, which decreases the probability to obtain the expected output [5]. Hence the need for noise analysis and reduction techniques to improve the resilience of quantum computing.

In this paper, accompanying a tutorial with the same title, we provide an introduction to QC and touch upon some aspects of QSE, namely quantum programming, as well as analysis, specification, and testing of quantum programs.

2   Background: Quantum Computing

In quantum computing, a system usually has two classical states, denoted $|0\rangle$ and $|1\rangle$. A qubit is in a *superposition* of these states $|\psi\rangle = \alpha|0\rangle + \beta|1\rangle$, where α and β are complex numbers called *amplitudes*. In polar coordinates, $\alpha = |\alpha|\, e^{i\varphi_\alpha}$ and $\beta = |\beta|\, e^{i\varphi_\beta}$, where φ_α and φ_β are called phases; $|\alpha|$ and $|\beta|$ are called magnitudes and satisfy $|\alpha|^2 + |\beta|^2 = 1$. A *quantum state* is the combination of several qubits, e.g., in $|01\rangle$, the first bit is $|0\rangle$ and the second is $|1\rangle$. Qubits that have correlated values are *entangled*, e.g., in $\frac{1}{\sqrt{2}}(|00\rangle + |11\rangle)$, the first qubit is $|0\rangle$ if and only if the second one is $|0\rangle$.

While in classical computing logic gates are the basic blocks of circuits, in quantum computing *quantum gates* are the basic blocks of *quantum circuits*. Quantum gates perform unitary transformations on one or several qubits at a time, updating the state of these qubits in a reversible way. A quantum state can be *measured*, in which case it collapses to a classical state, with a probability depending on the magnitude. For instance, a qubit $|\psi\rangle = \alpha|0\rangle + \beta|1\rangle$ can collapse either in state $|0\rangle$ with probability $|\alpha|^2$ or in state $|1\rangle$ with probability $|\beta|^2$.

Quantum operations are performed in a *quantum processing unit* (QPU), which can have various implementations. The *qubit connectivity* of the QPU is the physical connection allowing qubit interactions, with each qubit typically connected to only a few neighbors. As NISQ computers are noisy, QSE approaches have to consider quantum noise. It is possible to analyze QPUs or use models in quantum simulators to determine the largest sources of noise [21].

3   Quantum Programming

Quantum programming frameworks are very diverse. Quantum circuits are usually described using low-level programming languages embedded in classical languages [1]. Some ideas for higher-level quantum programming languages have been proposed, but they are not ready yet [6,22,26]. Common quantum frameworks, like Qiskit, Cirq, Tket, and PennyLane, implement a quantum platform on top of Python code, using a dedicated library for quantum-specific operations [20].

These frameworks also support essential steps in quantum software development. *Transpilation* is the translation of a circuit to another circuit (written at the same level of abstraction) that takes into account the topology of and the gates supported by the target QPU. *Uncomputation* consists in performing inverse quantum operations in backward order to undo any previously built entanglement, so qubits are ready for the next execution.

As quantum executions can be costly and noisy, quantum *simulators* can be useful to test quantum circuits on classical computers. During a simulation, the execution can be stopped at any moment so intermediate states as well as phase information can be observed at will, facilitating debugging. However, since quantum simulations do not benefit from the speed-up due to actual quantum superposition, simulators can be used only for small circuits, with a few qubits.

4   Quantum Software Engineering

QSE approaches need not only to adapt techniques from classical computing, but also to consider specificities of quantum computing. For instance, a *quantum bug* is a bug on a quantum algorithm (not on the language or implementation) that happens because of quantum considerations (as opposed to classical ones, like API usage) [3]. They often require domain-specific knowledge to fix [19]. Most of them occur in components independent of the execution environment, hence they can be triggered in simulators. They tend to manifest though unexpected outputs, i.e., a silent misbehavior, as opposed to crashes, which are more common for classical bugs. Several studies have investigated quantum bug patterns [14,19,29], e.g., the incorrect usage of quantum gates and incorrect measurement handling. Actually, most quantum bugs are API- or math-related, indicating a lack of proficiency by developers [14].

QSE approaches must face several challenges regarding quantum programs:

C1: Quantum states cannot be duplicated (as per the no-cloning theorem); therefore one may not extract a value and then study it while the execution resumes.
C2: Quantum states, when observed through a quantum measurement, collapse into (usually) classical states; consequently, it is challenging to investigate intermediate states to find quantum bugs.
C3: Intermediate states have a large size; this make them hard to interpret, even in simulation where they can be observed.
C4: Quantum state space is large: making it challenging to identify the input capable of triggering a quantum bug.
C5: Quantum programs have probabilistic outcomes, which means that quantum bugs may not manifest in the same way as in classical programs.

4.1   Quantum Program Analysis

Static analysis techniques can be applied to quantum programs without executing them. *Static analyzers* (like Qchecker [28] and LintQ [20]) are based on bug patterns or quantum abstractions; they generate bug reports with bug location and description. *Slicing techniques* address C3 by dividing the circuit in small subcircuits and removing qubits which are not involved in a particular slice [15]. *Probabilistic cloning* [9] tackles C1 as follows. While the no-cloning theorem prevents cloning quantum states using only unitary transformations, this technique performs unitary transformations and quantum measurements to produce, with a chance of failure, a clone that is not entangled with the state of interest. Such a state can then be used to obtain information about it without collapsing the computation.

4.2   Quantum Program Testing

To tackle C4, multiple approaches have been applied to generate and execute input qubits able to trigger quantum bugs. QuanFuzz mutates qubit inputs using common quantum gates [23]. QuBST uses a genetic algorithm to determine a subset of the initial test suite with enough failing tests [24]. QuCAT tests combinations of input qubits [25]. QuraTest generates small circuits to generate qubit inputs with diverse magnitude, phase, and entanglement [27].

One way to tackle C5 is repeating runs to determine the underlying output distribution; a test failure is either an unexpected output or an incorrect output distribution. *Statistical tests* on the output can be used to determine, e.g., if two qubits are equal or are entangled [7]. A recent work [18] has proposed to test qubit states after a *change of basis* (mixed Hadamard basis), depending on the expected state [18]. Such an approach can be used to tackle C3, as it leads to reduced output distributions (and thus smaller test cases), as well as to reduced sample size, reducing execution time while improving fault detection.

4.3   Specifications of Quantum Programs

Similarly to tests on the final state, *specifications* can be written and tested on intermediate states.

Huang and Martonosi [8] addressed C5 by proposing *statistical assertions*, i.e., measurements performed at breakpoints across multiple runs to approximate the underlying distribution. They can be used to determine, for example, whether a qubit is classical (i.e., it has almost always the same value), is in superposition (i.e., it consistently takes several values), or if two qubits are entangled (i.e., they tend to be correlated). Nevertheless, each quantum measurement stops the program execution while each assertion requires many runs to reach statistical significance.

To tackle C2, Liu et al. [12,13] proposed to instrument the source program with circuits checking for *dynamic assertions*, covering any state comparison and some entangled states. Li et al. [10] proposed a generalization of dynamic assertions with *projective predicates*, expressing that a state is in a given projective subspace. These predicates can then be combined using connectives to write more complex assertions. In the context of formal verification, Minh Do and Ogata [16] proposed to use linear temporal logic (LTL) to define properties of quantum programs and verify them using symbolic model checking.

5 Conclusion

In this paper, we have briefly discussed some challenges in QC (the no-duplication of quantum states, their collapse after observation, their size, their space size, and their probabilistic outcome) and reviewed how state-of-the-art approaches in QSE have tackled them.

The growing availability of powerful quantum computers capable to run complex and diverse programs calls for further research in QSE. This research is required to equip more software developers with the skills to master this novel computing paradigm. Given the interdisciplinary nature of the QC community, it is crucial to reach consensus on the *quantum abstractions* [4] that should be adopted when defining high-level quantum programming languages. These languages will facilitate improved compatibility among various quantum frameworks and simplify the development of quantum programs.

Acknowledgment. This project has received funding from SES and the Luxembourg National Research Fund under the Industrial Partnership Block Grant (IPBG), ref. IPBG19/14016225/INSTRUCT.

Disclosure of Interests. The authors have no competing interests to declare that are relevant to the content of this article.

References

1. Akbar, M.A., Khan, A.A., Mahmood, S., Rafi, S.: Quantum software engineering: a new genre of computing. In: Proceedings of QCE-NE. ACM (2024)
2. Arute, F., et al.: Quantum supremacy using a programmable superconducting processor. Nature **574** (2019)
3. Di Matteo, O.: On the need for effective tools for debugging quantum programs. In: Proceedings of Q-SE. ACM (2024)
4. Di Matteo, O.: The art of abstraction in quantum software. In: 2025 IEEE/ACM International Workshop on Quantum Software Engineering (Q-SE), pp. 25–26 (2025)
5. Ding, Y., Gokhale, P., Lin, S.F., Rines, R., Propson, T., Chong, F.T.: Systematic crosstalk mitigation for superconducting qubits via frequency-aware compilation. In: Proceedings of MICRO (2020)
6. Esposito, M., Sabzevari, M.T., Ye, B., Falessi, D., Khan, A.A., Taibi, D.: Classiq: towards a translation framework to bridge the classical-quantum programming gap. In: Proceedings of QSE-NE. ACM (2024)
7. Honarvar, S., Mousavi, M.R., Nagarajan, R.: Property-based testing of quantum programs in Q#. In: Proceedings of ICSEW. ACM (2020)
8. Huang, Y., Martonosi, M.: Statistical assertions for validating patterns and finding bugs in quantum programs. In: Proceedings of ISCA. ACM (2019)

9. Jiang, N., Wang, Z., Wang, J.: Debugging quantum programs using probabilistic quantum cloning (2023)
10. Li, G., Zhou, L., Yu, N., Ding, Y., Ying, M., Xie, Y.: Projection-based runtime assertions for testing and debugging quantum programs. Proc. ACM Program. Lang. **4** (2020)
11. Liimatta, P., Taipale, P., Halunen, K., Heinosaari, T., Mikkonen, T., Stirbu, V.: Research versus practice in quantum software engineering: experiences from credit scoring use case. IEEE Softw. **41** (2024)
12. Liu, J., Byrd, G.T., Zhou, H.: Quantum circuits for dynamic runtime assertions in quantum computation. In: Proceedings of ASPLOS. ACM (2020)
13. Liu, J., Zhou, H.: Systematic approaches for precise and approximate quantum state runtime assertion. In: Proceedings of HPCA. IEEE (2021)
14. Luo, J., Zhao, P., Miao, Z., Lan, S., Zhao, J.: A comprehensive study of bug fixes in quantum programs. In: Proceedings of SANER. IEEE (2022)
15. Metwalli, S.A., Van Meter, R.: A tool for debugging quantum circuits. In: Proceedings of QCE. IEEE (2022)
16. Minh Do, C., Ogata, K.: Symbolic model checking quantum circuits in maude. PeerJ Comput. Sci. **10** (2024)
17. Murillo, J.M., et al.: Quantum software engineering: roadmap and challenges ahead. ACM Trans. Softw. Eng. Methodol. **34**(5) (2025)
18. Oldfield, N.H., Laaber, C., Yue, T., Ali, S.: Faster and better quantum software testing through specification reduction and projective measurements (2024)
19. Paltenghi, M., Pradel, M.: Bugs in quantum computing platforms: an empirical study. Proc. Program. Lang. **6** (2022)
20. Paltenghi, M., Pradel, M.: Analyzing quantum programs with lintq: a static analysis framework for qiskit. Proc. Softw. Eng. **1** (2024)
21. Sarovar, M., Proctor, T., Rudinger, K., Young, K., Nielsen, E., Blume-Kohout, R.: Detecting crosstalk errors in quantum information processors. Quantum J. **4** (2020)
22. Varga, T., Aragonés-Soria, Y., Oriol, M.: Quantum types: going beyond qubits and quantum gates. In: Proceedings of Q-SE (2024)
23. Wang, J., et al.: Quanfuzz: fuzz testing of quantum program (2018)
24. Wang, X., Arcaini, P., Yue, T., Ali, S.: Qusbt: search-based testing of quantum programs. In: Proceedings of ICSE. ACM (2022)
25. Wang, X., Arcaini, P., Yue, T., Ali, S.: Qucat: a combinatorial testing tool for quantum software. In: Proceedings of ASE. IEEE (2024)
26. Waseem, M., et al.: Qadl: prototype of quantum architecture description language (2024)
27. Ye, J., et al.: Quratest: integrating quantum specific features in quantum program testing. In: Proceedings of ASE. IEEE (2024)
28. Zhao, P., Wu, X., Li, Z., Zhao, J.: Qchecker: detecting bugs in quantum programs via static analysis. In: Proceedings of Q-SE (2023)
29. Zhao, P., Zhao, J., Ma, L.: Identifying bug patterns in quantum programs. In: Proceedings of Q-SE (2021)

1st International Workshop on Analytics for Software Product and Process Improvement (A-SPPI 2025)

Object-Centric Analysis of XES Event Logs: Integrating OCED Modeling with SPARQL Queries

Saba Latif[1], Huma Latif[2], and Muhammad Rameez Ur Rahman[3]($\boxtimes$)

[1] Sapienza University of Rome, Rome, Italy
saba.latif@uniroma1.it
[2] University of Sahiwal, Sahiwal, Pakistan
[3] Ca' Foscari University of Venice, Venice, Italy
muhammad.rahman@unive.it

Abstract. Object Centric Event Data (OCED) has gained attention in recent years within the field of process mining. However, there are still many challenges, such as connecting the XES format to object-centric approaches to enable more insightful analysis. It is important for a process miner to understand the insights and dependencies of events in the event log to see what is going on in our processes. In previous standards, the dependencies of event logs are only used to show events, but not their dependencies among each other and actions in detail as described in OCEDO. There is more information in the event log when it is revealed using the OCEDO model. It becomes more understandable and easier to grasp the concepts and deal with the processes. This paper proposes the use of Object-Centric Event Data Ontology (OCEDO) to overcome the limitations of the XES standard in event logs for process mining. We demonstrate how the OCEDO approach, integrated with SPARQL queries, can be applied to the BPIC 2013 dataset to make the relationships between events and objects more explicit. It describes dealing with the meta descriptions of the OCEDO model on a business process challenge as an event log. It improves the completeness and readability of process data, suggesting that object-centric modeling allows for richer analyses than traditional approaches.

Keywords: XES · OCEDO · Object Centric Notations · SPARQL

1 Introduction

The XES standard[1] is an XML-based format for traditional event logs. The XES standard describes event logs where a single case notion, that is, a process instance, needs to be chosen, and it is part of the Task Force on Process Mining (TFPM)[2]. However, in real life, information systems like SAP ERP systems

---

[1] https://www.tf-pm.org/resources/xes-standard/about-xes.
[2] https://www.tf-pm.org/upload/1678694478319.pdf.

© The Author(s), under exclusive license to Springer Nature Switzerland AG 2026
G. Scanniello et al. (Eds.): PROFES 2025, LNCS 16362, pp. 171–182, 2026.
https://doi.org/10.1007/978-3-032-12092-2_12

support processes that cannot be converted into a single case notation. Many objects interact with each other, and these interactions overlap. A single uniform notation to represent this behavior is missing. This leads to major data loss and prevents the actual information about object dependencies from being shown, which may cause convergence or divergence problems and result in incomplete process models [12].

Object centric process mining is a new paradigm which focuses on the object centric event logs. There are many researchers exploring this paradigm as in [21]. The Object Centric Event Data (OCED) standard can handle processes in an object-centric way by allowing multiple notations and extracting the dependencies between them as in [3]. These types of logs are not flat logging formats as in XES. The purpose of this paper is to provide a general standard for Object-Centric Event Data ontology(OCEDO)[3] and to show its working using a GraphDB schema to solve BPIC 2013 challenge question as an example. This is a new perspective towards solving BPIC 2013 questions using a novel meta model in an object-centric way [5] using semantics. It is similar to the Object-Centric Event Logs (OCELs) [7][4], but while OCEL deals only with the logs, this approach deals with the data and their dependencies. Some logging formats have been defined to address this problem, as discussed before, but they were not widely used due to their complex structures and performance issues, for example, XOC allows reconstructing the entire database state [6]. This standard aims to provide a generic way to change event data using multiple case notations for exchanging data between process mining tools and information systems.

When developing the OCEDO standard[5], the goals were interoperability to handle many languages and enable understanding across systems and platforms, generalization to support storing and using events, objects, and their attributes with possible extensions, provision of a collection of examples related to event logs and supporting information from information systems, and tool or library support for implementation in custom applications like [7,13]. The advantages of using OCEDO are that it incorporates object-centric notions using ontology and has been extensively discussed within the working group. Simplicity compared to expressiveness has been considered so that the standard is easy to understand and grasp. Standardization versus adoption has also been considered, with a focus on ensuring conversion steps are minimal and clear using knowledge graphs as in [23]. The OCED meta-model has already been circulated to the community, and feedback was sought in 2022. By structuring event data through an object-centric lens, the OCED standard aims to make process data clearer, more complete, and better suited to modern, complex information systems. The meta-model has already been shared with the community, and feedback was gathered in 2022 to refine its design and usability as shown in Fig. 1 taken from [11].

---

[3] https://www.tf-pm.org/upload/1700818140843.pdf.

[4] https://ocel-standard.org/.

[5] https://www.tf-pm.org/resources/oced-standard.

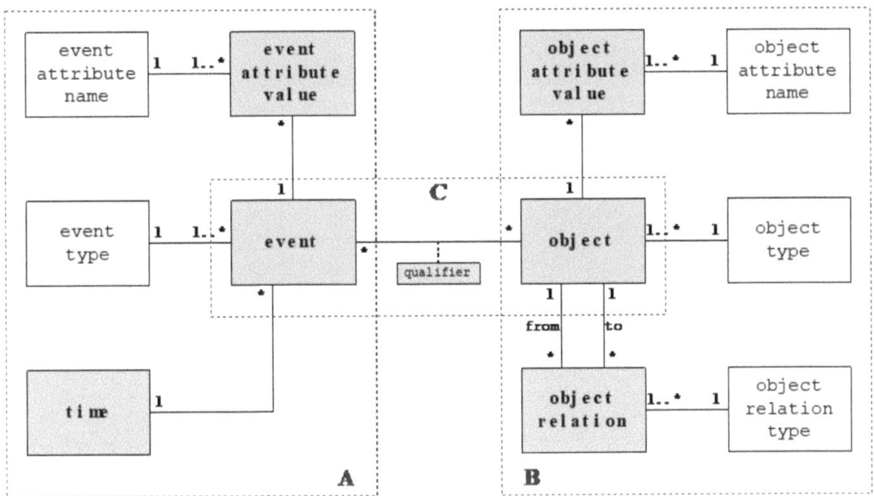

Fig. 1. The visualization of Object Centric Event Data(OCED) meta model.

This paper explores how Object-Centric Event Data Ontology(OCEDO) can enrich process mining, focusing on transforming the BPIC 2013 dataset into an object-centric representation. We argue that OCEDO captures dependencies and relationships that traditional XES-based event logs often miss. We describe the OCEDO meta-model, compare it to XES and OCEL, and demonstrate how event-object relationships can be queried using SPARQL to gain deeper insights. The main purpose of this work is to illustrate how OCEDO can be used to convert XES logs into an object-centric format, providing additional insights and more meaningful results. We address the technical aspects of process mining and event log modeling in an object-centric manner. The paper offers a concrete example of how OCEDO structures can be represented and queried using the BPIC 2013 event log and solving one question asked in BPIC 2013 event log. Additionally, OCEDO complements existing standards, such as OCEL 2.0. Its purpose is to work alongside these tools, offering an alternative or supplementary option based on the user's requirements.

In Sect. 2, we present the BPIC 2013 Challenge Event Log description and comparison of OCEDO with other approaches. Section 3 describes the explanation of the Event-Object Relationship of OCEDO in SPARQL Query. Section 4 discusses related work on existing standards and techniques for modeling event logs and object-centric data, and finally, Sect. 5 concludes the paper and outlines directions for future research.

2   BPIC 2013 Challenge Event Log

The BPIC 2013 event log [10] is a real-life dataset often used in process mining research. It contains events related to the customer service process of a large

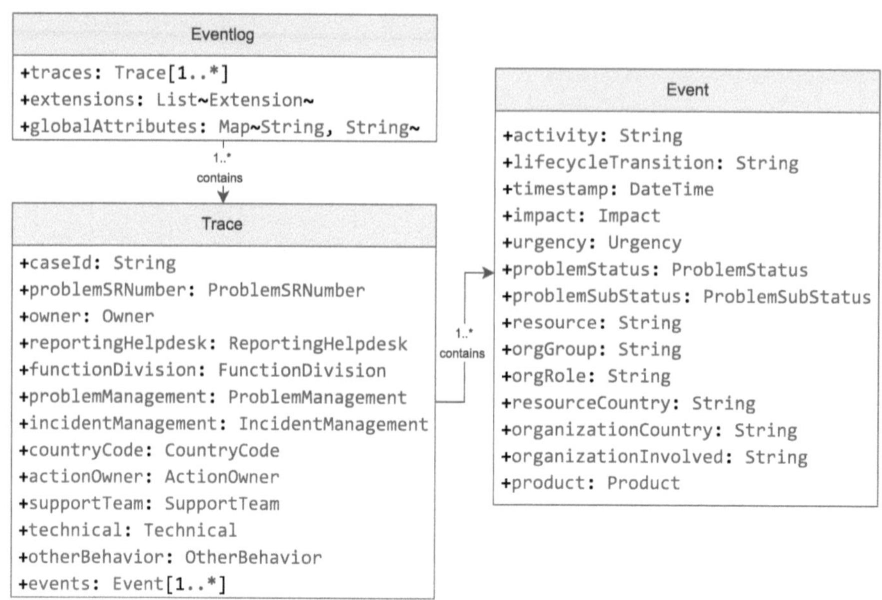

Fig. 2. The abstract class diagram of the BPIC 2013 event log in XES representing event log, trace, and event attributes. The full diagram is available at the link https://tinyurl.com/BPIC2013ClassDiagram

Dutch insurance company [1]. Each event in the log records activities like receiving, handling, and closing customer requests in process mining [2]. This event log is valuable because it shows how cases move through different departments and how long each step takes. It includes details such as the timestamp of each event, the resources involved (like employees or teams), and the type of service requested. Researchers and analysts use the BPIC 2013 log to discover patterns, find inefficiencies [9], and suggest improvements in business processes [20]. It helps in understanding what work happens and how it is compared to how it is supposed to happen. A class diagram of the whole BPIC 2013 challenge in XES format is shown in Fig. 2. By analyzing this event log, we can gain insights into real operational challenges and performance issues in service processes. An example of the BPIC 2013 challenge in the OCED meta model representation is shown in Fig. 2. We did this conversion by using the techniques of representing event logs in OCEDO model using semantics. A diagram showing BPIC 2013 event log example converted in OCEDO representation where events and objects are related with qualifiers and object to object relations 3. The final output of our technique is in turtle file format, which can be used as it is in SPARQL queries analysis. The representation is depicted in a turtle file in the OCED.

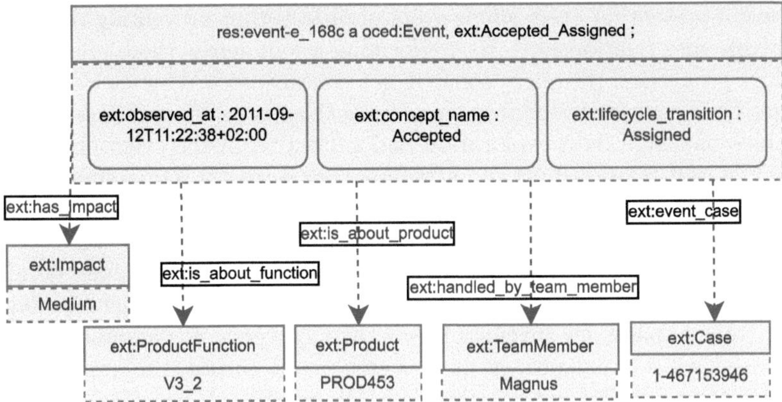

Fig. 3. An example showing BPIC 2013 event log example converted in OCEDO representation where events and objects are related with qualifiers and object to object relations in object centric manner.

3   Explanation of the Event-Object Relationship of OCEDO Into SPARQL Query

The demonstration of BPIC 2013 challenge into OCED is derived from the repository link[6]. Based on the information provided here, we are analyzing the BPIC 2013 event log. This section elaborates on the purpose, methodology, and advantages of the provided SPARQL query, specifically designed to interact with data structured according to the file named 2013 small integrated ttl. Based on the provided information, we analyze the BPIC 2013 event log and answer one of its questions to demonstrate the power of our approach.[7] The core question addressed by this query revolves around understanding the intricate relationships between events and objects within a given dataset. It seeks to uncover specific instances where an event is associated with an object, along with their respective classifications, types, and any relevant descriptive attributes. Fundamentally, it aims to provide a comprehensive, granular view of the event-object landscape as modeled by the OCED ontology(OCEDO), allowing for detailed data exploration. This question is precisely solved by leveraging the explicit ext:EventObject class and its foundational properties defined within the 2013 small integrated turtle file. The query systematically identifies every ext:EventObject instance, connecting an event (ext:event) to an object (ext:object). For each such connection, it proceeds to retrieve auxiliary information: an optional classifier value that might categorize the event object pairing; the event type and time for the associated event; and the object type for the related object. Crucially, the strategic use of OPTIONAL clauses ensures that the query remains robust, returning results even if certain attributes or proper-

---

[6] https://gitlab.isis.tuwien.ac.at/Ekaputra/ocedo.

[7] https://ceur-ws.org/Vol-1052/vinst_data_set.pdf.

ties are not present for every single event or object, thus preventing the exclusion of valuable core relationships. By performing a join across these related entities and their properties, the query constructs a cohesive record for each event-object linkage. The benefits derived from employing this query are multifaceted. Firstly, it enables thorough data exploration and validation of the event-object model, confirming that relationships and attributes are correctly represented as per the ontology's design. Secondly, it provides a foundational dataset for qualitative analysis, allowing users to identify specific event-object interactions, understand their context through types and classifiers, and examine granular details via attributes. This is particularly valuable for scenarios where understanding individual event impacts on specific objects, or vice versa, is paramount. Thirdly, by exposing all relevant properties in a structured output, the query facilitates further data processing and visualization. The results can be easily consumed by other tools or scripts for more advanced analytics, reporting, or graphical representations, aiding in pattern recognition and anomaly detection within event-object dynamics. Lastly, its adherence to the ontology's structure makes it a highly interpretable and maintainable query, directly reflecting the logical design of the knowledge graph as shown in Fig. 4.

3.1   Questions of BPIC 2013 Challenge

The process owner poses a number of possible questions on which answers are sought:

1. **Push to Front (incidents only)**: Is there evidence that cases are pushed to the 2nd and 3rd line too often or too soon?
2. **Ping Pong Behavior**: How often do cases ping pong between teams, and which teams are more or less involved in ping-ponging?
3. **Wait User Abuse**: Is the "wait user" substatus abused to hide problems with the total resolution time?
4. **Process Conformity per Organization**: Where do the two IT organizations differ, and why?

Ping-Pong Behavior. This analysis addresses Question 2 from the BPIC 2013 challenge, focusing on identifying ping-pong behavior between support teams. The objective is to quantify how frequently cases bounce between teams and determine which teams are most involved in this inefficient practice. Our solution implements a sophisticated pattern-matching approach that detects when a support team handles a case, transfers it to another team, and subsequently receives the case backâĂŤindicating workflow inefficiencies and potential process gaps. The analysis identifies the specific teams engaged in ping-pong exchanges, measures the frequency of such occurrences, and ranks teams by their level of involvement. By providing clear metrics on inter-team case transfers, this analysis enables organizations to pinpoint problematic handover patterns and implement targeted process improvements to reduce unnecessary case bouncing and improve overall support efficiency.

Ping-Pong Behavior Analysis. This section elaborates in detail on the purpose, methodology, and advantages of the provided SPARQL query, which is specifically designed to effectively interact with data structured according to the `2013_small-integrated.ttl` ontology. The core question addressed by this query revolves around understanding the intricate relationships between events and objects within a given dataset, with the explicit goal of identifying and quantifying the impact of the **'Ping-Pong behavior'** event on **accepted cases**. The analysis addresses the problem of detecting ping-pong behavior in support incident handling by implementing a sophisticated pattern matching approach. This solution identifies cases where a support team initially handles a case, transfers it to another team, and subsequently receives the case back a pattern that indicates inefficient workflow and potential process gaps. The core innovation lies in using an EXISTS subquery that searches for a specific three-event sequence: Team A handles the case at time T1, Team B handles it at a later time T2, and Team A again handles it at an even later time T3, with the critical constraint that Team A and Team B must be distinct entities. This approach successfully solves the detection problem by efficiently scanning event sequences without requiring consecutive event matching, thereby capturing ping-pong behavior even when intermediate handling events occur between the key transitions. The implementation aggregates results by case while calculating temporal boundaries, providing a comprehensive view of each case's lifecycle alongside a clear boolean indicator of ping-pong occurrence, enabling effective monitoring and process optimization.

```
 1  PREFIX ocedo: <https://w3id.org/ocedo/core#>
 2  PREFIX ext: <https://w3id.org/ocedo/ext#>
 3  PREFIX xsd: <http://www.w3.org/2001/XMLSchema#>
 4
 5  SELECT ?case
 6         (COUNT(?pingPong) > 0 AS ?hasPingPong)
 7         (MIN(?time) AS ?minTime)
 8         (MAX(?time) AS ?maxTime)
 9  WHERE {
10    {
11      SELECT ?case ?time (GROUP_CONCAT(?team) AS ?teams)
12      WHERE {\autoedited2{
13        ?}event ext:event_case ?case ;
14               ocedo:observed_at ?time ;
15               ext:handled_by_support_team ?team .
16      }
17      GROUP BY ?case ?time
18      ORDER BY ?case ?time
19    }
20    BIND(
21      EXISTS {\autoedited2{
22        ?}e1 ext:event_case ?case ;
23             ext:handled_by_support_team ?teamA ;
24             ocedo:observed_at ?time1 .\autoedited2{
```

```
25    ?}e2 ext:event_case ?case ;
26        ext:handled_by_support_team ?teamB ;
27        ocedo:observed_at ?time2 .\autoedited2{
28    ?}e3 ext:event_case ?case ;
29        ext:handled_by_support_team ?teamA ;
30        ocedo:observed_at ?time3 .
31    FILTER(?teamA != ?teamB && ?time1 < ?time2 && ?time2 < ?time3)
32    } AS ?pingPong
33  )
34 }
35 GROUP BY ?case
36 ORDER BY ?hasPingPong
```

	case		hasPingPong		minTime		maxTime	
1	res:object-o_ 0015cc277c538491174d3375a1375b6eb8f 16ae3		"true"^^xsd:boolean		"2012-05-02T12:51:53+02:00"^^xsd:dateTime		"2012-05-02T13:01:43+02:00"^^xsd:dateTime	
2	res:object-o_ 001ae2643c6f406ce8378d6b76e470d6751 0b8db		"true"^^xsd:boolean		"2012-05-01T12:36:34+02:00"^^xsd:dateTime		"2012-05-09T01:12:09+02:00"^^xsd:dateTime	
3	res:object-o_ 001ae84f05c4eb933de9043a35591aeb1e2 80866		"true"^^xsd:boolean		"2012-05-03T10:23:29+02:00"^^xsd:dateTime		"2012-05-12T01:17:14+02:00"^^xsd:dateTime	
4	res:object-o_ 00288de6c532142a833f6160e933ba8d8df 9c71a		"true"^^xsd:boolean		"2012-04-27T11:17:04+02:00"^^xsd:dateTime		"2012-05-12T01:18:44+02:00"^^xsd:dateTime	
5	res:object-o_ 00350e957a80f80f7445ea1703c54154135 2b5a4		"true"^^xsd:boolean		"2012-05-03T09:01:45+02:00"^^xsd:dateTime		"2012-05-11T01:19:26+02:00"^^xsd:dateTime	

Fig. 4. Result of BPIC 2013 in the form of a Graph in GraphDB extracted by running the above SPARQL Query.

4   Related Work

The field of *object-centric process mining* (OCPM) has emerged as a significant advancement beyond traditional event-centric approaches, enabling more comprehensive analysis of business processes involving multiple interacting objects. Also, event logs are the basis for applying process mining techniques. A typical event log consists of a case ID, which represents a unique instance of a process [5], for example, a student or any product available for sale online. It includes other tags such as an activity, a timestamp, and additional characteristics in the form of key-value pairs, such as login, booking a test, or placing an online order in the form of XES event logs. Further, the study focusing on how event logs are represented, as they are essential for process mining by recording the sequence, context, and relationships of activities, is presented in [4].

Recent research has made substantial contributions to this paradigm through theoretical foundations, practical frameworks, and novel applications. The conceptual foundation was established through the formalization of *object-centric*

Table 1. Comparison of OCEDO approach with XES and OCEL event logs providing difference and similarities

Key Aspect	OCEDO[a]	XES[b]	OCEL[c]
Flexibility	Focus on events and objects where object interactions trigger events	Stream of data as independent events in a generic, loosely-coupled manner	Object-centric, allowing events to relate to multiple objects, improving realism
Extensibility	Rigid standardized approach with predefined object attributes and behavior	Easier adaptation to changing requirements	Moderate supports extensions but still constrained by JSON/XML schema
Scalability	Challenges due to tightly coupled objects and complex events	Stream-based, more scalable with large volumes and parallel processing	Better scalability than XES by grouping events with multiple objects, though still bound by storage overhead
Interoperability	Generic knowledge graph format easily shared across systems	Tighter dependency on XML limits interoperability	Designed for interoperability, using JSON and XML formats widely supported
Event Processing	Event driven programming where events trigger specific object actions	Requires parsing of flat event streams; events not tied to objects	Supports querying across objects and events, better suited for complex analysis

[a] https://www.tf-pm.org/resources/oced-standard
[b] https://www.tf-pm.org/resources/xes-standard   [c] https://ocel-standard.org/

event logs (OCEL), with [7] introducing the OCEL 2.0 specification that standardizes representation formats. Building on this, [3] provided crucial definitions for cases and variants in object-centric contexts, while [6] developed the OC-PM framework for analyzing both event logs and process models from an object-centric perspective. Several extensions have enhanced the capabilities of object-centric approaches. [13] proposed methods for improving data-awareness in object-centric logs, and [21] introduced OCPM^2 to address event data extraction challenges. The practical implementation aspects were explored by [23] through knowledge graph representations. The examination of formal methods establishes essential groundwork for enhancing process mining approaches, especially within object-centric paradigms. Further, techniques from formal methods offer substantial methodological support that can strengthen process mining frameworks. TLA+ has proven effective for specifying and verifying concurrent processes in distributed systems [18], while finite automata provide systematic structures for modeling state-based control logic and checking event sequence compliance [22]. Graph based modeling demonstrates significant utility in representing complex relationships in resource allocation and state transition scenarios [17]. The application of formal verification methods to ensure smart contract robustness in blockchain contexts [15] indicates a viable approach for managing object-centric event log complexities. Additionally, formal taxonomies enable organized classification of security threats and process deviations [19], and complex event processing techniques facilitate real-time monitoring and analysis of event streams [16]. These established methodologies constitute the foundational basis for OCEDO, representing a new paradigm that integrates formal verification rigor with object-centric process mining principles. The BPIC 2013 dataset [10] has served as an important benchmark, with earlier process mining techniques [1,2,20] laying the groundwork for multi perspective analysis that later influenced object-centric approaches. Comparative studies like [9] demonstrated the advantages of richer log representations for variant analysis. Recent systematic evaluations by [8] have documented the field's progress while identifying remaining challenges. Emerging applications are expanding the paradigm's reach, including innovative work by [14] applying object-centric methods to blockchain transaction analysis. While these advances have established OCPM as a powerful paradigm, open challenges remain in areas of scalability, standardization, and integration with existing process mining infrastructures. In this Table 1, we are showing a comparison of OCEDO with other approaches to show its viability. We are presenting a comparison with XES, OCEL and OCEDO techniques from different perspectives including flexibility, extensibility, scalability, interoperability and event processing.

5   Conclusion

This paper explored the application of Object-Centric Event Data in the context of business process analysis, particularly in addressing the BPIC 2013 challenge questions. We demonstrated how event logs can be enriched to reveal deeper insights into process dependencies, interactions, and underlying behaviors going beyond traditional event-centric approaches that often overlook intricate relationships between events and objects. The study highlighted the advantages of OCEDO in enhancing process mining by providing a more comprehensive, structured, and intuitive representation of event data. Unlike conventional methods that primarily focus on sequential event logs, the OCED model captures object interactions, dependencies, and contextual attributes, enabling process miners to gain a more holistic understanding of process dynamics. This shift not only improves analytical depth but also simplifies the interpretation of complex process behaviors. Furthermore, the implementation of OCEDO on the BPIC 2013 dataset illustrated its practical utility in uncovering hidden patterns, improving traceability, and supporting more informed decision-making. By adopting an object-centric perspective, organizations can move beyond simplistic event logs and embrace a richer, more expressive framework for process analysis. Future research could explore the scalability of this approach, its integration with other process mining techniques, and its application across diverse industries. Furthermore, empirical evaluations, benchmarking, and validation on additional real-world datasets are planned.

References

1. van der Aalst, W.M.P., Adriansyah, A., van Dongen, B.F., Carmona, J., Verbeek, M., Wynn, M.: Packages: improving process mining results to align with the real process. In: Business Process Management Workshops (BPM 2013). Lecture Notes in Business Information Processing, vol. 171, pp. 407–414. Springer (2014)
2. van der Aalst, W.M.P., Adriansyah, A., Munoz-Gama, J., Carmona, J.: Multi-perspective process explorer: combining visual analytics and process mining. In: Enterprise, Business-Process and Information Systems Modeling (BPMDS/EMMSAD 2013). Lecture Notes in Business Information Processing, vol. 147, pp. 25–37. Springer (2013)
3. Adams, J.N., Schuster, D., Schmitz, S., Schuh, G., van der Aalst, W.M.: Defining cases and variants for object-centric event data. In: 2022 4th International Conference on Process Mining (ICPM), pp. 128–135 (2022)
4. et al., X.W.G.: IEEE standard for extensible event stream (XES) for achieving interoperability in event logs and event streams. IEEE Std 1849-2016 (2016)
5. Berti, A., van der Aalst, W.M.P.: An object-centric perspective on event logs. In: Business Process Management Workshops (BPM 2020 International Workshops). Lecture Notes in Business Information Processing, vol. 409, pp. 128–140. Springer (2021)
6. Berti, A., van der Aalst, W.M.: Oc-pm: analyzing object-centric event logs and process models. Int. J. Softw. Tools Technol. Transfer **25**(1), 1–17 (2023)
7. Berti, A., et al.: OCEL (object-centric event log) 2.0 specification. Tech. rep., RWTH Aachen University (2024)
8. Berti, A., Montali, M., van der Aalst, W.M.P.: Advancements and challenges in object-centric process mining: a systematic literature review. arXiv preprint arXiv:2311.08795 (2023)
9. Carmona, J., et al.: Benchmarking business process variant generation techniques using event logs. Softw. Syst. Model. **17**(2), 675–699 (2018)
10. van Dongen, B.F.: BPI challenge 2013 event log. Dataset (2013). https://data.4tu. nl/articles/dataset/BPI_Challenge_2013/12689204
11. Fahland, D., et al.: Towards a simple and extensible standard for object-centric event data (oced)–core model, design space, and lessons learned. arXiv preprint arXiv:2410.14495 (2024)
12. Ghahfarokhi, A., Park, G., van der Aalst, W.M.P.: Multi-dimensional event data in object-centric process mining. Inf. Syst. **115**, 102245 (2023). https://doi.org/10. 1016/j.is.2023.102245
13. Goossens, A., De Smedt, J., Vanthienen, J., van der Aalst, W.M.: Enhancing data-awareness of object-centric event logs. In: International Conference on Process Mining, pp. 18–30. Springer (2022)
14. Hobeck, R., Berti, A., Weber, I., van der Aalst, W.: Object-centric process mining for blockchain applications: extracting and representing ethereum execution data in OCEL 2.0. Enterprise Model. Inf. Syst. Architectures **20**(2), 1–15 (2025)
15. Latif, S.: Formal methods as a catalyst for robust smart contracts in blockchain. In: 2025 International Conference on Emerging Technologies in Electronics, Computing and Communication (ICETECC), pp. 1–6. IEEE (apr 2025)
16. Latif, S., Afzaal, H., Zafar, N.A.: Intelligent traffic monitoring and guidance system for smart city. In: 2018 International Conference on Computing, Mathematics and Engineering Technologies (iCoMET), pp. 1–6. IEEE (2018). https://doi.org/10. 1109/ICOMET.2018.8346360

17. Latif, S., Afzaal, H., Zafar, N.A.: Modelling of graph-based smart parking system using internet of things. In: 2018 International Conference on Frontiers of Information Technology (FIT), pp. 7–12. IEEE (2018). https://doi.org/10.1109/FIT.2018.00011

18. Latif, S., Rehman, A., Zafar, N.A.: Blockchain and IoT based formal model of smart waste management system using TLA+. In: 2019 International Conference on Frontiers of Information Technology (FIT), pp. 119–124. IEEE (2019). https://doi.org/10.1109/FIT47737.2019.00030

19. Latif, S., Zafar, N.A.: A survey of security and privacy issues in IoT for smart cities. In: 2017 Fifth International Conference on Aerospace Science & Engineering (ICASE), pp. 1–8. IEEE (2017). https://doi.org/10.1109/ICASE.2017.8374252

20. de Leoni, M., van der Aalst, W.M.P.: Data-aware process mining: discovering decisions in processes using alignments. In: Proceedings of the 23rd International Conference on Cooperative Information Systems (CoopIS 2013). Lecture Notes in Computer Science, vol. 8185, pp. 146–163. Springer (2013)

21. Miri, N., Khayatbashi, S., Zdravkovic, J., Jalali, A.: Ocpm 2: extending the process mining methodology for object-centric event data extraction. In: International Conference on Business Process Modeling, Development and Support, pp. 123–140. Springer (2025)

22. Rehman, A., Latif, S., Zafar, N.A.: Automata based railway gate control system at level crossing. In: 2019 International Conference on Communication Technologies (ComTech), pp. 30–35. IEEE (2019). https://doi.org/10.1109/COMTECH.2019.8737805

23. Swevels, A., Fahland, D., Montali, M.: Implementing object-centric event data models in event knowledge graphs. In: Process Mining Workshops – ICPM 2023 International Workshops, Lecture Notes in Business Information Processing, vol. 503, pp. 431–443. Springer (2024)

User Engagement and Adaptive Optimisation in Renewable Energy Communities

Daniele Marletta$^{(\boxtimes)}$ ⬤, Erika Scaletta ⬤, and Emiliano Tramontana ⬤

Dipartimento di Matematica e Informatica, University of Catania,
95125 Catania, Italy
`{daniele.marletta,erika.scaletta}@phd.unict.it,`
`tramontana@dmi.unict.it`

Abstract. The rapid growth of renewable energy sources is accelerating the transition towards decentralised electricity systems. However, the variable nature of such sources and user consumption profiles present a significant challenge to achieving a sustainable energy balance. This paper introduces an innovative software system for adaptive energy management in Energy Communities, where a data-driven aggregator collects energy data, defines flexible threshold-based balancing strategies, and coordinates user actions by means of a gamified mobile application. Hence, users would become active participants in the balancing process. We evaluated the proposed system using simulations based on publicly available data. The results showed that our system can be effectively used to address energy fluctuations through coordinated data-driven responses, harnessing the potential of a renewable energy infrastructure.

Keywords: Software system · Energy Community · Gamification

1 Introduction

In recent years, there has been a growing adoption of renewable energy sources (RES), mainly wind and solar photovoltaic (PV), whose share is projected to increase from 30% in 2023 to 46% in 2030 [12]. This trend reflects global efforts to decarbonise energy systems and reduce dependence on fossil fuels. However, RES are inherently variable, as their output depends on changing natural and meteorological conditions. These unpredictable fluctuations pose several challenges, including maintaining grid stability, balancing electricity supply with demand, and handling the inaccuracy of energy forecasts [28].

In this context, a promising solution is represented by Energy Communities (ECs), defined by European Union directives as open and voluntary organisations of citizens engaged in energy-related activities [8]. The new prosumer role was introduced, as the evolution of the traditional consumer, who can also generate electricity using RES, mainly solar PV and energy storage systems (ESS) [18]. PV-equipped prosumers can feed surplus energy into the electrical

G. Scanniello et al. (Eds.): PROFES 2025, LNCS 16362, pp. 183–192, 2026.
https://doi.org/10.1007/978-3-032-12092-2_13

grid, and ESS-enabled prosumers can strategically charge or discharge their batteries to maximise self-consumption [19]. Data measuring the power consumption, the generation and storage of EC members are remotely managed by the local aggregator, an entity that acts as a central orchestrator of distributed RES, and coordinates energy optimisation strategies to support grid operations [15]. To realise the full potential of ECs, active and sustained member participation is paramount. This can be fostered by methodologies and stimuli that promote energy-aware decisions. One such methodology is demand-response, where financial compensation is offered to users who adjust their energy usage in response to requests from an aggregator or system operator [11]. In addition, gamification has been applied in the energy domain [14]. The main idea is to apply elements of game design, such as challenges and leaderboards, to stimulate changes in energy consumption or production. Although these approaches have shown promising results, the integration of games with financial rewards and community-wide energy balancing strategies is still limited [24].

The distinctive element of our system lies in the demand adaptation mechanisms, which are based on continuous monitoring and stimuli sent to users when certain thresholds have been reached. The proposed approach aims to make users active participants in the balancing process. Unlike traditional approaches, which assume supply as a fixed constraint without requiring any modulation from users, our system integrates adaptive incentives and engagement mechanisms to obtain concrete contributions to the energy balance. Building on this concept, this paper proposes a software system that combines gamified engagement with data-driven balancing strategies, derived from the community's aggregated energy profile. Therefore, financial rewards and targeted challenges are proposed to EC members via a mobile application. The integration of incentives and socially engaging features should encourage users to align with the target energy use. Our main contributions include: (i) a software architecture for adaptive energy management in ECs, which combines monitoring, flexible threshold-based strategy definition, and member coordination via a mobile application; (ii) a gamified incentive mechanism based on financial rewards and targeted challenges to promote energy-aware decisions aligned with the community's welfare; (iii) the evaluation of the approach on multiple EC configurations using a publicly available dataset. We show that our approach can effectively tackle energy fluctuations by means of a coordinated response that builds on observed user patterns to better harness the renewable energy infrastructure.

The remainder of this paper is structured as follows. Section 2 presents related works in the field of energy management in EC. Section 3 presents our proposed software architecture. Section 4 describes our analysis and assessment on real-world data. Finally, Sect. 5 draws our conclusions.

2   Related Works

Several attempts have been made to address the challenge of energy balance in systems with a high share of renewables, and several strategies have been proposed to manage the inherent variability of production and demand.

Power systems that integrated renewable sources have highlighted the variability of production and consumption and the difficulty of ensuring stability. The analysis based on production and consumption behaviours allowed the formulation of sufficient conditions that guarantee stability and energy balance [13]. Focusing on short-term energy balance, an optimisation model was proposed for hybrid energy hubs, which operates at 15-min intervals. The approach focused on cost minimization while ensuring efficient integration of PV and storage at the building level [27]. In contrast, our work shifts from building-level optimisation to the broader context of ECs, highlighting the collective impact of production-consumption imbalances and proposing a control framework based on hourly adaptation proposals and real-time incentive signals.

A dynamic energy price strategy was proposed in a simulated microgrid to achieve an efficient balance between demand and generation from seven renewable sources [2]. Compared to this approach, our work focuses on ECs where an aggregator manages incentives and disincentives, and provides an analysis that more closely reflects real operating conditions, making it more useful for decision support. The framework presented in [6] implements a centralised strategy for optimal scheduling of storage systems in ECs under an incentive-based scheme. In contrast, our approach introduces an adaptive system that coordinates energy management by actively involving consumers through a gamified application. Other works address technical and economic aspects of distributed power systems, such as voltage control [29] and aggregator-based coordination to maximize profit and decrease cost [10].

In addition to these technical contributions, several studies have explored gamification as a tool to promote energy-related behavioural change. Some works focus on user engagement in smart communities through tailored interfaces and social competition [23], while others analyse consumer participation in virtual power plants using behavioural models and gamified applications [5]. The energy game presented in [17] enables users to cooperate and set targets in a virtual neighbourhood for maximising energy savings. In contrast, our approach integrates a gamified application into a comprehensive framework that actively monitors grid conditions and activates adaptive energy management strategies.

An interdisciplinary framework was proposed to promote residential user engagement through gamification techniques [3]. The adopted behavioural model (transtheoretical model) defines the requirements for behavioural change, which are supported by a technical architecture and game design elements classified into five categories. Unlike our approach, which relies on a software system integrating a gamified app with dynamic incentives, this study focuses on the motivational and social dimensions of behavioural change.

3   Proposed Energy Management System

We propose a software system for managing ECs designed to dynamically monitor energy flows, assess net energy balance, and coordinate adaptive energy balancing strategies.

Unlike traditional approaches, our work integrates consumption adjustment mechanisms based on continuous monitoring and threshold comparisons, aiming to provide consumers with incentives to contribute to balancing. Thanks to this strategy, consumers could receive benefits and become more active towards a common goal whereas the previous proposals do not seek a real-time modulation from users. Figure 1 illustrates the system architecture, showing the main entities and data flows.

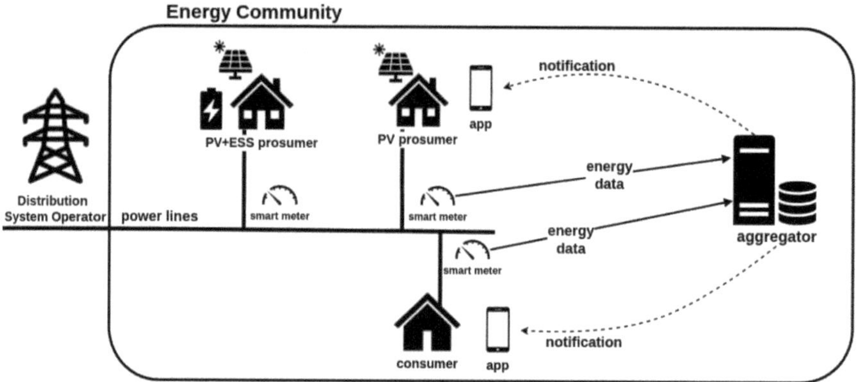

Fig. 1. Architecture diagram of the proposed software system for adaptive energy management in Energy Communities.

The distribution system operator (DSO) manages the electricity distribution networks and infrastructure and is responsible for delivering power to consumers and prosumers. In our system, we consider two types of prosumers: those equipped with PV panels and those with both PV panels and ESS. Smart meters (SMs) are embedded IoT devices installed on users' premises, integrating sensing and communication capabilities. These devices measure the incoming or outgoing flow of electricity and periodically transmit the recorded data, over the Internet, to the energy aggregator, which is one of the main components of our system. Data communication is supported by readily available technologies, such as Java RMI or HTTP REST (according to the characteristics of smart meters), which also cater for security requirements, such as authentication, data encryption, etc. [25]. Additionally, privacy and non-repudiation can be obtained using blockchain technology [20–22], and service availability by using microservice and cloud computing.

The aggregator is a cloud-based service that collects energy data from the SMs of community members and stores such data in a local database. By combining data from SMs, the aggregator actively monitors the net energy balance of the EC. Based on such data, it checks the real-time proximity to critical thresholds and readily detects abnormal fluctuations by comparing observed values with predefined limits. These thresholds are either derived from optimal consumption profiles or agreed upon with the DSO to maintain grid stability. The threshold value is set to a percentage of the desired overall energy profile, e.g. 1% below the maximum observed value of the consumption curve. However, this threshold value is considered provisional and is meant to be recalibrated after empirical validation in field trials, since the actual parameter cannot be uniquely determined in advance and depends on the characteristics of the community. The DSO itself must guarantee minimum and maximum levels of supply that vary over time with the load. Therefore, our thresholds are designed to follow these profiles: for instance, when consumption approaches its maximum and the system detects values within 1% of that limit, the aggregator triggers adaptive stimuli such as "reduce consumption" signals or incentives. This mechanism allows thresholds to act as flexible indicators, tuned to operational needs, and refined through real-world validation. The computational resources needed to calculate the aggregated energy consumption and compare this with the desired profile are very low and are dynamically provisioned in a cloud computing environment.

When net energy exceeds the thresholds, the aggregator sends a notification to users requesting changes in their energy consumption patterns. E.g., if monitoring data reveal that net energy falls below a predefined consumption threshold, users are signalled to reduce their energy demand, and ESS-enabled prosumers are requested to discharge their batteries into the grid. Conversely, in overproduction scenarios, ESS-enabled prosumers are notified to redirect their energy surplus to charging their batteries. According to user preferences, some devices can be deployed to have an automatic adjustment of consumption in the said scenarios.

Aggregator's requests are delivered to users via in-app notifications. The app includes gamification features and financial incentives, defined by the aggregator, to promote user participation [1,7]. Incentives can be defined according to several strategies, such as a fixed rate per kilowatt-hour [4,9]. These incentives are integrated into a gamified system that stimulates both individual and collective engagement. E.g., users can receive time-bound missions such as "reduce your consumption between 6 p.m. and 8 p.m. for three consecutive days", earning points and badges upon completion, which can then be converted into financial rewards. A leaderboard also rewards the consistency of positive behaviour over time, similar to streak-based systems, granting extra points to reliable users who continuously contribute to the balance.

In addition, community-wide challenges can be launched, where the entire group aims to collectively reduce a certain peak; if successful, all participants share in the rewards. These mechanisms combine personal motivation with social recognition, reinforcing sustained participation while directly supporting the adaptive balancing strategies of the aggregator. The adaptive strategies of the aggregator, combined with financial incentive schemes, enable a coordinated response to address energy fluctuations, illustrating the key role of the proposed software system in realising the full potential and flexibility of renewable energy infrastructure.

4   Experiments and Discussion

To evaluate the feasibility of our proposed software system, we performed an analysis and assessment of energy data using a dataset for residential consumers publicly available and presented in [30]. The dataset was built using real-world energy data from 2000 consumers living in the same neighbourhood, aggregated with renewable energy sources data such as the generation of PV panels and ESS operations. Specifically, the PV profiles were created using the solar ninja tool [26], and the ESS profiles were obtained from real-world industrial specification and data [30]. Each row in the dataset contains hourly energy consumption/production data in kilowatt-hour (kWh), labelled with a season.

Real-world ECs greatly vary among different countries, ranging from fewer than 50 members to over 2000 [16]. In our analysis, we considered the scenario of a medium-sized EC comprising 400 participants. In total, we designed and analysed ten different EC configurations. Two types of prosumers were considered: (i) PV-equipped prosumers, and (ii) PV+ESS-equipped prosumers. For each type, we modelled five ECs with prosumer ratios of 0%, 25%, 33%, 50%, and 75%, respectively. For each configuration, hourly energy profiles were obtained as follows. Based on the predetermined prosumer ratio, entries were randomly extracted from the consumer and prosumer datasets. To account for the variability introduced by randomness, the sampling process was repeated 500 times for each configuration. The final energy values were obtained by averaging the hourly data across all 500 iterations.

Figure 2 compares the seasonal energy profiles of ECs with 75% prosumers. Negative values on the y-axis indicate that energy is imported from the grid, while positive values represent energy that is exported to the grid.

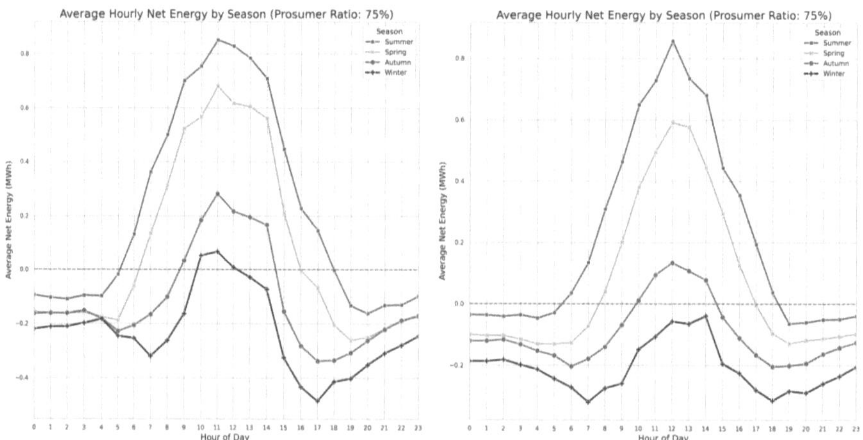

Fig. 2. Average hourly net energy by season for a community of 400 members, 75% prosumers having PV on the left, and having PV and ESS on the right.

Both EC configurations exhibit a similar trend, with surplus energy during daylight hours and net imports in the evening. However, the PV+ESS scenario features a smoother profile, with lower midday peaks and reduced evening demand. This suggests that ESS charge during peak solar generation and discharge their stored energy later in the day.

Table 1 and Table 2 show daily net energy balances (in MWh), for all seasons and different ratios of PV prosumers and PV+ESS prosumers, respectively.

Table 1. EC energy balance for several PV prosumers ratios (MWh)

	Prosumers Ratio				
Season	0%	25%	33%	50%	75%
Spring	−5.05	−2.77	−2.03	−0.47	1.81
Summer	−3.7	−0.71	0.25	2.28	5.24
Autumn	−4.94	−4.17	−3.93	−3.44	−2.69
Winter	−6.33	−6.06	−5.95	−5.77	−5.49

Table 2. EC energy balance for several PV+ESS prosumers ratios (MWh)

	Prosumers Ratio				
Season	0%	25%	33%	50%	75%
Spring	−5.06	−2.82	−2.11	−0.57	1.62
Summer	−3.7	−0.75	0.18	2.2	5.12
Autumn	−4.94	−4.08	−3.8	−3.2	−2.31
Winter	−6.32	−5.9	−5.75	−5.49	−5.06

The analysis of these tables reveals that the inclusion of prosumers significantly reduces the overall energy consumption in the EC. This effect is particularly noticeable in spring and summer, where a prosumer ratio of only 25% leads to a consumption decrease of approximately 45% and 80%, respectively. Both spring and summer feature a net daily surplus when the prosumer ratio is 75%, and summer in particular experiences a dramatic increase from the net consumption of -3.7 MWh (0% prosumers) to the net production of over 5 MWh. In seasons with less solar irradiance, while the net balance remains negative across all configurations, it can be observed that PV+ESS prosumers provide consistently lower values than the PV prosumers case.

Overall, the results of our experiments indicate that storage systems help mitigate peak consumption and suggest that ESS-enabled residential users actively engage in optimising battery usage, revealing an awareness of the strategic value of these storage devices at the individual level. The aggregator can capitalise on this trend by offering financial incentives that further promote and scale behaviours that align with optimal energy management. Its access to aggregated data enables the definition of adaptive strategies from a community-wide perspective. Consequently, the gamified app can present users with targeted and carefully designed challenges, such as "Maintain your battery charge above 50% throughout the week" or "Reduce your energy use by 20% between 6 p.m. and 8 p.m.". These challenges, supported by financial rewards and social features such as leaderboards, further reinforce user engagement and align with community-level balancing.

5   Conclusions

This paper presented an adaptive software system that enables coordinated energy management in energy communities. By collecting data from smart meters installed on consumer and prosumer premises, the community aggregator actively monitors the overall energy balance. When predefined usage thresholds are exceeded, the aggregator notifies users via a gamified app that promotes optimal energy use through financial incentives and targeted challenges. The key contribution lies precisely in the demand adaptation mechanisms, which combine continuous monitoring, threshold-based triggers, and user incentives to actively involve consumers in the balancing process.

The feasibility of our proposed system was evaluated by conducting simulations on a publicly available dataset based on real-world energy profiles. The results showed that prosumers have a significant impact on reducing overall consumption and that batteries can be strategically used to mitigate peak usage. In this context, the adaptive behaviour suggested by the aggregator can be effectively employed to tackle energy fluctuations with flexible strategies that fully harness the potential of renewable energy sources. Future developments in this research include the deployment of the proposed software system to assess its computational and economic viability.

Acknowledgments. We acknowledge the support of the University of Catania PIAC-ERI project TEAMS, PNRR project CN-HPC, Big Data and Quantum Computing, Spoke 2 Fundamental Research and Space Economy, and Innovation Grant Agri@Intesa.

Disclosure of Interests. The authors have no competing interests to declare that are relevant to the content of this article.

References

1. Abdurahmanovic, N., Cadenbach, A.: Enhancing energy efficiency through user engagement and behaviour change: a review on gamification approaches and serious games in energy systems. Energy 137496 (2025)
2. Albogamy, F.R.: An optimal adaptive control strategy for energy balancing in smart microgrid using dynamic pricing. IEEE Access **10**, 37396–37411 (2022)

3. AlSkaif, T., Lampropoulos, I., Van Den Broek, M., Van Sark, W.: Gamification-based framework for engagement of residential customers in energy applications. Energy Res. Soc. Sci. **44**, 187–195 (2018)
4. Astriani, Y., Shafiullah, G., Shahnia, F.: Incentive determination of a demand response program for microgrids. Appl. Energy **292**, 116624 (2021)
5. Behi, B., Arefi, A., Jennings, P., Pivrikas, A., Gorjy, A., Catalão, J.P.: Consumer engagement in virtual power plants through gamification. In: 2020 5th International Conference on Power and Renewable Energy (ICPRE), pp. 131–137. IEEE (2020)
6. Bianchini, G., Casini, M., Gholami, M.: Optimal prosumer storage management in renewable energy communities under demand response. Energies **18**(18), 4904 (2025)
7. Bradley, P., Coke, A., Leach, M.: Financial incentive approaches for reducing peak electricity demand, experience from pilot trials with a UK energy provider. Energy Policy **98**, 108–120 (2016)
8. European Parliament: Directive (EU) 2018/2001 of the European parliament and of the council of 11 December 2018 on the promotion of the use of energy from renewable sources (2018). https://eur-lex.europa.eu/eli/dir/2018/2001/oj
9. Gagne, D.A., Settle, D.E., Aznar, A.Y., Bracho, R.: Demand response compensation methodologies: Case studies for Mexico. Technical repo0rt, National Renewable Energy Lab.(NREL), Golden, CO (United States) (2018). https://doi.org/10.2172/1452706
10. Gržanić, M., Capuder, T.: Coordinated scheduling of renewable energy balancing group. Int. J. Electr. Power Energy Syst. **125**, 106555 (2021)
11. Honarmand, M.E., Hosseinnezhad, V., Hayes, B., Shafie-Khah, M., Siano, P.: An overview of demand response: From its origins to the smart energy community. IEEE Access **9**, 96851–96876 (2021)
12. International Energy Agency (IEA): Renewables 2024. https://www.iea.org/reports/renewables-2024
13. Javaid, S., Kaneko, M., Tan, Y.: Energy balancing of power system considering periodic behavioral pattern of renewable energy sources and demands. IEEE Access **12**, 70245–70262 (2024)
14. Johnson, D., Horton, E., Mulcahy, R., Foth, M.: Gamification and serious games within the domain of domestic energy consumption: A systematic review. Renew. Sustain. Energy Rev. **73**, 249–264 (2017)
15. Kerscher, S., Arboleya, P.: The key role of aggregators in the energy transition under the latest European regulatory framework. Int. J. Electrical Power Energy Syst. **134**, 107361 (2022)
16. Koltunov, M.: Mapping of energy communities in Europe: status quo and review of existing classifications. Sustainability **15**(10), 8201 (2023)
17. Lanezki, M., Siemer, C., Wehkamp, S.: changing the game neighbourhood: an energy transition board game, developed in a co-design process: a case study. Sustainability **12**(24), 10509 (2020)
18. Leal Filho, W., t al.: Prosumers and sustainable development: an international assessment in the field of renewable energy. Sustain. Futures **7**, 100158 (2024)
19. López, I., et al.: European energy communities: characteristics, trends, business models and legal framework. Renew. Sustain. Energy Rev. **197**, 114403 (2024)
20. Mandarino, V., Pappalardo, G., Tramontana, E.: Proof of flow: a design pattern for the green energy market. Future Internet **15**(9), 313 (2023)
21. Mandarino, V., Pappalardo, G., Tramontana, E.: A blockchain-based electronic health record (EHR) system for edge computing enhancing security and cost efficiency. Computers **13**(6), 132 (2024)

22. Marletta, D., Midolo, A., Tramontana, E.: A blockchain-based strategy for certifying timestamps in a distributed healthcare emergency response systems. Future Internet **17**(5), 210 (2025)
23. Méndez, J.I., Ponce, P., Meier, A., Peffer, T., Mata, O., Molina, A.: Empower saving energy into smart communities using social products with a gamification structure for tailored human-machine interfaces within smart homes. Int. J. Interact. Des. Manuf. (IJIDeM) **17**(3), 1363–1387 (2023)
24. Nykyri, M., Annala, S., Silventoinen, P., et al.: Review of demand response and energy communities in serious games. IEEE Access **10**, 91018–91026 (2022)
25. Orlando, M., et al.: A smart meter infrastructure for smart grid IoT applications. IEEE Internet Things J. **9**(14), 12529–12541 (2021)
26. Pfenninger, S., Staffell, I.: Long-term patterns of European PV output using 30 years of validated hourly reanalysis and satellite data. Energy **114**, 1251–1265 (2016)
27. Savolainen, R., Lahdelma, R.: Optimization of renewable energy for buildings with energy storages and 15-minute power balance. Energy **243**, 123046 (2022)
28. Wang, W., Yuan, B., Sun, Q., Wennersten, R.: Application of energy storage in integrated energy systems a solution to fluctuation and uncertainty of renewable energy. J. Energy Storage **52**, 104812 (2022)
29. Wasiak, I., et al.: Innovative energy management system for low-voltage networks with distributed generation based on prosumers active participation. Appl. Energy **312**, 118705 (2022)
30. Yuan, R., Pourmousavi, S.A., Soong, W.L., Black, A.J., Liisberg, J.A., Lemos-Vinasco, J.: A synthetic dataset of Danish residential electricity prosumers. Sci. Data **10**(1), 371 (2023). https://doi.org/10.1038/s41597-023-02271-3

Automated Classification of ADS Disengagements Using Convolutional Neural Networks

Elisabet Hein$^{(\boxtimes)}$, Ali Ihsan Güllü, Faiz Ali Shah, and Dietmar Pfahl

University of Tartu, Narva Mnt 18, 51009 Tartu, Estonia
{elisabet.hein,ali.ihsan.gullu,faiz.ali.shah,
dietmar.pfahl}@ut.ee

Abstract. Test-drives of Automated Driving Systems (ADS) generate a rich pool of data that can be used to analyze and improve the ADS software stack. In this context, disengagement events, i.e., situations where the safety driver takes over control of the ADS are of specific interest. While it is easy to automatically identify when a disengagement happens, it is a non-trivial, and therefore manually performed task to classify disengagements with regards to its cause. The goal of our study was to replace the current manual classification process with a more efficient, scalable and reliable automatic approach. To this end, using supervised learning, we developed and tested a set of eight CNN-based binary classifiers, one for each label type. The evaluation indicated a high performance for six of the eight label types. A follow-up SHAP analysis gave insights into the reasons for the good performance of the classifiers.

Keywords: Automated Driving System · Automated Classification · Disengagement Event Analysis · Convolutional Neural Networks · Explainable Artificial Intelligence

1 Introduction

Automated driving technology has been advancing rapidly during the past decade. Chu et al. [1], Khan et al. [2], and Karla et al. [3] have described how it is expected to play a significant role in humans' daily transportation, emphasizing its potential to improve road safety by reducing traffic-related fatalities and to enhance overall driving comfort. Chu et. al. [1] and McGehee et al. [4] also emphasize that entirely automated vehicles, i.e., Automated Driving Systems (ADS), have not yet been fully implemented nor tested, due to safety, technical or ethical reasons. Therefore, as of now, a safety driver is needed to supervise the ADS and always maintain situational awareness.

The transition from automated driving mode to manual driving mode is called a disengagement event, i.e., an instance where a safety driver takes control over driving and proceeds to continue driving manually. Events like these can be analyzed to find potential problems in the ADS software and potential improvement points, for example in perception or decision-making algorithms [5]. Disengagements could be triggered by various reasons and are typically classified into two main categories:

G. Scanniello et al. (Eds.): PROFES 2025, LNCS 16362, pp. 193–205, 2026.
https://doi.org/10.1007/978-3-032-12092-2_14

- Planned disengagements—Situations where the safety driver will intentionally take over driving or where the system is programmed to hand over control. This could be due to legal or predefined safety reasons, such as approaching a pedestrian crossing.
- Unplanned disengagements—Situations where the safety driver unexpectedly needs to take over driving. The reasons include problems in the system, or safety risks anticipated based on the safety driver's personal evaluation of the situation.

At the University of Tartu, the Autonomous Driving Lab[1] (ADL) plays a crucial role in developing and evaluating a software stack for an Automated Driving System (ADS). In this context, disengagement events, i.e., situations where the safety driver takes over control of the ADS are of specific interest. Currently, disengagement events are manually reviewed by examining image and video data to determine the reasons that caused a disengagement events. While we intend to replace the manual process by models that can do the classification automatically, the existing manually labeled datasets can be used as the ground truth for our modelling activities. And keep track of different rides and the classifications. The contributions of this paper are the following[2]:

1. A structured data processing pipeline to transform raw ADL-provided sensor data from test drives into a format suitable for neural network training.
2. An evaluated automated classification system for disengagement events using binary Convolutional Neural Network (CNN) models for each disengagement class.
3. An application of explanatory methods to interpret model predictions, building trust into the reliability of the classification system and providing insights into the classification process.

The paper has four Appendices available online in additional materials[3].

2 Background

This section provides an overview of the key concepts relevant to this study. It is divided into four subsections, beginning with an explanation of autonomous driving levels, detailing the varying degrees of system automation and human supervision, followed by an overview of the Autonomous Driving Lab. Next, a detailed description of disengagement events is presented, along with the classification structure used by the ADL. Finally, to support the proposed automation of disengagement classification, the choice of using a CNN is justified in the light of existing literature.

Levels of Automation in Automated Driving Systems. Autonomous vehicles have been a major focus of research and development in recent years, with the potential

---

[1] Information about the Autonomous Driving Lab is available at: https://adl.cs.ut.ee/

[2] All data, models and scripts are available in a GitHub repo at:

https://github.com/Elisabethein/Automating-the-Classification-of-Disengagements-using-Convolutional-Neural-Networks

[3] Link to materials: https://zenodo.org/records/15690286.

to revolutionize transportation by improving safety, efficiency, and accessibility. By leveraging advanced sensors, artificial intelligence, and machine learning (ML), these vehicles can assist or even replace human drivers in various driving tasks. However, the journey to fully autonomous driving is complex, requiring continuous advancements in technology, regulation, and infrastructure.

To better understand where this technology currently stands, SAE International (previously known as the Society of Automotive Engineers) defined six levels of driving automation[4], ranging from Level 0 (no automation) to Level 5 (fully automated). These levels help classify vehicle capabilities and the degree of human involvement.

The ADS used in our study falls into the category of partial automation, operating at a level between SAE Level 2 and Level 3—referred to as Level 2.5. This means that while the vehicle can perform certain automated driving tasks, the driver remains responsible for overall control and must be prepared to intervene when necessary.

Chu et al. [1] also highlight the importance of ADS safety for technical, legislative, or ethical reasons. Since partially automated vehicles, by definition, cannot drive autonomously in most driving scenarios, and fully automated vehicles at SAE Levels 4 and 5 have not yet been sufficiently well proven to be safe enough, it is common practice to have a human supervisor, the so-called safety driver, on-board during test drives.

The Autonomous Driving Lab (ADL). The ADL at the University of Tartu is a research laboratory, which was founded in 2019, in cooperation with the Estonian mobility unicorn Bolt. ADL uses a Lexus RX 450h SUV (see Fig. 1a), which is equipped with all sensors necessary, like lidars, cameras, a radar, and Global Navigation Satellite System (GNSS) equipment, to perform test drives with the vehicle running on in-house software. The test drive data used in this study were collected from the 16th of October 2023 to 3rd of November 2023 from drives on the route shown in Fig. 1b.

Fig. 1. (a) Lexus RX 450h SUV used for test drives. (b) Route used for the test drives.[5]

ADL Technologies. The ADL develops and uses a software called Autoware Mini, which is integrated with the ROS 1 platform[6]. Robot Operating System (ROS) is a

---

⁴ Link to SAE Levels of Driving Automation: https://www.sae.org/blog/sae-j3016-update.

⁵ Figure 1 is based on a personal communication with an ADL research engineer.

⁶ An introduction into ROS can be found at: https://wiki.ros.org/ROS/Introduction.

platform for software developers that provides different tools and libraries, which can be used in robot-based systems. ROS is an open-source system, which is running only on Unix-based operating systems. Bag file format is used by the ROS for saving logs and messages from different components of the system. The platform logs messages from nodes to topics. A self-driving car system has, for example, components that are responsible for the operation of gas and brake pedals. Messages from those components could be logged into one topic, which describes pedal data.

Disengagement Events. A disengagement event in the autonomous vehicle's driving process, is an instance where the safety driver sitting behind the steering wheel is required or decides to take control over driving. This is a transition from autonomous driving to manual driving. Disengagements can be classified as planned and unplanned. In the ADL, further sub-classification is done based on the reason for the disengagements—unplanned disengagements are divided into three sub-categories and planned disengagements are divided into five sub-categories.

Unplanned disengagement sub-categories:

(1) **"OBS"**—Situations where an obstacle is blocking the vehicle.
(2) **"Safety"**—Situations where the safety driver decides to take over driving for their safety based on their own judgement, for example, unstable driving.
(3) **"Localization"**—Situations where the vehicle had problems with localization, like misinterpreting its location or insufficient signals from satellites.

Planned disengagement sub-categories:

(1) **"Pedestrian crossing"**—Situations where a pedestrian is intending to cross the crosswalk; requires the safety driver to disengage for pedestrian safety.
(4) **"Give way"**—Situations where the vehicle is approaching a "give way" intersection; requires the safety driver to take over collision prevention.
(5) **"Turnback"**—Situations where the vehicle needs to perform a turnback, for example, turn back to drive back the same road it originally came from. This is done in manual mode because the autonomous vehicle in use cannot drive backwards autonomously.
(6) **"SPEED"**—Situations where the maximum allowed speed on the road exceeded the legally allowed one for the autonomous vehicle (50 km/h), therefore, manual driving is required to be used.
(7) **"STOP"**—Situations where the vehicle has stopped at a bus stop and needs to either do a turnback or drive back to the main road.

The automated solution for classifying disengagements developed in our study targets the above listed sub-categories.

3 Related Work

The goal of this study is to develop an effective ML model to classify disengagement events from log data. The model needs to accurately distinguish different disengagement categories while minimizing misclassifications, given the safety-critical nature of the application. Traditionally, CNNs are commonly associated with image processing. However, they can also be highly effective for classification of time-series data, particularly through 1D Convolutional Layers (Conv1D), which can be useful in tasks involving one-dimensional sequence data, such as audio analysis, time-series forecasting, or natural language processing. Conv1D layers aim to extract meaningful features that contribute to the model's task at hand, which would require understanding patterns in the data based on time and order.

Petnehazi [6] describes in their research how CNNs utilize sliding local receptive fields, enabling them to detect local patterns and correlations in sequential data. This is particularly useful for time series, where nearby values often hold meaningful dependencies. Their ability to capture short-to-mid-range dependencies makes them suitable for tasks where disengagement events are characterized by distinct, localized patterns in vehicle control and sensor data.

4 Development of the Disengagement Classification Models

This section explains the development of disengagement classification models, covering data gathering, data preprocessing, and model building and evaluation.

Data Gathering. To develop classification models for categorizing disengagements, a high-quality dataset must be obtained from a reliable source. The dataset must contain multiple instances of disengagements for each class being modeled. This guarantees that each class has sufficient samples for both training and testing.

Since autonomous driving vehicles typically log data in ROS (.bag) format, a total of 27 ROS bag files, containing 160 disengagement events, were selected. The data was sourced from the University of Tartu's ROSBAG cloud server[7] and collected during test drives conducted between October 16 and November 3, 2023. Of the 31 available test rides, four were excluded due to processing issues, leaving 27 usable ROS bag files.

Each ROS bag file contained logs from various sections of the test trail, capturing data across 136 topics from different autonomous vehicle components. The 27 files contained a total of 160 disengagement events, which are summarized in Table 1 with their respective counts. Note that column "Numerical Mapping" in Table 1 skips the value "5". Originally, we considered including the disengagement category "Bad Engage" (class 5) in our study. However, we later decided to exclude it, because it does not represent a distinct disengagement reason but rather an ongoing issue linked to a previous disengagement decision made by the safety driver.

Data Preprocessing. To facilitate further preprocessing, the ROS bag files are converted into a standardized CSV format using to ease the training and evaluating of ML models. Each selected topic, as listed above, was extracted and saved as a separate CSV file, resulting in nine CSV files per test drive. In total, 27 test drives were converted, ensuring a consistent and accessible format for model training. Once the relevant topics are converted to CSV format, the following additional preprocessing is performed to refine the dataset:

---

[7] ROSBAG database at https://bagdatabase.cloud.ut.ee/ (accessed on 27.10.2024) Direct access to the database is available on request by the ADL.

Table 1. Disengagement classes with their respective counts.

Disengagement Class	Numerical Mapping	Count
"OBS"	0	65
"Safety"	1	30
"Turnback"	2	14
"Pedestrian crossing"	3	24
"Localization"	4	13
"Give way"	6	12
"SPEED"	7	1
"STOP"	8	1
SUM		**160**

- Remove irrelevant columns such as component IDs and redundant values.
- Merge topic files into a single, unified CSV per ride, using timestamps as the primary key and keeping all unique timestamps.

Since ROS logs data asynchronously, timestamps across different topics may not always align, leading to missing values. To solve this problem, the Python Pandas library functions, forward filling and backward filling, are used to replace missing values with valid values; thus, maintaining the consistency of the dataset while also preserving the relationships across all topics. This result is a single combined CSV file per test drive, aligning data by timestamps.

Labeling and Isolating the Disengagement Events. To be able to classify disengagement events, these instances need to be identified and then isolated together with relevant context information from the complete ride dataset.

The identification of disengagement instances was done with the help of a Python script that identifies transitions from autonomous to manual driving mode. The isolation of the disengagement instances with appropriate context involved selecting a predefined timeframe that captures data leading up to each disengagement event. The extraction window typically ranges from 3 to 10 s. Ad-hoc experiments indicated that a time-window of 5 s provided a good balance between capturing sufficient pre-disengagement context and the computational load. Thus, for each disengagement event, a five-second window leading up to the switch from autonomous to manual driving is isolated and saved as a separate CSV file for model training, resulting in 160 CSV files, each representing a disengagement event with its driving data.

Preparing the Training, Validation, and Test Data. To train the models, a standardized structure for the input data frame must be established. The full dataset initially included 160 disengagement events available for both training and testing purposes. For the evaluation of classification models, 6 events were reserved for testing, selected from classes 0 to 6 (excluding class 5) to ensure that each class has at least one sample reserved for testing. This left 154 disengagement events for the training set.

Table 2. The count of disengagement classes for training after preprocessing.

Disengagement class	Count (unbalanced)	Count (after balancing)
0	64	320
1	29	320
2	13	320
3	23	320
4	12	320
6	11	320
7	1	320
8	1	320
SUM	**154**	**2560**

After separating the training and test sets, both sets were normalized to ensure consistent feature scaling, and padding was applied to ensure a fixed length for uniformity. The initial class distribution for the training set was highly imbalanced (cf. Table 2). To address this, data augmentation (data jittering) was applied to the training set, generating additional samples to balance the dataset. Each class in the training set was augmented to contain 320 samples. This number was chosen based on the typical requirement for a few hundred samples to train robust models, while also considering potential memory constraints due to the large size of the data.

The same technique we used for augmenting the training data was used to generate additional test samples. We ensure to have at least five test samples per disengagement class to create a balance between reliability and redundancy—too few samples may bias evaluation results, while too many have limited additional value, as augmented samples are derived from the same original data and thus tend to have similarities. For each target class, the following set of training and validation data sets is prepared:

- 320 samples from the target class were labeled as 1 [True].
- 320 samples were randomly selected from each of the other classes, ensuring an equal number of samples from each, and were labeled as 0 [False].
- The final dataset (640 samples per model) was split 80/20 and kept class balance:

  - Training set (80%): 256 samples from class 1 [True], 256 from class 0 [False].
  - Validation set (20%): 64 samples from class 1 [True], 64 from class 0 [False].

Building the Classification Models. For each disengagement class, a separate binary classification model is trained and validated (see Table 3) based on the data shown in Sect. 3.4. Each model is designed to determine whether a given input window belongs to a specific class it was trained to identify. The input to the model is a disengagement sequence with dimensions (timestamps, features). The output is a probability score indicating the likelihood that the input belongs to the target class. Each model uses a default classification threshold of 0.5.

For classification of disengagement events, a 1D Convolutional Neural Network (Conv1D) architecture is used, which is effective for sequential data by applying convolutional filters across time-series patterns. The architecture remains identical across all models, and with key characteristics as described below.

Table 3. Mapping between disengagement and numerical classes, with corresponding model name and model file name.

Disengagement Class	Numerical Mapping	Model Name	Model File
"OBS"	0	CL0	"model_class_0_final.h5"
"Safety"	1	CL1	"model_class_1_final.h5"
"Turnback"	2	CL2	"model_class_2_final.h5"
"Pedestrian crossing"	3	CL3	"model_class_3_final.h5"
"Localization"	4	CL4	"model_class_4_final.h5"
"Give way"	6	CL6	"model_class_6_final.h5"
"SPEED"	7	CL7	"model_class_7_final.h5"
"STOP"	8	CL8	"model_class_8_final.h5"

Input Shape

- Input: A sequence with dimensions (1304 timestamps, 484 features).

Feature Extraction Layers

- Conv1D Layers: Three convolutional layers with increasing filter sizes (128, 256, 512) were used to capture hierarchical features from the data.
- Kernel Regularization: L2 regularization was applied to reduce overfitting [7].
- Batch Normalization: Normalized the intermediate activations to stabilize and speed up training.
- MaxPooling1D: Reduced the temporal resolution, focusing on the most prominent features while down-sampling the sequence.

Global Feature Representation

- GlobalAveragePooling1D: Aggregated temporal features into a single feature vector by computing the average of all values in the feature map.

Classification Head

- Dense Layers: Fully connected layers with 128 units and a ReLU (rectified linear unit) activation learning higher-level representations; dropout (30%) was applied to prevent overfitting.
- Output Layer: A single neuron with a sigmoid activation function outputs a probability score, indicating whether the input belonged to the target class.

All CNN-based binary classification models were trained for 100 epochs using the Adam optimizer [8, 9] (learning rate = 0.0001) and a batch size of 8 with binary cross-entropy as the loss function [10]. Early stopping was used for monitoring validation loss, halting training after five epochs of no improvement, and restoring the best weights. Class weights were computed to balance class importance.

Evaluation Metrics. To assess model performance, four standard metrics are measured for each binary classification model, i.e., accuracy, precision, recall, and F1-score.

5 Evaluation of the Disengagement Classification Models

This section shows the confusion matrices and the corresponding performance metrics, which summarize how well the models classified the test samples. These results were derived from the models' predictions on the 30 test samples, ensuring a consistent evaluation framework across all models.

Each model's predictions were compared against the true labels to compute true positives (TP), true negatives (TN), false positives (FP), and false negatives (FN). For each model, a detailed breakdown of classification results per sample can be found in Tables 1 and 2 of Appendix A (see link in footnote 3). Based on the prediction outcomes, confusion matrices were constructed for each model and the evaluation metrics precision, recall, F1-score, and accuracy were derived to assess model effectiveness. Table 4 presents the confusion matrix of models CL0 to CL6, which share the same matrix. For models CL7 and CL8, the corresponding confusion matrix is shown in Table 5.

Table 4. The confusion matrix of models CL0 to CL6

	Actual Positive	Actual Negative
Predicted Positive	5 (TP)	0 (FP)
Predicted Negative	0 (FN)	25 (TN)

The confusion matrices indicate that all models performed flawlessly on the test set, with no false positives or false negatives. Consequently, the performance metrics—accuracy, precision, recall, and F1-score—were all 100% for each model.

Table 5. The confusion matrix of models CL7 and CL8

	Actual Positive	Actual Negative
Predicted Positive	0 (TP)	0 (FP)
Predicted Negative	0 (FN)	30 (TN)

6 Discussion

Explanation of Predictions. To better understand why the models performed so well, SHAP value analysis of each model was performed as follows [11, 12]:

- **Feature Aggregation**: The top five features per model were extracted separately from both the most positive and the most negative influences.
- **Feature Normalization**: Feature names with numerical suffixes were standardized (replacing numbers with "_i") to ensure consistency. If multiple features had the same base name with different suffixes, only the first occurrence was retained.
- **Value scaling**: SHAP values were scaled by a factor of one million to improve readability in visualizations, without altering their relative importance.
- **Sorting:** Feature names and model numbers were sorted alphabetically to ensure a structured visualization.

The full details of the SHAP value analysis are available in Appendix B (see link in footnote 3). The heatmap in Fig. 2 gives an overview of feature importance across different models, summarizing how various features influenced predictions. SHAP value analysis was performed separately for each model, with a focus on the distinct sets of positively (red) influencing features. This analysis helped interpret each model's behavior and assess whether the most influential features aligned with human intuition. For instance, in the Class 0 model, which classifies disengagements caused by obstacles, the most positively influential features were related to object detection, particularly position and dimension data (cf. Red cells in the first row of Fig. 2). These features highlight the model's reliance on spatial awareness, emphasizing the importance of nearby objects in classifying disengagements caused by obstacles blocking the vehicle's path. This focus on nearby objects aligns with human intuition where obstacle detection considers both their position and characteristics.

The heatmap can also be analyzed in terms of the shades of red (positive influence) and blue (negative influence). For instance, the Class 1 model (classifying disengagements caused by safety reasons) places high emphasis on the closest object's velocity, indicating that nearby objects moving quickly can trigger safety-critical situations. In contrast, the Class 0 model shows this feature as having a strong negative impact, suggesting that it does not focus on moving objects, which makes sense because obstacles tend to be static. For a comprehensive breakdown of the most important features in each class, along with their correlation to the disengagement categories, see Appendix C (see link in footnote 3).

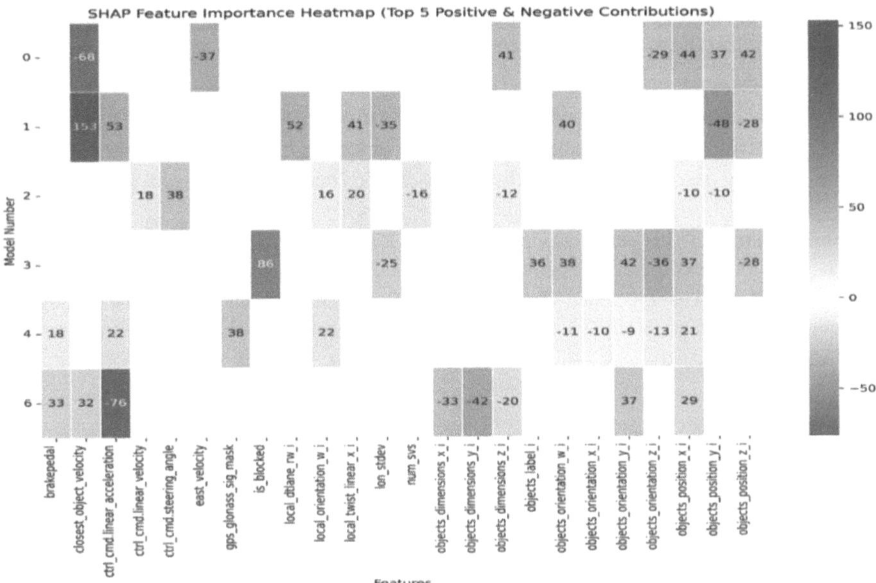

Fig. 2. SHAP feature importance heatmap.

Following the per-model analysis, the models were compared to assess how they performed as a set and how they differed from one another. The full comparative analysis is provided in Appendix D (see link in footnote 3).

Threats to Validity. The main threat to *internal validity* is the limited availability of raw data. Our dataset was selected due to the high quality of the labeling done by the ADL research engineer. Even though the augmentation of the original samples provided an avenue for increasing dataset size, more original samples are needed to enhance the models' validity. Especially problematic were disengagement classes 7 and 8, with only a single original sample for both classes, making proper training and testing difficult. Another issue related to *internal validity* is the choice of parameter values during the data pre-processing step. For example, a manually conducted ad-hoc analysis of the best time window to use before a disengagement suggested that 5 s are sufficient, but no systematic analysis was done to find the optimum value. The main threat to *external validity* and *reliability* is that definitions of disengagement categories may change over time. However, our approach of developing a set of binary classifiers for each disengagement makes the models reusable at least for those categories where definitions and sensor data types do not change.

7 Conclusion

Our research contributes to the advancement of post-drive analysis in autonomous driving and enhances safety by enabling accurate automated classification of disengagement events.

Beyond post-drive analysis, our solution could serve as a valuable software evaluation tool by monitoring trends in disengagement events and their types over time. By automatically identifying how certain disengagement events fluctuate across different driving scenarios and software updates, developers can assess the effectiveness of the ADS software more efficiently. This could enhance ADS development cycles and improve quality assurance by providing data-driven feedback on system performance.

Acknowledgments. This study was co-funded by BMIMI, BMWET, and the State of Upper Austria in the frame of the SCCH competence center INTEGRATE (FFG grant no. 892418) part of the FFG COMET Competence Centers for Excellent Technologies Programme and by Bolt Technology ÖU. We gratefully acknowledge the support received from the ADL and its research engineer Edgar Sepp.

Disclosure of Interests. The authors have no competing interests to declare that are relevant to the content of this article.

References

1. Chu, M., Zong, K., Shu, X., Gong, J., Lu, Z., Guo, K., Dai, X., Zhou, G.: Work with AI and work for AI: Autonomous vehicle safety drivers' lived experiences. In proceedings of the 2023 CHI Conference on Human Factors in Computing Systems (CHI '23). ACM, New York, NY, USA, Article **753**, 1–16 (2023). https://doi.org/10.1145/3544548.3581564
2. Khan, S.M., Salek, M.S., Harris, V., Comert, G., Morris, E.A., Chowdhury, M.: Autonomous vehicles for all? ACM J. Auton. Transport. Syst. **1**, 1, Article 3 (March 2024), 8 pages (2024). https://doi.org/10.1145/3611017
3. Kalra, N., Paddock, S.M.: Driving to safety: How many miles of driving would it take to demonstrate autonomous vehicle reliability? Transportation Research Part A: Policy and Practice **94**(2016), 182–193 (2016). https://doi.org/10.1016/j.tra.2016.09.010
4. McGehee, D.V., Brewer, M., Schwarz, C., Smith, B.W.: Review of automated vehicle technology: Policy and implementation implications. Iowa department of transportation 03/14/2016 (2016). https://iro.uiowa.edu/esploro/outputs/9984475729002771
5. Shokan, A., Mareček, J.: Could disengagement reports indicate evolution of autonomous vehicles? Vehicles **7**(2), 32 (2025). https://doi.org/10.3390/vehicles7020032
6. Petneházi. G.: Quantile convolutional neural networks for value at risk forecasting, MLWA, **6**, 100096 (2021). https://doi.org/10.1016/j.mlwa.2021.100096
7. Ma, T., Zhou, C.: Selection of regularization model for linear regression under high-dimensional data. In Proc. of the 7th Int. Conf. on Deep Learning Technologies (ICDLT '23). ACM, New York, NY, USA, 91–97 (2023). https://doi.org/10.1145/3613330.3613342
8. Harjai, A., Charan, A., Singhal, S.: Sentiment analysis of medications review using deepLearning algorithms. In Proc. of the 5th Int. Conf. on information management & machine intelligence (ICIMMI '23). ACM, New York, NY, USA, Article **2**, 1–5 (2024). https://doi.org/10.1145/3647444.3647828
9. Kingma, D.P., Ba, J.: Adam: A method for stochastic optimization. 2015 (2014). https://doi.org/10.48550/arXiv.1412.6980
10. Kulkarni, C.A., M. R, and Sharath, S.S.: Custom binary cross entropy based anomaly detection in bank transactions using deep convolutional neural network. In 23rd Int. Conf. on Inform. Integration and Web Intelligence (iiWAS2021). ACM, New York, NY, USA, 319–323 (2022). https://doi.org/10.1145/3487664.3487708

11. Jhumka, J., Auzine, M.M., Khan, M.H.-M., Casseem, S.M., Fedally, S.A., Mungloo-Dilmohamud, Z.: Explainable Chronic Kidney Disease (CKD) Prediction using deep learning and shapley additive explanations (SHAP). In Proc. of the 7th Int. Conf. on Advances in Artificial Intelligence (ICAAI '23). ACM, New York, NY, USA, 29–33 (2024). https://doi.org/10.1145/3633598.3633604
12. Cunha, B.M., Barbosa, S.D.J.: Evaluating the effectiveness of visual representations of SHAP values toward explainable artificial intelligence. In Proceedings of the XXIII Brazilian Symp. on Human Factors in Computing Systems (IHC '24). ACM, New York, NY, USA, Article **54**, 1–11 (2024). https://doi.org/10.1145/3702038.3702093

Toward Greener Background Processes: Measuring Energy Cost of Autosave Feature

Maria Küüsvek and Hina Anwar[(✉)][iD]

Institute of Computer Science, University of Tartu, Tartu, Estonia
{maria.kuusvek,hina.anwar}@ut.ee

Abstract. Background processes in desktop applications are often overlooked in energy consumption studies, yet they represent continuous, automated workloads with significant cumulative impact. This paper introduces a reusable process for evaluating the energy behavior of such features at the level of operational design. The process works in three phases: 1) decomposing background functionality into core operations, 2) operational isolation, and 3) controlled measurements enabling comparative profiling. We instantiate the process in a case study of autosave implementations across three open-source Python-based text editors. Using 900 empirical software-based energy measurements, we identify key design factors affecting energy use, including save frequency, buffering strategy, and auxiliary logic such as change detection. We give four actionable recommendations for greener implementations of autosave features in Python to support sustainable software practices.

Keywords: Green Software Engineering · Energy Profiling · Background Processes · Autosave

1 Introduction

Software energy consumption is emerging as a critical concern in sustainable computing, particularly in battery-constrained devices. While hardware efficiency has advanced, the energy footprint of software, especially background features, remains under-optimized. Huawei estimates that ICT will consume 9% of global energy by 2025, with projections reaching 21% by 2030 [1,7]. Yet, only 18% of developers consider energy efficiency during development [11].

Background process can be defined as a program component that executes alongside the primary foreground workflow, starting automatically or indirectly, running with no UI, and continuing to run despite user interactions[1,2].

Background processes are a particularly underexplored contributor to software energy waste. These processes, such as autosaving, syncing, or logging, operate without direct user interaction, yet they generate consistent CPU, memory,

---

[1] Microsoft - Introduction to Windows Service Applications. https://learn.microsoft.com/en-us/dotnet/framework/windows-services/introduction-to-windows-service-applications.

[2] Background Tasks Overview. Android Developers. https://developer.android.com/develop/background-work/background-tasks.

G. Scanniello et al. (Eds.): PROFES 2025, LNCS 16362, pp. 206–217, 2026.
https://doi.org/10.1007/978-3-032-12092-2_15

and I/O activity over time. Although their energy footprint may appear minimal in isolation, their continuous nature and high execution frequency can lead to meaningful cumulative costs, especially at scale.

In this paper, we present a feature-level energy measurement process for background processes in interactive software. The process focuses on decomposing background features into their constituent operations (e.g., file writing, change tracking, metadata handling), and empirically benchmarking their energy consumption under controlled conditions. It is designed to support practical energy awareness during feature design, offering a lightweight and reproducible approach for profiling real-world implementations.

We instantiate the process via a case study of the autosave feature in three open-source Python-based desktop text editors. The study isolates key implementation differences across the editors, conducts 900 controlled measurements across multiple file sizes and autosave variants, and extracts practical insights on which design decisions drive energy usage. This case study was conducted originally in the context of the first author's MSc thesis at the University of Tartu, and serves here as a concrete instantiation of the presented process.

Our results show that save frequency, write buffering, and metadata operations significantly influence energy use in the autosave feature, with one implementation reducing energy by up to 83% through simple parameter adjustments. Based on these findings, we offer four actionable guidelines for developers implementing autosave or similar background features in Python.

The contributions of this paper include:

- A reusable process that formalizes the steps needed to carry out a valid empirical experiment for measuring the energy consumption of background processes.
- A fully published and reusable instantiation of the process as well as its output[3], including development, application, and evaluation of a measurement testbed for autosave energy consumption in real-world applications.
- Actionable guidelines for developers to move towards greener implementations of the autosave feature.

These findings aim to inform greener software design practices and support energy-aware development of background features.

2   Feature-Level Energy Measurement Process

Background processes such as logging, syncing, and silent updates are pervasive in modern software systems. Operating without direct user interaction, they are typically triggered by time intervals, system events, runtime conditions, or idle states. Despite their cumulative energy impact, these features are often overlooked during the design and evaluation phases. To address this gap, we propose a lightweight, feature-level energy measurement process for analyzing and

---

[3] The MSc thesis by M. Küüsvek is available at https://thesis.cs.ut.ee/250643ac-df5e-4993-9b73-a51d9b5d4d3f.

benchmarking the energy behavior of background operations. The measurement process presented here builds upon established methodologies in software energy analysis [2,4,9] but is tailored to the specific context of background processes. Whereas existing studies often evaluate energy consumption at the level of entire applications or functional modules, our process focuses narrowly on the isolated impact of background operations. This specialization enables a more precise examination of design trade-offs that might otherwise be obscured in broader analyses.

At its core, the process treats background features as composed of discrete atomic operations, the smallest functional units that can be individually isolated and profiled for energy consumption. It also emphasizes the importance of trigger mechanisms, which define the temporal or conditional context in which these operations are executed. By decomposing features into these elements, the process enables systematic energy profiling across implementations and contexts.

The feature-level energy measurement process proceeds in three Phases: 1) feature decomposition, 2) operational isolation, and 3) controlled measurement. A high-level schematic of the process is shown in Fig. 1

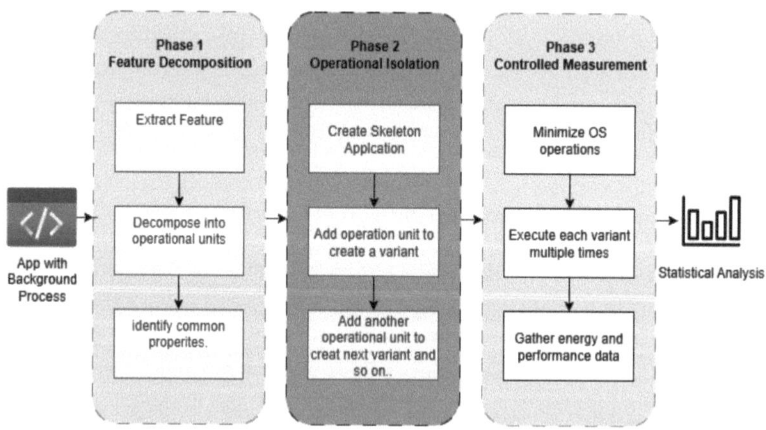

Fig. 1. Overview of Energy measurement process for Background Processes

2.1   Phase 1: Feature Decomposition

The first stage involves breaking down a background process into its constituent atomic operations, defined here as the smallest self-contained units of work that (a) perform a discrete functional task, and (b) can be instrumented and executed independently. Depending on the feature, these may include file access, state monitoring, data transformation, or network communication.

Alongside operational decomposition, common properties of the background process also need to be identified. These properties affect how demanding the background process is and how much energy it uses. The properties and their possible values are listed in Table 1. There is no consolidated list of common properties for background processes, and the ones shown in Table 1 are extracted from industry[4] and online [10, 15] sources.

Table 1. Core Properties of Background Processes

Property	Description
Trigger	How the process is started: **Schedule-driven** (e.g., Time-based (i.e., periodic execution), **Event-based** (i.e., triggered after system or user input), **Idle-based** (i.e., syncing when the system is inactive), Reactive (e.g., triggering after buffer thresholds are exceeded).
Frequency	How often the process runs: **Periodic** (fixed intervals), **Aperiodic** (irregular timing), or **Sporadic** (event-driven with minimum time between activations).
Persistence	How long the process remains active or enabled: **Immediate** (short-lived), **Long-running**, **Deferrable** (can be delayed), or **Persistent** (remains across reboots).
Resource Usage	The primary hardware resources consumed: e.g., **CPU**, **disk I/O**, **network**, **sensors**, etc.
Scope	Whether the process executes **locally** (on-device operations) or interacts with **external systems** (e.g., network, cloud, peripherals).

2.2 Phase 2: Operational Isolation

The second stage focuses on isolating the core functionality of a background process within a skeleton application, a minimal working implementation that includes only the target feature, stripped of unrelated UI elements, services, or unrelated logic. This isolation allows for focused energy analysis by minimizing confounding variables.

Each atomic operation is introduced incrementally in a series of controlled application variants. For example, one variant might perform only buffer monitoring, while the next variant includes monitoring plus file I/O. This incremental setup supports analysis, enabling measurement of the marginal energy impact of each added component.

---

[4] https://dev.to/rajrathod/background-jobs-473j,   https://learn.microsoft.com/en-us/azure/architecture/best-practices/background-jobs,   https://developer.android.com/develop/background-work/background-tasks/persistent.

2.3   Phase 3: Controlled Measurement

The final stage involves collecting statistically reliable energy measurements in a consistent testing environment as described in existing literature [2,4,9].

Environment Setup and Preparation: This includes minimizing OS and system background activity, fixing CPU frequency or disabling turbo modes (if applicable), and using high-resolution energy tools, such as Intel RAPL, via access layers like perf or pyRAPL. Such preparation reduces external variability and ensures that observed differences can be attributed to the feature under test.

Performing Measurements: Each variant is executed multiple times across controlled parameters (e.g., data size, trigger frequency, I/O load). Multiple runs are required to achieve statistically reliable results and to smooth out noise introduced by the system environment. This process captures both the total energy consumed and the execution patterns of the background feature.

Data Analysis and Reporting: Collected measurements are averaged and subjected to statistical treatment to account for natural variability across runs. Analysis focuses not only on total energy consumed but also on the relationship between operational design decisions (e.g., batching, buffering, trigger thresholds) and energy behavior. This allows for identifying trade-offs between performance and efficiency that might otherwise remain hidden.

3   Case Study: Autosave Feature in Text-Editors

To evaluate the proposed feature-level energy measurement process, we applied it to the autosave feature in three real-world text editors: Mu[5], Leo[6], and novelWriter[7]. This case study serves as a practical demonstration of how the described process can be used to isolate and quantify energy usage in real software systems.

3.1   Context

Autosave is a widely used background feature in text editors, designed to protect users from data loss by saving content periodically or in response to user activity. While the functionality is similar across applications, the underlying implementation strategies vary significantly, particularly in terms of trigger mechanisms, file handling, and auxiliary operations such as logging and change detection.

Based on the context and objective, the following RQs are formed

RQ1: *What operations within the autosaving feature are most energy-intensive?*

RQ2: *How do different implementations of the autosave feature differ in energy consumption in selected text editors?*

RQ3: *How do file size and save frequency impact the energy consumption of autosaving implementations in selected text editors?*

---

[5] https://github.com/mu-editor/mu.
[6] https://github.com/leo-editor/leo-editor.
[7] https://github.com/vkbo/novelWriter.

The case study focused exclusively on Python-based desktop text editors using the Qt[8] framework to ensure consistency in architecture and UI behavior.

3.2 Applying Phase 1: Feature Decomposition

The autosave feature was decomposed into its core operations by inspecting the source code and runtime behavior of three open-source Python-based editors: Mu, Leo, and novelWriter. Three fundamental operations were consistently identified: 1) **file writing:** the act of persisting the active document or project state to disk, 2) **change detection:** logic to verify whether the document has changed since the last save, 3) **logging:** optional recording of autosave activity to console or log files. These operations were chosen for isolation because they represent the typical energy-consuming steps in autosave cycles. Table 2 summarizes the most impactful implementation differences in selected editors The autosave behavior across the three editors was governed by distinct trigger mechanisms. Each editor used a different type of trigger: Mu used a high-frequency timer (QTimer), triggering saves every 5 s. NovelWriter used a lower-frequency timer set to 30 s. Leo relied on an idle-time detection hook, firing autosave only after 5 min of user inactivity. These differences affect not only when energy is consumed but also how frequently background processes interrupt system idle states. The case study captured these distinctions by configuring test variants that preserved original triggering behaviors wherever possible. Other common properties of the autosave feature across applications are shown in Table 3, while Fig. 2 provides an overview of the energy measurement process in the context of the case study:

Table 2. Autosave Implementation Differences

Text Editor	Trigger Type	textbfFile Writing	Change Detection	Logging
Mu	QTimer (5s)	Direct write + `fsync()`	Built-in Qt flag	File + Stream
novelWriter	QTimer (30s)	Temp file → overwrite	Custom flag	`stderr` only
Leo	Idle-time hook (300s)	Backup copy → overwrite	Manual flag	`print()` (optional)

Table 3. Properties of Autosave Background Process

Property	Value
Trigger	Schedule driven
Frequency	Periodic
Persistence	Asynchronous
Resource	usage Disk I/O
Scope	Local

---

[8] https://doc.qt.io/qtforpython-6/.

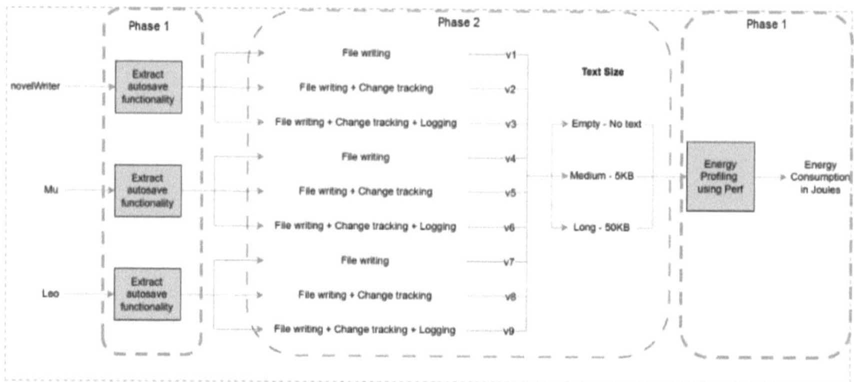

Fig. 2. Overview of energy measurement process in the context of case study

3.3   Applying Phase 2: Operational Isolation

To isolate autosave energy use from unrelated system activity, each editor was reduced to a skeleton application. These lightweight Qt-based programs retained only the core autosave logic and a minimal text editing interface. All non-essential features, such as UI rendering, network access, or non-autosave I/O, were removed.

For each editor, three controlled variants were implemented using the skeleton application: 1) **Base:** Implementing only the file writing operation, 2) **Change:** Implementing file writing + change detection, 3) **Logging:** Implementing file writing + change detection + logging. These variants enabled incremental assessment of each operation's energy cost while maintaining functional realism. Autosaving is carried out at identical intervals of 10 s (i.e., executed 12 times) in the skeleton application. To examine scalability, three file sizes were used in each test variant: 1) **0 KB:** Empty file (baseline behavior), 2) **5 KB:** Small document (code snippet or note), 3) **50 KB:** Large document (e.g., markdown or essay). All variants are available in the GitHub repository[9].

3.4   Applying Phase 3: Controlled Measurement

Each variant was tested in a controlled Linux environment using the Intel RAPL interface (via perf) to measure CPU and DRAM energy consumption. Autosave was triggered via each editor's native mechanism, and artificial text edits were simulated to activate the feature reliably. Experimentation is carried out on an HP Elitebook with Lubuntu 24.04 LTS. Each measurement followed a fixed cycle: start the app, wait 5 s, start Perf profiling, execute the test, let Perf finish, close the app, pause 5 min, then repeat. Each configuration of test variant was executed 30 times, resulting in 900 total measurements ((3 editors × 3 variants × 3

---

[9] https://github.com/MariaKuusvek/MSc-Thesis.

file sizes $\times$ 30 repetitions) + 90 control test measurements). **Comparative Profiling:** The data collected across all configurations was used to compare energy usage patterns across editors and variants. Statistical analysis was performed to reveal significant differences in energy consumption.

4   Results

We report on 900 measurements: 810 test case measurements and 90 control test measurements were carried out. The average values for each control test scenario were subtracted from the relevant main test to receive the delta energy value for autosaving. The full set of measurements taken is found in the CSV file in the GitHub repository (See footnote 9). Below, only the conclusions are discussed[10].

Result of RQ1: *(In-app Comparison)* The basic file-writing operation was consistently the least energy-intensive across all editors, forming the baseline for autosave. Adding change tracking generally produced little to no additional cost, except in Mu (see Fig. 3), where medium and large files consumed an extra 5.83 J and 5.61 J, suggesting that its implementation of modified-flag checks is less efficient. Adding logging also had no statistically significant impact in any editor; in fact, raw means often indicated slight energy reductions, with the largest observed overhead being only 3.62 J, which is negligible compared to other operational differences.

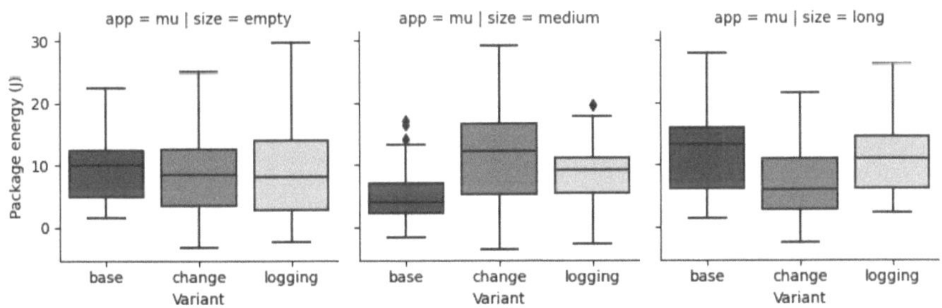

Fig. 3. Box plot of energy distribution in variants of Mu in all three file sizes.

Result of RQ2: *(Inter-app Comparison Results)* The energy measurements revealed significant differences across autosave implementations (see Table 4), particularly in relation to trigger frequency and file write strategy. Mu, which uses high-frequency writes with fsync(), consistently consumed more energy than Leo and novelWriter. Leo's idle-triggered backup system was the most energy-efficient overall, especially for small files, while novelWriter performed well under moderate workloads.

---

[10] For full hypothesis testing results, see https://docs.google.com/spreadsheets/d/
14lV3lX50QL54Ocp-foSjeYGQ2VO_ROkp_NZSYdc1Z-w/edit?usp=sharing.

Table 4. Summary of statistically significant pairwise differences in autosave energy consumption

Pairwise Comparison	File Size	p-value	Higher Energy User	Δ Energy (J)
Mu base vs Mu change	5 KB	0.0029	Mu change	5.83
Mu base vs novelWriter base	5 KB	0.003	novelWriter base	6.84
Mu base vs Leo base	5 KB	0.046	Leo base	4.04
Mu change vs Leo change	5 KB	0.015	Mu change	6.23
Mu change vs novelWriter change	5 KB	0.000037	Mu change	10.37
Leo change vs Mu change	50 KB	0.0001	Leo change	7.83
Leo change vs novelWriter change	50 KB	0.016	Leo change	5.01
Leo logging vs novelWriter logging	0 KB	0.0155	Leo logging	5.12
Mu logging vs novelWriter logging	5 KB	0.032	Mu logging	3.75
Mu logging vs Leo logging	50 KB	0.0021	Mu logging	5.96

Result of RQ3: *Scalability (File Size & Save Frequency).*

Scaling analysis showed that file size (see Fig. 4) had only a minor impact, while save frequency dominated energy consumption (see Table 5). All three editors used 0.83–0.92 J per save, independent of file size. However, their default save intervals led to dramatic differences in hourly energy use: Mu's 5-s interval resulted in 619.2 J/hour, compared to novelWriter's 99.6 J/hour at 30 s and Leo's 11.04 J/hour at 300 s. Aligning Mu's interval with novelWriter's would reduce its energy consumption by 83%.

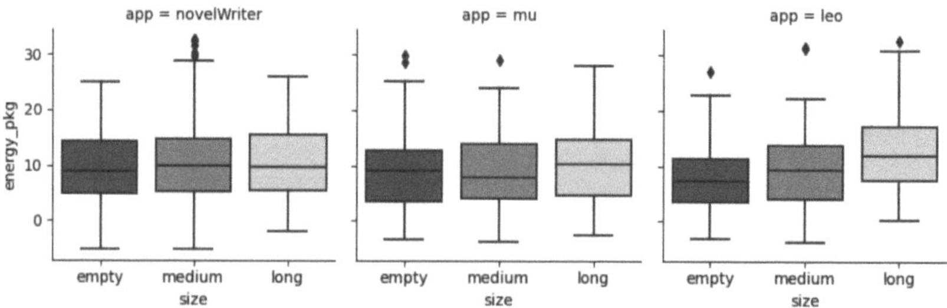

Fig. 4. Box plot of application-specific joule distribution by file size.

Table 5. Estimated hourly cost of autosaving in each application (RQ3).

Editor (change+logging)	Avg J (12 saves)	Avg J per save	Frequency	Calls/hr	Joules/hr
novelWriter	9.98	0.83	30 s	120	99.6
Mu	10.3	0.86	5 s	720	619.2
Leo	11.07	0.92	300 s (idle)	12	11.04

5   Guidelines for Developers

Based on the results of the case study, we propose four practical guidelines for developing an energy-efficient autosave feature in Python:

- *Minimize Save Frequency:* High-frequency autosave (e.g., every 5s) consumes significantly more energy than longer intervals. Use change-aware triggers or debounce logic to avoid redundant saves.
- *Prefer direct file writes for autosave:* If stronger crash safety is required, a temp-file→rename approach can be used, but it was still less efficient than directly overwriting the original file in our tests.
- *Use dedicated change-tracking for autosave:* Avoid heavyweight/built-in modified flags; add a separate flag so autosave stops re-writing once changes cease, preventing unnecessary writes.
- *Don't fear logging:* Adding logging showed no statistically significant energy overhead across editors; treat logging placement as a maintainability/usability choice rather than an energy constraint.

6   Threats to Validity

This process is intended to be flexible and extensible. While our use case focuses on a single background process in a very limited set of real-world applications, we believe the described process can be applied to other background features (such as syncing, telemetry, and auto-formatting etc.) and platforms, provided that atomic operations can be isolated or mocked, trigger conditions can be emulated, and energy usage can be measured meaningfully. However, there are limitations, such as the process assumes background features are discrete and isolatable. Highly integrated or event-cascading systems may require adaptation. Energy measurements are subject to system-level variability (e.g., caching, OS scheduling), even in controlled settings. Skeleton applications suggested in phase two of the process may not capture all side effects present in real-world systems. Despite these caveats, this process provides a practical pathway for incorporating energy awareness into both research and design workflows.

Captured measurements provide clear comparative insights; however, the study is limited to a single hardware configuration and focuses on desktop applications written in Python and Qt. Results may vary on mobile devices, SSDs with different write performance, or platforms with advanced power management. Expanding the scope to other architectures or feature types is an important direction for future work.

7   Related Work

This section presents the most relevant literature related to the case study. Measuring the energy usage of software systems has gained momentum in sustainable computing research. Prior studies have explored energy implications from two perspectives: code-level implementation practices and system-level or environmental factors.

At the code level, Sahin et al. [13] and Şanlıalp et al. [14] showed that even basic code refactorings (e.g., "extract local variable", "simplify nested loops") can influence energy usage by ±5–8%. Chowdhury et al. [3] isolated the impact of logging in Android apps, showing that high-frequency logging ($\geq$ 10 messages/sec) significantly increases energy usage due to disk I/O flushes, while low-frequency logging has a negligible impact. These findings support feature-level energy analysis as a method for guiding software design decisions.

Environment-level studies have examined broader structural attributes such as programming languages and software metrics. Mancebo et al. [8] and Hindle [4] found that lines of code and churn metrics correlate with energy use. Pereira et al. [12] conducted a benchmark across 27 languages, finding that compiled languages like C and Rust are more energy-efficient than interpreted languages like Python. This contextualizes our case study, which focuses on implementations of background processes in Python, a widely used but energy-inefficient language.

Despite this progress, few studies have analyzed individual software features across multiple applications in a controlled, empirical setting. Jagroep et al. [5] and Jimenez et al. [6] looked at feature-level consumption, but did not isolate internal operations or background processes.

Autosave implementations differ in key dimensions: trigger mechanisms (timers vs. idle hooks), write strategies (buffered vs. unbuffered), and metadata handling. Yet no empirical study has systematically compared these factors in terms of their energy impact.

8   Conclusion

This paper introduced a reusable process for analyzing the energy behavior of background software features and demonstrated its application through a detailed case study of autosave implementations in three real-world text editors. By decomposing the feature, isolating operations, and profiling energy consumption under controlled conditions, we exposed measurable tradeoffs in trigger design, file handling, and auxiliary logic. Save frequency emerged as the dominant factor, with the Base variant in Mu consuming up to 83% more energy than Leo under identical file sizes. Additional overhead from change detection and logging was observable but less pronounced; for example, logging added an average of 3–7% energy cost depending on the editor and file size. The process proved effective for empirical energy evaluation and yielded four practical guidelines for designing greener autosave features. We believe this approach can be adapted to other background processes such as syncing, telemetry, and auto-formatting, and encourage further exploration in both research and development settings.

Acknowledgments. We would like to thank all internal reviewers at the University of Tartu for their valuable feedback.

Disclosure of Interests. The authors have no competing interests to declare that are relevant to the content of this article.

References

1. Andrae, A.: Total consumer power consumption forecast. Nordic Dig. Bus. Summit **10**, 69 (2017)
2. Ardito, L., Coppola, R., Morisio, M., Torchiano, M.: Methodological guidelines for measuring energy consumption of software applications. Sci. Program. **2019**(1), 5284645 (2019)
3. Chowdhury, S., Di Nardo, S., Hindle, A., Jiang, Z.M.: An exploratory study on assessing the energy impact of logging on android applications. Empir. Softw. Eng. **23**(3), 1422–1456 (2018)
4. Hindle, A.: Green mining: a methodology of relating software change and configuration to power consumption. Empir. Softw. Eng. **20**(2), 374–409 (2015)
5. Jagroep, E.A., et al.: Software energy profiling: comparing releases of a software product. In: Proceedings of the 38th International Conference on Software Engineering Companion, pp. 523–532 (2016)
6. Jimenez, E., Pulido, C., Calero, C., Moraga, M.Á., García, F., Gordillo, A.: Analysing instagram's energy consumption: Tips for an eco-friendly use. IADIS Int. J. WWW/Internet **22**(1) (2024)
7. Jones, N., et al.: How to stop data centres from gobbling up the world's electricity. Nature **561**(7722), 163–166 (2018)
8. Mancebo, J., Calero, C., García, F.: Does maintainability relate to the energy consumption of software? a case study. Software Qual. J. **29**(1), 101–127 (2021)
9. Mancebo, J., Calero, C., García, F., Moraga, M.Á., de Guzmán, I.G.R.: Feetings: framework for energy efficiency testing to improve environmental goal of the software. Sustain. Comput. Inf. Syst. **30**, 100558 (2021)
10. Mercer, C.W.: An introduction to real-time operating systems: scheduling theory. Unpublished manuscript (1992)
11. Pang, C., Hindle, A., Adams, B., Hassan, A.E.: What do programmers know about software energy consumption? IEEE Softw. **33**(3), 83–89 (2015)
12. Pereira, R., et al.: Ranking programming languages by energy efficiency. Sci. Comput. Program. **205**, 102609 (2021)
13. Sahin, C., Pollock, L., Clause, J.: How do code refactorings affect energy usage? In: Proceedings of the 8th ACM/IEEE International Symposium on Empirical Software Engineering and Measurement, pp. 1–10 (2014)
14. Şanlıalp, İ, Öztürk, M.M., Yiğit, T.: Energy efficiency analysis of code refactoring techniques for green and sustainable software in portable devices. Electronics **11**(3), 442 (2022)
15. Zsak, N., Wolff, C.: Impact of video quality and wireless network interface on power consumption of mobile devices. arXiv preprint arXiv:1407.7667 (2014)

Key Factors in Data-Driven Green-Lighting: An Empirical Investigation

Sarath Mookola Raveendran[1(✉)], Sebastian Herold[1], Per Kristensson[2], and Siri Jagstedt[2]

[1] Department of Computer Science and Engineering, Karlstad University, Universitetsgatan 2, 651 88 Karlstad, Sweden
{sarath.mookola.raveendran,sebastian.herold}@kau.se
[2] Service Research Center, Karlstad University, Universitetsgatan 2, 651 88 Karlstad, Sweden
{per.kristensson,siri.jagstedt}@kau.se

Abstract. Video game companies often have to choose among thousands of ideas to decide which ones to turn into video games. Despite the huge amount of money at stake, this process known as green-lighting in the game industry is largely a guesswork based on experts' experience and intuitions. In this paper, through a case study with a prominent Swedish gaming company we identify the key factors influencing green-lighting decisions and develops a typology for evaluating game concepts more effectively. These factors can be used to build a data-driven model that integrates domain knowledge with AI/ML techniques, including natural language processing (NLP), to predict a game's potential return on investment (ROI) during the funding request process. Further, the typology provides a structured framework for decision-makers, helping to reduce risk and ensure investments are aligned with market demand.

Keywords: Game development · Pre-release · Green-lighting · Key factors · Typology · Data driven decision making

1 Introduction

Creative industries, including gaming [16,19], film making [13], and startups [23], have long been characterized by inherent uncertainty. Traditionally, decision-making in these fields has relied heavily on intuition and gut feelings, with executives and developers using experience, market instincts, and past successes to guide critical choices [9,17]. In the gaming industry, for instance, the green-lighting process that decides whether to commit resources to a game concept has often been based on subjective assessments. However, as these industries grow more complex and competitive, the limitations of intuition [12] become apparent which leads to the need for data-driven solutions. While data science offer a more promising future in terms of predicting success and minimizing risks [14], the transition from "just knowing" to science-based decision-making is far from reality especially in early phases like Greenlighting.

G. Scanniello et al. (Eds.): PROFES 2025, LNCS 16362, pp. 218–231, 2026.
https://doi.org/10.1007/978-3-032-12092-2_16

For example, predictive analytics in film has been used to estimate box office performance [2,6], while startups rely on market testing and early feedback to evaluate potential success. However, most studies in these fields focus on post-release data [22], analyzing outcomes after a product has launched. In contrast, the gaming industry faces unique challenges in predicting the success of a project before its release [1,18]. Unlike movies, which tend to have clearer metrics early on [22], video games require continuous player engagement and long-term retention to determine success, making pre-release decisions even more critical.

Our research focuses on this underexplored gap in gaming: data-driven decision-making during the funding request process phase of game development, where key decisions are made about whether a game should move forward to full production. The challenge here is that the gaming industry is highly dynamic, with rapidly changing player preferences and technological advancements that make predicting success before release particularly difficult. We aim to address this problem by identifying and analyzing the key factors influencing green-lighting decisions and proposing a typology to assess game concepts more effectively. The contribution of this paper is two-fold: First, it identifies and categorizes the key factors influencing green-lighting decisions in the gaming industry based on expert interviews. Second, it develops a typology of green-lighting decisions to guide future industry practices. The identified categories and typology were then validated with a prominent Swedish gaming company, ensuring the results are grounded in real-world industry practices. Our findings ensure both relevance and applicability to future industry practices. From an academic perspective, this work contributes to the relatively underexplored field of pre-launch decision-making in creative industries, offering new insights into the factors that shape early-stage decision-making in game development. While much of the existing literature focuses on post-release success predictions, our study addresses an important gap by providing theoretical insights into pre-launch evaluation processes.

The structure of this paper is as follows: Sect. 2 provides an overview of the background and related works. In Sect. 3, we outline the research methodology employed in this study. Sections 4 and 5 present the key findings of the research. Finally, Sect. 6 offers a summary of the conclusions and concludes the paper.

2 Background and Related Works

Data-driven methods for predicting success have gained momentum in creative industries such as film, gaming, and startups. Traditionally, green-lighting decisions relied on intuition and expert judgment, introducing considerable uncertainty. Recent advances in predictive analytics, machine learning (ML), and data mining now provide valuable insights that help reduce uncertainty in early-stage project evaluations.

In the film industry, predicting box office success has long been a focus. Early studies, such as Litman [8], considered budget, genre, and star power, but these models relied heavily on post-production data, limiting predictive accuracy. Recent approaches use ML techniques. For instance, Kim et al. [6] applied

Latent Dirichlet Allocation (LDA) to movie scripts, extracting latent topics that improved box office prediction prior to production. Similarly, Eliashberg et al. [2] used a bag-of-words model along with domain knowledge to predict ROI, highlighting the value of textual features in early-stage decisions. While bag-of-words models are limited in capturing semantic nuance, LDA and advanced text-mining techniques provide more precise insights, enhancing prediction [6] [15].

In the startup domain, predictive analytics has been applied to forecast venture success. Sharchilev et al. [10] demonstrated that early-stage features, such as investor counts, funding amounts, crowdfunding pledges, and backer engagement, significantly influence funding decisions. Lin et al. [7] similarly highlighted the role of early market validation, including user feedback and crowdfunding support, in predicting long-term viability [6,15].

Crowdfunding platforms, in particular, provide rich early-stage data. Colletta et al. [5] found that early backer engagement strongly predicts project success, while Oduro et al. [11] used ML models with early feedback and social media sentiment to forecast outcomes. Such data-driven approaches are increasingly adopted by both entrepreneurs and investors for project selection [6,11].

Overall, the growing body of literature emphasizes the importance of data-driven decision-making in creative industries. While most studies focus on post-release performance, our study specifically examines the application of data-driven approaches during the early stages of game development, providing timely insights for green-lighting decisions.

3   Research Methodology

This empirical study adopts a Qualitative Interpretive Case Study approach [3,21] to examine the key factors influencing decision-making during the funding request phase. We collaborated with a Swedish gaming company focused on development and publishing. Initial meetings ensured alignment of research objectives and access to key personnel and data. We then conducted ten one-hour interviews with experts evaluating and funding game concepts, enabling in-depth insights into qualitative decision-making processes. The Gioia Methodology [4] guided our analysis, systematically translating first-order concepts into second-order themes and aggregate dimensions, providing a clear understanding of decision patterns despite the limited sample size.

3.1   Data Collection

We conducted semi-structured interviews with professionals from a game development company, gamers, and an academic expert to explore the factors influencing funding decisions during the funding request phase. The interview transcripts served as the primary data source, while reports from SVT Nyheter [20], a leading Swedish news outlet, were used as secondary data to provide context and triangulate our findings. This approach enabled validation by cross-referencing industry trends and challenges reported in the media with insights from the interviews. The first author developed an interview guide, which was reviewed and refined by all co-authors, resulting in 30 questions organized into four thematic sections: (1) interviewees' professional background and roles, (2) factors influencing funding decisions, (3) game feasibility considerations, and (4) integration of data-driven decision-making in the green-lighting process. Initial interviews included senior experts such as the senior finance leader and members of the finance control team. Remaining participants were selected through purposive sampling with the assistance of the Senior finance leader. Most interviews were conducted face-to-face, with one via video conference, each lasting 6090 min. All sessions were audio-recorded with consent, transcribed, and summarized for analysis.

3.2   Data Analysis

We employed the Gioia Methodology [4], an inductive approach for qualitative data analysis, to systematically extract themes from the interview transcripts. Initially, transcripts were coded to identify first-order concepts, representing participants' direct responses. These concepts were then abstracted into second-order themes, which were further grouped into aggregate dimensions. This structured process allowed us to develop a comprehensive understanding of the key factors influencing game funding decisions during the funding request phase. Throughout the analysis, we maintained an open stance, guided only by the context of the company allowing patterns and themes to emerge organically from the data, ensuring transparency and rigor while grounding findings in participants' own language and experiences.

First Order Concepts: The analysis continued by identifying additional key concepts that influence game evaluation decisions. Concepts like "Pitch Presentation," "Portfolio," and "Audience" highlight the importance of the game's creative potential, the quality of the idea's presentation, and the studio's ability to connect with its target audience. Other concepts, such as "Studio," "AAA projects" (high-budget, high-quality games often developed by major studios with advanced graphics and expansive gameplay), "Developer track record," and "Bug fixing server," emphasize the technical capabilities of the studio and the need for reliable post-launch technical support. Additional factors like "Intellectual Property (IP) Strength," "Geographical alignment," "Royalty fee," and "Risk" reflect concerns related to cost, development time, and expected ROI. Lastly, external influences such as "COVID," "Pandemic," and "Market saturation" were also highlighted, illustrating emerging market trends and external factors that shape the decision-making process.

Second Order Themes: After identifying the 1st order concepts (raw, unfiltered data), first author grouped them into 2nd order themes to begin abstracting the raw data into more interpretable and theoretical categories. 1st order concepts are mapped to Creative Track Record, Storyline of the Game, Pitch Presentation, Studio Portfolio Alignment, Target Audience, and Creative Concept Development. These themes represent various creative elements considered by evaluators when deciding if a game should move forward in development. Themes like Technical Track Record, Team Capability & Team Track, and Post-launch Technical Support reflect the importance of the studio's technical history and ability to handle the game's technical demands, as well as the support required once the game is launched. Themes like IP Strength, IP Licensing Cost & ROI, Initial Investment, Expected ROI, Development Time, Marketing Costs, Maintenance cost, Release Time, Regional Alignment of IP & Studio and Multi-Language Accessibility are critical financial and marketing considerations that directly impact the feasibility of funding a game. External Events such as pandemic (e.g., COVID, market disruptions), Market Saturation, and Post-Announcement Search are mapped into contextual and strategic factors.

Aggregate Dimensions: The second-order themes were consolidated into four aggregate dimensions capturing the core factors influencing game funding decisions during the funding request phase. The creative dimension covers the game's storyline, concept development, and the studio's prior creative achievements, reflecting project originality and appeal. The technical dimension highlights the studio's capabilities, team expertise, and reliability of post-launch support, emphasizing execution feasibility. The business and marketing dimension includes investment costs, expected ROI, and marketing strategies, ensuring funding decisions are financially sound. Finally, the contextual and strategic dimension accounts for external influences, such as market conditions, industry trends, and unexpected events, shaping project timing and strategic alignment. Together, these dimensions provide a comprehensive framework for understanding how multiple factors guide green-lighting decisions.

4   Key Factors Influencing Green-Lighting Decisions

This section presents factors that should be considered during the green lighting process of game development. We have organized the factors into four categories as shown in Fig. 1

4.1   Creative Factors

The creative aspects of a game encompass how original and engaging the game's content is, how well it is presented, and how it aligns with player expectations or introduces new, exciting ideas.

Creative Track Record: A studio's creative track record reflects its history of producing innovative, high-quality games, demonstrating strengths in storytelling, art direction, or mechanics. Proven creative work builds trust with decision makers and boosts internal confidence and stakeholder support.

"Creative people who come up with new ideas, especially those who have done it before, bring a lot of value to the table."- Expert 3

"Information on similar games already available in the market and the track record of those games, as well as the games made by the studio previously, is crucial."- Expert 7

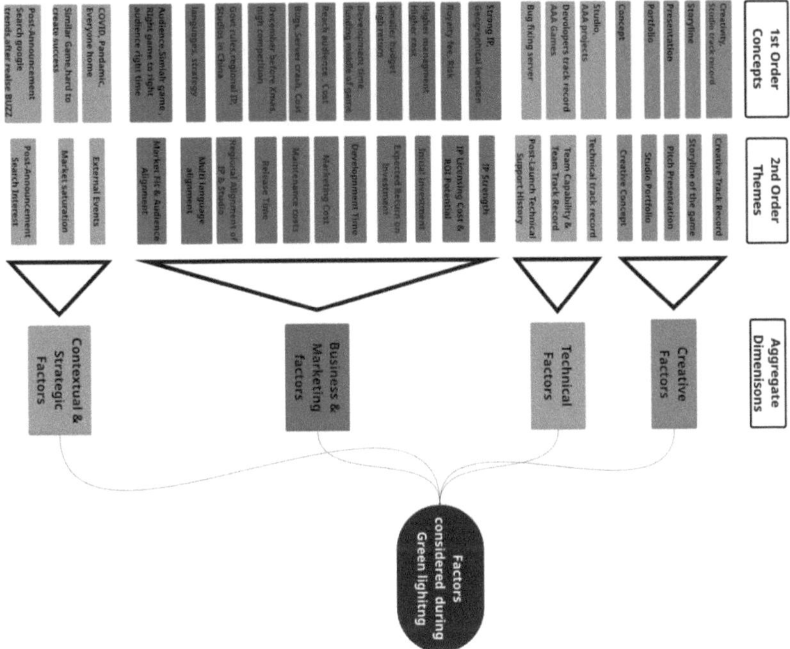

Fig. 1. Data structure created by Gioia Methodology

Storyline: It is the narrative framework of a game that elevates it beyond just game play mechanics, transforming it into an emotionally engaging experience, often becoming the reason stakeholders get excited and want to invest.
"Different studios believe they have a strong case for the game they want to invest in and are eager to start the project."- Expert 9
"Often, you just have key art and a basic storyline, and that's the type of game you're going to make."- Expert 2

Pitch Presentation: A pitch presentation is a studio's formal opportunity to present their game concept during the green-lighting phase to secure funding and approval. It includes key elements such as game-play footage, character designs, and sales projections, helping decision-makers visualize the game's potential and creative direction. A strong, clear pitch builds confidence in the project and the team, increasing the chances of funding. However, a vague or poorly delivered pitch can lead to rejection, even if the game concept is strong.
"You have a pitch with the storyline in a standard format, along with financials, and then often a sales pitch, which is a PowerPoint that tells the story they want to sell."- Expert 2

Studio's Portfolio Alignment: A studio's portfolio is a collection of its past projects, demonstrating its creative capabilities, execution skills, ability to meet deadlines and quality standards. If a studio's portfolio doesn't align with a new game, there is a higher risk in funding the project.

"If you look at the company, well, the studios are more or less acquired because they fit into our portfolio. We acquire them based on the level of competence, ability to create AAA games, handle smaller indie games and live-up games. Our portfolio is designed to be diversified ."- Expert 5

Creative Concept Development: While some genres may experience market saturation, the right creative concept has the potential to break through and capture player interest, even in crowded spaces. The key to success is not just introducing something novel but also aligning it with the market conditions and player demand. Understanding market saturation helps mitigate the risk of launching a conceptually similar game that doesn't stand out.

"Creative people who come up with new ideas, especially those who have done it before, bring a lot of value to the table. But, uncertainty increases when there is a new IP, but it becomes more important to assess its potential." - Expert 3

"No one had ever done it before, and we were like, 'OK, how can this be successful? It's so stupid that it's not... it's so strange.' And then it just hit the market, and everyone loved it." - Expert 2

"We believed in the studio, but not in the game." - Expert 2

4.2   Technical Factors

A game with poor technical quality whether due to bugs, performance issues, or platform incompatibility, will frustrate players, damage the studio's reputation, and ultimately fail to meet financial expectations. The technical can be divided into sub-factors identified through the interview study.

Technical Track Record: Technical track record refers to a studio's history of delivering high-quality, technically sound games, demonstrating expertise, consistency, and problem-solving. It includes managing challenges, meeting milestones, and success with AAA projects. Decision-makers trust the studio's past performance even if the current game's concept is unproven.

"When you look at what the game studio has made before, if they've only made games that have proven to have bad quality, that's an indication that it might be a higher risk." - Expert 3

Team Capability and Track Record: A team's capability and track record refer to the past experience and expertise of developers working in the studios. Developers with a background in major game studios, having contributed to successful games, bring valuable experience, industry knowledge, and best practices that can elevate a new game's quality. For AAA games, where the project scale is large and expectations are high, it is crucial to have experienced developers who can handle both technical and creative demands. Further, having the right team size ensures the game has adequate resources.

"We believed in the studio, but not in the game." - Expert 2

"We were at company-A before, and they have a track record of making successful games. We can look at that history, and also consider the studio's track record to assess the potential success." - Expert 5

Post-launch Technical Support History: Post-launch support refers to a studio's efforts to maintain and improve a game after its release, including addressing technical issues, providing updates and ensuring ongoing player engagement. Games that lack ongoing support often face issues like server insta-bility, buggy game play, and negative player sentiment, which can hurt long-term success. While these issues cannot found out during green-lighting phase, the studio's history provides valuable insight into their reliability, responsiveness, and ability to sustain long-term player trust and technical performance.

"They are continuously working in different phases to find bugs." - Expert 3

"The game is a live-op game, and the servers crash because too many players are trying to access it." - Expert 3

4.3   Business and Marketing Factors

A solid budget and marketing ensures that the game is not only well-developed but also well-promoted. An effective marketing plan helps ensure that the game reaches its target audience, builds excitement, and generates long-term sales.

IP Strength: IP strength refers to the value of an intellectual property (IP) based on its brand recognition, fan base, and established reputation in the market. Strong IP strength provides built-in brand recognition, trust, and community interest, which can significantly reduce marketing costs and increase player acquisition. Established IPs often generate excitement on the first day, higher conversion rates, and long-term engagement through fan loyalty.

"One IP may succeed in a small region with many people." - Expert 2

"Uncertainty increases when there is a new IP, but it becomes more important to assess its potential." - Expert 2

IP Licensing Cost and ROI Potential: IP licensing cost refers to the fees and legal constraints involved in using an existing intellectual property (IP), while the ROI potential measures the potential return on investment that an IP can generate. Strong IPs can reduce marketing risk and help with discoverability. But they often come with high licensing fees, legal constraints, and ROI pressure. New/original IPs are riskier, but offer long-term ownership and creative freedom.

"For IPs you don't own, include the agreed royalty payments to the IP owner to calculate financial upside." - Expert 2

Initial Investment: Initial investment refers to the capital required to start a project, which includes development costs, marketing expenses, and any other upfront financial commitments. The size of the initial investment plays a key role in green-lighting decisions. Higher-cost projects require greater justification, carry more financial risk, and often trigger internal review processes and approval from higher management.

"We have a threshold below a certain level, they can make decisions on their own. Above that level, management needs to be involved and have a say on whether we should continue with a project." - Expert 2

"A small investment requires less risk, so we expect a lower return. It's also a matter of the investment level, how much money should be invested in each case, and what the risk and return are in each case." - Expert 3

Expected Return on Investment: Expected Return on Investment (ROI) refers to the anticipated financial return that a project is expected to generate compared to its initial cost, helping to assess the financial viability of a project. Some games with small budgets may have a huge commercial potential, while others with higher costs may show weaker returns. Understanding expected ROI helps prioritize projects that strike the best balance between risk and reward and ensures that investment is aligned with financial goals and market realities. *"A small investment requires less risk, and so we expect a lower return. It's also a matter of the investment level, how much money should be invested in each case, and what the risk and return are."* - Expert 3

Game Development Time: Game development time is the estimated duration needed to complete a game, from initial concept to final release. A well-estimated timeline is essential for financial planning, resource allocation, and market positioning. Unrealistic or extended timelines can lead to cost overruns, delayed releases, and missed market opportunities, especially if trends shift or competitive titles release first. Insufficient development time can significantly impact the quality and stability of the game and often leads to unresolved bugs, technical issues, and missed opportunities to improve the game play and features.
"How many months of development do you believe this will take?" - Expert 1
"The budget at the pitching time is set, but depending on what happens during the project, you might need to adjust it-either increase the budget or recognize that it will cost more." - Expert 1
"When you green-light a project, it might seem like a huge success, but if your competition releases a similar game a year before you, then..." - Expert 3

Marketing Cost: Marketing cost involves expenses associated with promoting a game, including advertising, outreach, and strategies to build awareness and drive sales. A strong marketing push is essential for commercial success, especially in competitive genres or new IPs. Even the release of a new game with few modifications from previous version needs marketing cost to reach the audience.
"If you spend a lot on marketing and other things to reach the audience you require..." - Expert 10

Maintenance Cost: Maintenance cost include ongoing expenses required to support and update a game post release, particularly for games with online components or live services. Even games with minimal content updates may require consistent infrastructure, monitoring, and support. Ignoring these costs during green-lighting can lead to underestimating total investment and strain post-launch operations.
"Games where you always have a server online, and nothing much changes year over year, but you still need to maintain the game and keep it alive." - Expert 8

Release Time: The timing of a game's launch significantly impacts its market reception, PR effectiveness, campaign reach and overall success. Releasing during a crowded window, such as when other high-profile games are launching or during peak seasons, can limit visibility and make it harder to stand out in the market. For example, while December offers strong sales due to the holidays, it also brings high competition, making it a double-edged sword. For sequels, releasing too soon after the previous game risks lower engagement, as players may not have had enough time to fully enjoy or get excited about the original title.

"Before Christmas is a big season, but there is quite heavy competition in that release window as well. It doesn't necessarily make sense to release a game before Christmas because of the competition." - Expert 3

"You have a pretty interesting case this autumn when, between September and December, GTA6 is rumored to be released. It's not confirmed yet, but I don't think any other studios around the world will release a game during that time." - Expert 2, SVT Nyheter

"That implied my kids. They released another one the next year. Now it's too much. I don't want to hold." - Expert 3

Regional Alignment of IP and Studio: Regional alignment of IP & studio refers to how well a game and its associated IP align with the cultural, regulatory, and market preferences of specific regions. Commercial success is often tied to how well it fits with regional expectations and preferences. Some IPs are extremely powerful in specific countries but lack recognition in other countries. Studios in certain regions can navigate local regulations more easily, making development smoother and more cost-effective. Understanding these regional dynamics enables better market targeting, forecasting, and investment.

"One IP may succeed in a small region with many people." - Expert 2

"Chinese developers have an easier time considering the government's rules and regulations compared to Western developers. But in Western European or Canadian markets, the strength of the IP is more of a focus." - Expert 2

"I think there are a lot of regional differences depending on the type of game and how it's developed." - Expert 2

Multi language alignment: Multi-language support is vital for expanding the reach of the game's market and commercial viability. Games available in multiple languages are more likely to attract and engage a global audience, increasing the chances of success of the game in non-native markets. Further, language alignment does not just mean direct translation, it also involves cultural adaptation. A game that aligns its story, humor, and themes with regional preferences can gain a competitive advantage over games that are simply translated without cultural consideration. This includes adjusting certain references or content to better resonate with players in different regions (e.g., local jokes, cultural references, or adjusting content for regulatory standards).

"I think the number of languages is an important part of the strategy to target the right audience for the game." - Expert 3

Market fit and Audience Alignment: Market fit & Audience Alignment involve gathering data to ensure a game aligns with player interest, genre demand, and commercial viability, reducing failure risks. Without proper validation, teams may invest in concepts that don't resonate with the audience.

"The right game for the right audience at the right time." - Expert 3

"But when they pitch a game, they have a targeted audience in mind and an assumption of who is going to play this game." - Expert 3

4.4 Contextual and Strategic Factors

Contextual and Strategic Factors highlight external risks and opportunities affecting a game's market success.

External Events Impact: External events impact refers to unforeseen events or global situations that can disrupt game development, alter market conditions, and influence player behavior. For example, the COVID-19 pandemic caused widespread production delays but also boosted interest in certain genres. Factoring in these situational risks helps ensure the game's plan remains realistic and adaptable to broader industry and global conditions.

"When they released the game, it was a good time. It was the beginning of the pandemic, everyone was at home, and suddenly a game-A survival game sells for over a billion." - Expert 2

Market Saturation: Market saturation refers to the extent to which a specific game genre or market is filled with competing titles, making it harder for new games to stand out. Over-saturation in a genre can make it difficult even for well-designed games to succeed. If the market is crowded and the game doesn't have a clear differentiator, it may struggle to attract attention. This factor helps to assess competitive risk and the importance of unique positioning.

"Competition is like, 'This is the game we want to make,' and then we tweak it a little bit. Often, it's not about new ideas; you just take what's already there and modify it a bit to create a new game." - Expert 2

"These are the coolest games coming up for next year, and it's quite fun because every game looks the same, and it takes 3–4 years to make a game. So, three years ago..." - Expert 1

Post-announcement Search Interest: Post-announcement search interest measures the level of online search activity and public curiosity about a game after its announcement, indicating potential demand and market interest. Early search interest is a reliable leading indicator of demand. High spikes after a reveal suggest strong concept resonance, good marketing execution, and potential commercial traction. Although this cannot be assessed during the funding request phase, trends can be analyzed by looking at similar games.

"When an announcement is made, you can also track online search traffic. With tools like Google Trends, you get a lot more information compared to before the announcement when nobody knows what you're working on." - Expert 1

"After release as the release week and month are crucial for game." - Expert 2

5 Typology of Green-Lighting Decisions

In this study, we organized the key factors in green-lighting decisions into four main categories: Creative, Technical, Business & Marketing, and Contextual & Strategic factors. Through qualitative coding of interviews and case materials, we observed recurring patterns that formed three distinct decision-making typologies: Safe Bets, Risky Innovators, and Committee Compromises 1. Each typology represents a characteristic combination of factors that influence whether a project receives funding.

To support cross-typology comparison and aid visual interpretation, we assigned illustrative scores (15) to each main factor for the three typologies. These scores were not derived from quantitative analysis but were constructed interpretively by assessing the relative frequency, emphasis, and strength of presence of each factor in our qualitative data. Frequency indicates how often a factor appeared in interviews and case discussions. Frequently mentioned factors received higher scores. Emphasis is how strongly the factor was highlighted by interviewees in shaping decisions. Strongly emphasized factors received higher scores. Strength of Presence means how central or critical a factor was in the decision-making process. Dominant factors received higher scores. The final score for each main factor is calculated as the average of these three dimensions, providing a heuristic profile to visualize qualitative distinctions among the typologies rather than a precise measurement (Table 1).

Sample Score Calculation: Creative Factors are often central to Risky Innovators and drive decisions. It is frequently discussed, strongly emphasized, and consistently present, leading to a high illustrative score of 5. Business & Marketing factors are important for Committee Compromises but are not dominant.

Table 1. Typology of Green-lighting Decisions

Category	Safe Bets	Risky Innovators	Committee Compromises
Creative Factors	Familiar, well-aligned (3)	Bold, original experimental(5)	Moderate, compromised concepts (3)
Technical Factors	Proven team, high stability (5)	Unproven or unconventional (4)	Adequate, sufficient execution (3)
Business & Marketing Factors	Clear ROI, low risk (4.33)	High risk, niche appeal (3)	Balanced, acceptable margins (4.33)
Contextual & Strategic Factors	Stable market timing, aligned (5)	Trend-driven, reactive (4)	Seasonality-driven, strategic filler (3)

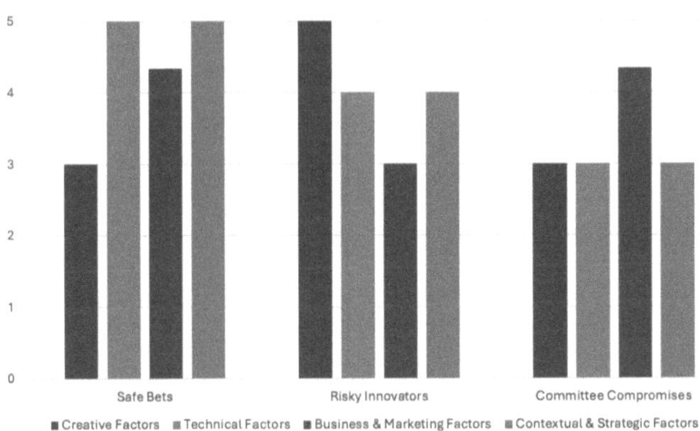

Fig. 2. Grouped Bar chart for typology of green-lighting decisions (Color figure online)

Moderate emphasis and presence yield a score of 4.33. The illustrative scores are summarized in 1 and visualized in Fig. 2.

Each group shows how factors shape different typologies: Safe Bets stress technical and strategic strength with reliable market backing, Risky Innovators highlight bold creative vision supported by strategy, and Committee Compromises balance all factors with an emphasis on business and marketing to ensure alignment and steady output though rarely aiming for standout innovation.

6   Conclusions

Our empirical study has identified and analyzed the key factors influencing data-driven decision-making in the game green-lighting process. We have formulated a typology providing a structured framework for evaluating the critical factors that drive strategic decisions. Moreover, the categorization and typology can address the potential selective memory problem among experts involved in the green-lighting process. By relying on structured data instead of subjective recollections, this research can help reduce biases arising from past experiences, personal preferences, or human errors. Through the identification of these critical factors, this research provides valuable insights for game studios and publishers, enabling them to navigate the complexities of the green-lighting process more effectively, reduce financial risks, align projects with market demand, and ultimately increase the likelihood of a game's commercial success. Thus, our study has the potential to serve as an important step towards reducing the inherent uncertainties in the gaming industry, using data to make more reliable and informed green-lighting decisions. Future research could focus on developing a data-driven model of the green-lighting process, which can be further enhanced by integrating emerging technologies such as AI and ML to support more informed and objective decision-making.

References

1. Divakaran, P.K.P.: Pre-release member participation as potential predictors of post-release community members' adoption behaviour: Evidence from the motion picture industry. Behav. Inf. Technol. **32**(6), 545–559 (2013)
2. Eliashberg, J., Hui, S.K., Zhang, Z.J.: From story line to box office: a new approach for green-lighting movie scripts. Manage. Sci. **53**(6), 881–893 (2007)
3. Flyvbjerg, B.: What Is a Case Study? (2011)
4. Gioia, D.A., Corley, K.G., Hamilton, A.L.: Seeking qualitative rigor in inductive research: Notes on the gioia methodology. Organ. Res. Methods **16**(1), 15–31 (2013)
5. Kao, S.C.: A crowdfunding prediction model: a data-driven approach. In: Proceedings of the 8th Multidisciplinary International Social Networks Conference, pp. 63–70 (2021)
6. Kim, J., Lee, Y., Song, I.: From intuition to intelligence: a text mining-based approach for movies' green-lighting process. Internet Res. **32**(3), 1003–1022 (2022). https://doi.org/10.1108/INTR-11-2020-0651

7. Li, Y., Zadehnoori, I., Jowhar, A., Wise, S., Laplume, A., Zihayat, M.: Learning from yesterday: predicting early-stage startup success for accelerators through content and cohort dynamics. J. Bus. Ventur. Insights **22**, e00490 (2024)
8. Litman, B.R.: Predicting success of theatrical movies: an empirical study. J. Popular Culture **16**(4), 159 (1983)
9. Matzler, K., Bailom, F., Mooradian, T.A.: Intuitive decision making. MIT Sloan Manag. Rev. **49**(1), 13–21 (2007)
10. Ningrum, I.W.K., Ridho, F., Wijayanto, A.W.: Predicting startup success using machine learning approach. J. Appl. Inform. Comput. **8**(2), 280–290 (2024)
11. Oduro, M.S., Yu, H., Huang, H.: Predicting the entrepreneurial success of crowdfunding campaigns using model-based machine learning methods. Int. J. Crowd Sci. **6**(1), 7–16 (2022)
12. Perkins, D.N.: The limits of intuition. Leonardo, pp. 119–125 (1977)
13. Pokorny, M., Miskell, P., Sedgwick, J.: Managing uncertainty in creative industries: film sequels and hollywood's profitability, 1988–2015. Competition Change **23**(1), 23–46 (2019)
14. Provost, F., Fawcett, T.: Data science and its relationship to big data and data-driven decision making. Big Data **1**(1), 51–59 (2013)
15. von Rimscha, M.B., Albarran, A., Faustino, P., Santos, R.: Packaging a movie project-a resource based perspective (2009)
16. Sarioğuz, O., Miser, E.: Data-driven decision-making: Revolutionizing management in the information era. J. Artif. Intell. General Sci. (JAIGS) **4**(1), 179–194 (2024)
17. Sauter, V.L.: Intuitive decision-making. Commun. ACM **42**(6), 109–115 (1999)
18. Schaer, O., Kourentzes, N., Fildes, R.: Estimating the market potential with pre-release buzz. Lancaster University Management School, Management Science Paper Series (2019)
19. Serova, E.: Data-driven analysis of project portfolio dimensions in the video game industry (2024). unpublished
20. Spelutvecklaren, S.: Gta 6: Hela kulturvärlden påverkas (2023). https://www.svt.se/kultur/svenska-spelutvecklaren-om-gta-6-hela-kulturvarlden-paverkas. Accessed 20 July 2023
21. Starman, A.B.: The case study as a type of qualitative research. J. Contemporary Educ. Stud./Sodobna Pedagogika **64**(1), 15–25 (2013)
22. Varghese, R.R., et al.: A novel approach to predict success of online games using random forest regressor for time series data. In: International Conference on Advances in Electrical and Computer Technologies, pp. 100–110. Springer, Singapore (2021)
23. Yusupova, G.R., Nesmeyanova, E.I.: Financial uncertainty of a startup (2024)

AppChallenge: Integrating Software Engineering, Business Development, and Coaching in Challenge-Based Learning

Rita Francese[(✉)] [iD]

University of Salerno, Fisciano, Italy
`francese@unisa.it`

Abstract. We present *AppChallenge*, a software-analytics pipeline embedded in a eleven-edition, challenge-based learning program that engages students in the design and development of innovative applications. The initiative integrates academic supervision, company coaching, busisness development, and multi-stakeholder evaluation, functioning both as an educational framework and as a research environment. A central element of this pipeline is its dual-assessment structure, which combines the perspectives of a *Technical Jury* of experts with those of a *Young Jury* of high school students. This design captures both professional standards of quality and youth perceptions of engagement and motivation. Results revealed that experts expressed highly consistent scoring and an exceptional NPS of 77.8, surpassing benchmarks of leading companies, while students revealed greater variability and a more moderate but still positive NPS. Qualitative feedback further indicates that experts valued professionalism, applicability, and continuity, whereas students appreciated interactivity, diversity of ideas, and the motivational experience of participation. The findings demonstrate that AppChallenge trains students in technical and collaborative skills and provides a replicable methodology for bridging expert and young perspectives, strengthening its dual role as a professional training ecosystem and an instrument for inspiring future generations.

Keywords: Project-based learning · Challenge-based learning · Coaching · Enterprise Applications · Busisness Development

1 Introduction

Universities are increasingly asked to prepare software engineers who can navigate real-world constraints, collaborate across roles, and deliver maintainable products, not just toy assignments, as well as to develop soft skills [13]. To respond to this need, we proposed *AppChallenge*[1], an eleven-edition, challenge-based, coached innovation course of the Computer Science master program at the University of Salerno, named *enterprise mobile application development*. Since

---

[1] https://www.appchallenge.it/.

2014, AppChallenge has connected the university with industry partners and secondary schools, acting as a bridge for knowledge transfer and community-facing innovation promoting busisness development. It builds on preliminary Project-Based Learning (PBL) experiences in our context [5], where the process was at an early stage. Within this ecosystem, small student teams design and implement running, enterprise-grade applications that answer concrete needs proposed by external stakeholders. AppChallenge is a data-driven intervention that treats a semester-long, coached challenge as a software analytics pipeline. The program continuously collects evaluation and process traces, rubric scores from an industry Technical Jury, ratings and Net Promoter Score (NPS) from a both the techinical and a school-based Youth Jury, open comments, milestone adherence, and repository/CI activity, and analyzes them for process improvement.

It is important to point out that AppChallenge is based on two pedagogical pillars: team-based learning (TBL), which structures small groups into accountable, high-performance teams, and challenge-based learning (CBL), which frames authentic, community-relevant problems that culminate in public dissemination [6–8,10]. A relevant feature is structured, continuous coaching by professionals from leading companies, aligned to each team's topic and skills, consistent with evidence that externally mentored, authentic tasks strengthen learning and professional readiness [13]. The program culminates in a public road show assessed by two juries, a Technical Jury of industry experts and a Young Jury drawn from secondary schools, to balance professional rigor with user-facing freshness, as in juried showcases and hackathon-style evaluations [2,12]. Involving schools also aligns with evidence on the benefits of outreach learning activities for secondary students.

Beyond pedagogy, AppChallenge is designed as a bidirectional technology-transfer mechanism. On the university side, sustained engagement with firms includes academic engagement, collaborative research, consulting, and other knowledge interactions linked to positive outcomes for research and education. On the industry side, partnerships provide access to emerging technologies, prototypes, and talent pipelines.

The paper contribution may be summarized as follows:

- a replicable description of the AppChallenge methodology that integrates CBL, TBL, busisness development and industry coaching in a single, annually repeatable format;
- a mixed-methods evaluation, combining rubric-based technical assessment and Youth Jury ratings with user-facing measures (e.g., NPS);
- actionable lessons for university, industry, school collaboration, including implications for course design, employability signaling, and STEM promotion.

In the most recent edition (February 2025), 40 students collaborated with 13 partner companies, supported by academic mentors and industry coaches, and were evaluated by 36 members of the Technical Jury alongside Young Jury of secondary school students. The projects showcased advanced technological integration, frequently employing artificial intelligence, cloud infrastructures, and immersive interfaces. Post-event analyses revealed strong indicators of impact and transfer: the Technical Jury reported an exceptionally high Net Promoter

Score (NPS) of 77.8, reflecting near-unanimous endorsement and professional recognition of the initiative's value, while the Young Jury expressed a positive but more heterogeneous response, with an NPS of 40.0 that highlighted both enthusiasm and a degree of critical variability among participants. Complementary survey data also highlighted the educational relevance of the program, with technical jurors rating coaching as highly useful for student development and students emphasizing the motivational and exploratory dimension of participating as evaluators.

Paper Organization. Section 2 discusses the background; Sect. 3 details the proposed methodology. Section 4 reports results of the last challenge while Sect. 5 discusses implications and lessons learned. Finally, Sect. 6 concludes the paper with final remarks and future work.

2   Background

Our methodology adopts CBL in computing by structuring authentic, stakeholder-driven problems over a semester and culminating in public dissemination. Prior research has highlighted the benefits of CBL for engagement, transversal skills, and authenticity in engineering education [6], while recent computing education studies have explored design adaptations for large cohorts and technical contexts [14]. *AppChallenge* extends this line of work by combining CBL with team-based learning (TBL), which has shown strong impact on accountability and learning outcomes in computing courses [10], and with continuous industry coaching, a practice increasingly recognized as essential for bridging academic and professional standards [4].

Our approach also connects with research on involving external stakeholders in capstone and project-based courses [3]. Studies consistently report that industry clients and mentors enhance authenticity and employability signals, though they introduce supervision and assessment complexities [13]. Public showcases and hackathons have similarly emerged as experiential formats for surfacing real-world quality attributes, but they are often short-term and judged by a single panel [2,12]. By contrast, AppChallenge embeds a semester-long process and formalizes a dual-jury evaluation, separating industry assessment of rigor from youth appraisal of appeal. Finally, assessment of learning and impact has been approached through rubrics, reflective measures, and external examiners [1], with growing interest in compact indicators such as the Net Promoter Score (NPS) [9]. Our model leverages both rubrics and NPS to capture complementary perspectives. Beyond pedagogy, AppChallenge also acts as a technology-transfer mechanism: it has produced concrete innovation outcomes (e.g., the Commigo SRL startup) and fostered sustainable community engagement, with former students returning as jurors in later editions.

Earlier at our institution, the preliminary mobile app version of this course used PBL with industry judges, yielding positive results [5]. AppChallenge generalizes this model with structured coaching, broader technologies, and a dual-jury design.

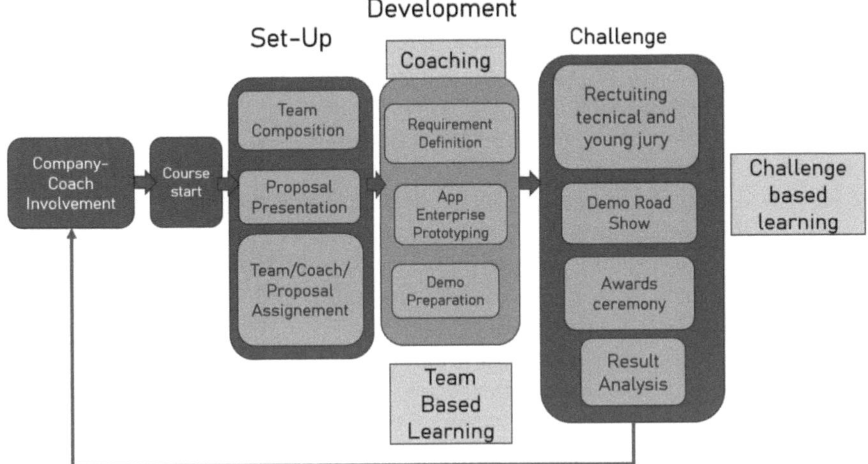

Fig. 1. AppChallenge process from challenge launch to public road show.

3   Methodology

This section describes the methodological design of *AppChallenge*: a semester-long, challenge-based intervention embedded in a Master's course and supported by continuous industry coaching. Figure 1 depicts the overall workflow from the challenge launch to public road show, detailed in the following.

Setting and Participants. *AppChallenge* is embedded in the *Enterprise Mobile Application Development* course of the Master's in Computer Science at the University of Salerno. Each edition enrolls ≈40–50 Master's students. Students are assigned to permanent teams of 3–4 based on a short skills survey (backend, frontend/mobile, data/AI, UX) and schedule compatibility. Partner companies (IT, consulting, telecom, fintech, healthcare) nominate coaches who propose the application idea in a prlenary session (proposal presentation); the teaching staff matches teams and coaches by topic and skill fit.

Process and Timeline. The program uses CBL blended with TBL and continuous industry coaching (Fig. 1). In addition to technical delivery, teams explicitly develop a *Business Model Canvas (BMC)*, cohesive *brand design*, and an investor/customer-ready *pitch*. The semester is organized into milestones:

M0: Challenge scoping (wk 1–2)—select/refine a company brief; draft the problem statement, priority users, and success criteria; produce a fist version of the *Business Model Canvas (BMC)* (segments, value proposition, pains/gains, channels, early cost/revenue hypotheses).

M1: Concept & prototype (wk 3–5)—architecture sketch, UX flows, clickable prototype; begin *brand design* (name exploration, positioning statement, initial visual directions). An intermediate presentation involved the coaches and the teams for monitoring the state of the projects and get feedback from the other coaches.

M2: Alpha (wk 6–8)—core features, data model, running backend; formative demo with coach feedback; refine BMC (pricing, key resources/partners); outline the *pitch narrative* (problem, solution, demo storyline, competitors, evidence/risks, monetization).

M3: Beta (wk 9–11)—feature-complete build, basic tests; finalize *brand design* (logo, palette, type, accessibility checks) and publish a lightweight brand guide; create a marketing landing page; develop *pitch deck v1*.

M4: Release candidate (wk 12) - stabilization, performance / usability refinement, security pass; deploy to production or production-like; assemble public demo assets; deliver *pitch deck v2* and a live pitch of 3–5 min. Provide an app brochure to distribute to the juries.

Teams may use cross-platform frameworks, cloud backends, AI/ML, or immersive/VR, but must meet *enterprise-grade* criteria, such as authentication, persistence, and deployment.

Coaching and Academic Supervision. Each team has a named *industry coach* who provides technical/product feedback via scheduled touchpoints (minimum: biweekly). Faculty supervisors conduct readiness checks at M1-M4, ensure ethical compliance, and supervise scope changes or any difficulty.

Public Evaluation. The course concludes with a public road show, featuring a one-minute pitch and a live demo for each team. Two juries provide complementary judgments:

- *Technical Jury (TJ):* industry professionals and faculty apply a structured rubric to *Adequacy to need, Technical complexity, Usability/UX*, and *Presentation*, using a 15 scale. They also answer several questions concerning their perception of the event and NPS, reported in Table 1.
- *Youth Jury (YJ):* secondary-school students rate the projects on a scale 1–10 and their perception filling in the questionnaire reported in Table 2.

Data Collection and Management. Rubric and survey forms are collected digitally and bound to team IDs. basic process metrics (milestone compliance, repository activity) are adopted to grade the participants.

Analysis. We analyze the evaluation data collected from the two juries and their perception questionnaires reported in Tables 1 and 2 and compute the Net Promoter Score (NPS) [11]. In particular, NPS is a metric used to assess loyalty and satisfaction, based on how likely respondents are to recommend a service or organization. Respondents rate on a scale from 0 to 10 and are categorized into three groups based on their score: Promoters (those who respond with a score of 910), Passives (score of 78), and Detractors (score of 06).

The score is calculated as:

$$\text{NPS} = \%\text{Promoters} - \%\text{Detractors}$$

NPS ranges from -100 to $+100$: positive values indicate more promoters than detractors (favorable sentiment), while negative values indicate the opposite.

Continuous Improvement and Entrepreneurship Integration. Annual retrospectives with coaches, the data analysis, and the two juries open comments provide

Table 1. Technical Jury—Final perception questions.

QID	Question
GT-01	How do you rate the overall impact of App Challenge on promoting a culture of innovation?
GT-02	Did the event foster dialogue between companies, students, and institutions?
GT-03	Was collaboration with company coaches useful for the teams?
GT-04	Did the event help students develop practical and professional skills?
GT-05	Does the initiative contribute to promoting innovation among students?
GT-06	Would you recommend a colleague to take part as a juror in future editions?
GT-OPEN-01	What impressed you most in the projects presented?
GT-OPEN-02	What were the main weaknesses you observed?
GT-OPEN-03	What suggestions do you have to improve the event or the evaluation process?

Table 2. Young Jury—Final perception questions.

QID	Question
YJ-01	How interesting did you find the initiative?
YJ-02	How engaged did you feel during the event?
YJ-03	Did you learn anything new by participating in the App Challenge?
YJ-04	Do you think the initiative helped you better understand the academic and/or professional world?
YJ-05	How much did the event inspire you to consider university studies in science or technology?
YJ-06	Would you recommend a friend to take part in this initiative?
YJ-OPEN-01	What impressed you most in the projects presented?
YJ-OPEN-02	Describe the negative aspects of the initiative.
YJ-OPEN-03	What suggestions do you have to improve the event in future editions?

feedback for the improvement of the process and the organization. As an example, we introduced the questionnaires and the NPS analysis in the X Edition.

4 Evaluation

In this section, we investigate how different juries, with distinct evaluation instruments and perspectives, assessed the student-developed applications in the AppChallenge. In particular, we focus on both the project scores and the perceptions expressed by the jurors. Based on this objective, we address the following research question:

- **RQ1.** How do technical expert and youth juries differ in their evaluation and perception of student-developed applications in the AppChallenge?

We discuss the results of the XI Edition, held in the first semester (fall) 2024, involving 40 Master's students in Computer Science who, in small teams, delivered running, enterprise-grade applications. The final road show competition was held February 18, 2025. 12 projects were proposed by coaches and reflected market and territorial needs, integrating AI for healthcare (e.g. chronic back pain support, schizophrenia monitoring, chatbot triage), education (mathematics and literature tools), civic services (damage detection, video anonymization), cybersecurity through serious games, and local tourism through personalized itineraries; most apps used modern cross-platform stacks with cloud back ends and, in several cases, immersive/VR components.

University Computer Science teachers and twenty companies of national and international relevance (e.g., Google, Accenture, NTT Data, IBM, Engineering) contributed as coaches and/or Technical Jury members. 25 secondary school students participated as members of the Young Jury, strengthening dialogue among pupils, university students, and industry professionals.

Net-Promoter Score. As summarized in Table, the Technical Jury achieved an NPS score of 77.8, while the Young Jury obtained an NPS of 40.0.

Table 3. Net Promoter Score (NPS) Summary

Group	Promoters	Detractors	Total	NPS Score
Technical Jury	29	1	36	77.78
Young Jury	14	4	25	40.00

Project Evaluation. The comparison between the mean of Technical and Young Jury scores on the normalized 1–20 scale (Fig. 2), shows very similar central tendencies. The Technical Jury reached a median score of 11.8 and a mean of 11.9, while the Young Jury obtained a median of 11.6 and a mean of 11.6 (Table 4). The variability was slightly lower for the Technical Jury (SD = 1.58) compared to the Young Jury (SD = 1.77). Scores ranged from 9.22 to 15.6 in the Technical Jury and from 8.33 to 14.0 in the Young Jury.

Table 4. Descriptive statistics of normalized average project scores for the Technical and Young Jury (n. projects = 12).

Jury	Median	Mean	SD	Min	Max
Technical Jury	11.8	11.9	1.58	9.22	15.6
Young Jury	11.6	11.6	1.77	8.33	14.0

The Technical Jury's assessment across the four evaluation dimensions produced relatively homogeneous results (Table 5, Fig. 3), in a scale 36–180. The mean scores were close in value, ranging from 105.5 for Presentation to 107.4 for Usability & UX, while medians varied only slightly between 105.0 and 106.5. The dispersion of the scores, however, showed moderate variability: the lowest standard deviation was recorded in Adequacy (SD = 13.37), whereas Usability &UX displayed the highest (SD = 15.20). The range of observed scores highlighted that some projects received relatively low evaluations, such as 77 in Presentation and 81 in Usability & UX, while the top-performing projects achieved high totals, including 143 in Technological Difficulty and 142 in Usability & UX. Overall, the distributions shown in the boxplot confirm that the Technical Jury's evaluations were balanced across dimensions, with no dimension being systematically favored or penalized.

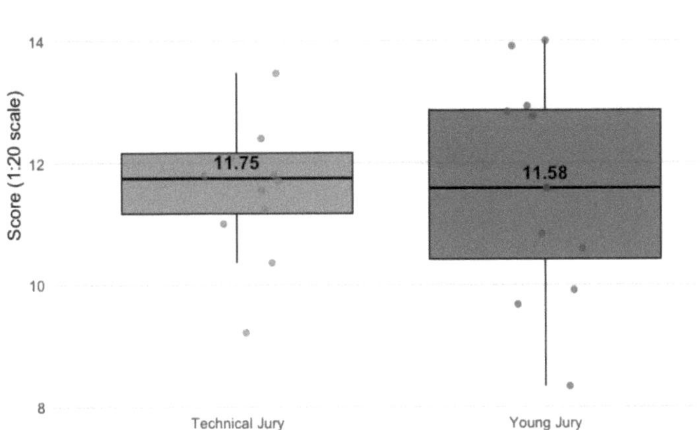

Fig. 2. Boxplot of the score comparison of the Technical vs Young jury on a normalized on a 1–20 scale.

Table 5. Descriptive statistics of project scores by dimension.

Dimension	Mean	Median	SD	Min	Max
Adequacy	107.17	105.0	13.37	86	139
Presentation	105.50	105.0	15.24	77	138
Technological Difficulty	106.58	106.5	14.77	88	143
Usability & UX	107.42	106.0	15.20	81	142

Post Rating Questionnaires. The final post-event questionnaires provided complementary perspectives from the Technical Jury (Fig. 4) and the Young Jury (Fig. 5). The Technical Jury consistently reported high levels of satisfaction across all six closed questions, with medians at or close to the maximum value of 10. In particular, questions concerning the overall impact of the initiative on promoting innovation (GT-01) and the willingness to recommend participation to colleagues (NPS/GT-06) scored at the very top of the scale, indicating unanimous endorsement. Only GT-02, related to fostering dialogue between companies, students, and institutions, showed slightly more variation, with a few responses falling below the maximum.

The Young Jury also rated the initiative positively, though with a wider range of responses. Median scores ranged between 7 and 9 depending on the question. High ratings were observed for YJ-01 (interest in the initiative) and NPS/YJ-06 (recommendation to a friend), both clustering near the maximum. By contrast, YJ-05 (inspiration to consider scientific or technological studies) exhibited greater variability, with some scores dropping as low as 2, highlighting a diversity of reactions among younger participants.

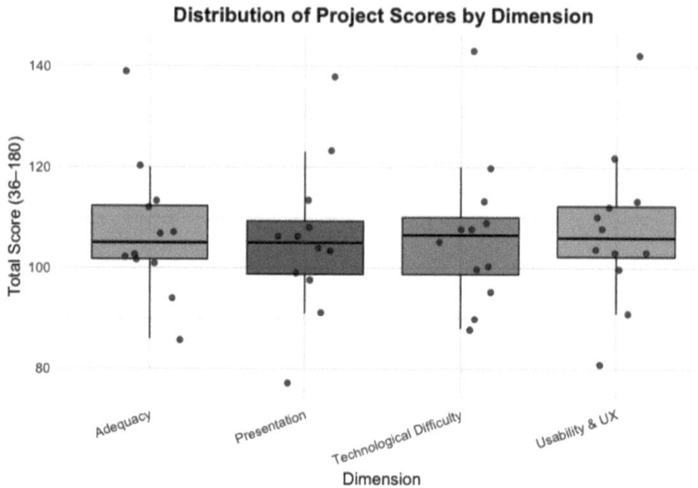

Fig. 3. Boxplot of the TJ score of the projects by dimension.

5   Discussion and Lessons Learned

The analysis addressed our main research question:

RQ1. How do technical expert and youth juries differ in their evaluation and perception of student-developed applications in the AppChallenge?

The exceptionally high NPS of the Technical Jury (77.8, Table 3) reveals an almost unanimous positive endorsement, surpassing benchmarks typically reported for leading global companies, such as Google's range of 4258. By contrast, the Young Jury reported a more moderate NPS (40.0), highlighting greater diversity of opinions. Despite this gap, both groups converged on very similar mean and median project scores, indicating that while advocacy differed, overall evaluations of project quality were aligned. The Technical Jury also showed narrower score dispersion, reflecting consistency in applying professional standards, whereas the Young Jury's wider spread points to heterogeneous user perspectives.

Dimension-level analysis further confirms this distinction. Experts assessed adequacy, usability, technical difficulty, and presentation in a balanced manner, with variability concentrated in usability and presentation (see Fig. 3 and Table 4). Their holistic approach was confirmed in comments describing the apps as "high technical quality" and "concrete and competent work, with products almost ready for the market." Youth jurors, while also valuing professionalism, highlighted features such as "the use of Artificial Intelligence" and "the variety of themes." These remarks confirm that experts privilege systemic rigor, while younger participants respond more to visible novelty and presentation.

Perception questionnaires reinforced these differences. The Technical Jury unanimously endorsed the event as impactful for innovation and employability,

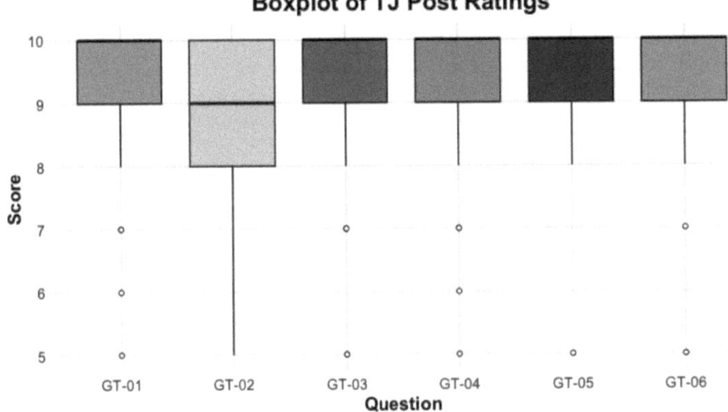

Fig. 4. Boxplot of the final questionnaire for TJ.

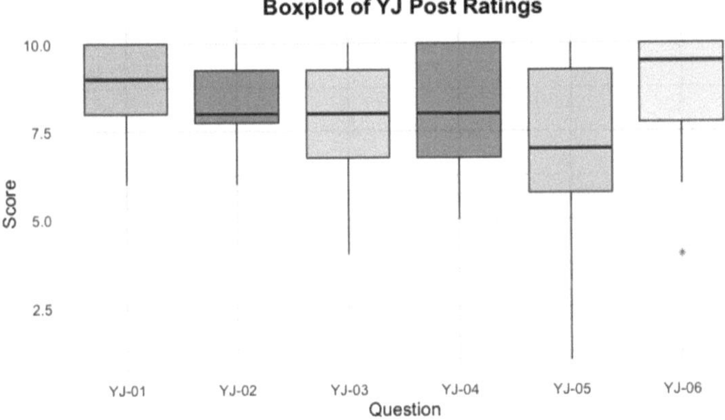

Fig. 5. Boxplot of the final questionnaire for YJ.

noting it "stimulates student learning, prepares them for the job market, and favors collaboration with companies." The Young Jury, while generally positive, showed greater variability, especially on STEM inspiration (YJ-05). Their comments emphasized personal engagement: "the feeling of having a responsibility" and "talking with those who developed the apps", confirming that outreach effects are meaningful. Some contrasts also emerged regarding logistics. Professionals pointed to "too much confusion during the demos" and suggested better space management, while students appreciated "the opportunity to test all the apps" and "listening to all the beautiful ideas." This confirms that experts focus on organizational efficiency, while youth prioritize the experiential aspects of participation.

Together, these results provide a clear answer to RQ1: both juries endorsed the initiative, but differed in consistency, intensity, and framing. Experts represent professional rigor and homogeneous validation of project quality, while students contribute heterogeneous, user-centered perspectives. This dual evaluation framework is therefore complementary, simultaneously validating employability outcomes and highlighting areas for stronger youth engagement.

Finally, the lessons learned inform improvements in logistics, time management, code quality and sustainability, continuity, and stakeholder communication. Embedding analytics, structured feedback, and juror commentary ensures continuous alignment of pedagogical, professional, and outreach objectives. In the next editions, we plan to structure suggestions through focus groups involving all the stakeholders in a post-mortem discussion.

5.1 Threats to Validity

Internal validity may be affected by the self-selection of Technical and Young Jury members, whose prior exposure to informatics or industry may have influenced their ratings. While the use of structured rubrics and standardized NPS questions mitigates subjectivity, individual biases cannot be fully excluded. *Construct validity* relates to the measures adopted. NPS, though widely applied in industry and increasingly in education, remains a proxy for advocacy, and open comments may not fully capture nuanced perceptions. Regarding *external validity*, the study involves a single institution and specific partner companies, which may constrain the generalizability of results. This restriction is also intentional: broadening participation to students from other programs or institutions could compromise the high technical quality of the teams' products, which is central to the initiative's objectives. Nevertheless, the presence of multiple cohorts across eleven editions and recurring juror participation (including former students returning as jurors) strengthens confidence in the replicability of our approach. Finally, the relatively small sample size of the Youth Jury can impact *conclusion validity*, though triangulation of quantitative scores and qualitative feedback helps confirm observed patterns.

6 Conclusions

We presented AppChallenge, a methodology that integrates challenge- and team-based learning with industry coaching, combining product development, business modeling, and advanced technologies to deliver authentic educational and innovation outcomes. The dual-jury evaluation confirmed its value, blending professional rigor with youth perspectives, while future work will refine logistics, continuity, and feedback for greater scalability and impact. Beyond its educational value, AppChallenge has generated concrete technology transfer results, including the creation of the startup *Commigo SRL*[2] and the return of former students as jurors (e.g., winners of the VI edition joining the XI). These outcomes confirm its sustainability as a training ecosystem and an innovation pipeline.[3]

---

[2] https://www.commigo.it/.
[3] https://www.appchallenge.it/partners.

Acknowledgements. The authors gratefully acknowledge all partner companies, the secondary school students, and the students of the *Enterprise Mobile Application Development* course that participated in the XI editions of the AppChallenge.

References

1. Abdulmawjood, K., Zilany, M.S., Sheet, M.: An in-depth examination of assessment methods for capstone projects—measuring success. In: 2024 ASEE Annual Conference & Exposition (2024)
2. Afshar, Y., Bahrehvar, M., Moshirpour, M., Behjat, L.: Hackathon as an effective learning and assessment tool: an analysis of student proficiency against bloom's taxonomy. In: Proceedings of the Canadian Engineering Education Association (CEEA) (2022)
3. Bruegge, B., Krusche, S., Alperowitz, L.: Software engineering project courses with industrial clients. ACM Trans. Comput. Educ. (TOCE) **15**(4), 1–31 (2015)
4. Bunse, C., Grutzner, I., Peper, C., Steinbach-Nordmann, S., Vollmers, C.: Coaching professional software developers-an experience report. In: 19th Conference on Software Engineering Education & Training (CSEET'06), pp. 123–130. IEEE (2006)
5. Francese, R., Gravino, C., Risi, M., Scanniello, G., Tortora, G.: Using project-based-learning in a mobile application development course—an experience report. J. Vis. Lang. Comput. **31**, 196–205 (2015)
6. Gallagher, S.E., Savage, T.: Challenge-based learning in higher education. Teach. High. Educ. **28**(8), 1494–1512 (2023)
7. Johnson, L.F., Adams, S., Smythe, J.T.: Challenge based learning: The report from the implementation project. Tech. rep, New Media Consortium (with Apple Education) (2011)
8. Johnson, L.F., Smith, R.S., Smythe, J.T., Varon, R.K.: Challenge-based learning: An approach for our time. Tech. rep, The New Media Consortium, Austin, TX (2009)
9. Kara, A., et al.: An application of the net promoter score in higher education. J. Educ. Bus. **99**(5), 303–314 (2024)
10. Michaelsen, L.K., Knight, A.B., Fink, L.D.: Team-Based Learning: A Transformative Use of Small Groups in College Teaching. Stylus/Routledge, Sterling, VA (2004)
11. Reichheld, F.F.: The one number you need to grow. Harv. Bus. Rev. **81**(12), 46–54 (2003)
12. Schulten, C., et al.: How do we learn in and from hackathons? a systematic review. Education and Information Technologies (2024)
13. Shah, R., Gillen, A.L.: A systematic literature review of university–industry partnerships in engineering education. Europ. J. Eng. Educ., 1–27 (2024)
14. Taconis, R., Bekker, T.: Challenge based learning as authentic learning environment for stem identity construction. Front. Educ. **8** (2023)

1st International Workshop on Promoting and Dealing with Advanced Technology in Healthcare (PATH 2025)

RespirAction: Remote Respiratory Rehabilitation Supported by Innovative Sensor Technology

Alessia Bramanti[1], Elisa Anna Contursi[1], Giuseppe De Filippo[2(✉)],
Simona De Santis[1], Gianluca Fimiani[1], Marina Garofano[1],
Francesco Pio Matassino[1], Andrea Marino[1], Gabriele Mongelli[1],
Colomba Pessolano[1], Simranjit Singh[2], and Gianpiero Sisto[2]

[1] University of Salerno, Fisciano, Italy
[2] MediNet S.r.L., Milan, Italy
`g.defilippo@medinetsrl.eu`

Abstract. RespirAction is an ongoing industry-academic collaboration aimed at advancing the use of new technologies (e.g. innovative wearable sensors and an IoT platform) in the healthcare field and, specifically, in the context of remote respiratory rehabilitation. Targeting patients with chronic respiratory conditions such as Chronic Obstructive Pulmonary Disease, the project is developing a novel system based on chest and abdominal strain sensors to monitor breathing patterns and provide real-time biofeedback. Integrated with an established telerehabilitation platform, the system supports personalized and home based training via modular applications and exergames. RespirAction combines software engineering, clinical practice, and user-centered design to deliver an evidence-based, scalable, and engaging rehabilitation experience. Its empirical component includes the design and future execution of a clinical feasibility study involving (at least) 60 patients, evaluating usability, adherence, and preliminary outcomes. The final goal of RespirAction is to contribute to the digital transformation of healthcare, with implications for remote monitoring and rehabilitation technologies.

Keywords: Telerehabilitation · Research Project · Empirical Assessment

1 Motivation and Research Context

Chronic respiratory diseases, particularly Chronic Obstructive Pulmonary Disease (COPD) and dyspnea, represent a major global health burden [15], compromising quality of life and leading to frequent hospitalizations. Respiratory rehabilitation mitigates these effects, but traditional programs face barriers in accessibility, continuity, and adherence [9]. While telemedicine has gained momentum,

G. Scanniello et al. (Eds.): PROFES 2025, LNCS 16362, pp. 247–253, 2026.
https://doi.org/10.1007/978-3-032-12092-2_18

Table 1. Project summary information.

Name:	RespirAction
Website:	https://tinyurl.com/4nepnvwp
Duration:	12-months (from December 3rd, 2024)
Funding Agency:	Italian Ministry of the University and Research MUR
Participants:	University of Salerno
Principal Investigators:	Alessia Bramanti
Funding Received	291,584.00
Industrial Partners:	MediNet S.r.L. (https://www.medinetsrl.eu)
	Khymeia S.r.L. (https://khymeia.com/en/)
Technology Readiness Level (TRL)	8
Status:	Ongoing

current digital solutions remain limited in personalization, user engagement, and evaluation in real-world contexts [1].

RespirAction is a research-industry collaboration addressing these challenges through innovative wearable sensors and an IoT-based platform. The system employs strain sensors embedded in elastic thoracoabdominal belts for precise, non-invasive monitoring of respiratory patterns, integrated with a telerehabilitation platform to deliver interactive biofeedback modules and exergames for improved breathing control and engagement. The project combines expertise from software engineering, clinical medicine, human-computer interaction, and rehabilitation science, following empirical methods to ensure user-centered design and evaluation. We report further details on RespirAction in Table 1. The rest of the paper is organized as follows: Sect. 2 reviews related work, Sect. 3 outlines project objectives, Sect. 4 presents its structure, Sect. 5 and Sect. 6 report preliminary results and expected impact.

2   State of the Art

This section reviews the background underlying the RespirAction project, focusing on: (i) respiratory rehabilitation and biofeedback, (ii) wearable solutions for respiratory monitoring, and (iii) exergaming approaches for rehabilitation.

Respiratory Rehabilitation and Biofeedback. Respiratory rehabilitation is a cornerstone of COPD treatment, improving quality of life, exercise tolerance, and symptom management. Breathing retraining is often supported by biofeedback, which provides real-time visualization of parameters such as respiratory rate or effort, fostering awareness and self-regulation. Biofeedback has been linked to reduced anxiety and dyspnea in chronic patients [11]. Continuous feedback also sustains adherence and reinforces proper breathing techniques [3], offering tangible progress indicators that increase satisfaction and compliance.

Wearable Technologies for Respiratory Monitoring. Wearables devices enable continuous, non-invasive monitoring of respiratory rate, thoracoabdominal motion and breathing patterns using piezoelectric, inductive, or resistive strain sensors. Each modality has specific advantages and limitations. Piezoelectric sensors are compact and low-cost but lose accuracy in static breathing phases [16,17]. Inductive sensors, particularly those based on magnetic induction or mutual inductance, allow flexible textile integration but are prone to interference and signal drift [12,13]. Strain sensors, instead, capture both dynamic and static respiratory phases without high-pass filtering, preserving low-frequency components essential for evaluating breath-holding, inspiratory/expiratory pauses, and thoracoabdominal symmetry. Their sensitivity to slow, controlled respiratory motions makes them ideal for clinical applications such as biofeedback or diaphragmatic training, despite higher cost and manufacturing complexity [7].

Exergaming in Respiratory Rehabilitation. Exergaming, combining physical exercise with interactive gaming, has emerged as a motivating adjunct to Pulmonary Rehabilitation (PR) programs. Reviews and trials report improvements in lung function and exercise capacity when PR is enhanced with Virtual Reality (VR) or exergames [10]. By incorporating real-time feedback, goal-oriented tasks, and gamified elements, these systems promote higher engagement than conventional regimens [2]. In chronic respiratory diseases, exergaming can extend access to rehabilitation in home settings, supporting adherence and long-term participation.

3 Objectives

The objectives of the RespirAction project are summarized as follows:

O1: Develop and validate an innovative wearable device for respiratory monitoring. The project aims to design and validate a wearable device based on chest and abdominal belts integrated with strain sensors.

O2: Integrate the device into an existing telerehabilitation platform. The wearable device will be integrated into the VRRS Home Kit by Khymeia, enhanced with modular components to support home-based respiratory rehabilitation. The system will ensure usability and accessibility for patients with COPD and dyspnea, promoting adherence and continuity of care across clinical and domestic settings. Particular attention will be paid to privacy and security, ensuring GDPR compliance and building trust among patients and healthcare providers.

O3: Develop modular training and exergaming applications. Customizable exergaming software modules will guide respiratory training with visual and auditory biofeedback, encouraging thoracic and abdominal control, paced breathing, and diaphragmatic exercises. Additional modules will focus on reducing breathlessness, improving lung capacity, and combining relaxation with light movements. All tools will be adaptable to individual needs, supporting personalized and scalable rehabilitation.

O4: Conduct a clinical feasibility study. A feasibility study will assess usability, patient acceptance, and therapeutic value of the developed solutions in real-world clinical settings, providing feedback to refine both the wearable device and training applications.

O5: Promote innovation in respiratory rehabilitation. RespirAction showcases how advanced wearable technology and telerehabilitation platforms can enhance outcomes for chronic respiratory patients. Results will inform best practices and guidelines for secure, patient-centered telerehabilitation, addressing data protection and cybersecurity requirements. Through its collaboration with public healthcare stakeholders (e.g., Tuscany Health Ecosystem), RespirAction also contributes to policy innovation, paving the way for more structured integration of telerehabilitation within national healthcare frameworks.

4   Project Structure

Given the objectives described above, the RespirAction project is structured into three main Work Packages (WPs), each designed to tackle specific scientific, technical, and clinical challenges. In Table 2, we provide details on each of the WPs. It is worth mentioning that all the WPs are led and coordinated by the Department of Medicine at the University of Salerno, which is the principal investigator of the project.

5   Preliminary Results

WP1: Clinical Study Design and Laboratory Setup. WP1 established the foundation for the clinical study, defining protocol, inclusion/exclusion criteria, outcome measures, and intervention strategies. The protocol foresees two supervised sessions and one month of telerehabilitation using the VRRS Home Kit (Fig. 1, left-hand side), combining synchronous and asynchronous activities. Outcome measures include the Six-Minute Walk Test (6MWT), Short Physical Performance Battery (SPPB), Mini-Mental State Examination (MMSE), Short Form-36 (SF-36), and the Modified Medical Research Council (mMRC) Dyspnea Scale. Usability and satisfaction are assessed through the System Usability Scale (SUS) and Client Satisfaction Questionnaire (CSQ-8).

WP2: Development of Innovative Rehabilitation Content. Innovative and modular contents were integrated into the VRRS Home Kit using Unity [14], with real-time communication enabled by Khymeia's Kloud [8] platform. This setup allows therapists to remotely monitor patients and guide sessions. The rehabilitation library includes exercises for respiratory, motor, and cognitive functions. Respiratory modules feature progressive training for thoracic and abdominal control, paced breathing, diaphragmatic exercises, and exergames driven by breathing rhythms. We also integrated validated neuromotor [5], orthopedic [6], and cognitive [4] exercises involving upper and lower limbs, trunk mobility, and mental stimulation tasks. The system relies on multiple sensors, including an inertial unit, a spirometer, and a prototype elastic belt with strain gauges (Fig. 1, right-hand side), ensuring accurate monitoring and biofeedback.

Particular attention was devoted to data protection. The Kloud platform provides GDPR-compliant management of health data through encryption, strict

Table 2. Description of the RespirAction work packages.

WP1: Clinical Study Design and Lab Setup (M1-M3)[a]	
Objective: Design of the clinical study protocol and preparation of the laboratory (RI)	
WP Breakdown:	– Detailed design of the clinical study, including the process for obtaining ethical approval (M1-M2)
	– Acquisition and installation of all necessary equipment to enable clinical testing for telerehabilitation (M1-M2)
	– Coordination and alignment with the Tuscany Health Ecosystem program (M1-M2, and beyond if necessary)
Deliverable(s): Clinical study protocol (M2)	
WP2: Innovative Rehabilitation Content} (M1-M5)	
Objective: Development and testing of innovative rehabilitation content (RI)	
WP Breakdown:	– Design of at least 12 innovative rehabilitation scenarios, 2 per type (M1-M2)
	– Development of rehabilitation content in Unity and integration into the VRRS Home Kit platform, with technical support from the manufacturer (M3-M4)
	– Iterative testing and refinement of the content based on clinical feedback (M4-M5)
Deliverable(s): A suite of rehabilitation scenarios, including development and testing report (M5)	
WP3: Clinical Validation Trial and Dissemination of Results} (M6âĂŞM12)	
Objective: Functional validation of the integrated platform and dissemination of results (SS)	
WP Breakdown:	– Clinical trial with patients with COPD and dyspnea to assess reliability and usability in home settings; 60 patients will be recruited from the Department of Medicine and the Cardiac Rehabilitation Unit at AOU San Giovanni di Dio e Ruggi d'Aragona. Data collected includes medical, demographic, and clinical profiles. Each patient will complete at least two clinical rehab sessions before using a Home Kit for one month of synchronous (weekly) and asynchronous (5Œ/week) telerehabilitation, with sessions lasting at least 40 min.
	• Six Minute Walking Test (6MWT)
	• Short Physical Performance Battery (SPPB)
	• Mini-Mental State Examination (MMSE)
	• Quality of Life (SF-36)
	• Dyspnea assessment (Modified Medical Research Council âĂŞ MMRC scale) (M6-M11)
	– Analysis of trial data using SUS and CSQ8 to measure usability and patient satisfaction (M12)
	– Preparation of a scientific publication summarizing trial results and providing guidelines for future development (M9-M12)
	– Communication of results in alignment with Tuscany Health Ecosystemt (M9-M12)
Deliverable(s):	– Clinical trial report including usability analysis and functional feedback (M12)
	– Draft of the first scientific publication (M12)
	– Coordination report with Tuscany Health Ecosystem (M12)

[a] "M" stands for "Month".

access controls, and customizable privacy policies. These measures ensure confidentiality, integrity, and reliability in home-based rehabilitation.

A pilot study involving healthcare professionals and healthy volunteers was conducted to test feasibility and usability. The results confirmed the robustness of the setup, the reliability of the wearable system, and the overall reliability of the sensors, providing critical input before the clinical study.

WP3: Clinical Trial and Dissemination of Results. WP3 focuses on validating the integrated platform in real-world clinical settings. The study has received ethical approval, and recruitment is underway, with a target of 60 patients from the Department of Medicine and the Cardiac Rehabilitation Unit at AOU "San Giovanni di Dio e Ruggi d'Aragona."

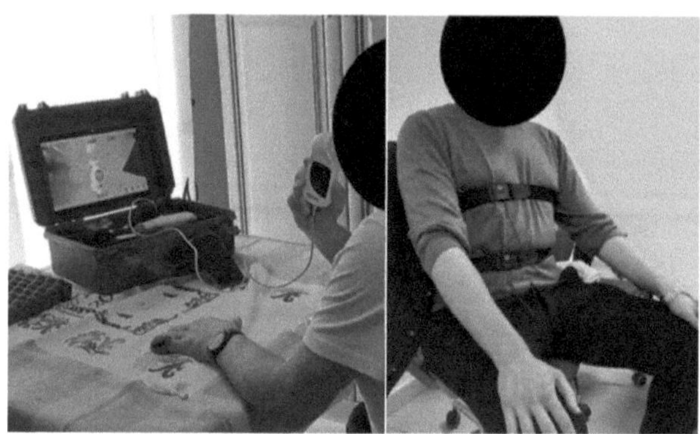

Fig. 1. VRRS Home Kit, spirometer, and elastic belts

6   Conclusion and Expected Impact

RespirAction aims to develop novel thoracoabdominal tracking technologies, based on exergaming and sensors designed to support both the measurement and training of breathing techniques. RespirAction solutions (particularly suited for home use) enhance patient engagement and adherence to respiratory rehabilitation while enabling early detection of deteriorating respiratory patterns and continuous, home-based symptom management. By integrating real-time monitoring, interactive visual feedback, and guided breathing exercises, RespirAction offers a personalized, accessible, and continuous therapeutic experience. Its low-cost design further promotes widespread adoption, especially in settings with limited access to conventional rehabilitation services.

Acknowledgments. This project has been financially supported by the Italian Ministry of the University and Research MUR (M4C2) as part of the project "Tuscany Health Ecosystem" - THE - Spoke 10 - CUP - B83C22003920001.

References

1. Barbosa, M.T., Sousa, C.S., Morais-Almeida, M.: Telemedicine in the management of chronic obstructive respiratory diseases: an overview (2022)
2. Burkow, T.M., et al.: Comprehensive pulmonary rehabilitation in home-based online groups: a mixed method pilot study in COPD. BMC. Res. Notes **8**, 1–11 (2015)
3. Chen, Y.J., Huang, L.H., Perng, W.C.: Biofeedback for improving the effectiveness of pulmonary rehabilitation exercise in patients with chronic obstructive pulmonary disease. Eur. Respir. J. **46**(suppl 59) (2015). https://doi.org/10.1183/13993003.congress-2015.PA542
4. Contrada, M., et al.: Multidomain cognitive tele-neurorehabilitation training in long-term post-stroke patients: an RCT study. Brain Sci. **15**(2), 145 (2025). https://doi.org/10.3390/brainsci15020145
5. Contrada, M., : Stroke telerehabilitation in Calabria: a health technology assessment. Front. Neurol. **12**, 777608 (2022). https://doi.org/10.3389/fneur.2021.777608
6. Galasso, O., et al.: Accelerating recovery: a case report on telerehabilitation for a triathlete's post-meniscus surgery comeback. Healthcare (Basel) **13**(4), 406 (2025). https://doi.org/10.3390/healthcare13040406
7. Hussain, T., Ullah, S., Fernández-García, R., Gil, I.: Wearable sensors for respiration monitoring: a review. Sensors **23**(17) (2023).https://doi.org/10.3390/s23177518, https://shorturl.at/M9Tb8
8. Khymeia Group: Kloud – piattaforma di riabilitazione remota (2025). https://khymeia.com/it/products/kloud/. Accesso: 23 luglio 2025
9. Lamberton, C.E., Mosher, C.L.: Review of the evidence for pulmonary rehabilitation in COPD: clinical benefits and cost-effectiveness. Respir. Care **69**(6), 686–696 (2024)
10. Patsaki, I., Avgeri, V., Rigoulia, T., Zekis, T., Koumantakis, G.A., Grammatopoulou, E.: Benefits from incorporating virtual reality in pulmonary rehabilitation of COPD patients: a systematic review and meta-analysis. Adv. Respir. Med. **91**(4), 324–336 (2023)
11. de Souto Barbosa, J.V., et al.: Effectiveness of paced breathing guided by biofeedback on clinical and functional outcomes patients with chronic obstructive pulmonary disease: an uncontrolled pilot study. Appl. Psychophysiol. Biofeedback **48**(4), 423–432 (2023)
12. Teichmann, D., De Matteis, D., Bartelt, T., Walter, M., Leonhardt, S.: A bendable and wearable cardiorespiratory monitoring device fusing two noncontact sensor principles. IEEE J. Biomed. Health Inform. **19**(3), 784–793 (2015)
13. Teichmann, D., Kuhn, A., Leonhardt, S., Walter, M.: The main shirt: a textile-integrated magnetic induction sensor array. Sensors **14**(1), 1039–1056 (2014)
14. Unity Technologies: Unity real-time development platform (2025). https://unity.com/. Accesso: 30 maggio 2025
15. Viegi, G., Pistelli, F., Sherrill, D.L., Maio, S., Baldacci, S., Carrozzi, L.: Definition, epidemiology and natural history of COPD. Eur. Respir. J. **30**(5), 993–1013 (2007)
16. Wang, Q., Ruan, T., Xu, Q., Yang, B., Liu, J.: Wearable multifunctional piezoelectric mems device for motion monitoring, health warning, and earphone. Nano Energy **89**, 106324 (2021)
17. Zeng, X., Deng, H.T., Wen, D.L., Li, Y.Y., Xu, L., Zhang, X.S.: Wearable multi functional sensing technology for healthcare smart detection. Micromachines **13**(2), 254 (2022)

SENTIRE: An Intelligent System for Hearing Protection and Human-Machine Interaction in Industrial Environments

Rosaria Del Sorbo[✉], Gabriele Mongelli, Maria Pia Di Palo, Massimo Giordano, Marianna Bartolomeo, Elisa Anna Contursi, Chiara Maria Ragusa, Colomba Pessolano, Andrea Marino, Simona De Santis, and Giuseppe Del Sorbo

University of Salerno, Salerno, Italy
rdelsorbo@unisa.it

Abstract. The SENTIRE—DPI-uAI project aims to develop an intelligent active hearing protection device for workers in high-noise industrial environments. Combining Internet of Things (IoT) technologies, Machine Learning algorithms, and edge-cloud architectures, SENTIRE enables selective noise filtering to preserve safety-relevant sounds while suppressing harmful ones. At the core of the system are noise-canceling headphones connected via BLE to a wearable device that integrates a DSP module for acoustic signal pre-processing and an embedded CPU for contextual analysis and sound classification. Edge communication is handled via MQTT protocol, while a serverless infrastructure enables interaction with the smart factory. The system demonstrates robust latency and classification performance, confirming the feasibility of selective audio filtering and sub-meter localization accuracy in industrial scenarios [5, 6].

Keywords: Smart PPE · Industrial acoustics · Artificial intelligence · Edge computing · Occupational safety · Embedded systems · Active noise control · Wearable technology

1 Introduction and Technological Background

Noise pollution in industrial environments remains a persistent issue that directly affects workers' hearing health. Conventional passive hearing protectors indiscriminately attenuate all sound frequencies, reducing not only harmful noise but also critical auditory cues such as alarms, verbal instructions, or acoustic variations in machinery, thus increasing the risk of accidents. In this context, the evolution toward Industry 4.0 requires a radical revision of the approach to hearing protection: not indiscriminate acoustic isolation, but distributed contextual intelligence. The SENTIRE—DPI-uAI project follows this direction by proposing a smart device that operates as an adaptive filter and, simultaneously, as a communication interface between the oper-ator and the environment (Table 1).

G. Scanniello et al. (Eds.): PROFES 2025, LNCS 16362, pp. 254–259, 2026.
https://doi.org/10.1007/978-3-032-12092-2_19

Table 1. Project Summary

Name	DPI-uAI BRIC 2022—ID 48
Duration	1 June 2023—31 December 2025
Founding Agency	INAIL
Partecipants	University of Salerno
Principal Investigator	Francesco Antonio Salzano
Founding Received	€ 305.000,00
Technology Readiness Level (TRL)	5
Status	Ongoing

2 Related Work

Conventional hearing protectors and Active Noise Control (ANC) systems represent the most widely adopted solutions for occupational hearing protection. However, these approaches indiscriminately attenuate both harmful noise and safety-relevant sounds, such as alarms or verbal instructions, thereby compromising situational awareness in noisy environments. Several research efforts have attempted to inte-grate IoT and ANC for occupational safety [7, 10]. For example, Serizel et al. [8] investigat-ed integrated ANC and noise reduction strategies in hearing aids, while Shen et al. [9] proposed MUTE, an IoT-based noise cancellation system. Marques and Pitarma [11], and Said et al. [12], designed IoT-based monitoring systems for acoustic comfort in industrial workplaces. Despite their contributions, these approaches are often limited to passive monitoring or global noise attenuation without adaptive filtering of specific acoustic events. Fur-thermore, many studies (e.g., Mihalache et al. [1], Korkmaz and Boyacı [2], Wilkinson and Niesler [3], Ding et al. [4]) focused primarily on voice activity detection for speech recognition, with little attention to safety-critical industrial contexts. In contrast, SENTIRE introduces an integrated approach that combines selective noise suppression, real-time acoustic event classifi-cation, and contextual interaction with the industrial environment, unlike previous approaches that either rely on global ANC (Serizel, Shen), focus on IoT monitoring without filtering (Marques), or are limited to speech-focused VAD models (Mihala-che, Korkmaz). SENTIRE ensures selective acoustic event filtering with <50 ms la-tency and seamless integration into industrial IoT frameworks.

3 Objectives of the Sentire System

SENTIRE aims to develop a wearable device that integrates acoustic analysis, adap-tive filtering, and contextual interaction with the industrial environment. The system must be capable of real- time sound recognition, distinguishing be-tween background noise, alarm signals, human speech, or characteristic machine sounds. Based on the classification, the device activates the most appropriate filter to protect hearing without compromising safety. At the same time, the system can receive signals from surrounding machinery via BLE modules and MQTT protocols, converting them into acoustic messages for the user. It also collects environmental and postural data to build a dynamic individual risk profile, useful for proactive safety management.

4 Technological Architecture

The SENTIRE architecture (Fig. 1) follows a modular and scalable design, combining robustness with real-time signal processing. It is structured in two main layers:

- **Pre-processing layer:** a DSP module performs signal conditioning (filtering, normalization, compression) and extracts acoustic features such as spectral energy and Mel coefficients.
- **Classification and decision layer:** an ARM-based embedded platform runs lightweight ML models (TensorFlow Lite Micro) for event recognition, dynamically activating adaptive filters. The processing chain guarantees end-to-end latency below 50 ms, essential for safety.
- **Communication and HMI subsystem:** BLE 5.0 and MQTT protocols, with audio, LED, and vibro-feedback, connect the device to the smart factory. Secure data exchange and OTA updates allow remote management and integration in Safety 4.0 workflows.

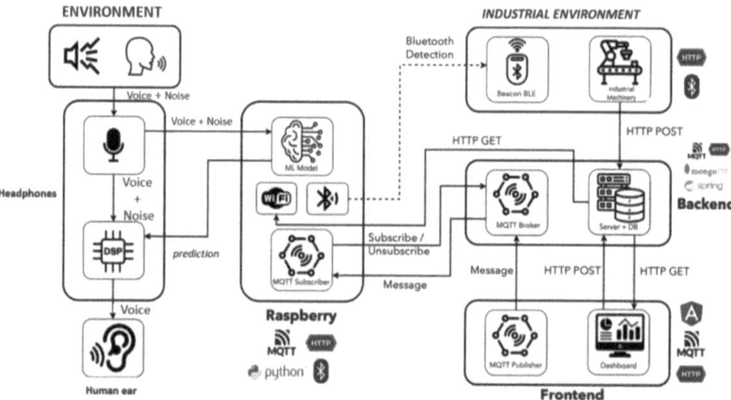

Fig. 1. Logical architecture of the SENTIRE system showing interactions between headset, edge module, cloud interface, and notification systems.

5 Prototype

The developed prototype consists of smart headphones and a wearable edge-based module. The noise-canceling headphones host directional MEMS micro-phones and transducers for communication. The onboard DSP processes the signal in real time. A Raspberry Pi Zero 2 W performs intelligent processing, implementing a Voice Activity Detection (VAD) algorithm and selecting the most ap-propriate acoustic filter, as illustrated in Fig. 2.

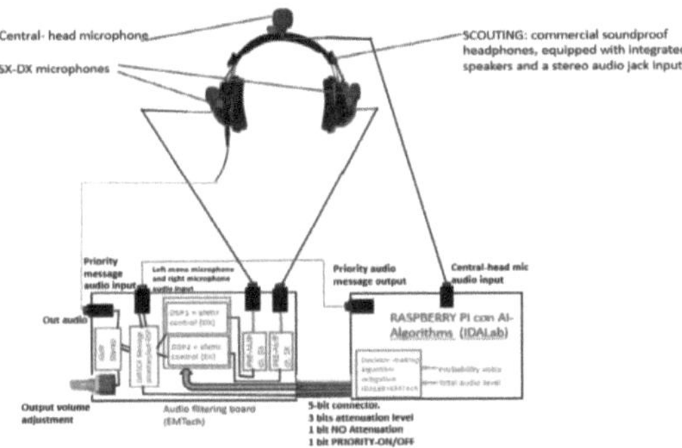

Fig. 2. Prototype of the wearable device with embedded computing unit and integrated acoustic interfaces.

5.1 Engineering Details: Architecture and Testing

The processing chain performs feature extraction (STFT and Mel spectrogram), real-time voice activity detection with the lightweight Silero DNN model [13], and activation of adaptive DSP filters that preserve alarms and speech while attenuating background noise. Classical ML models (e.g., logistic regression, random forest, CNNs) were evaluated but discarded due to latency and computational costs. Preliminary tests in mixed noise–speech scenarios showed ~ 85% VAD accuracy, latency below 50 ms, and BLE localization error under 1 m. These early results confirm system feasibility, although full validation is ongoing.

5.2 Design and Development of the Shield Module for Raspberry Pi

To reduce wiring and improve integration, a compact shield was designed for the Raspberry Pi. The board includes audio connectors and a dedicated power interface that isolates the DSP from the main supply. Electromagnetic interference was mitigated by decoupling capacitors and increased physical separation from the SoC. After these modifications, background noise was eliminated and signal stability improved, allowing reliable integration and testing at the IDA Lab.

6 Clinical Evaluation and Medical Protocols

A prospective observational study, approved by the Campania 2 Ethics Commit-tee (ref. 4194/2025), is assessing the SENTIRE system in 50 adult participants exposed to occupational noise. Multidimensional evaluations include audiological tests, cognitive tasks, and standardized questionnaires (HHIA, WHOQOL-BREF, SF-36). Data are collected via REDCap with GDPR compliance. At sub-mission, baseline (T0) assessments were completed, and follow-up visits are on-going. The study aims to evaluate protective effectiveness, psychophysical well-being, and user experience, with future validation planned in real industrial environments.

7 Discussion

The SENTIRE system demonstrates the potential of edge intelligence in industrial safety, ensuring real-time responsiveness and privacy without cloud dependence. Preliminary tests confirmed feasibility in terms of latency, VAD accuracy, and BLE localization, but broader statistical validation is required. The BLE/MQTT interface positions the device as a connected node within the smart factory, sup-porting Safety 4.0 applications. Clinically, the ongoing study will provide multi-dimensional evidence of impact, though challenges remain in user variability and replicating workplace complexity. Future work will extend validation in real industrial settings and assess long-term ergonomics and compliance.

8 Conclusions and Future Developments

SENTIRE advances beyond traditional ANC by selectively filtering acoustic events while ensuring < 50 ms latency in safety-critical contexts. Its integration of BLE localization and MQTT communication enables interoperability and scalability within smart factories. The modular design and ongoing clinical study position the system for future industrial deployment. Next steps include validation in real environments and long-term assessment of ergonomics and user acceptability.

Acknowledgments. The SENTIRE–DPI-uAI project was funded by INAIL (Italian National Institute for Insurance against Accidents at Work) under the BRIC 2022 Call (ID 48), supporting scientific research on health and safety in the workplace. We thank all scientific and industrial partners for their multidisciplinary contributions to system development.

References

1. Mihalache, S., Ivanov, I.-A., Burileanu, D.: "Deep neural networks for voice activity detection," in *Proc. 44th Int. Conf. Telecommunications and Signal Processing (TSP)*, Brno, Czech Republic, pp. 191–194 (2021)
2. Korkmaz, Y., Boyacı, A.:"Hybrid voice activity detection system based on LSTM and auditory speech features," *Biomed. Signal Process. Control*, **80**, p. 104408 (2023)

3. Wilkinson, N., Niesler, T.: "A hybrid CNN- BiLSTM voice activity detector," in *Proc. IEEE Int. Conf. Acoustics, Speech and Signal Processing (ICASSP)*, Toronto, Canada, pp. 6803–6807 (2021)

4. Ding et al., S.: "Personal VAD 2.0: optimizing personal voice activity detection for on-device speech recognition," in *Proc. Interspeech*, Incheon, South Korea, pp. 3744–3748 (2022)

5. Spachos, P., Plataniotis, K.N.: "BLE beacons for indoor positioning at an interactive IoT-based smart museum," *IEEE Syst. J.*, **14**(3), pp. 3483–3493 (2020)

6. Jeon, K.E., She, J., Soonsawad, P., Ng, P.C.: "BLE beacons for internet of things applications: survey, challenges, and opportunities," *IEEE Access*, **6**, pp. 29309–29330 (2018)

7. Jiang et al., Y.: "An integration development of traditional algorithm and neural network for active noise cancellation," *Appl. Acoust.*, **189**, p. 108603 (2022)

8. Serizel, R., Moonen, M., Wouters, J., Jensen, S.H.: "Integrated active noise control and noise reduction in hearing aids," *IEEE Trans. Audio, Speech Lang. Process.*, **18**(6), pp. 1333–1343 (2009)

9. Shen et al., S.: "MUTE: bringing IoT to noise cancellation," in *Proc. 16th ACM Conf. Embedded Networked Sensor Syst. (SenSys)*, Shenzhen, China, Nov., pp. 285–298 (2018)

10. Diao, Z., Jin, C.: "Review of ANC algorithm," in *Proc. IEEE Int. Conf. Signal Process.* (2022)

11. Marques, G., Pitarma, R.:"A real-time noise monitoring system based on internet of things for enhanced acoustic comfort and occupational health," *Int. J. Environ. Res. Public Health*, **17**(15), p. 5602 (2020)

12. Said et al., M.A.M.: "Design and develop low- cost device for monitoring occupational noise exposure toward workers in factory," in *Proc. Int. Conf. Smart Comput. Commun. (ICSCC)* (2020)

13. Ramírez et al., J.:"Efficient voice activity detection algorithms using long-term speech information," *Speech Commun.*, **42**(3– 4), pp. 271–287 (2004). https://doi.org/10.1016/j.specom.2003.10.002

Agility Under Fire: What Healthcare Can Learn from Crisis-Driven Accelerated Technology Development and Adoption

Aapo Koski[1]([envelope]) [ID], Tommi Mikkonen[2] [ID], and Laura-Maria Peltonen[3] [ID]

[1] Tampere University and 61N Solutions Oy, 33100 Tampere, Finland
`aapo.koski@tuni.fi`
[2] University of Jyväskylä, Jyväskylä, Finland
`tommi.j.mikkonen@jyu.fi`
[3] University of Eastern Finland and Kuopio University Hospital, Kuopio, Finland
`laura-maria.peltonen@uef.fi`
`https://www.tuni.fi` , `https://www.jyu.fi` , `https://www.uef.fi`

Abstract. Healthcare systems around the world are under pressure to adopt advanced technologies, yet innovation is often stalled by rigid regulatory frameworks, complex procurement procedures, and risk-averse cultures. In contrast, societal crises, such as a pandemic and wartime, catalyze rapid user-driven development and deployment of technologies such as drones, telehealth platforms, and situational awareness systems, demonstrating that even high-risk domains can innovate and rapidly deploy new technologies under extreme conditions. This paper explores what healthcare can learn from these innovation models of social crises, focusing on how agility, minimal viable products (MVPs) and close end-user collaboration can coexist with safety and ethical oversight. By examining real-world cases and drawing parallels with healthcare, we propose actionable strategies to accelerate responsible innovation in healthcare.

Keywords: Healthcare systems · Societal crises · Agile methods · Regulated software development

1 Introduction

The integration of advanced technologies, such as drones, AI-driven diagnostics, and real-time communication platforms, has the potential to revolutionize healthcare. Yet, in most health systems, such innovations face resistance. Regulatory constraints, siloed organizations, slow procurement cycles, and a strong emphasis on zero-risk deployments tend to suppress experimentation. As a result, even technologies with proven value struggle to gain traction in healthcare.

In contrast, societal crises such as pandemics and wartime conditions have created an ecosystem where innovation thrives under pressure [4]. For example, constrained by time, resources, and existential threat, Ukrainian developers, defense actors, and civil society organizations have successfully deployed complex technologies such as drone swarms, distributed logistics platforms, and digital battlefield medicine tools in remarkably short time-frames. These efforts

G. Scanniello et al. (Eds.): PROFES 2025, LNCS 16362, pp. 260–265, 2026.
https://doi.org/10.1007/978-3-032-12092-2_20

demonstrate how agility, iterative design, and end-user participation can lead to rapid high-impact outcomes, even in safety-critical environments.

We argue that healthcare systems, while rightly committed to safety and ethics, would benefit from the adoption of key elements of the innovation models of social crises. Rather than viewing regulation and complexity as fixed barriers, healthcare actors would benefit from seeking structured ways to enable controlled experimentation and lean innovation. Drawing parallels to lessons learned in the wartime settings (Ukraine), this paper examines how healthcare can adopt faster feedback loops, minimally viable deployments, and sandbox-style regulatory models, without compromising core values. In doing so, it contributes to the ongoing discourse on responsible, adaptive innovation in socio-technical systems.

This paper is positioned as a conceptual engineering short paper. Goal is not to provide an empirical evaluation but rather to synthesize qualitative evidence from wartime innovation and articulate a set of actionable strategies for healthcare systems. The contribution lies in offering a structured lens through which policymakers and engineers can consider responsible acceleration of innovation.

2   Rapid Innovation in Wartime Ukraine

Wartime Ukraine has become a living laboratory for technological innovation, fundamentally shaping the future of technology and innovations in warfare. Facing existential threats and urgent need to outmaneuver a technologically superior adversary, Ukrainian society has responded with an unprecedented surge in agile, grassroots-driven technological development. This section highlights key characteristics of this innovation model through examples from the defense technology domain, particularly drones and battlefield digital systems.

Scaling Innovation Through Decentralization. Unlike traditional defense procurement models, Ukraine's wartime innovation ecosystem is characterized by a decentralized, startup-driven approach. The government has provided strategic direction, but the technological progress has emerged from volunteer tech groups, small companies, and informal networks that work directly with end-users on the front lines. Such decentralization enables rapid iteration: End-user feedback is directly integrated into the development cycle, within days.

Lean Cycles and Minimal Viable Products. The pressure of the battlefield has led to the adoption of lean development principles. The prototypes are tested in live environments, refined iteratively, and deployed incrementally, instead of a rigid, preplanned strategy. Rather than waiting for fully mature systems, teams prioritize functional solutions that solve critical problems now. Reconnaissance drones were rapidly deployed and iteratively upgraded, first with basic thermal vision, later with swarm coordination and AI-based target recognition, entirely guided by frontline feedback.

Embedded End-Users and Tactical Feedback Loops. A crucial success factor has been the direct involvement of military personnel in the design. Unlike traditional top-down R&D pipelines, Ukraine's approach enables real-time tactical feedback to shape product evolution. Short feedback loops foster a culture of experimentation and continuous learning, one that healthcare innovation efforts rarely achieve due to layers of abstraction between developers and practitioners.

Dual-Use Technologies and Civil Resilience. Many of the tools developed for military use, such as low-cost drones, mesh networks, and telehealth tools, have found applications in civilian contexts, from infrastructure monitoring to emergency response. This dual-use orientation underscores the societal resilience benefits of agile tech ecosystems.

Importantly, Ukraine's wartime context has also accelerated healthcare-specific innovation, such as telemedicine networks connecting frontline medics with specialists, the digitalization of field hospital records, and mental health support platforms for soldiers and civilians. These provide concrete evidence that the same innovation dynamics seen in defense also extend to healthcare delivery.

The Ukrainian experience illustrates how extreme constraints can catalyze innovation, not suppress it. By embracing decentralization, embedding users in the development loop, and favoring rapid iteration over bureaucratic perfectionism, Ukraine has managed to field advanced adaptive technologies in real-world conditions. These mechanisms are not exclusive to war, they reflect general principles of agile and user-centered innovation that could be translated, with appropriate safeguards, into other high-stakes domains. While Ukraine's innovation environment thrives under pressure, the healthcare sector operates under a very different set of institutional incentives, as explored next.

3   Obstacles in Healthcare Innovation

While the healthcare sector operates under conditions that are often just as mission-critical as military environments, its capacity for rapid innovation is limited by deep-rooted structural and cultural barriers. These obstacles reflect a system optimized for risk elimination rather than adaptive learning, prioritizing stability over speed, and compliance over iteration.

Regulatory and Legal Complexity. Healthcare innovation is tightly bound by legal frameworks designed to protect patient safety, privacy, and ethical standards. These frameworks are essential, but are often rigid. For example, in the EU, the Medical Device Regulation (MDR) has been criticized for creating significant bottlenecks for innovative digital health solutions, especially from small and mid-sized enterprises. Similarly, in the U.S., while the FDA has introduced emergency-use pathways, most technologies still face a lengthy approval process that does not accommodate iterative development. In other words, in healthcare, innovation moves at the pace of regulation, not at the pace of need.

Risk Aversion and Accountability Layers. Healthcare organizations tend to exhibit a strong aversion to uncertainty, which results in long procurement cycles, multistage assessments, and reliance on heavily vetted solutions. Unlike military environments, where failure in the field often drives improvement, failure in healthcare settings is politically and legally sensitive.

Separation of Innovators from End-Users. Another major issue is the gap between developers and practitioners. Health tech developers are often separated legally, geographically, and operationally from real-world clinical settings. This inhibits direct feedback loops, real-time experimentation, and rapid problem-solving. 5 In contrast to Ukraine's frontline-driven innovation, many healthcare systems lack mechanisms for structured co-creation with health professionals, patients, or emergency responders.

Procurement and Scalability Challenges. Procurement processes in healthcare systems – especially public ones – are often linear, slow, and compliance-heavy, designed for purchasing well-established technologies, not iterative development partnerships. Contracts tend to favor long-term stability over rapid value delivery. Even when a pilot project succeeds, scaling it within or across systems is difficult due to fragmentation in governance, financing, and infrastructure.

Combined, the above factors form a system that favors caution over curiosity. Although this protects patients from harm in the short term, it can hinder their access to life-saving innovations in the long term. Unlike the Ukrainian model, where innovation is seen as a necessity for survival, healthcare innovation often becomes a bureaucratic exercise rather than a continuous adaptive process.

4   Bridging the Gap: Translating Lessons Into Healthcare

The Ukrainian innovation model cannot be directly transplanted to healthcare but offers valuable principles for safe, context-sensitive adaptation We outline four levers that healthcare could adopt to foster faster, adaptive innovation.

Embrace Regulatory Sandboxes for Real-World Testing. A promising model is systematically providing access for researchers and developers to the regulatory sandbox, a controlled environment where new technologies are tested with real users under regulatory supervision. This approach, already piloted in finance and more recently in healthcare (e.g. the UK's MHRA AI Airlock [5]), allows developers and regulators to co-evolve rules and designs in real time.

Institutionalize End-User Feedback Loops. Healthcare technologies often fail because they are designed without deep engagement from the people who will use them. Systematically establishing co-creation as standard practice and taking advantage of Ukraine's embedded co-creation model, health systems could institutionalize mechanisms for real-time feedback from health professionals, patients, and emergency responders into development lifecycles. Keeping the user constantly in the loop [1] includes (i) the systematic implementations of "innovation units" embedded in healthcare organizations; (ii) Short-cycle test-and-learn pilots with embedded evaluation; and (iii) Participatory design sessions structured around real healthcare workflows.

Redesign Procurement for Iteration, Not Perfection. Procurement processes must shift from waterfall-style vendor selection to agile-oriented partnerships. Contracts should allow iterative development, outcome-based metrics, and

Table 1. Opportunities for Translating Wartime Innovation Practices to Healthcare

Wartime Practice	Barrier	Adapted Strategy for Healthcare
Decentralized, user-embedded development	Centralized, abstracted tech design	Create embedded healthcare innovation units for co-creation with real end-users
Iterative MVPs deployed in live conditions	Rigid, linear validation and approval paths	Use regulatory sandboxes to safely test early-stage solutions in real-world environments
Tactical feedback loops with frontline users	Limited or delayed feedback from healthcare users	Institutionalize rapid feedback loops via short test cycles and real-world pilot programs
Dual-use civilian-military tech repurposing	Siloed development and limited cross-sector flow	Promote civil-military innovation corridors for dual-use technologies

mid-course corrections, in the spirit of calm compliance [2]. This mirrors how Ukrainian tech teams deploy first versions quickly, then improve on the basis of the user experience. Suggested mechanisms include (i) Challenge-based procurement; (ii) Outcome-focused milestones; and (iii) Pre-commercial procurement models, already piloted in the EU.

Support Dual-Use and Civil-Military Innovation Corridors. Finally, healthcare can benefit from cross-sectoral collaboration with defense, civil protection, and emergency management communities, especially for technologies such as drones, autonomous vehicles, and secure communications. Structured dual-use innovation corridors [3], or collaborative ecosystem designed to foster the development and application of dual-use technologies, could accelerate the translation of field-tested technologies into civilian health contexts.

As summarized in Table 1, the wartime innovation model offers actionable strategies that healthcare systems can adopt to overcome institutional inertia and accelerate responsible innovation. The goal is not to replicate wartime dynamics in healthcare, but to learn from them. By selectively borrowing key principles like rapid cycles, user co-creation, iterative validation, and controlled flexibility, health systems become more responsive, resilient, and patient-centered.

Risks and Ethical Considerations. Translating wartime innovation practices into healthcare is not without risk. While speed and flexibility are essential for progress, they must be carefully balanced with the ethical and legal responsibilities unique to healthcare environments. Next, we list key concerns that must be addressed in any effort to responsibly accelerate innovation.

- *Patient Safety Must Remain Paramount.* Rapid iteration cannot come at the expense of harm prevention. Unlike battlefield technologies, where iterative failure can be tolerated as part of tactical risk, healthcare systems must maintain a do-no-harm baseline. Regulatory sandboxes and testbeds must, therefore, include robust safety nets, professional oversight, data monitoring, and clear exit criteria for failing pilots.
- *Data Privacy and Informed Consent.* Technologies such as AI and remote monitoring often require access to sensitive health data. Unlike combat environments where operational necessity can override privacy, healthcare systems

must comply with legal frameworks like GDPR or HIPAA. Innovation environments must therefore incorporate privacy-by-design and ensure meaningful informed consent, even under accelerated timelines.

- *Wartime Exceptionalism vs. Sustainable Governance.* Romanticizing wartime innovation is dangerous. What works under existential threat may not translate neatly into peacetime governance. Innovation-by-crisis is not a sustainable model; healthcare systems must build institutionalized mechanisms for rapid response, not rely on emergency culture.

5   Call to Action

Healthcare innovation today is at a crossroads. Tools exist to radically improve care, access, and resilience, but the systems needed to deploy them remain constrained by risk-averse structures, fragmented processes, and extremely slow-moving regulation. The wartime innovation ecosystem in Ukraine, while born of crisis, offers a powerful counterexample: decentralized, iterative, and user-embedded innovation can thrive under the most challenging conditions.

We have argued that healthcare systems should selectively borrow from this model by (i) Establishing regulatory sandboxes to enable real-world validation under controlled conditions; (ii) Creating embedded feedback loops between developers and health professionals; (iii) Reforming procurement processes to support iteration and agility; and (iv) Supporting cross-sector innovation corridors, particularly in dual-use technology domains. These shifts do not require abandoning safety or ethics. What they require, is reimagining how innovation is governed, moving from control to coordination, from compliance to collaboration. We strongly believe that only by doing so can healthcare keep pace with the needs of the 21st century.

References

1. Evers, C., Kniewel, R., Geihs, K., Schmidt, L.: The user in the loop: enabling user participation for self-adaptive applications. Futur. Gener. Comput. Syst. **34**, 110–123 (2014)
2. Granlund, T., Stirbu, V., Mikkonen, T.: Medical software needs calm compliance. IEEE Softw. **39**(1), 19–28 (2021)
3. Guo, Y., Chen, P., Wan, Y., Zhu, Y., Cao, X., Zeng, G.: Technology transfer in asymmetric innovation corridors: theory and empirical evidence from china. Appl. Geogr. **178**, 103599 (2025)
4. Hakmeh, J.: What Ukraine can teach europe and the world about innovation in modern warfare. Chatham House (2025). https://www.chathamhouse.org/2025/03/what-ukraine-can-teach-europe-and-world-about-innovation-modern-warfare
5. Medicines and Healthcare products Regulatory Agency (MHRA): AI Airlock: the regulatory sandbox for AIaMD. Gov.uk (2025). https://www.gov.uk/government/collections/ai-airlock-the-regulatory-sandbox-for-aiamd

TED – The intElligent Doctor at Your Home

Massimo Giordano, Rosaria Del Sorbo, Elisa Anna Contursi,
Chiara Maria Ragusa, Maria Pia Di Palo, Andrea Marino,
Giuseppe Del Sorbo, Gabriele Mongelli, Colomba Pessolano, Simona de Santis,
and Marianna Bartolomeo[✉]

Università degli studi di Salerno, Fisciano, Italy
mbartolonco@unisa.it

Abstract. Chronic diseases represent a growing challenge for healthcare systems worldwide, particularly in aging populations like Italy, where multimorbidity and functional decline significantly impact care needs. This paper analyzes the epidemiological, clinical, and organizational aspects of chronic disease management, focusing on type 2 diabetes and heart failure. It reviews national care models, including the Chronicity National Plan and Diagnostic-Therapeutic Care Pathways (PDTA), and explores the integration of digital health tools, such as telemedicine, in addressing continuity of care and patient empowerment. Within this framework, the paper presents the TED – The intElligent Doctor at your home project, developed by DIPMED UNISA, as an innovative response to the need for home-based, patient-centered chronic care. TED integrates certified medical devices, telemonitoring platforms, virtual voice assistants, and Internet of Medical Things (IoMT) technologies to enable real-time health monitoring and AI-driven decision support. Designed using a Patient-Centered Design methodology, TED is currently undergoing a controlled clinical trial involving patients with type 2 diabetes and heart failure. The system aims to improve therapeutic adherence, quality of life, and reduce social isolation. In line with Italy's National Recovery and Resilience Plan (PNRR), TED proposes a scalable, sustainable, and technologically advanced care model for frail and chronic patients.

Keywords: Chronic disease · Digital health · Telemedicine · loMT · Ambient Assisted Living (AAL) · Artificial Intelligence · Virtual Assistants · Patient-centered care · Home monitoring · GDPR

1 Introduction

In recent years, non-communicable diseases (NCDs) have emerged as a critical global health concern, accounting for 74% of worldwide mortality and placing an immense burden on healthcare systems. Managing these chronic conditions–such as cardiovascular disease, diabetes, and chronic respiratory illness–requires

G. Scanniello et al. (Eds.): PROFES 2025, LNCS 16362, pp. 266–272, 2026.
https://doi.org/10.1007/978-3-032-12092-2_21

long-term strategies that integrate clinical support, behavioral monitoring, and patient empowerment. Within this evolving landscape, voice assistants (VAs) have gained traction as promising tools in digital healthcare. A systematic review by Bramanti et al. (2025) highlights that VAs can effectively support self-management and patient engagement, particularly in elderly populations or those with limited digital literacy. While clinical and quality-of-life improvements remain moderate, the review emphasizes meaningful behavioral outcomes, including enhanced physical activity, improved problem-solving skills, and greater adherence to therapy. However, the authors also identify significant challenges, such as privacy concerns, speech recognition errors, and uneven accessibility across user groups.

Building upon this technological and clinical context, the TED (The intElligent Doctor at your home) project, funded under the PRIN 2022 call, introduces a novel patient-centered solution that integrates voice-based interaction with telemedicine services. TED is designed to support chronic and frail patients through a modular IoMT (Internet of Medical Things) system that includes certified monitoring devices, environmental sensors, and a virtual voice assistant. Its goal is to promote autonomy in daily activities, enable continuous health monitoring, and reduce social isolation. What distinguishes TED is its systemic interoperability–designed to integrate seamlessly with regional healthcare platforms such as COReHealth and Sinfonia–and its ability to tailor services according to individual pathologies and degrees of autonomy. Moreover, TED adheres to privacy-by-design principles, ensuring full GDPR compliance in managing sensitive health data .

Together, these contributions underscore a growing convergence between technological innovation and personalized chronic care. While the use of voice assistants in healthcare is still maturing, their integration into structured, patient-centric frameworks like TED may represent a pivotal step forward in making digital health solutions more accessible, effective, and human-centered.

Table 1. Project Summary

Project Summary	
Name	TED: The intElligent Doctor at your home
Duration	Nov 2023 – Feb 2026
Funding	MIUR – 319,100 €
Participants	Univ. of Salerno, Univ. of Salento
PI	Prof. Alessia Bramanti
TRL	5–6 (Clinical Validation)
Status	Ongoing

TED's main goal is to develop and validate a modular, interoperable platform that:

- Collects vital and environmental data using certified IoMT sensors
- Processes health information through AI algorithms
- Communicates with patients via voice-based virtual assistants
- Provides personalized reminders, alerts, and lifestyle coaching
- Facilitates remote consultations and telerehabilitation
- Ensures compliance with GDPR and national data protection regulations

The system will undergo a clinical trial involving patients with diabetes and heart failure to evaluate its impact on health outcomes, adherence, quality of life, and social isolation.

2   Technological Framework

The TED system is built on a modular, scalable, and privacy-preserving infrastructure to support home-based chronic disease management. It combines Ambient Assisted Living (AAL) principles with certified IoMT devices, a voice-based virtual assistant, secure communication protocols, and AI algorithms. The system runs on a containerized microservices architecture to ensure maintainability, security, and interoperability (Fig. 1).

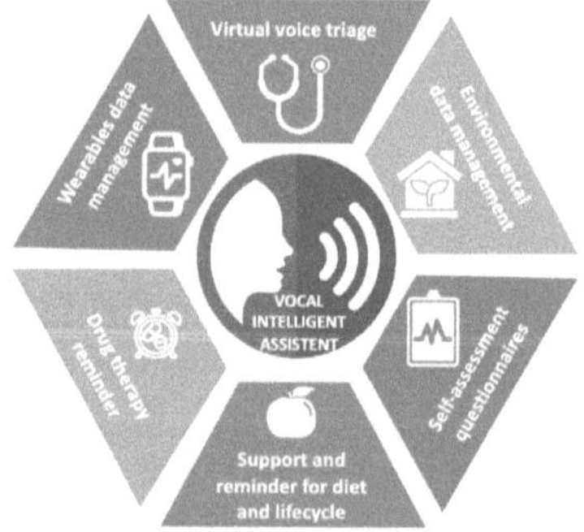

Fig. 1. Functional architecture of the TED system's Vocal Intelligent Assistant: (i) virtual voice triage; (ii) environmental data management; (iii) self-assessment questionnaires; (iv) support and reminders for diet and lifestyle; (v) drug therapy reminders; and (vi) wearable data management.

At the foundation, AAL strategies and IoMT devices continuously collect vital and environmental data such as blood glucose, blood pressure, heart rate, oxygen saturation, weight, posture, and movement. Devices include wearable sensors (e.g., Comftech Howdy Senior), ambient sensors, and embedded systems chosen for medical certification, usability, and edge-processing capability. The hardware platform is a Raspberry Pi 5 connected to a 7-inch touch display, supporting wired and wireless peripherals and providing sufficient computational power for containerized services.

TED's software stack uses Docker to isolate core services: Rhasspy for offline voice interaction, Node-RED for workflow orchestration and dashboard management, InfluxDB for time-series sensor data storage, and Mosquitto MQTT broker for lightweight, secure publish/subscribe communication. Rhasspy enables wake word detection, speech-to-text, intent recognition, and text-to-speech synthesis, integrating with Node-RED to trigger actions, retrieve sensor data, and deliver spoken feedback. Users interact via voice or touch, with support for multimodal input and fully offline operation.

Node-RED manages the system logic by receiving sensor data, triggering alerts, querying InfluxDB for trend visualization, and controlling the user interface for patients and caregivers. Data are timestamped and stored locally in InfluxDB, allowing efficient querying and real-time dashboards while ensuring temporal integrity. The local-first design maximizes privacy, avoids cloud dependence, and complies with GDPR and Italian data protection regulations. Well-defined APIs and standardized data formats guarantee interoperability with external platforms such as EHRs and telemedicine portals, with future extensions planned for additional sensors and clinical workflows.

This integrated, containerized, and privacy-by-design framework enables TED to deliver a secure, adaptive, and robust solution for home-based care of chronic conditions.

3   User Experience and Design Approach

TED adopts a Patient-Centered Design (PCD) methodology, placing the patient at the core of the development process. Patients, caregivers, and clinicians are actively involved in co-design workshops, ensuring that TED addresses real-world needs and overcomes key barriers–especially for elderly users with limited digital literacy or cognitive decline. The interaction model combines voice commands, powered by Rhasspy (an offline, open-source voice assistant), with a fallback touchscreen interface using a 7" HDMI capacitive display. This multimodal approach ensures usability even in the presence of speech or motor impairments. The system is built using a modular microservices architecture based on Docker, allowing for scalable deployment and simplified maintenance. Node-RED serves as the orchestration engine and dashboard interface, MQTT manages inter-device communication, and InfluxDB stores and manages health data over time. This architecture ensures interoperability and robustness while operating entirely offline for enhanced data protection.

TED's design was inspired by findings from Bramanti et al. (2025), which highlighted the role of voice assistants in enhancing behavioral engagement and self-management in chronic patients, while also stressing usability challenges in real-world settings. As such, TED undergoes continuous usability testing and iterative refinement. Emotional design elements, drawn from the Voice4Health model, promote empathy, reduce isolation, and enhance long-term adherence to care routines. Patients have reported a sense of companionship and greater confidence in managing their condition daily.

4 Privacy and Data Protection

Privacy is a core foundation of the TED ecosystem. The system is fully compliant with the EU General Data Protection Regulation (GDPR) and Italian national standards. Unlike most commercial voice assistants, TED processes all sensitive data–including biometrics, user commands, and sensor inputs–locally, avoiding cloud-based dependencies.

The platform employs data minimization, pseudonymization, role-based access control, and audit trails to ensure security. A Data Protection Impact Assessment (DPIA) has been completed, and all interactions are logged and encrypted. MQTT communication between modules takes place on a secured local network, while Docker containers isolate services to prevent cross-service data leaks.

By eliminating data transfer to external servers and prioritizing a privacy-by-design approach, TED builds user trust and ensures legal compliance–particularly important for older and vulnerable populations.

5 Clinical Trial and Application Scenarios

To assess TED's clinical and user experience impact, a controlled six-month trial is underway in the Campania region with 100 patients diagnosed with type 2 diabetes and/or heart failure. Participants are randomized to either TED plus standard care or standard care alone. The study evaluates primary clinical outcomes such as HbA1c, blood pressure, and hospital admissions, alongside secondary measures including therapy adherence, quality of life, and perceived social support. Data are collected via REDCap eCRFs, pseudonymized, and securely stored in compliance with ethical guidelines. Usability is assessed using standardized instruments such as the System Usability Scale (SUS), EQ-5D, and SF-36, providing insights for both clinical validation and future improvements of TED.

TED is designed for diverse home and institutional healthcare environments. In daily home use, it delivers real-time monitoring, medication reminders, and behavioral guidance, while post-discharge it facilitates remote monitoring and telerehabilitation to reduce readmission risk. For multimorbid patients, TED integrates data from multiple sources, offering shared dashboards for coordinated care among specialists, general practitioners, and caregivers. The system supports family members with alerts, trend visualizations, and actionable insights. Its modular and scalable architecture also allows deployment in rural areas, ICUs, nursing homes, rehabilitation centers, and future scenarios including pediatric care, neurodegenerative conditions, and long-COVID rehabilitation.

6 Impact, Expected Outcomes, and Future Perspectives

TED aims to transform chronic disease management through proactive, personalized, and digital-first interventions. It is expected to improve key health metrics (e.g., glycemic and blood pressure control), reduce avoidable hospitalizations, and enhance patient engagement. Socially, it can decrease isolation and improve autonomy and quality of life, while economically it supports sustainable healthcare by enabling remote monitoring and reducing in-person service demand. Its alignment with Italy's National Recovery and Resilience Plan (PNRR) reinforces its role in public health digital transformation.

TED's offline, privacy-preserving, and patient-centered architecture distinguishes it from commercial alternatives. By combining AI, IoMT, and human-centered care, it provides a scalable, ethically sound response to the growing burden of chronic diseases. Future developments include extending TED to conditions such as COPD and neurodegenerative disorders, implementing advanced predictive analytics, AI-driven triage, and integration with national EHR platforms. With ongoing clinical validation, TED is poised to become a reference model for smart, sustainable, home-based healthcare in Europe and beyond.

References

1. Bramanti, A.: Exploring the role of voice assistants in managing noncommunicable diseases: a systematic review on clinical, behavioral outcomes, quality of life, and user experiences. Healthcare. **13**, 517 (2025). https://doi.org/10.3390/healthcare13050517
2. Italian Ministry of Health: Piano Nazionale della Cronicità (2016). https://www.salute.gov.it
3. European Parliament and Council: Regulation (EU) 2016/679 (General Data Protection Regulation). Official Journal of the European Union (2016). https://eur-lex.europa.eu
4. WHO: Noncommunicable diseases. World Health Organization (2022). https://www.who.int/news-room/fact-sheets/detail/noncommunicable-diseases
5. Golinelli, D., Boetto, E., Carullo, G., Nuzzolese, A.G., Landini, M.P., Fantini, M.P.: Adoption of digital technologies in health care during the COVID-19 pandemic: systematic review of early scientific literature. J. Med. Internet Res. **22**(11), e22280 (2020). https://doi.org/10.2196/22280
6. European Commission: Recovery and Resilience Facility: Italy's National Recovery and Resilience Plan (2021)
7. DataWizard. Voice4Health: Using Voice Assistants to Promote Positive Ageing. https://datawizard.it/en/voice4health-using-voice-assistants-to-promote-positive-ageing/ Accesso: 15 settembre 2025
8. McCabe, C., McCann, M., Brady, A.M.: Home telemonitoring for chronic disease management: a systematic review and meta-analysis. Int. J. Nurs. Stud. **117**, 103890 (2021). https://doi.org/10.1016/j.ijnurstu.2021.103890
9. Tuckson, R.V., Edmunds, M., Hodgkins, M.L.: Telehealth. N. Engl. J. Med. **377**(16), 1585–1592 (2017). https://doi.org/10.1056/NEJMsr1503323
10. Dorsey, E.R., Topol, E.J.: Telemedicine: lessons learned during the COVID-19 pandemic and beyond. Nat. Rev. Clin. Oncol. **17**(9), 573–584 (2020). https://doi.org/10.1038/s41571-020-0410-5

11. Mehta, N., Pandit, A., Shukla, S.: Artificial intelligence in home-based healthcare: a scoping review. npj Digital Medicine, vol. 5, p. 92 (2022). https://doi.org/10.1038/s41746-022-00694-0
12. Dinesen, B., Nonnecke, B., Lindeman, D., et al.: Personalized telehealth in the future: a global research agenda. J. Med. Internet Res. **18**(3), e53 (2016). https://doi.org/10.2196/jmir.5257

AI-Driven Intervention with Wearable Remote Monitoring Devices for Human Health

Response to Action: Telerehabilitation Smoking Cessation Program Assisted by Wearable Remote Monitoring Devices

Maria Pia Di Palo[(✉)] [ID], Rosaria Del Sorbo, Colomba Pessolano, Gabriele Mongelli, Marianna Bartolomeo, Giuseppe Del Sorbo, Massimo Giordano, Elisa Anna Contursi, Andrea Marino, Simona De Santis, and Chiara Maria Ragusa

University of Salerno, Via S. Allende, 84081 Baronissi, SA, Italy
mdipalo@unisa.it

Abstract. In recent years, wearable remote monitoring devices have been increasingly utilized across various healthcare domains and have gained attention as a potential tool for the smoking events detection. Given the substantial impact of smoking on global public health—and according to the designation of smoking treatment as a "priority objective" requiring innovative methodologies development—this paper presents a study proposal for an AI-driven intervention program that integrates wearable devices, telemedicine, and personalized support strategies to assist smokers in a novel, personalized, and multimodal telerehabilitation smoking cessation program. As a project proposal, this work aims to provide the conceptual and methodological foundation for subsequent clinical studies. The project seeks to monitor changes in cardiopulmonary, oral health, and quality-of-life (QoL) parameters throughout the smoking cessation process, also assessing patient adherence, usability, and satisfaction. Wearable devices will be employed to detect smoking-related gestures, monitor vital signs, and support adherence, whereas telemedicine platforms will facilitate continuous monitoring, enhance communication and program personalization. Expected outcomes include improvements in nicotine dependence severity, QoL, cardiopulmonary and oral health parameters, along with higher adherence and satisfaction than traditional programs. The proposed intervention holds the potential to enhance smoking cessation strategies effectiveness, reduce smoking-related morbidity and healthcare expenditures. Nonetheless, issues related to data security, privacy, and integration into existing healthcare systems must be carefully addressed.

Keywords: Smoking cessation · Wearable device · Telemedicine

© The Author(s), under exclusive license to Springer Nature Switzerland AG 2026
G. Scanniello et al. (Eds.): PROFES 2025, LNCS 16362, pp. 273–279, 2026.
https://doi.org/10.1007/978-3-032-12092-2_22

1   Introduction

In recent years, wearable remote monitoring devices have been widely used to track medical parameters in several fields [1–3], targeting all ages and physiologi-cal/pathological health conditions [4–8]. Wearable remote monitoring devices were used to perceive, register, analyze, monitor, manage the lifestyle, remotely adjust treatment plans, or treat diseases [2, 3]. These goals were obtained by integrating ad-vanced technologies for identification, sensing, connectivity, and cloud-based storage [2, 3]. In the past decades, several technology-based smoking assessments were inves-tigated, like expired carbon monoxide monitoring and biomarkers. However, no pat-terns of smoking habits could be derived from these approaches [9]. For this reason, a portable monitoring device was developed to record cases of smoking. However, this device requires that subjects smoke all their cigarettes using the portable monitoring device, and not all smokers adhere to these instructions, therefore incorrect smoking patterns were recorded due to the device's obtrusiveness and large size [9]. To over-come all these limitations, wearable remote monitoring devices have caught attention [9].

The World Health Organization estimates >8 million deaths each year due to tobacco smoke and 1.2 million to second-hand tobacco smoke; (65.000 children) [10, 11]. Tobacco smoking represents the leading risk factor for chronic non-communicable diseases, as cardiovascular and respiratory diseases, periodontitis and malignant cancers [10–13], characterized by increased risk of complications, frequent hospitali-zations, disability, and mortality, with a significant burden on the National Health Service [14].

Traditional smoking cessation services are associated with high economic costs and low levels of patient satisfaction due to the time and effort required to access [15, 16]. In contrast, e-health technologies may offer accessible and cost-effective alternatives [15, 16]. However, a primary limitation of m-health interventions is the reliance on self-reported abstinence data, not corroborated by objective systemic markers [15, 16].

This research project aims to evaluate the effectiveness of an integrated telemedicine system combined with wearable remote monitoring devices in supporting patients undergoing smoking cessation. The objectives include monitoring longitudinal changes in cardiopulmonary, oral health, and quality-of-life parameters, as well as assessing patient adherence, usability, and satisfaction with telerehabilitation inter-ventions.

2   Response to Action

The project proposes a personalized and multimodal telerehabilitation program for smoking cessation supported by wearable remote monitoring devices and integrated-telemedicine platforms to smokers of heat and heat-not-burn tobacco and nicotine-containing products who wish to undertake the program at hospitals, anti-smoking centers, or who are referred by general practitioners. The project involves a large specialists network (cardiologists, pulmonologists, dentists, engineers, and telemedicine experts).

The systems include the telerehabilitation smoking cessation program (Fig. 1):

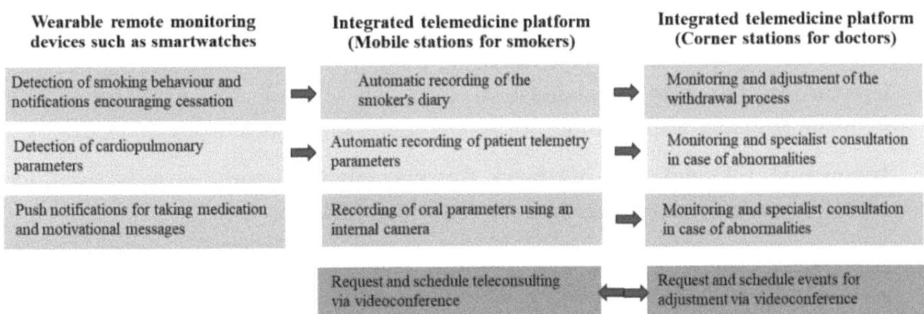

Fig. 1. Interconnection between wearable remote monitoring devices and the integrated telemedicine platform

Wearable remote monitoring devices: smartwatch and smart wristband worn bilaterally to ensure accurate detection of patient gestures and continuous monitoring of vital parameters even on the non-habitual side of the smoke. Their main functions are:

- **Detection of smoking gestures:** the wearable devices are equipped with accelerometers and gyroscopes motion sensors that record arm movements associated with smoking. AI analyzes movements and distinguishes them from similar actions. If a smoking gesture is detected, the device emits a vibrational/auditory signal to encourage patient to stop. These data are transmitted in real-time to the telemedicine platform.
- **Automatic uploading of the Smoker's Diary:** each smoking episode is automatically recorded on the integrated-telemedicine platform. If the patient forgets to wear the device, they can still manually upload smoking episodes.
- **Real-time monitoring of vital parameters:** heart rate, respiratory rate, oxygen saturation, and blood pressure data are transmitted in real-time to the platform.
- **Support for treatment adherence:** the wearable remote monitoring devices track wearing time and send reminder notifications on the platform if not worn.

Integrated-telemedicine platform for smokers: a web-based and mobile application, accessible via smartphones/tablets on Android or iOS systems. The main functions are:

- **Viewing the Smoker's Diary:** smoking episode is automatically recorded in the platform, so smokers can track smoking frequency over time to monitor progress. If needed, they can manually upload smoking episodes if they forget to wear the devices.
- **Real-time health monitoring:** smokers can check their real-time vital signs recorded by wearable devices. If abnormalities are detected, they receive a notification and can request a medical consultation.
- **Oral health support:** the platform allows smokers to take pictures of oral cavity using their smartphone camera to monitor gum bleeding after brushing. If abnormalities are detected, they receive a notification and can request a dentist consultation.
- **Reminders and personalized notifications:** the integrated-telemedicine platform sends push notifications for: medication reminders for patients with comorbidities;

motivational text messages, images, or videos to encourage smoking cessation; and alerts if the wearable devices are not being used, promoting adherence.

- **Teleconsultation with specialists:** smokers can schedule tele visits through the platform, reducing waiting times for access to traditional healthcare services.

Integrated telemedicine platform for specialist doctors: a web-based tool accessible from dedicated corner stations. The main functions are:

- **Viewing the Smoker's Diary and smoking event analysis:** each smoking episode is automatically recorded in the integrated-telemedicine platform, so smokers can track their smoking frequency over time to monitor progress. AI analysis differentiates between actual smoking gestures and similar movements, reducing false positives.
- **Real-time vital parameters monitoring and analysis:** doctors can view real-time vital parameters and intervene in not normal case. AI highlights critical situations.
- **Oral health support:** dentists can view the oral status based on the pictures uploaded by the smokers in the integrated-telemedicine platform, as well as, monitor the periodontal status through the gum bleeding after brushing, to intervene in case of abnormalities. Data is processed by AI algorithms, which highlight any critical situations.
- **Personalization of smoking cessation programs:** doctors can adjust the rehabilitation program at any time and configure personalized support messages.
- **Teleconsultation with smokers:** the integrated-telemedicine platform allows video consultations with smokers when needed, reducing the need for in-person visits.
- **Analysis and reporting:** the integrated-telemedicine platform for doctors generates graphs and reports tracking smokers' progress and vital parameters over time. Data security and privacy are handled through pseudonymization of patient records, encrypted transmission, and role-based access control within the platform. These measures are essential to ensure patient confidentiality and system integrity.

3   Evaluation Plan

The evaluation plan will be scheduled as follows:

Baseline assessment (T0): sociodemographic and medical history, smoking habits (including daily number of cigarettes); nicotine dependence (Fagerström Test) [20]; motivation to quit (National Institute of Health smoking cessation test) [11]; health-related quality of life (HRQoL) and Oral health-related quality of life (OHRQoL, OHIP-14) [20]; self-assessment of periodontal status and home oral hygiene habits.

Daily monitoring using the wearable remote monitoring devices: cardiovascular (heart rate, blood pressure) and pulmonary parameters (respiratory rate, oxygen saturation); oral parameters: bleeding on brushing.

Quarterly assessments: nicotine dependence (Fagerström Test) [19]; usability, acceptance, and satisfaction of the platform and devices; HRQoL and OHRQoL (including OHIP-14); in-person cardiology, pulmonology and dental visit.

4 Expected Outcomes and Potential Impact on Human Health

The expected outcomes are improvements in nicotine dependence severity, cardio-pulmonary, oral parameters, and perceived QoL and oral health, in line with scientific literature for former smokers in the short term (<12 months) [17]. An increase in reported bleeding on brushing is expected, as tobacco is known to fictitiously mask gingival bleeding. It is anticipated that the worsening of self-reported gingival bleeding will nevertheless be associated with an improvement in periodontal parameters assessable by the dentist. The improvement in QoL is attended considering the possibility of synchronization between specialists and patients. Considering the patient reported outcomes, greater adherence and satisfaction than traditional smoking cessation program is expected in line with the reported findings in the literature regarding mAdherence [18, 19]. To strengthen feasibility, the project will include a pilot phase with a small group of participants. This phase will be designed to obtain preliminary data on usability, acceptance, and early clinical indicators, which will be used to refine the intervention prior to the full clinical trial. This is expected to reduce waiting times, effort, costs, and the need for travel.

A key strength of this project is its multidisciplinary approach, which fosters comprehensive patient care to optimize outcomes.

5 Conclusions and Future Prospectives

In the healthcare field, wearable remote monitoring devices facilitate connectivity between specialist physicians, patients, and platforms, thereby enhancing multidisciplinary care planning. The integration of emerging technologies, such as AI-driven medical interventions combined with wearable monitoring systems, may represent a significant advancement in public health by improving population health outcomes and reducing the economic burden on healthcare systems. From a broader perspective, these devices could also support national epidemiological surveillance and preventive health strategies. However, it also presents critical challenges. This involves establishing robust legal frameworks to support the secure collection, transmission, storage, and exchange of data across diverse healthcare organizations. Legal structures must address potential issues such as misdiagnoses or missed diagnoses resulting from unreliable, delayed, or false-alarm data. Data security and privacy are of paramount importance given the highly sensitive nature of the information collected. To fully harness the potential of these technologies, it is imperative to develop comprehensive strategies that ensure data protection and build public trust.

It should be emphasized that this paper presents a project proposal, the pilot investigations on usability and patient acceptance are planned as preliminary steps to confirm the feasibility of the proposed system and will serve for subsequent clinical validation, while addressing data security, integration, and legal framework challenges.

Disclosure of Interests.. The authors have no competing interests to declare that are relevant to the content of this article.

References

1. Chen, X., Kim, D.H., Lu, N.: Introduction: Wearable devices. Chem. Rev. **124**(10), 6145–6147 (2024). https://doi.org/10.1021/acs.chemrev.4c00271
2. Lu, L., Zhang, J., Xie, Y., et al.: Wearable health devices in health care: Narrative systematic review. JMIR Mhealth Uhealth **8**(11), e18907 (2020). https://doi.org/10.2196/18907
3. Cheng, Y., Wang, K., Xu, H., Li, T., Jin, Q., Cui, D.: Recent developments in sensors for wearable device applications. Anal. Bioanal. Chem. **413**(24), 6037–6057 (2021)
4. Koenig, C., Ammann, R.A., Kuehni, C.E., Roessler, J., Brack, E.: Continuous recording of vital signs with a wearable device in pediatric patients undergoing chemotherapy for cancer-an operational feasibility study. Support. Care Cancer **29**(9), 5283–5292 (2021)
5. Wakefield, C., Yao, L., Self, S., et al.: Wearable technology for health monitoring during pregnancy: an observational cross-sectional survey study. Arch. Gynecol. Obstet. **308**(1), 73–78 (2023). https://doi.org/10.1007/s00404-022-06705-y
6. Luo, J., Zhang, K., Xu, Y., Tao, Y., Zhang, Q.: Effectiveness of wearable device-based intervention on glycemic control in patients with type 2 diabetes: A system review and meta-analysis. J. Med. Syst. **46**(1), 11 (2021). https://doi.org/10.1007/s10916-021-01797-6
7. Park, Y.S., An, C.S., Lim, C.G.: Effects of a rehabilitation program using a wearable device on the upper limb function, performance of activities of daily living, and rehabilitation participation in patients with acute stroke. Int. J. Environ. Res. Public Health **18**(11), 5524 (2021). https://doi.org/10.3390/ijerph18115524
8. Scataglini, S., Van Dyck, Z., Declercq, V., et al.: Effect of music based therapy rhythmic auditory stimulation (RAS) Using wearable device in rehabilitation of neurological patients: A systematic review. Sensors (Basel). **23**(13), 5933 (2023)
9. Imtiaz, M.H., Ramos-Garcia, R.I., Wattal, S., Tiffany, S., Sazonov, E.: Wearable sensors for monitoring of cigarette smoking in free-living: A systematic review. Sensors (Basel). **19**(21), 4678 (2019)
10. World Health Organization (WHO). Tobacco. https://www.who.int/news-room/factsheets/detail/tobacco (accessed online 21 March 2025) (2023)
11. Ministero della Salute.: Tabagismo., https://www.salute.gov.it/portale/fumo/dettaglioContenutiFumo.jsp?id=5579&area=fumo&menu=vuoto (accessed online 21 March 2025) (2024)
12. Ford, P.J., Rich, A.M.: Tobacco use and oral health. Addiction **116**(12), 3531–3540 (2021). https://doi.org/10.1111/add.15513
13. Raspini, M., Cavalcanti, R., Clementini, M., et al.: La parodontite e gli italiani (2016–2020): necessità di linee guida per implementare una terapia efficace. Società Italiana di Parodontologia (SIdP). Dental Cadmos. **89**(5), 346–356 (2021)
14. Hoogendijk, E.O., Afilalo, J., Ensrud, K.E., et al.: Frailty: implications for clinical practice and public health. Lancet. **394**(10206), 1365–1375 (2019)
15. Guo, Y.Q., Chen, Y., Dabbs, A.D., Wu, Y.: The effectiveness of smartphone app-based interventions for assisting smoking cessation: Systematic review and meta-analysis. J. Med. Internet Res. **25**, e43242 (2023). https://doi.org/10.2196/43242
16. Mersha, A.G., Bryant, J., Booth, K., Watson, L., Kennedy, M.: The effectiveness of internet-based group behavioural interventions on lifestyle modifications: A systematic review. Prev. Med. **186**, 108099 (2024). https://doi.org/10.1016/j.ypmed.2024.108099
17. Cho, E.R., Brill, I.K., Gram, I.T., Brown, P.E., Jha, P. Smoking Cessation and Short- and Longer-Term Mortality. NEJM Evid. **3**(3), EVIDoa2300272 (2024)
18. Klonoff, D.C.: Improved outcomes from diabetes monitoring: the benefits of better adherence, therapy adjustments, patient education, and telemedicine support. J. Diabetes Sci. Technol. **6**(3), 486–490 (2012). https://doi.org/10.1177/193229681200600301

19. Basit, S.A., Mathews, N., Kunik, M.E.: Telemedicine interventions for medication adherence in mental illness: A systematic review. Gen. Hosp. Psychiatry **62**, 28–36 (2020)
20. Fagerström KO, Kunze M, Schoberberger R, Breslau N, Hughes JR, Hurt RD, Puska P, Ramström L, Zatoński W.: Nicotine dependence versus smoking prevalence: comparisons among countries and categories of smokers. Tob Control. Spring; **5**(1), 52–6 (1996)

Structured Clinical Reasoning in AI: Comparing LLMs and Curated, Ontology-Grounded Multi-Agent Systems

Francesco Barbato[1]($\boxtimes$), Filippo Sorichetti[2,3], Emanuele Ielo[1], and Lorenzo Megliola[2,4,5]

[1] Bergamo, Italy
info@kaimed.eu
[2] KaiMed, Cagliari, Italy
[3] Scuola Universitaria Superiore IUSS, Pavia, Italy
[4] H-FARM College, Roncade, Italy
[5] University of Chichester, West Sussex, UK

Abstract. In high-stakes domains like medicine, AI systems must do more than generate fluent responses—they must ensure that clinical reasoning is safe, auditable, and grounded in verified knowledge. This paper presents a comparative analysis of reasoning outputs produced by large language models and by curated, ontology-grounded AI systems. We use KaiMed—a hybrid multi-agent platform built on GPT-4o-mini and structured medical knowledge—as a representative of the latter approach. Unlike single-model pipelines, KaiMed decomposes reasoning into modular, role-specific agents specialized in diagnosis, treatment planning, literature validation, and safety filtering. Each agent operates over a semantically structured knowledge base, comprising a proprietary clinical ontology and two curated layers: a graph of clinical trials and a semantic retriever built on peer-reviewed literature. This architecture enables traceable, constraint-aware, and clinically aligned reasoning. Our hypothesis is that in medicine, the source, structure, and semantic integrity of knowledge are not technical details—they are prerequisites for reliability and trust. We evaluate both systems on complex prompts in two domains: Inflammatory Bowel Disease (IBD) and Chronic Rhinosinusitis with Nasal Polyps (CRSwNP). Results show that while GPT-4o-mini generates plausible responses, it lacks epistemic grounding and fails to surface non-obvious or investigational options. KaiMed, by contrast, consistently produces evidence-aligned, phenotype-specific recommendations—demonstrating that in Clinical AI, the key differentiator is not model size, but the structure and orchestration of knowledge.

Keywords: Structured Clinical Reasoning · Ontology-Based AI · Medical Knowledge Graphs · Multi-Agent Clinical AI Systems · Evidence-Based AI in Medicine

Independent Researcher, Contributor to the KaiMed Initiative (non-institutional affiliation).

G. Scanniello et al. (Eds.): PROFES 2025, LNCS 16362, pp. 280–285, 2026.
https://doi.org/10.1007/978-3-032-12092-2_23

1   Introduction

Recent advances in large language models (LLMs) have enabled systems capable of generating fluent, human-like responses to clinical queries. However, in high-stakes domains such as medicine, **fluency is not enough**. Clinical reasoning depends not only on information access, but on the **source, structure, and verifiability** of that information. Unverified or hallucinated content can directly impact patient safety—making **knowledge integrity** a central concern for Clinical AI.

In this paper, we investigate how different approaches to knowledge grounding affect the reliability of AI-driven medical reasoning. Specifically, we compare the outputs of GPT-4o-mini, used both as a standalone LLM and as the core language model within *KaiMed*, a curated, ontology-grounded multi-agent system for clinical reasoning. While both systems share the same base model, their outputs diverge significantly due to the way they access and structure medical knowledge.

KaiMed combines peer-reviewed knowledge sources with a proprietary clinical ontology and modular reasoning agents responsible for diagnosis, treatment planning, evidence retrieval, and safety validation. This architecture aims to ensure not only accuracy, but traceability and clinical coherence. Through comparative prompts in the domains of Inflammatory Bowel Disease (IBD) and Chronic Rhinosinusitis (CRS), we show how knowledge representation directly influences output quality.

Ultimately, we argue that in Clinical AI, **not all knowledge is equal**—and that **what the model knows, and how it knows it**, is as important as what it says.

2   Related Work

Traditional Clinical Decision Support Systems (CDSS) have long been used in healthcare settings, offering safety through rule-based or guideline-driven recommendations [5]. However, these systems lack adaptability and often fail to handle ambiguous or evolving clinical contexts.

More recent approaches leverage large language models trained on biomedical corpora—such as Med-PaLM [4]—to generate open-ended clinical suggestions. While promising, these models often suffer from **hallucinated content, unverifiable claims, and inconsistent recommendations** [1].

Retrieval-Augmented Generation (RAG) frameworks [2] offer partial mitigation by grounding outputs in external documents. Yet they still rely on unstructured evidence, lack ontological constraints, and struggle with knowledge consistency.

Ontology-based systems present an alternative: they encode medical knowledge into structured, queryable formats that support transparent reasoning and enforce domain-specific constraints [3]. However, such systems remain underutilized in conjunction with modern language models.

In this context, we present *KaiMed*, a curated, multi-agent clinical reasoning system that combines structured ontologies with modular LLM orchestration—designed to address the limitations of both rule-based CDSS and unstructured generative models.

3   Knowledge Curation in KaiMed

In *KaiMed*, clinical reasoning is grounded in a semantically curated knowledge infrastructure, explicitly designed to prioritize reliability, traceability, and interpretability. Unlike systems that rely on general web-scale corpora, *KaiMed* draws exclusively from **peer-reviewed sources**, processed through a controlled and auditable ETL pipeline.

The knowledge architecture consists of two complementary layers:

- **A symbolic knowledge graph**, derived from clinical trials indexed in Europe PMC and filtered through strict inclusion criteria (e.g., peer-reviewed, post-2015, trial-type only, no preprints).
- **A semantic vector space**, populated by embedding vetted journal articles and reviews, used for semantic retrieval during reasoning.

The ETL process is fully automated and scoped by domain. It queries Europe PMC, extracts metadata and content, filters by publication type and date, and ingests articles into a MongoDB instance. From there:

- Clinical trials are parsed by LLM agents into structured triples (e.g., *Disease - Treated With - Drug*) and stored in a Neo4j-based knowledge graph.
- Journal articles are embedded using sentence-transformers and indexed via Qdrant to support retrieval-augmented generation (RAG).

Central to the symbolic layer is a **proprietary medical ontology**, hand-crafted to represent clinically meaningful distinctions (e.g., *First-Line Therapy, Contraindicated In, Has Risk Factor, Has Complication*). This ontology underpins the graph schema and enforces semantic disambiguation during triple extraction and reasoning. Unlike open biomedical ontologies, the schema is optimized for inference tasks and real-world case mapping. Concretely, it encodes relations such as *Has Symptom, Treated With, Contraindicated In*, and *Has Risk Factor*, each qualified by attributes like severity, therapeutic line, or degree of risk. This allows reasoning agents to enforce therapeutic sequencing and patient-specific safety constraints rather than simply retrieving associations. For example, it can represent *"Crohn's Disease—Treated With—Upadacitinib (Second-Line Therapy)"* together with *"Upadacitinib—Contraindicated In—Pregnancy (Absolute)"*. The design is general-purpose yet extensible, so new relations (e.g., *biomarkers in oncology*) can be added without disrupting the core schema.

This curated knowledge base supports a **modular multi-agent system**. Each agent is explicitly configured to interact with one or more knowledge layers:

- **Diagnosis Agent**: evaluates differential hypotheses by querying both the symbolic graph and the semantic retriever.

- **Treating Agent**: proposes evidence-based therapies, grounded in trial-derived structured data and ontological constraints.
- **Scientist Agent**: retrieves literature with semantic filtering to justify or extend reasoning paths.
- **Guardrails Agent**: enforces safety and regulatory boundaries (e.g., excluding unapproved or contraindicated therapies).

Through this layered and role-specific orchestration, *KaiMed* ensures that clinical reasoning is not only generated, but **structured, validated, and explainable**.

4   Comparative Evaluation

4.1   Evaluation Setup

To assess how knowledge structure influences clinical reasoning, we compared two AI-based systems built on the same foundational model (GPT-4o-mini):

1. a **generic standalone LLM**, operating without clinical structure or memory; and
2. *KaiMed*, a **multi-agent architecture** grounded in structured, evidence-aligned clinical knowledge.

For both settings, we used GPT-4o-mini with temperature $= 0.0$ and web search disabled, ensuring deterministic outputs and full reliance on the respective reasoning architectures.

We designed a set of **high-complexity clinical prompts** in two domains—Inflammatory Bowel Disease (IBD) and Chronic Rhinosinusitis with Nasal Polyps (CRS/wNP)—selected for their **high inter-patient variability**, involvement of **investigational treatment pathways**, and prevalence of **mismanagement**.

Each prompt described a clinical picture, including **detailed patient phenotype**, **prior treatment history** (including investigational agents), and documented **treatment failures or resistance**. Cases required **diagnostic and therapeutic ambiguity** handling, **prioritization**, and **pattern recognition**.

Outputs were then **blindly evaluated** by two clinical domain experts per case. Reviewers were blinded to the model source. Experts assessed each output using a **structured evaluation framework**, aligned with **established clinical best practices**. Criteria included clinical accuracy, therapeutic appropriateness and sequencing, contextual reasoning, and **evidence traceability**.

4.2   Comparative Case Summary

Case 1 — Crohn's Disease. *Prompt:* "Refractory IBD with failure of multiple biologics. What experimental options exist?"

- **Standalone LLM**: Recommends surgery as fallback and ignores the experimental dimension despite the explicit prompt.

- **KaiMed**: Suggests trial enrollment (e.g., TRIBUTE), considers JAK inhibitors and combination therapy, and recommends immunologic profiling. Cites relevant trials.

Case 2 — CRS/wNP with Eosinophilia. *Prompt:* "Severe eosinophilic rhinosinusitis unresponsive to mepolizumab, omalizumab, dupilumab. Are there other options to manage polyp recurrence without surgery?"

- **Standalone LLM**: Proposes dupilumab and gives a generic mention of anti-IL-5 therapies. Omits benralizumab and gives no trial referral.
- **KaiMed**: Identifies anti-IL-5 pathway options—including depemokimab, reslizumab, and benralizumab—and explains mechanisms. Cites ongoing trials and justifies choices based on phenotype and history.

This summary highlights how the systems diverge under epistemic uncertainty and complex therapeutic requirements.

4.3 Key Findings

In both scenarios, the standalone LLM generated **fluent** but **generic** outputs, defaulting to **conventional pathways** and overlooking **patient-specific details**. Even when prompted, it failed to explore **phenotype-matched** or **investigational alternatives**, and offered limited therapeutic breadth.

KaiMed, by contrast, delivered:

- **Evidence-aligned, phenotype-specific** recommendations;
- **Context-aware treatment sequencing**, with explicit rationales;
- References to **clinical trials** with identifiers and literature citations.

These differences stem not from **model capacity**, but from **knowledge design**. Performance deltas remained **consistent across prompt variations**.

5 Conclusion and Implications

The comparison highlights two approaches to Clinical AI: one driven by general fluency, the other by structured, context-aware reasoning. In Crohn's disease and eosinophilic CRS/wNP, the standalone LLM defaulted to plausible but generic answers, failing to recognize investigational or phenotype-specific paths. This reflects absence of **structured, auditable knowledge**.

KaiMed combines a **curated trial graph**, a **semantic retriever** based on peer-reviewed literature, and a **domain-specific ontology**. Each reasoning agent— diagnosis, treatment, literature validation, safety—operates over a specific substrate, enforcing role accountability and semantic traceability.

These principles enable *KaiMed* to propose **clinically aligned, evidence-grounded**, and **forward-looking recommendations**, even in edge cases. While we report two scenarios here, the broader evaluation encompassed over sixty cases. Future work will extend to additional conditions and systematic comparisons with other hybrid reasoning methods.

Ultimately, in **Clinical AI**, trust does not stem from *fluency* but from the *integrity* and *structure of knowledge*. By making reasoning *auditable, constrained,* and *clinically aligned,* systems like KaiMed show that reliable intelligence emerges less from model capacity than from how knowledge is *curated, represented,* and *orchestrated.*

References

1. Ji, Z., Lee, N., Frieske, R., Yu, T., Su, D., Xu, Y., et al.: Survey of hallucination in natural language generation. ACM Comput. Surv. **55**(12), 1–38 (2023)
2. Lewis, P., Perez, E., Piktus, A., Petroni, F., Karpukhin, V., Goyal, N., et al.: Retrieval-augmented generation for knowledge-intensive nlp tasks. In: Adv. Neural Inf. Process. Syst. (2020)
3. Rotmensch, M., Halpern, Y., Tlimat, A., Horng, S., Sontag, D.: Learning a health knowledge graph from electronic medical records. Sci. Rep. **7**, 5994 (2017)
4. Singhal, K., Azizi, S., Tu, T., Mahdavi, S.S., Wei, J., Chung, H.W., et al.: Large language models encode clinical knowledge. In: Proc. NeurIPS 2022 Med. AI Workshop (2023)
5. Sutton, R.T., Pincock, D., Baumgart, D.C., Sadowski, D.C., Fedorak, R.N., Kroeker, K.I.: An overview of clinical decision support systems: benefits, risks, and strategies for success. NPJ Digit. Med. **3**, 17 (2020)

Optimizing Smart Hospitals with Deep Learning and Indoor Navigation: The Shkodra Case Study

Erisa Bekteshi[1]([✉]) [iD], Eliesa Bekteshi[2] [iD], Edoardo Polimeno[1] [iD], and Francesco Tommasi[1] [iD]

[1] University of Salento, Lecce, Italy
{erisa.bekteshi,edoardo.polimeno,
francesco.tommasi}@unisalento.it
[2] Regional Hospital of Shkoder, Shkodra, Albania

Abstract. Hospitals in Albania are constantly growing as a structure, offering more services, in the context of caring for the health of people, whose average life expectancy has increased. Hospitals in urban areas are being grouped into regional hospitals, increasing the range of services, improving quality, and modernizing them. An example of a regional hospital is the Shkodra Regional Hospital, located in Shkodra that offer services to more than 190 thousand people.

Direction of patients and visitors to the hospital is usually done by directional signs placed inside and outside the hospital structures, and direction for patients and visitors visiting the hospital for the first time presents difficulties.

The results of the questionnaire conducted with first-time or infrequent patients and visitors indicate the need to build an internal localization and navigation system in the hospital.

We propose implementing AI-powered indoor positioning and navigation systems in the Regional Hospital of Shkodra that represents a strategic advancement toward the realization of a smart hospital environment.

Keywords: Regional Hospital Shkodra · Indoor positioning and navigation · Deep learning

1 Introduction

The average duration of human existence on Earth continues to grow over time. [1]. This extension in the average human lifespan, combined with the growing ability to overcome severe medical conditions, presents numerous complexities for healthcare infrastructures across the world, transforming the adaptation of advanced technolog-ical solutions from a beneficial addition into an essential necessity. [2]. These facts present challenges to medical care systems that face increasing pressures to improve the quality of care for the population, reduce service costs, and increase efficiency in patient care. The growth of healthcare services and their concentration in hospitals has led to the growth of hospital structures. Hospitals are becoming increasingly complex structures that aim to provide an ever-increasing range of services to the population. In these complex structures, service must be fast and efficient because delays in finding patients, staff, or equipment's can negatively impact patient health and service efficiency.

© The Author(s), under exclusive license to Springer Nature Switzerland AG 2026
G. Scanniello et al. (Eds.): PROFES 2025, LNCS 16362, pp. 286–298, 2026.
https://doi.org/10.1007/978-3-032-12092-2_24

There is a growing trend toward the incorporation of advanced technological innova-tions aimed at optimizing operational processes, refining clinical workflows, and ele-vating the quality of patient care and experience. Over time, researchers have active-ly examined and responded to the continuous emergence of technological innova-tions. From this standpoint, technology has not only advanced significantly but has also under-gone a profound transformation within the medical field in recent decades. This evolution has opened a broad spectrum of opportunities to improve the delivery and effectiveness of public health services. Moreover, an additional research focus involves analyzing the heterogeneity of specific target populations and user profiles, which may influence the adoption and outcomes of these technological advance-ments [3–5]. Artificial Intelli-gence (AI) has advanced rapidly in medicine—especially in diagnostics, clinical decision support [6–8] and predictive analytics [9–11].

AI algorithms such as predictive analytics [12], machine learning [13, 14], and data mining [15] are employed to forecast patient flow, allocate staff and medical equip-ment efficiently, and automate administrative tasks. The integration of these tech-nologies enables context-aware, location-based services that support emergency rout-ing, infection control, and asset tracking.

Within such intricate and multifaceted healthcare environments—where even brief delays in locating patients, medical personnel, or essential equipment may detrimen-tally affect both the quality and efficiency of care—the integration of Artificial Intel-ligence (AI) with Indoor Positioning and Navigation Systems (INS) holds the potential to foster intelligent hospital ecosystems. These advanced settings are capable of adaptively managing resources, minimizing patient waiting periods, and significantly improving the overall delivery of healthcare services. [3]

2 Indoor Positioning and Navigation in Health Structures

Indoor positioning involves determining the location of individuals or items within build-ings using a range of technologies. Positioning systems intended to provide position estimation inside buildings are known as Indoor Positioning Systems (IPS) [16].

Many navigation studies primarily concentrate on refining positioning techniques or enhancing contextual understanding of the environment, often overlooking the com-plexities of indoor navigation [17]. Consequently, these approaches demand a robust infrastructure for effective indoor positioning and must be tailored to the specific envi-ronment. Positioning techniques in an enclosed environment such as hospitals have attracted the attention of many researchers who have adapted various techniques for indoor localization and navigation. [18–21].

According to Montello [22] navigation is typically described as the process through which the direction and movement of various modes of transport—such as cars, ships, aircraft, or even people—are managed to reach a particular destination.

Indoor navigation systems designed for buildings, hospitals, schools, and other objects do not use GPS signals, so recently lot of other technologies are used for such systems. The development of indoor navigation systems has been the focus of numerous research projects because of the incompatibility and poor accuracy of the standardized technology of such systems [17, 23, 24].

Actually, indoor positioning and navigation technologies including BLE beacons [25–27], Wi-Fi triangulation, [28–30] and LiDAR [31, 32], mobile-based navigation system [33, 34] are utilized to locate destination and to guide patients and staff in real time through complex healthcare facilities. Combining these technologies enables real-time, intelligent management of hospital resources and patient movement, improving workflow, safety, and the patient experience.

Studies are reported for efficient use of indoor positioning and navigation systems, such studies reported for Nottingham University Hospital Trust (Queens Medical Centre and City Hospital) [35] and the hospital of Santa Maria alle Scotte, Siena, Italy [36], which served as testbeds to evaluate implementations in smart hospitals indoor positioning and navigation., The findings suggest that the synergy between AI and indoor navigation holds transformative potential for the future of healthcare systems globally.

Building on these findings and recognizing the potential of such technologies in healthcare environments, the objectives of the present study are as follows:

- To evaluate the implementation potential, benefits, and challenges of introducing an indoor positioning and navigation system at the Regional Hospital of Shkodra, as a key step toward developing a smart hospital environment that enhances patient experience and operational efficiency, via mobile devices such as smartphones.
- To analyze the current navigation difficulties faced by patients, visitors, and staff within the Regional Hospital of Shkodra.
- To examine how indoor navigation can improve: 1) Wayfinding for patients and visitors; 2), Time management for healthcare professionals; and 3) Tracking of medical equipment and assets.

3   Methodology

This study adopts a "single case study approach" [37, 38], focusing on the Regional Hospital of Shkodra to explore the challenges and opportunities in implementing indoor navigation systems in a regional healthcare setting. During this study, a mixed qualitative and quantitative method was used to describe the current management system and the needs for a new system based on the implementation of artificial intelligence in indoor navigation within the hospital. Data collection methods were with observation the navigation of the patients and visitors during the navigation in hospitals and asking for the facilities in finding position and navigation with questionnaire.

3.1   Regional Hospital in Shkodra

Regional hospitals in Albania are typically extensive and intricate facilities, often posing navigational challenges for patients and visitors [39]. A prime example is the Regional Hospital of Shkodra, which provides a wide range of medical services. Regional Hospital of Shkodra (RHS) is the only governmental hospital in Shkodra city and north Albania that offers main health services for people who live in Shkodra, Malesia e Madhe and rural area around the cities, with a population of more than 190 thousand people. The number of medical staff that work in the RHS is about 400 people (where 100 is medical staff, 270 nurses and 30 maintenance staff).

Due to its size and complexity, locating specific areas—such as patient rooms, medical personnel, or equipment—can be difficult without staff assistance. This highlights the necessity of implementing indoor navigation systems within the hospital. Such systems can facilitate wayfinding for patients and visitors, enable real-time tracking of medical equipment and personnel, and enhance emergency response times [40, 41], contributing not only to a more positive patient experience but also to increased operational efficiency.

3.2 Current Navigation Challenges Faced by Hospital Users

At RHS, patient and visitor navigation are guided by direction signs located both outside and inside the hospital. However, these signs often prove insufficient for visitors, patients, individuals with disabilities, and others unfamiliar with the hospital layout, making orientation challenging. In Fig. 1, some examples of direction signs at RHS are shown.

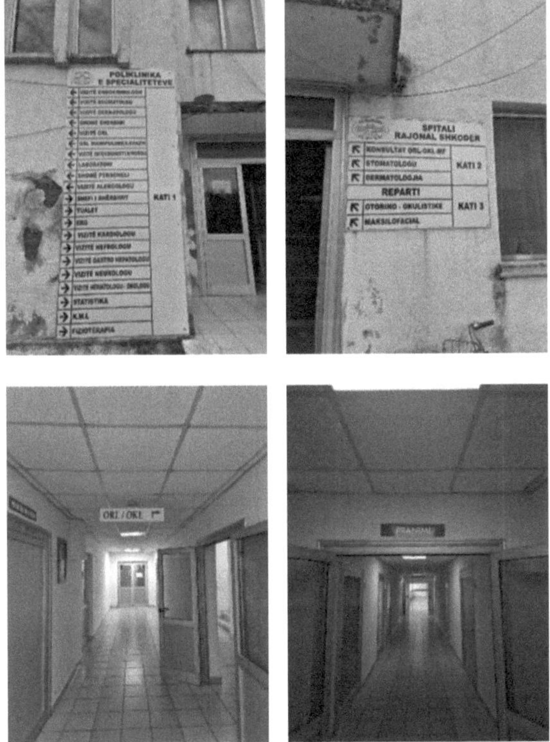

Fig. 1. Some direction signs used to direct patients and visitors in RHS

Navigating inside the hospital becomes more difficult as there are no maps with the "you are here" sign, nor markings on the turns to get to the equipment or the medical staff rooms.

The initial point of contact between users and the hospital often occurs through a medical appointment—either in emergency situations or via a referral letter. These forms of engagement typically provide the first navigational cues, ranging from detailed written instructions to merely stating the name of the clinic, staff member, or service to be visited. In many cases, patients, and visitors unfamiliar with the hospital layout rely on stopping uniformed personnel to request directions. This informal method of guidance can significantly affect hospital operations, often leading to inefficient use of staff time or requiring dedicated volunteers. To overcome such issues a host of 'non-technical' navigational and locative aids have been incorporated into hospital environments, based upon a well-documented understanding of spatial cognition [42], wayfinding [42] and signage design [43]. Within the Regional Hospital of Shkodra (RHS), the most used navigation method remains human assistance, whether through verbal instructions.

3.3 Use of AI to Implement Indoor Positioning and Navigation

Implementing an indoor positioning and navigation system within the hospital can greatly assist medical staff, patients, and visitors in finding their way more efficiently. The proposed system will be based on advanced positioning and navigation technologies and will incorporate Artificial Intelligence (AI) to address challenges related to orientation and directional guidance.

In order to introduce the positioning and navigation system inside RHS a survey was conducted with 60 patients and visitors in the RHS.

Participation in the study was based on three categories of participants: hospitalized patients, outpatients and visitors. The criteria for participation in the study are described as follows:

- All participants were selected from the categories presented in the RHS for participation in the study on a voluntary basis. At the outset, participants were informed about the purpose of the study and introduced to the idea of implementing a mobile-based navigation system within hospital [44].
- The presentation to the hospital was for the first time or was not a regular attender to the hospital.
- The selected participants were chosen from the biggest departments of the RHS.
- The participation was based on full of anonymity.

Table 1 shows the composition of samples chosen to participate in the survey.

Table 1. Composition of the population participated in the survey

Participant in the study	Number (%)	Department (Number)
Outpatients	28 (46.7%)	Emergency (12) Reception (16)
Patients	18 (30%)	Cardiology (8) Neurology (6) Surgery (4)
Visitors	14 (23.3%)	Emergency (4) Pediatrics (8) Obstetrics (2)

All the participants had to fill out the questionnaire, that was brief and focused on key details, such as the applicant's position in the hospital and the method used to determine proper patient positioning. Questionnaires were prepared in hard copy and they are filled by the participants in the presence of the study leader.

4   Discussion

Finding the desired destination in a large hospital is recognized as a difficult problem, not only for patients and visitors who may be unfamiliar with the environment, but even for hospital staff, who spend a great amount of their daily time in its premises [35]. The fact that staff members can face wayfinding difficulties can lead to cost and efficiency issues, putting aside potential cases of exposing patients' safety to risk. Also, if staff members may face difficulties in wayfinding, it is only natural that such difficulties will be greater for visitors, who will naturally stop and ask staff members for instructions. The fact that staff members are often stopped and asked for direction instructions can be often ineffective, as they might not know the answer or might be interrupted from important tasks they are supposed to be undertaking. Problems like this should be clearly identified, reported, and understood before proceeding in finding appropriate solutions.

Observations of patient and infrequent visitor navigation within RHS revealed that their routes through the hospital were often significantly longer than necessary. Additionally, requests for directions from the medical staff were frequent.

The results of the study expressed in questionnaires yielded the following results given in Table 2.

Table 2. Results of the questionnaire of study

Questions	Results	% Of Participants
Which are most important points you need to locate in hospitals	Medical equipment	50
	Medical staff room	80
	Patients room (for visitors)	30
	Supply medications room	25
How many times have you visited hospital	1—time	35
	2—times	40
	3 – times	25
Are you familiar with the use of applications in cellular	Yes	65
	Not so familiar	25
	No	10

Mean age of the participants was 62.5 years old, and based of the study done by [45, 46] people in Albania are using mobile telephony for different applications and are familiar with its use as internet applications are used in everyday life now.

Patients and visitor can determinate two or more points they need to localize in hospital. Results of the questionnaire with the patients and visitors show that the most important point for the interviewees was the doctor's room, where 80% expressed their need to find its location as quickly as possible, followed by medical equipment room 50%, patients' room 30% and supply medical room 25%. The results show that most of the interviewees are in the hospital to make medical visits to a specialist doctor or to be diagnosed with equipment.

As the results show a smartphone-based application for indoor navigation on the hospitals can be used from most of the patients and visitors (90% are familiar or less familiar with the use of smartphone applications).

Based on the Table 1 we build the Fig. 2 that illustrates the integration of Artificial Intelligence (AI) in smart hospitals for indoor positioning and navigation, showcasing how both technologies interact and their impact areas.

The diagram highlights the role of AI in optimizing indoor spatial awareness and navigation efficiency within smart hospital systems.

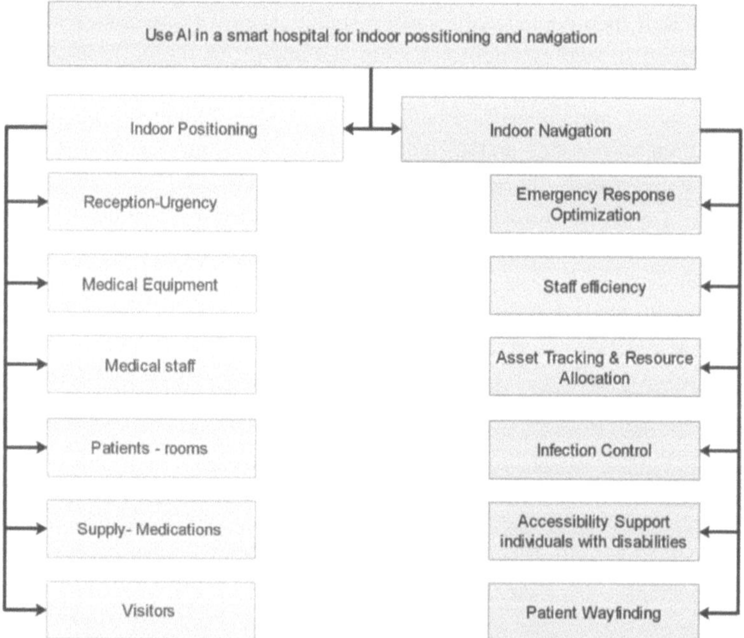

Fig. 2. Conceptual schema shows integration of AI in indoor positioning and navigation in smart hospital

- Left Side – Indoor Positioning:
    Positioned at the left side of the schema, indoor positioning refers to tracking the location of people and objects inside the hospital in real time. It includes:
    Reception-Urgency: Tracking urgent cases and their arrival times.
    Medical Equipment: Locating essential tools and devices when needed.
    Medical Staff: Knowing where staff is to improve response and coordination.

Patients – Rooms: Real-time tracking of patients (especially vulnerable ones such as elderly, children, or those with dementia).

Supply – Medications: Managing inventory and quick access to medication.

Visitors: Ensuring visitors can be tracked or guided for security and assistance.

- Right Side – Indoor Navigation:

On the other side of the schema, indoor navigation involves guiding or directing people and assets through the hospital. It supports:

Emergency Response Optimization: Rapidly identify the location of patients or staff in emergency situations as described in [47]. Determine and guide resuscitation teams responders along the quickest route. Automatically activate the nearest safe exits during evacuation procedures.

Staff Efficiency: Allow nurses, doctors, and technicians to: 1) Navigate the shortest path to patient rooms or clinical departments; 2), locate nearby available medical equipment (such as ECG machines); and 3), identify and reach other staff members quickly for urgent collaboration.

Asset Tracking & Resource Allocation: Instantly track the location of mobile medical equipment, minimizing time lost searching for essential tools. Gain insights into equipment usage patterns and monitor real-time availability to improve operational efficiency.

Infection Control: Monitor the movement of infected patients or staff to accurately trace contact pathways described by [48]. Restrict navigation routes during outbreaks to help prevent cross-contamination and contain the spread of infection.

Accessibility Support (Individuals with Disabilities): Provide navigation support for individuals with disabilities, voice directions, wheelchair-friendly routes, visual aids, and sign interpretation.

Patient Wayfinding: Guides patients to their appointments, reducing confusion and delays.

There is a two-way arrow between Indoor Positioning and Indoor Navigation, showing that accurate positioning data enhances navigation. Navigation needs reliable positioning to function effectively.

Based on the results we propose the following schema shown in Fig. 3.

The system illustrates how AI-powered indoor positioning and navigation systems can enhance hospital operations by increasing efficiency, improving safety, and creating a more patient-centered environment. It highlights practical applications such as real-time tracking of staff and equipment, optimizing emergency response times, and assisting patients and visitors in navigating the often-complex hospital infrastructure.

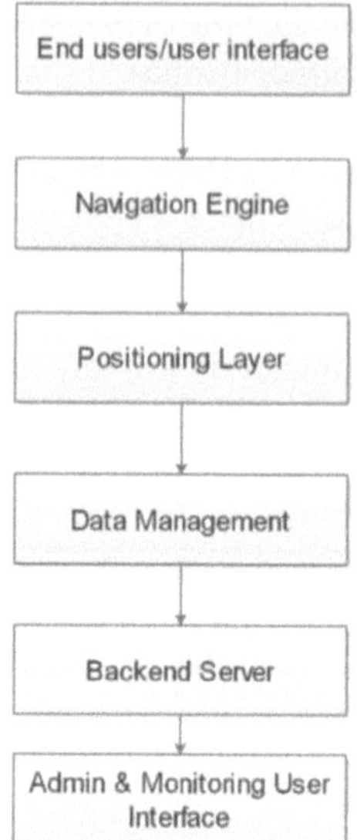

Fig. 3. Indoor navigation system proposed for RHS

5 Conclusion and Future Work

This article examined the importance of indoor positioning and navigation at the Regional Hospital of Shkodra from the viewpoints of patients, and visitors. Establishing such a system within the hospital would significantly support the orientation and movement of individuals within the facility, reducing confusion and delays. The study, conducted with especially first-time or infrequent patients and visitors, shows the need for indoor positioning and navigation in order to reduce the time required to locate specific destinations.

The implementation of AI-enhanced indoor positioning and navigation systems in Shkodra's regional hospital signifies a key step toward developing a smart healthcare environment. Utilizing technologies such as Bluetooth Low Energy (BLE) beacons, Wi-Fi-based triangulation, and machine learning–driven localization algorithms, the hospital would gain high-accuracy, real-time tracking capabilities for medical assets, personnel, and patients.

This technological integration with deep learning not only streamlines hospital operations and clinical coordination but also contributes to a safer and more user-friendly experience for patients and visitors. As a major healthcare institution in northern Albania, the Regional Hospital of Shkodra is well-positioned to lead the way in the country's digital healthcare transformation.

References

1. Mathers, C.D., Stevens, G.A., Boerma, T., White, R.A., Tobias, M.I.: Causes of international increases in older age life expectancy. The Lancet. **385**(9967), 540–548 (2015). https://doi.org/10.1016/S0140-6736(14)60569-9

2. Röcker, C., Ziefle, M., Holzinger, A.: From computer innovation to human integration: current trends and challenges for pervasive health technologies. In: Holzinger, A., Ziefle, M., Röcker, C. (eds.) Pervasive health, pp. 1–17. Springer, London (2014)

3. Röcker, C.: Smart medical services: A discussion of state-of-the-art approaches. In: S. Thatcher (Ed.): Proceedings of the International IEEE Conference on Machine Learning and Computing (ICMLC'11), **1**, 334–338 (2011)

4. Holzinger, A., Röcker, C., Ziefle, M.: From smart health to smart hospitals, in: Holzinger, A., Röcker, C., Ziefle, M. (Eds.), Smart health: Open problems and future challenges. Springer International Publishing, Cham, pp. 1–20 (2015). https://doi.org/10.1007/978-3-319-16226-3_1

5. Garg, N., 2021.: Technology in healthcare: Vision of smart hospitals, in: Handbook of Research on Engineering, Business, and Healthcare Applications of Data Science and Analytics. IGI Global Scientific Publishing, pp. 346–362. https://doi.org/10.4018/978-1-7998-3053-5.ch016

6. Sadr, H., Nazari, M., Khodaverdian, Z., et al.: Unveiling the potential of artificial intelligence in revolutionizing disease diagnosis and prediction: a comprehensive review of machine learning and deep learning approaches. Eur. J. Med. Res. **30**, 418 (2025). https://doi.org/10.1186/s40001-025-02680-7

7. Khalifa, M., Albadawy, M., Iqbal, U.: RETRACTED: Advancing clinical decision support: The role of artificial intelligence across six domains, Computer Methods and Programs in Biomedicine Update, **5**, (2024) https://doi.org/10.1016/j.cmpbup.2024.100142

8. Kumar, Y., Koul, A., Singla, R., et al.: Artificial intelligence in disease diagnosis: a systematic literature review, synthesizing framework and future research agenda. J Ambient Intell Human Comput **14**, 8459–8486 (2023). https://doi.org/10.1007/s12652-021-03612-z

9. Soenksen, L.R., Ma, Y., Zeng, C., Boussioux, L., Villalobos Carballo, K., Na, L., Wiberg, H.M., Li, M.L., Fuentes, I.,Bertsimas, D.: Integrated multimodal artificial intelligence framework for healthcare applications. NPJ digital medicine, **5**(1), p. 149 (2022) https://doi.org/10.48550/arXiv.2202.12998

10. Anuyah, S., Singh, M.K., Nyavor, H.: Advancing clinical trial outcomes using deep learning and predictive modelling: Bridging precision medicine and patient-centered care. arXiv preprint arXiv:2412.07050 (2024)

11. Morid, M.A., Sheng, O.R.L., Dunbar, J.: Time series prediction using deep learning methods in healthcare. ACM Trans. Manag. Inf. Syst. **14**(1), 1–29 (2023)

12. Van Calster, B., Wynants, L., Timmerman, D., Steyerberg, E.W., Collins, G.S.: Predictive analytics in health care: how can we know it works? J. Am. Med. Inform. Assoc. **26**, 1651–1654 (2019). https://doi.org/10.1093/jamia/ocz130

13. Habehh, H., Gohel, S.: Machine Learning in Healthcare. Curr. Genomics **22**, 291–300 (2021). https://doi.org/10.2174/1389202922666210705124359

14. Rajkomar, A., Dean, J., Kohane, I.: Machine learning in medicine. New England J. Med. **380**, 1347–1358 (2019). https://doi.org/10.1056/NEJMra1814259

15. Boukenze, B., Mousannif, H., Haqiq, A.: Predictive analytics in healthcare system using data mining techniques, in: Computer Science & Information Technology (CS & IT). Presented at the The Fourth International Conference on Database and Data Mining, Academy & Industry Research Collaboration Center (AIRCC), pp. 01–09 (2016). https://doi.org/10.5121/csit.2016.60501

16. Brena, R.F., García-Vázquez, J.P., Galván-Tejada, C.E., Muñoz-Rodriguez, D., Vargas-Rosales, C.,Fangmeyer, J., Jr.: Evolution of indoor positioning technologies: A survey. Journal of Sensors **2017**, 2630413 (2017). https://doi.org/10.1155/2017/2630413

17. Perez-Navarro, A., Montoliu, R., Torres-Sospedra, J.: Advances in indoor positioning and indoor navigation. Sensors **22**, 7375 (2022). https://doi.org/10.3390/s22197375

18. Marini, G.: Towards indoor localisation analytics for modelling flows of movements. In Adjunct Proceedings of the 2019 ACM International Joint Conference on Pervasive and Ubiquitous Computing and Proceedings of the 2019 ACM International Symposium on Wearable Computers (UbiComp/ISWC '19 Adjunct). Association for Computing Machinery, New York, NY, USA, 377–382 (2019). https://doi.org/10.1145/3341162.3349306

19. van der Ham, M.F.S., Zlatanova, S., Verbree, E., Voûte, R.: Real time localization of assets in hospitals using quuppa indoor positioning Ttechnology. ISPRS annals of the photogrammetry, remote sensing and spatial information sciences IV-4-W1, 105–110 (2016). https://doi.org/10.5194/isprs-annals-IV-4-W1-105-2016

20. Guerriero, F., Miglionico, G., Olivito, F.: A decision support system for localisation and inventory management in healthcare. In Bilski, P., & Guerriero, F. (Eds.). (2017). Computer systems for healthcare and medicine (1st ed.). River Publishers (2017). https://doi.org/10.1201/9781003337683

21. Wichmann, J.: Indoor positioning systems in hospitals: A scoping review. DIGITAL HEALTH 8 (2022). https://doi.org/10.1177/20552076221081696

22. Montello, D.R.: Navigation. In P. Shah (Ed.) & A. Miyake, The cambridge hand-book of visuospatial thinking (pp. 257–294). Cambridge University Press (2005). https://doi.org/10.1017/CBO9780511610448.008

23. Jung, S., Lee, S., Han, D.: A crowdsourcing-based global indoor positioning and navigation system. Pervasive Mob. Comput. 31, 94–106 (2016). https://doi.org/10.1016/j.pmcj.2016.02.002

24. Roy, P., Chowdhury, C.: A region-wise indoor localization system based on unsupervised learning and ant colony optimization technique. Appl. Soft Comput. 157, 111509 (2024). https://doi.org/10.1016/j.asoc.2024.111509

25. Kriz, P., Maly, F., Kozel, T.: Improving indoor localization using bluetooth low energy beacons. Mob. Inf. Syst. (2016). https://doi.org/10.1155/2016/2083094

26. Shipkovenski, T., Kalushkov, E., Petkov, Angelov, V.: "A beacon-Based Indoor Positioning System for Location Tracking of Patients in a Hospital," 2020 International Congress on Human-Computer Interaction, Optimization and Robotic Applications (HORA), Ankara, Turkey, pp. 1–6, (2020). https://doi.org/10.1109/HORA49412.2020.9152857

27. Sherif, F.F., Ahmed, K.S. (2024). Medical Equipment Real-Time Locating System in Hospitals Based on Bluetooth Low Energy. In: Rojas, I., Ortuño, F., Rojas, F., Herrera, L.J., Valenzuela, O. (eds) Bioinformatics and Biomedical Engineering. IWBBIO. Lecture Notes in Computer Science, 14848 (2024). Springer, Cham. https://doi.org/10.1007/978-3-031-64629-4_11

28. Mosaif, A., Rakrak, S.: A Li-Fi based wireless system for surveillance in hospitals. Biomedical Spectroscopy and Imaging. 8(3–4), 81–92 (2019). https://doi.org/10.3233/BSI-200191

29. Okoniewska, B., Graham, A., Gavrilova, M., Wah, D., Gilgen, J., Coke, J., Burden, J., Nayyar, S., Kaunda, J., Yergens, D., Baylis, B., Ghali, W.A., on behalf of the Ward of the 21st Century team: Multidimensional evaluation of a radio frequency identification wi-fi location tracking system in an acute-care hospital setting. J. Am. Med. Inform. Assoc. 19, 674–679 (2012). https://doi.org/10.1136/amiajnl-2011-000560

30. Vieira Brodt, J.P., Lopes Rijo, R.P.C., Alves, D.: Improving hospital experience through indoor localization implementation. Procedia Computer Science, CENTERIS - International Conference on ENTERprise Information Systems / ProjMAN - International Conference on Project MANagement / HCist - International Conference on Health and Social Care Information Systems and Technologies 256, 1326–1332 (2025). https://doi.org/10.1016/j.procs.2025.02.245

31. Ryoo, Y.-K.: A Patient Movement Monitoring Method Using 2D Lidar. J. Health Care and Life Science 9, 297–302 (2021). https://doi.org/10.22961/JHCLS.2021.9.2.297

32. Islam, M.M., Fukuda, H., Kobayashi, Y., Kuno, Y.: DNN and LiDAR sensor based crowd avoidance method for nurse-following robot in Healthcare, in: Kaiser, M.S., Mahmud, M., Al Mamun, S. (Eds.), Rhythms in healthcare. Springer Nature, Singapore, pp. 79–93 (2022). https://doi.org/10.1007/978-981-19-4189-4_6,

33. Chen, R., Pei, L. and Chen, Y.: A smart phone based PDR solution for indoor navigation. In Proceedings of the 24th international technical meeting of the satellite division of the institute of navigation (ION GNSS 2011) (pp. 1404–1408) (2011)

34. Fang, J., et al.: High-speed indoor navigation system based on visible light and mobile phone. IEEE Photonics J. 9(2), 1–11 (2017)

35. Hughes, N., Pinchin, J., Brown, M., Shaw, D.: Navigating in large hospitals, in: 2015 International Conference on Indoor Positioning and Indoor Navigation (IPIN). Presented at the 2015 International Conference on Indoor Positioning and Indoor Navigation (IPIN), pp. 1–9 (2015). https://doi.org/10.1109/IPIN.2015.7346758

36. Luschi, A., Borsani Villa, E.A., Gherardelli, M., Iadanza, E.: Designing and developing a mobile application for indoor real-time positioning and navigation in healthcare facilities. (2022) https://journals.sagepub.com/doi/full/10.3233/THC-220146

37. Katsanis, S.H., Javitt, G., Hudson, K.: A case study of personalized medicine. Science 320, 53–54 (2008). https://doi.org/10.1126/science.1156604

38. Hersen, M.: Single-case experimental designs, in: Bellack, A.S., Hersen, M., Kazdin, A.E. (Eds.), International handbook of behavior modification and therapy: Second Edition. Springer US, Boston, MA, pp. 175–210 (1990). https://doi.org/10.1007/978-1-4613-0523-1_9

39. Hajrulla, D., Hajrulla, G., Hajrulla, S.: Healthcare policy in Albania compared to the healthcare system in the world and methods to achieve success. International Journal of Advanced Natural Sciences and Engineering Researches 8(2), 82–90 (2024)

40. Overmann, K.M., Wu, D.T., Xu, C.T., Bindhu, S.S., Barrick, L.: Real-time locating systems to improve healthcare delivery: A systematic review. J. Am. Med. Inform. Assoc. 28(6), 1308–1317 (2021)

41. Ezeuko, F., Ezennia, I.S., Jude, B., Calistus, O., Akametalu, C.: Using way finding as a tool to enhancing quality health care delivery. Int J Innov Environ Stud Res 11, 68–74 (2024)

42. Thorndyke, P.W., Goldin, S.E.: Spatial Learning and Reasoning Skill. In: Pick, H.L., Acredolo, L.P. (eds) Spatial Orientation. Springer, Boston, MA (1983). https://doi.org/10.1007/978-1-4615-9325-6_9

43. Calori, C., Vanden-Eynden, D.: Signage and wayfinding design: a complete guide to creating environmental graphic design systems. John Wiley & Sons (2015)

44. Aoki, R., Yamamoto, H. and Yamazaki, K.: February. Android-based navigation system for elderly people in hospital. In 16th International Conference on Advanced Communication Technology (pp. 371–377). IEEE Vorakulpipat C, Rattanalerdnusorn E, Sirapaisan S, Savangsuk V, Kasisopha N A Mobile-Based Patient-Centric Passive System for Guiding Patients Through the Hospital Workflow: Design and Development JMIR Mhealth Uhealth 2019;7(7), e14779 (2014) https://doi.org/10.2196/14779

45. Sherifi, I.: Internet usage on mobile devices and their impact on evolution of informative websites in Albania 3. European Journal of Business, Economics and Accountancy 3(6), 2015 (2015)

46. Spaho, A.B., Kraja, A.: Modeling and Forecasting the Diffusion of Mobile Telephony in Albania and Turkey. JETAS 4, 115–124 (2019). https://doi.org/10.30931/jetas.599517

47. Chiou, S.-Y., Liao, Z.-Y.: A real-time, automated and privacy-preserving mobile emergency-medical-service network for informing the closest rescuer to rapidly support mobile-emergency-call victims. IEEE Access **6**, 35787–35800 (2018). https://doi.org/10.1109/ACCESS.2018.2847030
48. Fitzpatrick, F., Doherty, A., Lacey, G.: Using artificial intelligence in infection prevention. Curr. Treat. Options Infect. Dis. **12**(2), 135–144 (2020)

Federated Learning for Pre-operative Detection of Triple-Negative Breast Cancer from Multiparametric MRI: Preliminary Results

Giorgio De Nunzio[1,2,3] [iD], Luana Conte[3,4] [iD], Vincenzo Taormina[5] [iD], Alessandro Crisci[6], Giovanni Vincenzo Donatiello[1] [iD], Rocco Rizzo[1,2,6(✉)] [iD], and Donato Cascio[4] [iD]

[1] Dept of Mathematics and Physics "E. De Giorgi", University of Salento, 73100 Lecce, Italy
{giorgio.denunzio,rocco.rizzo1}@unisalento.it,
giovannivincenzo.donatiello@studenti.unisalento.it
[2] National Institute for Nuclear Physics (INFN), 73100 Lecce, Italy
[3] Laboratory of Interdisciplinary Research Applied to Medicine (DReAM), University of Salento & ASL Lecce, 73100 Lecce, Italy
luana.conte@unipa.it
[4] Dept of Physics and Chemistry "E. Segrè", University of Palermo, 90128 Palermo, Italy
donato.cascio@unipa.it
[5] Dept of Mathematics and Informatics, University of Palermo, 90128 Palermo, Italy
vincenzo.taormina@unipa.it
[6] Dept of Engineering for Innovation, University of Salento, 73100 Lecce, Italy
alessandro.crisci@studenti.unisalento.it

Abstract. Triple-negative breast cancer (TNBC) is an aggressive subtype with poor prognosis and limited treatments, for which accurate pre-operative prediction is essential for guiding therapy. While multiparametric MRI is highly sensitive, its use in multi-center AI workflows is hampered by inter-scanner variability. This study explores Federated Learning with radiomic features from DCE-MRI, and assesses the role of image standardization in improving TNBC classification performance. Data were split across 5 virtual clients to simulate hospitals, each training locally within a federated MLP framework. Results show that image standardization markedly improves TNBC classification, highlighting the role of preprocessing in federated AI pipelines.

Keywords: Triple-Negative Breast Cancer · Radiomics · Federated Learning · Neural Networks · Machine Learning · MRI · Image standardization

1 Introduction

Triple-negative breast cancer (TNBC) is a subtype of BC characterized by the absence of estrogen receptor (ER), progesterone receptor (PR), and human epidermal growth factor receptor 2 (HER2) [1]. This limits treatment options and is associated with

G. Scanniello et al. (Eds.): PROFES 2025, LNCS 16362, pp. 299–305, 2026.
https://doi.org/10.1007/978-3-032-12092-2_25

high tumor aggressiveness [2]. Early diagnosis is critical, as timely treatment significantly impacts outcomes, and the ability to predict TNBC preoperatively could inform clinical decision-making by guiding neoadjuvant chemotherapy and surgical planning, thereby enhancing personalized treatment. However, TNBC classification relies on histopathological/immunohistochemical analysis in biopsy [3].

Magnetic Resonance Imaging (MRI), when combined with Artificial Intelligence (AI) and radiomics analysis, has shown excellent performance in characterizing breast lesions [4], particularly in TNBC [5, 6]. However, clinical translation remains challenged by image heterogeneity. MRI scans are acquired using different field strengths, coils, and acquisition protocols: as a result, the same anatomical region can yield non-overlapping signal intensities, undermining the consistency of radiomics features [7] and the development of robust AI models [8, 9]. Moreover, the development of large-scale, centralized imaging datasets is often hindered by strict data protection regulations: to address these limitations, Federated Learning (FL) has emerged as a promising approach that enables collaborative model training across institutions without exchanging raw data [10, 11]. Instead, model parameters are shared and aggregated centrally, allowing institutions to retain full control over their local datasets while contributing to the development of a global AI model. Being aware that the widespread adoption of this approach requires adequate computational and organizational infrastructures, we designed a FL framework to support the preoperative prediction of TNBC using radiomic features extracted from DCE-MRI. To account for the heterogeneity of MRI data, we evaluated the performance of the FL model with and without intensity standardization.

2 Materials and Methods

2.1 Dataset

This study was conducted using the MAMA-MIA dataset [12], designed to support the development and evaluation of AI-based models for BC imaging. This dataset comprises 1,506 DCE-MRI scans collected from publicly accessible datasets within *The Cancer Imaging Archive* (TCIA): ISPY1, ISPY2, NACT-Pilot, and DUKE. All cases are provided with 3D tumor segmentations. The dataset includes both pre-contrast and multiple post-contrast acquisitions.

We selected 1,271 patients from DUKE [13] and ISPY2 [14] cohorts, with DCE-MRI sequences and TNBC status labels. For each patient, we used the pre-contrast and the last post-contrast T1-weighted axial scans. This choice was made to capture both baseline characteristics and delayed enhancement patterns relevant to radiomics.

2.2 Methods

Pre-processing and feature extraction. For each patient, the provided masks were used to delineate the region of interest (ROI) on both the pre-contrast and last post-contrast T1-weighted DCE-MRI acquisitions. The images were resampled to isotropic voxel spacing $1.0 \times 1.0 \times 1.0$ mm^3. For standardization, intensity values were scaled to the [0, 255] range using percentile-based normalization (1st–99th percentile). Percentile parameters were first computed locally on each client on the training set, then averaged across clients, and the resulting global percentiles were used to normalize all images.. A total of 200 features per scan were extracted using the PyRadiomics library [15], including shape descriptors, 1st order statistics, and texture features. The features were normalized by Z-score normalization and Min–Max scaling. Normalization parameters were estimated from the training data and subsequently applied to the corresponding validation and test sets to ensure unbiased evaluation.

Experimental Design and Federated Learning Protocol. Data were split across 5 virtual clients by MRI vendor, so ensuring inter-client heterogeneity and partial intra-client homogeneity to simulate a realistic multicenter FL scenario. We adopted the Federated Averaging (FedAvg) protocol [16] where a central server aggregates local model weights into a global model without exchanging raw data. Each client used a 60:30:10 train–validation–test split, with preprocessing parameters estimated on training data. Two strategies were tested: a Local approach, with parameters computed and applied independently at each client, and a Global federated approach, where local parameters were averaged on a central server and redistributed to clients. The task was a binary classification of tumor subtype TNBC vs. non-TNBC, using immunohistochemical status as ground truth. Training used a 1-hidden-layer Multilayer perceptron (32 ReLU units, dropout 0.2, sigmoid output) optimized with Adam and binary cross-entropy. Training followed the FedAvg protocol [16] over 10 rounds. Each client was trained using an early stopping strategy. Local models were aggregated on the server and the global model evaluated on the clients. The experiment was repeated over 10 cycles with randomized intra-client splits to assess robustness. The pipeline was tested with/without intensity standardization, and both local and global standardization and feature normalization were evaluated.

3   Results

The experiments were conducted using Google COLAB. Results on the test sets, averaged over 10 repetitions, are shown in the following table as "mean (std)":

	Standardization	BAC	F1-score	Precision	Recall	**AUC**
On-site	None	.545 (.030)	.402 (.046)	.412 (.037)	.424 (.069)	**.550 (.047)**
	Lin	.558 (.046)	.445 (.058)	.409 (.054)	.513 (.085)	**.597 (.044)**
Fed Avg	None	.585 (.020)	.389 (.040)	.501 (.045)	.374 (.047)	**.612 (.015)**
	Lin	.582 (.042)	.435 (.051)	.453 (.050)	.443 (.051)	**.632 (.030)**

The table compares Local (on-site) and federated (FedAvg) approaches. FL generally outperforms Local models while preserving privacy, and applying linear standardization further improves results. The Global strategy consistently achieves the best performance, e.g., mean AUC rises from 0.612 (Local) to 0.632 (Global) in the federated setting. For feature normalization, unlike standardization, the Local approach generally performs slightly better. Among the two strategies tested (Z-score and Min-Max), Min-Max typically yields slightly superior results; therefore, the results reported in the table use Min-Max normalization with the Local approach.

Figure 1 illustrates a single training cycle, showing AUC progression over 10 federated rounds for 5 clients, with mean and std across clients highlighted. FL outperforms on-site training by enabling collaborative model updates without sharing raw data, and intensity standardization further boosts performance.

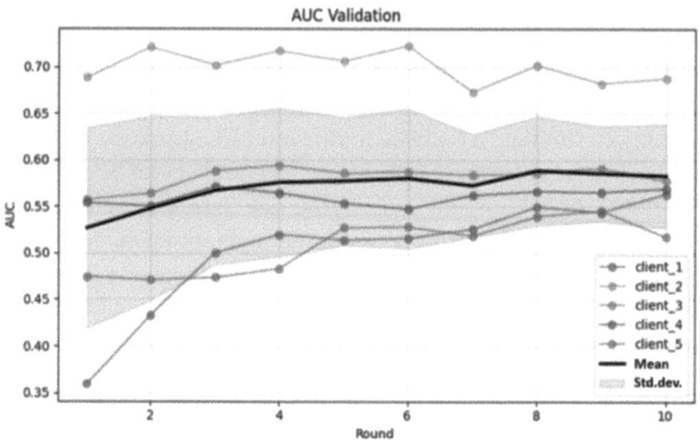

Fig. 1. AUC progression over 10 FL rounds in one training cycle, showing individual clients (colored lines) and the mean ± std (bold line with shaded area) on validation sets. Clients 1 and 5 had less populated datasets and clearly show to benefit from the FL process

4 Discussion

This study implemented a FL framework to predict TNBC from multiparametric DCE-MRI radiomic features in a simulated multicenter setting, showing that FL can build effective predictive models while preserving patient privacy.

Previous studies have explored the application of FL in BC contexts. Ogier du Terrail et al. [17] showed that FL improves prediction of histological response to neoadjuvant chemotherapy in TNBC using multi-institutional whole-slide images. Similarly, Selvakanmani et al. [18] proposed a federated transfer learning framework combining ResNet and domain adaptation, achieving 98.8% benign vs malignant tumor classification accuracy across multi-hospital mammography and MRI. Recently [19], multimodal MRI, combining DCE-MRI and DWI, achieved AUC of 0.89 for predicting pathological complete response to neoadjuvant chemotherapy. Kim and Park [20] developed a multimodal self-attention network integrating DCE-MRI and ADC features, further improving treatment response prediction. Xu et al. [21] showed that whole-volume radiomics combining DCE-MRI and ADC maps predicts TNBC with 88% accuracy, outperforming single-modality models.

Our experiments highlight that intensity standardization improves classification performance in FL, reinforcing evidence that scanner variability affects radiomic feature reproducibility [22]. This is also in agreement with phantom studies, which confirm many features are sensitive to acquisition settings, emphasizing the need for robust strategies to handle inter- and intra-institutional variability in multicenter radiomics. [23]. Unlike previous efforts, our study uniquely assessed intensity standardization in a federated setting, showing it reduces inter-client variability and improves model consistency, advancing clinically actionable federated workflows for preoperative DCE-MRI in oncology. Despite the encouraging results, limitations include testing only one intensity standardization method and not applying data augmentation; future work will explore multiple standardization techniques and augmentation strategies to better handle inter-scanner variability and increase feature heterogeneity. Future work will explore convolutional neural networks (CNNs) to eliminate manual feature extraction and possibly to reduce the importance of prior standardization.

5 Conclusions

This study shows that FL can enable privacy-preserving preoperative TNBC prediction from multiparametric DCE-MRI. While preliminary, results highlight the key role of intensity standardization in improving model performance and emphasize the need to address image heterogeneity in federated radiomics pipelines.

Acknowledgments. This study was partially funded by the Future Artificial Intelligence Research (FAIR) Foundation, project "A feDerAted learning approach To ImproVe Edgebased AI in iot-aware pervasive environments, ADAPTIVEAI" (CUP H97G22000210007). It was also partly funded by the National Institute for Nuclear Physics (INFN) within the AIM_MIA (Artificial Intelligence in Medicine: focus on Multi Input Analysis) project (INFN-CSN5).

Disclosure of Interests.. The authors declare no conflict of interest.

References

1. Emara, H.M., Allam, N.K., Youness, R.A.: A comprehensive review on targeted therapies for triple negative breast cancer: an evidence-based treatment guideline. Discov. Oncol. **16**, 547 (2025). https://doi.org/10.1007/s12672-025-02227-6

2. Li, Y., Zhang, H., Merkher, Y., Chen, L., Liu, N., Leonov, S., et al.: Recent advances in therapeutic strategies for triple-negative breast cancer. J. Hematol. Oncol. **15**, 121 (2022). https://doi.org/10.1186/s13045-022-01341-0

3. Conte, L., Rizzo, E., Civino, E., Tarantino, P., De Nunzio, G., De Matteis, E.: Enhancing breast cancer risk prediction with machine learning: Integrating BMI, smoking habits, hormonal dynamics, and BRCA gene mutations—A game-changer compared to traditional statistical models? Appl. Sci. **14**, 8474 (2024). https://doi.org/10.3390/app14188474

4. Zhao, J., Zhang, Q., Liu, M., Zhao, X.: MRI-based radiomics approach for the prediction of recurrence-free survival in triple-negative breast cancer after breast-conserving surgery or mastectomy. Medicine (Baltimore). **102**, e35646 (2023). https://doi.org/10.1097/MD.000000 0000035646

5. Sha, Y.S., Chen, J.F.: MRI-based radiomics for the diagnosis of triple-negative breast cancer: a meta-analysis. Clin. Radiol. **77**, 655–663 (2022). https://doi.org/10.1016/j.crad.2022.04.015

6. Cheng, C., Wang, Y., Zhao, J., Wu, D., Li, H., Zhao, H.: Deep learning and radiomics in triple-negative breast cancer: Predicting long-term prognosis and clinical outcomes. J. Multidiscip. Healthc. **18**, 319–327 (2025). https://doi.org/10.2147/JMDH.S509004

7. Schopp, J.G., Polat, D.S., Arjmandi, F., Hayes, J.C., Ahn, R.W., Sullivan, K., et al.: Imaging challenges in diagnosing triple-negative breast cancer. RadioGraphics. **43** (2023). https://doi.org/10.1148/rg.230027

8. Conte, L., Tafuri, B., Portaluri, M., Galiano, A., Maggiulli, E., De Nunzio, G.: Breast cancer mass detection in DCE–MRI using deep-learning features followed by discrimination of infiltrative vs. In Situ carcinoma through a machine-learning approach. Appl. Sci. **10**, 6109 (2020). https://doi.org/10.3390/app10176109

9. Conte, L., Rizzo, R., Sallustio, A., Maggiulli, E., Capodieci, M., Tramacere, F., et al.: Radiomics and machine learning approaches for the preoperative classification of In situ vs. Invasive breast cancer using dynamic contrast-enhanced magnetic resonance imaging (DCE–MRI). Appl. Sci. **15**, 7999 (2025). https://doi.org/10.3390/app15147999

10. Sandhu, S.S., Gorji, H.T., Tavakolian, P., Tavakolian, K., Akhbardeh, A.: Medical imaging applications of federated learning. Diagnostics. **13**, 3140 (2023). https://doi.org/10.3390/diagnostics13193140

11. Zhu, Y., Yin, X., Liew, A.W.-C., Tian, H.: Privacy-preserving in medical image analysis: A review of methods and applications. (2024)

12. Garrucho, L., Kushibar, K., Reidel, C.-A., Joshi, S., Osuala, R., Tsirikoglou, A., et al.: A large-scale multicenter breast cancer DCE-MRI benchmark dataset with expert segmentations. Sci. Data. **12**, 453 (2025). https://doi.org/10.1038/s41597-025-04707-4

13. Saha, A., Harowicz, M.R., Grimm, L.J., Kim, C.E., Ghate, S.V., Walsh, R., et al.: A machine learning approach to radiogenomics of breast cancer: a study of 922 subjects and 529 DCE-MRI features. Br. J. Cancer **119**, 508–516 (2018). https://doi.org/10.1038/s41416-018-0185-8

14. Li, W., Newitt, D.C., Gibbs, J., Wilmes, L.J., Jones, E.F., Arasu, V.A., et al.: I-SPY 2 breast dynamic contrast enhanced MRI trial (ISPY2) (Version 1). Cancer Imaging Arch. (2022). https://doi.org/10.7937/TCIA.D8Z0-9T85

15. van Griethuysen, J.J.M., Fedorov, A., Parmar, C., Hosny, A., Aucoin, N., Narayan, V., et al.: Computational radiomics system to decode the radiographic phenotype. Cancer Res. **77**, e104–e107 (2017). https://doi.org/10.1158/0008-5472.CAN-17-0339

16. Beutel, D.J., Topal, T., Mathur, A., Qiu, X., Fernandez-Marques, J., Gao, Y., et al.: Flower: A friendly federated learning research framework. (2022)

17. Ogier du Terrail, J., Leopold, A., Joly, C., Béguier, C., Andreux, M., Maussion, C., et al.: Federated learning for predicting histological response to neoadjuvant chemotherapy in triple-negative breast cancer. Nat. Med. **29**, 135–146 (2023). https://doi.org/10.1038/s41591-022-02155-w

18. S, S., Dharani Devi, G., V, R., Jeyalakshmi, J.: Privacy-preserving breast cancer classification: A federated transfer learning approach. J. Imaging Informatics Med. **37**, 1488–1504 (2024). https://doi.org/10.1007/s10278-024-01035-8

19. Mohamed, R.M., Panthi, B., Adrada, B.E., Boge, M., Candelaria, R.P., Chen, H., et al.: Multiparametric MRI–based radiomic models for early prediction of response to neoadjuvant systemic therapy in triple-negative breast cancer. Sci. Rep. **14**, 16073 (2024). https://doi.org/10.1038/s41598-024-66220-9

20. Kim, J., Park, H.: . (2024). https://doi.org/10.1109/ISBI56570.2024.10635671

21. Xu, T., Zhang, X., Tang, H., Hua, BD, T., Xiao, F., Cui, Z., et al.: The value of whole-volume radiomics machine learning model based on multiparametric MRI in predicting triple-negative breast cancer. J. Comput. Assist. Tomogr. **49**, 407–416 (2025). https://doi.org/10.1097/RCT.0000000000001691

22. Teng, X., Wang, Y., Nicol, A.J., Ching, J.C.F., Wong, E.K.Y., Lam, K.T.C., et al.: Enhancing the clinical utility of radiomics: Addressing the challenges of repeatability and reproducibility in CT and MRI. Diagnostics. **14**, 1835 (2024). https://doi.org/10.3390/diagnostics14161835
23. Lee, J., Steinmann, A., Ding, Y., Lee, H., Owens, C., Wang, J., et al.: Radiomics feature robustness as measured using an MRI phantom. Sci. Rep. **11**, 3973 (2021). https://doi.org/10.1038/s41598-021-83593-3

1st International Workshop on Quality Evaluation of ML-based Software Systems (QUEMALES 2025)

Alignment and Complementarity Between AI-FSM and ASPICE MLE: Findings from the Assessment of the SAFEXPLAIN Railway Demo

Carlo Donzella[1]([✉]), Giuseppe Nicosia[1], Fabio Bella[2,3], Irune Agirre[3], Javier Fernandez[4], Lorea Belategi[4], and Joanes Plazaola[4]

[1] Exida Development S.R.L, Via Ribes 5, 10010 Colleretto Giacosa (TO), Italy
carlo.donzella@exida-dev.com
[2] Regional Representative for iNTACS, Herderstr. 7, 5114 Köln, Germany
[3] UL Solutions, Leibnizstrasse 11, 70806 Kornwestheim, Germany
[4] Ikerlan Technological Research Center, Basque Research and Technology Alliance, 20500 Arrasate, Spain

Abstract. This paper has the goal of investigating the degree of alignment and complementarity between AI-FSM (an AI-oriented Functional Safety process model) and the MLE processes integrated in ASPICE PAM 4.0. The paper examines the degree of alignment of two standards/models as deployed in the demo of a safety-critical ML system in the railway domain.

The mapping of their lifecycle shows a strong compatibility, with some warning and limitations. The high-level process correspondences are useful, but this is not sufficient to ensure comprehensive alignment, and for this reason, a deeper mapping effort is required, covering practices, sub-practices, and work products content.

The SAFEXPLAIN railway demo provides a real case study of the application of ASPICE MLE in a safety-related context. The project outcomes validate the applicability of the AI-FSM in an ASPICE context. A significant number of improvement opportunities for both models are identified and described and will be directly followed up by the authors, who are directly involved in the relevant working groups.

Keywords: AI-FSM · ASPICE · Machine Learning · MLE · SAFEXPLAIN · processes · PAM · Functional Safety

1 Short Intro to the Model of ASPICE for Machine Learning

ASPICE (Automotive –Software Process Improvement and Capability Determination) is a process assessment model (PAM, which includes also a process reference model, PRM) that provides an objective and repetitive method to assess the capability of project

Note: The SAFEXPLAIN project has received funding from the European Union's Horizon Europe programme under grant agreement number 101069595.

G. Scanniello et al. (Eds.): PROFES 2025, LNCS 16362, pp. 309–322, 2026.
https://doi.org/10.1007/978-3-032-12092-2_26

processes in areas such as software, hardware, systems, management, and more, to improve the development phase to:

- Increase the quality (e.g., process, work products, organization quality, …)
- Reduce costs (e.g., timely identification and correction of defects, avoid duplication, rework, …)
- Manage process-related risks (e.g., timely risks identification and risks management, …)
- Satisfy customer expectations.

To address the needs arising from modern Automotive development approaches involving multiple disciplines, including artificial intelligence, the latest version of ASPICE (PAM 4.0) has been extended to accommodate ML-based systems, which are inherently data-driven and probabilistic in nature.

The ASPICE set of processes, as defined in [2], is shown in Fig. 1.

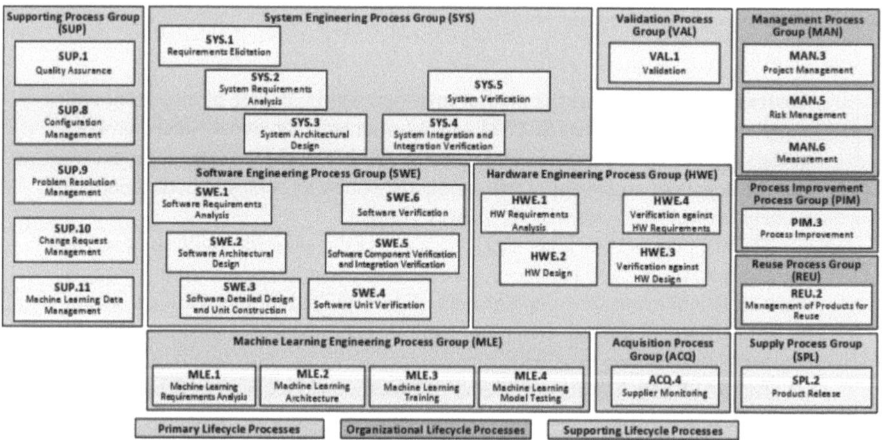

Fig. 1. Automotive SPICE process reference model.

As part of this extension, the Machine Learning Engineering (MLE) process group has been introduced to describe ML practices within the automotive domain. This process group includes processes such as:

- MLE.1 Machine Learning Requirements Analysis, whose purpose is to refine the machine learning-related software requirements into a set of Machine Learning (ML) requirements.
- MLE.2 Machine Learning Architecture, whose purpose is to establish an ML architecture supporting training and deployment, consistent with the ML requirements, and to evaluate the ML architecture against defined criteria.
- MLE.3 Machine Learning Training, whose purpose is to optimize the ML model to meet the defined ML requirements.
- MLE.4 Machine Learning Model Testing, whose purpose is to ensure compliance of the trained ML model and the deployed ML model with the ML requirements.

In addition, a new supporting process was created:

- SUP.11 Machine Learning Data Management, whose purpose is to define and align ML data with ML data requirements, maintain the integrity and quality of the ML data, and make them available to affected parties.

These processes support the development of machine learning applications within larger systems, according to the ASPICE model, ensuring reliable and consistent outcomes.

2 Short Intro to the Model of AI-FSM, AI Safety Process Model Developed Within the SAFEXPLAIN Project

AI-FSM is an extension to the traditional FSM (Functional Safety Management) to specifically address the nuances and novelties of the AI lifecycle. It is grounded in state of the art practices from functional safety according to standards such as IEC 61508 and ISO 26262 [5] as well as in emerging initiatives in the topic of AI safety, such as the EASA Concept Paper [12], AMLAS [14], and ISO/IEC TR 5469 [15]. The ML Development Lifecycle presented in DEVCOMM AvMC's paper is rather similar [13]. ASPICE for ML [included in 2] is the first *process quality* assessment model for ML. AI-FSM is publicly available at [10].

The V-based lifecycle, traditionally followed by FSM, has been expanded considering the peculiarities of the AI lifecycle. According to the realization phase it includes three new phases which were not considered for traditional systems: Data Management, Learning Management, and Inference Management.

Starting from the traditional FSM, due to the AI components integrated into safety-critical systems, the AI-FSM complementary procedure used in the SAFEXPLAIN project was defined to include additional steps, actions and considerations related to AI-based systems to addresses issues such as representativeness of the dataset, scenario completeness, and traceability between AI artifacts and safety requirements.

The process affected by including an AI-based system is highlighted in red in the picture below [4].

The process that is undoubtedly most affected is that relating to the realization of safety systems/software (see box 10 in Fig. 2), which, in Ikerlan's proposal, shown in the Fig. 3, consists of 8 phases, from Ph0 Overall Lifecycle to Ph7 Validation Testing.

The lifecycle shown above has been further expanded with the AI-FSM, see Fig. 4, to include the following MLE-related processes, not considered in the traditional FSM, such as:

- Ph1 DL-Related Concept Specification (add-on of already existing Ph1 E/E/PE/ System Concept Specification)
- Ph2 DL Requirements Specification (add-on of already existing Ph2.2 Software Safety Requirement Specification)
- PhDM Data Management
- PhLM Learning Management
- PhIM Interference Management

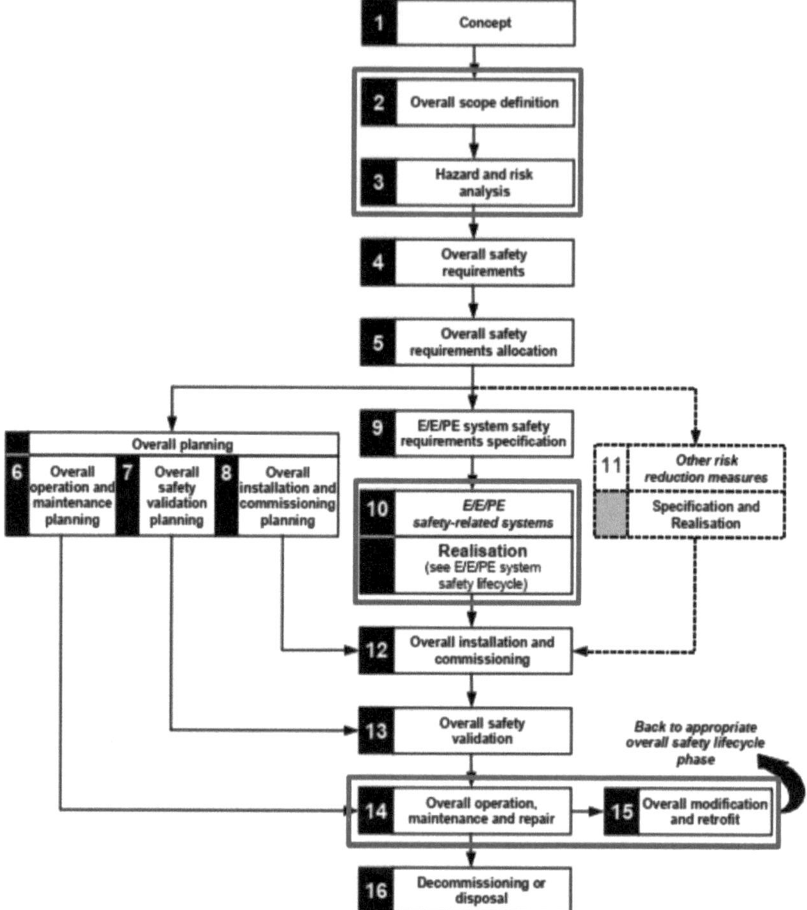

Fig. 2. Overall Safety Lifecycle [4].

Note: As the SAFEXPLAIN project was focused on Deep Learning, the original acronym used for AI-FSM was 'DL' instead of 'ML'. However, the model has been conceived of as applicable for the wider scope of Machine Learning, too.

The updated lifecycle includes both system and software phases, as well as purely ML-related processes. A brief introduction to them follows:

- Ph0 AI Overall Lifecycle, collects all AI-related project information (documents, organization charts and tools).
- Ph1 DL-Related Concept Specification, related to the definition of the DL operational design domain and applicable operational scenarios.
- Ph2 DL Requirements Specification, related to refining SW requirements into functional and non-functional ML requirements. *Note: this Ph has proved to be the most critical for an appropriate mapping with highly 'process-oriented' ASPICE MLE. See Sect. 5.*

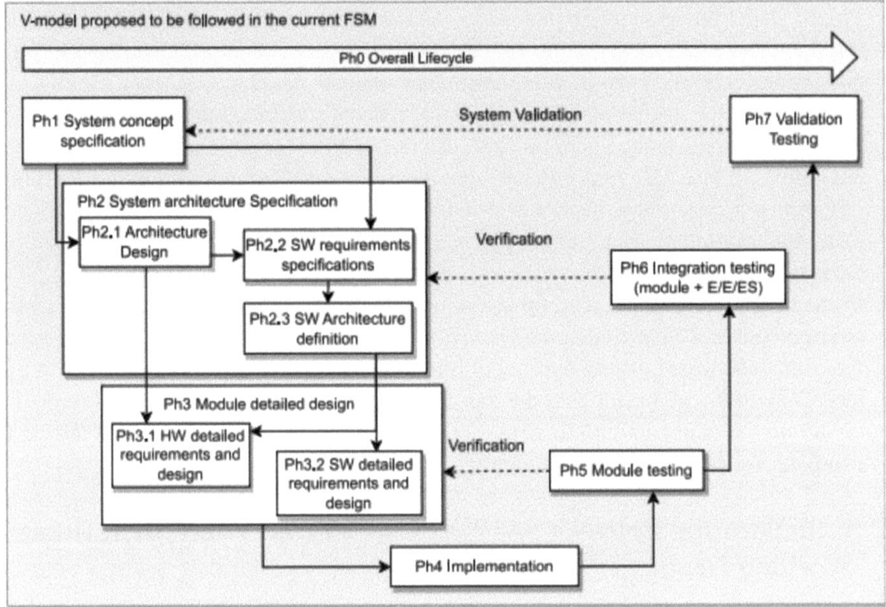

Fig. 3. E/E/PE system/software safety lifecycle [1].

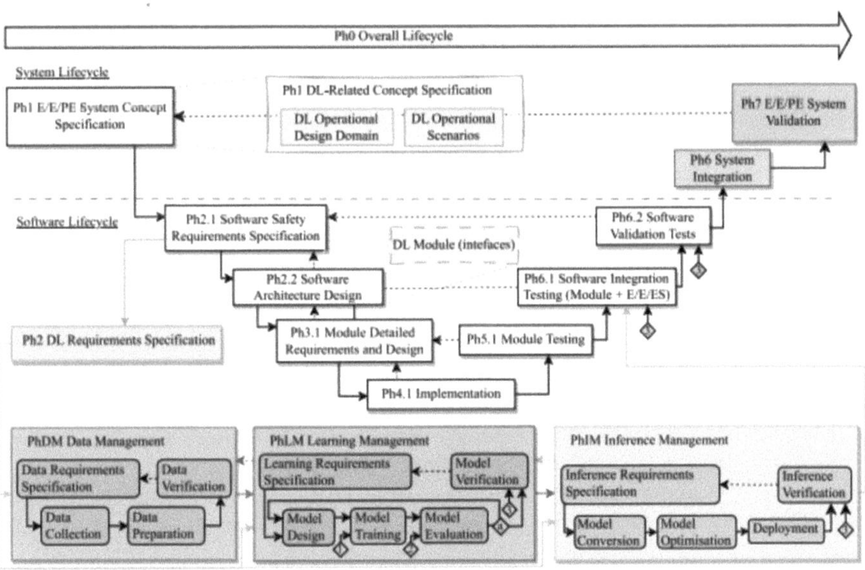

Fig. 4. IEC 61508 traditional functional safety lifecycle (Software V-model) + AI lifecycle [1].

- PhDM Data Management, in this phase, datasets are collected and prepared by defining the data requirements, collecting data to generate the dataset, cleaning and processing the data, and verifying its compliance with the data requirements. Finally, the coherence of the dataset with the data requirements specification is checked.
- PhLM Learning Management, the process responsible for generating the DL model according to the DL requirement specification, involving defining the learning requirements, designing the model to satisfy the application needs, training the model using the training dataset, and testing and verifying the model using the verification dataset to identify potential issues and ensure coherence with the requirements.
- PhIM Inference Management, this phase adapts the DL model to the target hardware environment and ensures that the DL requirements are met by defining the inference requirements, transforming the model into the correct format for deployment in the target environment, optimizing the model to improve its performance, deploying the model on the platform, and finally evaluating the model's capabilities and testing it using the verification dataset to identify potential issues.

3 Collaboration Between SAFEXPLAIN Project and MLE Intacs Working Group

3.1 Collaboration and Research Goals

During the early stage of the SAFEXPLAIN project (see: https://safexplain.eu/), a formal collaboration channel was established between the SAFEXPLAIN consortium and the ASPICE for Machine Learning (ASPICE-ML) working group. It took the form of an NDA allowing exchange of early unpublished documents, and it was signed by BSC as SAFEXPLAIN coordinating partner and Intacs as convener of the ASPICE MLE WG.

The ASPICE-ML working group has shown interest in the results of the SAFEXPLAIN project, as it provides a good opportunity to observe the direct application of ASPICE for Machine Learning practices in a safety-related context.

The WG has expressed interest in using this case study to improve the training material by providing practical examples that are/will be openly available, something that is proving unlikely for highly competitive automotive projects for autonomous driving.

Conversely, the AI-FSM will potentially get traction in more industrial-oriented communities, beyond the R&D audience.

The research goal of this paper is strictly associated to the collaboration goal: AI-FSM is essentially a new Process Development Model in the tradition of Functional Safety standards, while ASPICE MLE is (part of) a well-know and well-established tradition of (quality-oriented) Process Assessment Model standards. An ASPICE MLE Assessment of a project developed according to AI-FSM is an exceptional well-suited case-study for the validation of both models, spotting eventual weaknesses in practical use to eventually propose model improvements.

It is worth noting that the assessed project is a research demo (not an industrial development) and that it is in the *railway* domain, not in the *automotive* one. Far from being limitations (as initially feared), those two aspects proved to be advantages.

Being an activity framed within a (European) research project, all involved parties were amenable to consider (most of) the results to be publicly available; hardly this could be the case for industrial projects.

The railway domain, too, proved to be an initially unexpected advantage. Firstly, it proved to be more manageable for a restricted but significant demo: involved safety scenarios for an Obstacle Detection System are less complex in the railway rather than in the automotive domain. Secondly, assessment has shown that there are no limitations for the ASPICE MLE to be applied to other domains (at least, to other 'adjacent' surface transportation domains).

4 How the SAFEXPLAIN Railway Demo Was Developed to Be Compliant with Both AI-FSM and ASPICE MLE

An MLE ASPICE assessment on the DEMO Railway of the SAFEXPLAN project (which was created following the AI-FSM model) have been agreed between project partners, with Ikerlan's responsible unit being assessed by two qualified assessors from Exida Development.

In this context, the assessment does not only address compliance with MLE ASPICE but also collects findings on the compatibility/alignment/integration between the two standards.

From this multi-standard viewpoint, several observations can be already described as follows.

From the comparison viewpoint, MLE.1 ML Requirement Analysis can be seen as follows:

- Identification and specification: According to ASPICE, ML requirements are of different types: functional ML requirements, non-functional ML requirements, and data requirements. In AI-FSM, this process is addressed during the initial data, learning, and inference management phases, when the requirements for each part are specified. Furthermore, AI-FSM introduces the Ph1 DL-Related Concept Specification process, where the Operational Design Domains (ODDs) and applicable operational scenarios in which the ML component will operate are defined starting from the system requirements. It can be provisionally concluded that the ASPICE MLE aspect related to the identification and specification of requirements is covered by the activities envisaged by AI-FSM.
- Structure and prioritization: AI-FSM does not mandate a specific format for structuring or categorizing ML requirements; however, it encourages organizing them according to life cycle phases. For instance, within the Data Management phase, requirements may be structured around data attributes, datasets, and data preparation. The AI-FSM proposes these categories, although safety designer can adapt them according to peculiarities of their specific project. Additionally, AI-FSM suggests prioritizing requirements based on model selection criteria, which become relevant when the safety or AI engineer must choose among multiple models that meet performance requirements such as accuracy, precision, or mean inference time. *Note: see methodological conclusions in Sect. 5, raising concerns on this approach and suggestion amendments.*

- Correctness and verifiability analysis: This phase involves assessing whether the ML requirements are correct, complete, and verifiable. AI-FSM supports this by encouraging the formulation of measurable and testable criteria, especially in the Learning and Inference Management phases. Although AI-FSM does not prescribe a fixed methodology, it aligns with traditional safety practices by requiring that each requirement be subject to verification and validation strategies.
- Impact analysis on the ML operating environment: According to AI-FSM, the ML system's interaction with its operational environment must be analysed to ensure robustness and functional safety. This includes evaluating how changes in the environment—such as sensor input variability or dataset shifts—can impact the behaviour and safety performance of the ML model. This is particularly emphasized in the Inference Management phase.

From the comparison viewpoint, MLE.2 ML Architecture can be seen as follows:

- Definition of the ML architecture, hyperparameter ranges and initial values. ASPICE requires the documentation and specification of ML architectural elements, along with all relevant information needed to support generation, training, testing, and deployment of the ML model. In alignment with this, AI-FSM states that the safety designer must integrate the learning requirements—defined during the Learning Management phase—with their technical expertise during the Model Design step. *Note: see methodological conclusions in Sect. 5, raising concerns on this approach and suggestion amendments.*
- Define interfaces of the ML architectural elements. AI-FSM proposes defining the interfaces of the ML constituent during the "Ph2.2: Software Architecture Design" phase of the traditional FSM. In this phase, the ML component is treated as a black box, with defined inputs and outputs. Subsequently, the pre-processing and post-processing interfaces are specified during the "Ph2: DL Requirements" phase of AI-FSM.
- Define resources of the ML architectural elements. AI-FSM proposes that resource constraints be defined and documented in the Learning and Inference Requirements Specification documents. Additionally, it recommends measuring the mean inference execution time on both the training and inference platforms to establish a performance relationship. This relationship serves as a guiding metric for model redesign, particularly in cases where the model fails to meet the inference execution time requirements on the target hardware platform.

From the comparison viewpoint, MLE.3 ML Training can be seen as follows:

- Specification of ML training and validation criteria approach. ASPICE requires the definition of the training and validation environments, including their entry and exit criteria, as well as approaches for hyperparameter tuning and optimization. According to AI-FSM, this information is documented in two project-specific documents: the Model Election Log and the Learning Requirements Specification. While AI-FSM provides recommendations for these documents, it encourages—rather than mandates—the AI designer to complete them based on their expertise. An additional aspect to be addressed in this subprocess is the definition of an approach for dataset creation and modification, which AI-FSM covers under the Data Requirements Specification, established during the Data Management phase.

- Creation of ML training and validation datasets. ASPICE treats SUP.11 (Machine Learning Data Management) as a supporting, horizontal process, applicable across ML use cases, not necessarily linked to specific projects. AI-FSM defines a project-specific Data Management phase that governs the collection and preparation of datasets based on the Data Requirements Specification and the DL-Related Concept Specification.

- Creation and optimization of ML model. According to AI-FSM, the AI designer must document the model design and training process in accordance with the Learning Requirements Specification. Every new iteration or experimental adjustment is to be documented, ensuring full traceability of the model optimization process. *Note: evaluation of 'consistency and traceability' according to MLE.3 and MLE-3 proved to be a sore point; the ASPICE MLE model requires traceability to 'ML datasets', without giving any hint on how this could be interpreted in terms of specific elements to be traced, acceptable granularity, etc.... this is another area that could be further addressed to improve objectivity and repeatability of assessment results.*

- Verification of ML Training Results. In AI-FSM, this aspect is addressed primarily through the Learning Management and Inference Management phases. AI-FSM recommends defining quantitative performance metrics (e.g., *accuracy, precision, recall, mean inference time*) in the Learning Requirements Specification, and verifying these metrics against the results of the training process.

- To support functional safety, AI-FSM emphasizes that model selection decisions must be traceable and justified based on verification results. When performance thresholds are not met on the target inference platform, AI-FSM encourages the use of reference measurements from the training platform as fallback indicators, guiding model redesign efforts in subsequent development iterations.

From the comparison viewpoint, MLE.4 Model Testing can be seen as follows:

- Specification of a ML test approach. ASPICE requires to provide evidence to demonstrate the compliance of the trained and deployed ML model with the defined ML requirements. To support this, AI-FSM utilizes the verification dataset generated during the Data Management phase. This dataset is constructed in alignment with the ODD and the operational scenarios defined in the "Ph1: DL-Related Concept Specification" phase, ensuring that verification activities accurately reflect the intended deployment context of the model. It is important to highlight that during the Data Requirements Specification step, a set of test cases is defined to ensure that the dataset meets its specified requirements. These test cases include not only the expected results, but also verifications related to dataset attributes, such as class distribution within images, dataset balance, and other quality-related properties that influence model performance and safety assurance.

- Creation of a ML test dataset. This step is one of the defined processes and produces a key artifact within the Data Management phase. As in ASPICE, AI-FSM clearly distinguishes between the training dataset and the ML test dataset—the latter referred to as the verification dataset in AI-FSM.

- The trained ML model is tested. ASPICE specifies that the trained ML model must be tested according to a defined ML test approach, using the appropriate ML test dataset, and that both test results and their assessment must be documented. This is fully aligned with AI-FSM, which requires the trained ML model to be tested based on the procedures outlined in the Learning Verification Test Definition document, using the verification dataset. The test outcomes are recorded in the Learning Verification Test Results document, which must include not only the raw results but also an assessment of whether the model meets the defined learning requirements.
- The deployed ML model is derived from the trained ML model and tested. AI-FSM and ASPICE barely differ in that subprocess. AI-FSM considers that in the process there will be a set of requirements specifications (not only performance but also process-associated) associated with the deployment of the model in the target hardware platform. All actions performed to convert and optimize the model must be documented, and as in ASPICE, the model must be reassessed to verify that adaptation to the target hardware does not entail misalignment with the inference requirements specifications.
- ASPICE and AI-FSM show minimal differences in this subprocess. AI-FSM acknowledges that the deployment process must be governed by a set of requirement specifications, which include not only performance-related criteria but also process-associated requirements relevant to the deployment on the target hardware platform. All actions related to the conversion, optimization, and adaptation of the model for deployment must be thoroughly documented. As with ASPICE, AI-FSM requires that the deployed model be reassessed to ensure that its adaptation to the target hardware does not lead to any deviation from the defined inference requirements. This ensures consistency between the trained model's behaviour and its deployed counterpart within the operational context.

From the comparison viewpoint, SUP.11 Machine Learning Data Management can be seen as follows:

- Establish a ML data management system. It includes not only the management activities, but also the ML data lifecycle, supporting interfaces to affected parties and relevant sources of ML data. The way the AI-FSM proposes to that is gathered in Data Management Guideline document, which guides through all the activities, the artifacts to be generated and refer to the affected parties that must be communicated once each activity is carried out.
- Determine a ML data quality approach. AI-FSM does not force the definition of a particular ML data quality approach but encourages the user to define a set of data requirements specifications with this aim. Particularly, this can be mapped with the data attributes and dataset requirements specification categories within the data requirements.
- Collect ML data. In contrast with ASPICE approach and related to item's specific safety aspects, AI-FSM considers that the collection of ML data is project-specific and must be performed according to the data requirements specifications defined, fulfilling the ODD and operational scenarios previously defined in the DL-Related Concept Specification phase.

- Process ML data. This subprocess is fully aligned with AI-FSM. All data preparation activities must be thoroughly documented and executed in accordance with the Data Requirements Specification, specifically under the Data preparation requirements subcategory defined in the Data Management phase of the AI-FSM.
- Assure quality of ML data. ASPICE defines that all data-related activities must be performed in accordance with the ML data quality approach, in order to meet the defined ML data quality criteria. This is fully aligned with AI-FSM, which specifies a set of data requirements to be followed throughout the data lifecycle. The fulfilment of these requirements must be verified at the conclusion of the Data Management phase in the verification step. *Note: assessment made clear that just one practice to describe and rate this very wide activity (actually a structured set of tasks, as "SUP.1 Quality assurance" shows) is a severe under-definition that leaves too much space for interpretation, potentially undermining objectivity and repeatability of evaluation.*

The figure below shows the mapping between the ASPICE and AI-FSM processes and provides a graphical representation of the relationship between the two standards(Fig. 5).

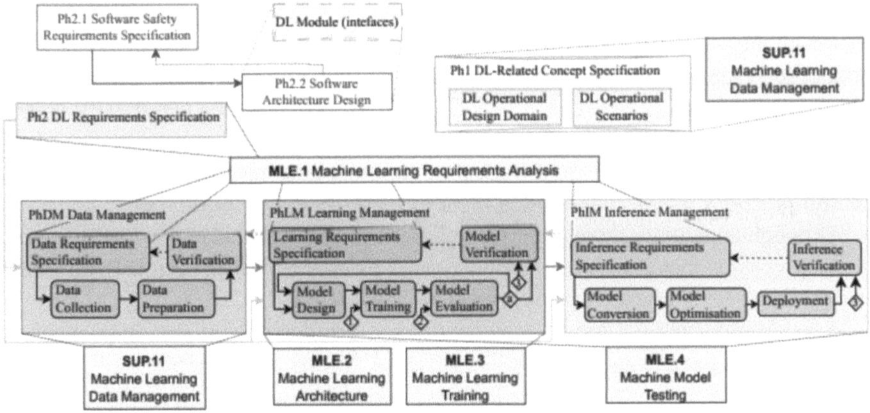

Fig. 5. AI-FSM Lifecycle + ASPICE ML Processes.

5 Major Findings of ASPICE MLE Pre-Assessment (July'25) and Assessment (Sept.'25) of the Railway Demo

The Pre-Assessment of the SAFEXPLAIN Railway Demo against the ASPICE MLE framework, which involved IKERLAN's Cybersecurity and Dependability Dept. Organisational unit based in Arrasate-Mondragón and ASPICE assessors from Exida Development's team, was performed in July 2025. This assessment aimed to provide a preliminary evaluation of compliance and process capability to guide the needed improvement and reach a complete compliance and process capability before the Final assessment scheduled for September 2025 and gather information about the comparability of (MLE) ASPICE 4.0 and AI-FSM.

For the reasons already mentioned in Sect. 3.the assessed project is the demo of a railway project, not an automotive one.

The scope of the assessment was limited to the following processes:

- SWE.1 - Software Requirements Analysis
- MLE.1 - Machine Learning Requirements Analysis
- MLE.2 - Machine Learning Architecture
- MLE.3 - Machine Learning Training
- MLE.4 - Machine Learning Model Testing
- SUP.11 - Machine Learning Data Management

Even at 'pre-'assessment stage, all processes have achieved PA1.1 rated as "L", so the CL1 target has been achieved, a very significant and not at all obvious result.

Some weaknesses have been found, some of that related to ongoing efforts still to be completed, other related to the complex 'cross' compliance between ASPICE MLE and AI-FSM.

Concerning the first kind of weaknesses, already well known by the team under assessment, the indication is to complete the planned work before the official assessment.

Concerning the second kind of weaknesses, some were anticipated, others were discovered only thanks to the pre-assessment itself, and guidance to remediation will be given with the full assessment report. For instance, what is exactly expected to be traced for data sets (see MLE.3.BP4 and MLE.3.BP6) is open to interpretation.

About the mapping between ASPICE MLE and AI-FSM, the complexity is much higher than previously thought. To 'survive' an ASPICE MLE assessment equipped with AI-FSM-structured processes and work-products, mapping has to go deeper to practices and sub-practices, notes, diagrams, content of work-products, terminology, etc....

Although apparently there are no practices/information items in the ASPICE MLE-related processes that are completely uncovered by AI-FSM, the previously informally available high-level mapping proved valid but insufficient.

A figure reporting the pre-assessment process profile follows. Pre-assessment was performed with the assistance of the TRACE tool, V5, by Sharpen360.:

ID	Name	BP1	BP2	BP3	BP4	BP5	BP6	BP7	GP1.1.1	PA1.1	CL
Automotive SPICE 4.0											
SWE.1	Software Requirements Analysis	L	L	P	P	L	L		L	L	1
MLE.1	Machine Learning Requirements Analysis	L	L	L	L	P	L		L	L	1
MLE.2	Machine Learning Architecture	P	F	L	L	F	P	L	L	L	1
MLE.3	Machine Learning Training	L	F	F	P	L			L	L	1
MLE.4	Machine Learning Model Testing	L	L	F	F	F	L	L	L	L	1
SUP.11	Machine Learning Data Management	L	L	F	F	L	L		L	L	1

Fig. 6. Pre-assessment processes rating summary table.

The official assessment was performed in Sept'25 as scheduled. Assessment was enriched by the presence of two members of the iINTACS ASPICE MLE Working Group participating as guest assessors and having access to all relevant data. Assessment results were much as expected, with some significant improvement in ratings (see Fig. 6 below) but especially with some further enlightening methodological insights over the some most challenging structural differences between AI-FSM and ASPICE MLE. More specifically, two significant' process-related structural weaknesses' have been noticed for AI-FSM:

1. ***Ph2*** is called *"Requirements Specification"* but, in fact, it abuses/misuses (i.e.: it stretches excessively) the meaning of 'requirement'; whatever is expected to be specified is called 'requirement'. This makes almost impossible to apply and verify systematically the strict rules of 'good requirements' to all type of (improperly defined) requirements. It might be better call just *"LM Specifications"* and have chapters on properly said *requirements*, but also on *design aspects, inspection criteria, verification measures*, etc....

2. *ML Architectural Design*, is an official process in ASPICE MLE, but in fact does not exist as such in AI-FSM... all aspects of design are absorbed into 'requirements', making to be compliant to all practices of MLE.2 almost impossible; content can be mostly there but specific practices such as *design analyses, traceability...* are very hard to be properly identified and rated. With a dedicated 'design' chapter within "ML Specifications", this model shortcoming could be amended with limited impact on the overall model.

A figure reporting the assessment process profile follows. Assessment was performed with the assistance of the TRACE tool, V6, by Sharpen360 Fig. 7:

ID	Name	BP1	BP2	BP3	BP4	BP5	BP6	BP7	PA1.1	CL
Automotive SPICE 4.0										
SWE.1	Software Requirements Analysis	F	F	F	L	L	L	L	F	1
MLE.1	Machine Learning Requirements Analysis	F	F	L	P	L	L		L	1
MLE.2	Machine Learning Architecture	L	F	L	L	F	P	L	L	1
MLE.3	Machine Learning Training	F	F	F	L	L			F	1
MLE.4	Machine Learning Model Testing	F	F	F	F	F	L	L	F	1
SUP.11	Machine Learning Data Management	F	F	F	F	L	L		F	1

Fig. 7. Assessment processes rating summary table.

6 Conclusions on Complexity and Advantages of Joint Compliance to AI-FSM and ASPICE MLE

It can be concluded that AI-FSM and ASPICE v4.0 are compatible to a large degree in terms of lifecycle, process goals, documentation, and traceability, and can be aligned to support the development of AI-based *safety-critical* systems.

However, the complexity of the mapping between ASPICE MLE and AI-FSM is significantly higher than initially expected. While the available simple, high-level mapping is valid as a first step, it is insufficient as a full guideline for both assessors and practitioners. In practice, a deeper mapping shall be developed, also counting on the results of the reported assessment. Despite this complexity, it is worth noting that no ASPICE

MLE process elements appears to be completely uncovered by AI-FSM. A recommendation for a relatively simple amendment of the AI-FSM model has been formulated. Indications for potential Change Requests to ASPICE MLE have been noted, and will be further discussed in appropriate fora, namely a planned dedicated Gate4SPICE and the iINTACS ASPICE MLE Working Group. The presence of authors of this paper in all the relevant groups is a guarantee that there will be an adequate follow up.

References

1. Fernández, J., Belategi, L., Agirre, I.: 2EU.0691_Ph0D0001_AI_FSM_Procedure. IKER-LAN (2025)
2. Automotive-SPICE-PAM-v40. VDA Working Group 13 (2023)
3. AI-FSM: Towards Functional Safety Management for Artificial Intelligence-based Critical Systems, 2024. https://safexplain.eu/wp-content/uploads/2024/04/Javier_CARS_2024_04_08.pdf
4. IEC 61508-1 Functional safety of electrical/electronic/programmable electronic safety-related systems – Part 1: General requirements, IEC (2010)
5. ISO 26262(-1/11): Road vehicles — Functional safety. International Organization for Standardization (ISO) (2018)
6. ISO/IEC WD 5338: Information technology — Artificial intelligence — AI system life cycle processes. International Electrotechnical Commission (IEC), 2023. https://www.iso.org/standard/81118.html
7. IEC TS 6254: Information technology — Artificial intelligence — Objectives and approaches for explainability of ML models and AI systems. International ElectrotechnicalCommission (IEC), [Under Development]
8. ISO/CD PAS 8800:2024 Road Vehicles — Safety and artificial intelligence. ISO/TC 22/SC 32 Electrical and electronic components and general system aspects (2024)
9. Perez-Cerrolaza, J. et al.: Artificial intelligence for safety-critical systems in industrial and transportation domains: a survey. acm computing surveys, association for computing machinery (2023). https://doi.org/10.1145/3626314
10. Fernández, J. et al.: AI-FSM. Zenodo (2024), version 2.0. https://doi.org/10.5281/zenodo.10964402
11. Jiao, L. et al.: A survey of deep learning-based object detection. IEEE Access, **7**, 128837–128868 (2019). https://doi.org/10.1109/ACCESS.2019.2939201
12. European Union Aviation Safety Agency (EASA): EASA Concept Paper—Guidance for Level 1 & 2 Machine Learning Applications. European Union Aviation Safety Agency (2023)
13. Carter, H., Chan, A., Vinegar, C., & Rupert, J.: Proposing the use of hazard analysis for machine learning data Sets. J. Syst. Safety **58**(2), 30–39 (2023). https://doi.org/10.56094/jss.v58i2.253
14. Hawkins, R. et al.: Guidance on the Assurance of Machine Learning in Autonomous Systems (AMLAS). [arXiv preprint] (2021). https://arxiv.org/abs/2102.01564
15. ISO/IEC CD TR 5469: Artificial Intelligence — Functional Safety and AI Systems. International Organization for Standardization (ISO) and International Electrotechnical Commission (IEC)
16. Bosch, J.: Automotive SPICE in practice: experiences from industry. Softw. Qual. J. (2020). https://doi.org/10.1007/s11219-020-09505-0

A Survey of Existing Standards Addressing AI-Based Technologies

Francesco Merola[(✉)] and Giuseppe Lami

Istituto Di Scienza E Tecnologie Dell'Informazione "A.Faedo", Consiglio Nazionale Delle Ricerche, Pisa, Italia

{francesco.merola,giuseppe.lami}@isti.cnr.it

Abstract. The rapid integration of Artificial Intelligence (AI) into software systems across many domains, including critical ones such as healthcare, transportation, and public administration, has intensified the need for robust, reliable, and transparent quality evaluation methods. While numerous standards and regulatory initiatives have emerged and many more are being worked on, the current landscape remains fragmented with varying scopes, definitions, and enforcement mechanisms. This paper provides a structured, yet not exhaustive, overview of current international standards, regulatory instruments, and soft-law guidelines relevant to AI-based software quality evaluation. The purpose of this paper is to provide a starting point for practitioners and researchers for understanding the status, as well as the short-coming evolution, of the standards addressing AI-based technologies and for orienting their efforts to contribute to fill the existing lacks and weaknesses in the standard corpus.

Keyword: Standards · AI-based Technologies · Quality Evaluation

1 Introduction

Artificial Intelligence (AI)-based technologies are today pervasive in the every-day life. AI-based technologies are often crucial for the business of companies and organizations as several vital functions of organizations are reliant on them. From a technological perspective we witnessed a dramatic (and sometimes messy) growth in the performance of AI-based solutions, which has pushed their application also in several safety-critical contexts (as for instance in the transportation or healthcare domains). In such a situation the need of commonly accepted and sound reference points addressing both the development, and the verification and validation of AI-based technologies is more and more pressing.

Machine Learning (ML) is a specific subset of AI that focuses on developing algorithms enabling systems to learn from data and improve their performance over time. This ability to learn and the data-centric nature of these approaches are what fundamentally distinguishes them from traditional ones. ML is a broad field and encompasses various algorithms and techniques for enabling systems to learn from data and make predictions or decisions accordingly. Many recent approaches, however, make use of

G. Scanniello et al. (Eds.): PROFES 2025, LNCS 16362, pp. 323–333, 2026.
https://doi.org/10.1007/978-3-032-12092-2_27

Artificial Neural Networks (ANN), a specific type of model inspired by the structure and function of the human brain. ANNs used for complex tasks typically contain a very large number of parameters (or weights) that are tuned during the learning process. This complexity makes them opaque and difficult for humans to interpret, which in turn further complicates their validation and deployment in real-world scenarios.

International standards play a crucial role in getting new technologies and their application mature. Usually, when a new technology booms, accompanied by the related original technical development paradigms and the specific organizational and process changes, we witness an initial period of uncertainty due to the lack of adequate, sound, and generally accepted approaches to face the demands related to such a new technology. This uncertainty is mostly due to lack of standards. Standards are developed through consensus by experts' committees (usually having an international composition) and represent the reference guidance for the global community of interest. The standardization organizations (e.g., ISO, IEC, SAE, ...) are aware of the substantial inadequacy of existing standards for AI-based technologies, as these were conceived for different technologies requiring different development paradigms. They are therefore working hard to provide developers, users, and governance authorities with state-of-the-art and sound standards tailored to AI. However, as of today, such a standardization effort is not yet completed, as several key standards (both generic and domain-specific) are still in progress.

The availability of a complete picture of existing (and upcoming) standards is a key factor, as they represent the most sound and reliable reference for those who are involved in the quality evaluation of AI-technology. The purpose of this paper is therefore to provide an overview of the current state of the available AI-related standards and regulations. We address not only the public available standard, but, to some extent, those that are still in the preliminary stages of development. Moreover, for space and clarity concerns, we mainly focus on cross-domain standards, which will hopefully serve as a foundation for the development and application of domain-specific ones.

This paper is structured as follows: Sect. 2 provides a brief background on AI- and ML-based systems, discussing the characteristics that differentiate them from traditional ones and place them partially outside the scope of existing regulations. Sect. 3 presents an overview of currently available and emerging standards and regulations, discussing their role in the current landscape. Finally, Sect. 4 offers some concluding remarks.

2   Background

The principal characteristic of emerging AI-based systems is the ability to improve, using specific algorithms (often based on Artificial Neural Networks), their problem-solving capabilities through a "learning" process triggered by exemplary input [1, 2]. This feature makes the use of this kind of approach particularly suitable in scenarios in which there is no detailed, complete, or predictable information about the problem. Another relevant feature is their parallel structure, which benefits from the use of powerful hardware to obtain timely and thus usable computation results.

From an architectural perspective, these AI-based systems often present a completely different structure with respect to the "traditional" software-based systems (i.e., those systems composed of software components running on a specific hardware). In many cases, this architectural difference derives from the employment of ANNs, whose structure is defined by attributes such as the number of layers, the number of units (also called "nodes") per layer, and the number of connections per unit. These attributes, known as hyper-parameters, determine the adjustment of the network's weights during training and consequently the behavior of the resulting model or AI-based system.

For these reasons the consolidated development paradigms applied for the development of software-based systems different than ML-based ones are no longer applicable. The same is for the quality evaluation techniques and methods developed for decades for assessing the quality of software products and related development processes.

The picture depicted above, impacts on the need for standards regulating or guiding system and software engineering of ML-based technologies.

3 Overview of Existing Standards and Regulations

The quality evaluation of AI-based (and particularly ML-based) software systems is hindered by the lack of tailored and widely adopted standards. While several existing standards from traditional software engineering provide partial guidance and emerging AI-specific frameworks are being rapidly worked on, the current landscape of regulations often falls short in addressing the dynamic, data-centric, and opaque nature of ML systems. In this regard, to offer clarity on how AI systems that use ML operate and interact, the ISO/IEC 22989 [3] and ISO/IEC 23053 [4] standard offer the related conceptual framework and shared terminology. More precisely, the former provides standardized concepts and terminology to help AI technology to be better understood and used by a broader set of stakeholders, while the latter defines the components and functions of ML-based AI systems within the broader AI ecosystem and establishes a unified vocabulary.

In the following sub-sections, we present and shortly describe the most relevant standards and regulatory frameworks currently available, with a critical lens on their applicability to ML-based software systems. To provide a possibly ordered and clear representation of the relevant standards and regulations, we structure this section by grouping them according to the topic they address (organizational and risk management, quality evaluation of AI-based systems, life cycle processes). We reserve a specific group for international and public bodies regulations.

3.1 AI-Related Standards for Organizational and Risk Management

AI has a significant impact on the management of organizations, both those developing AI-based technologies and those integrating them into their operations at any level. This impact calls for regulation and the development of specific standards to ensure responsible implementation. The following section briefly discusses several key documents related to these standards.

The recently released standard ISO/IEC 42001 [5] addresses the AI Management System (AIMS). AIMS disciplines the way an organization oversees and implements functions around AI technologies in a responsible way. The ISO/IEC 42001 encompasses practices for the deployment, operation, and continual improvement of AI applications, ensuring ethical use, transparency, and accountability in AI-related processes and decisions. In particular, it specifies requirements for establishing, implementing, maintaining and continuously improving an AI Management System using a Plan-Do-Check-Act cycle. The standard covers aspects like risk, impact, transparency, supplier management, data governance, ethics, accountability, and continual improvement across all lifecycle stages.

Very recently, the ISO/IEC 42006 [6] was released to complement the necessary competences needed by certification bodies that audit and certify AIMSs. Recognizing that credible certification depends on the auditors themselves having specialized knowledge and clear assessment guidelines, ISO/IEC 42006 aims to ensure that the audit and certification of AI management systems is performed consistently and credibly. This gives customers and stakeholders confidence that certified organizations meet the expectations set out in ISO/IEC 42001.

ISO/IEC 23894 [7] is also particularly relevant as it offers tailored guidance for managing AI-specific risks. It serves as an extension of ISO 31000 [8], the widely recognized standard for risk management principles and guidelines and is intended to be used alongside it. The extension focuses specifically on risks associated with AI, aiming to help organizations integrate risk management processes into the design, development, deployment, and operation of AI systems. It also outlines procedures for the effective implementation and integration of AI risk management. More precisely, ISO/IEC 23894 is structured around three main clauses: Principles, which describe the foundational concepts of risk management in the context of AI; Framework, which supports organizations in systematically integrating risk management into key activities and functions; and Processes, which involve the structured application of policies, procedures, and practices to assess, treat, monitor, review, record, and report risk.

3.2 Standards Addressing Quality Evaluation of AI-Based Products

Quality evaluation is the process of systematically assessing a software product to determine how well it meets its specified requirements and the needs of its users. The evaluation of AI-based software systems still largely relies on established software engineering standards, many of which were developed before AI technologies became pervasive. While these provide a solid foundation, they often fall short in addressing the unique characteristics of AI systems, such as data-driven functionality, non-deterministic behavior, and evolving models. In response, several new standards and technical reports are emerging to address these peculiarities and help bridge the gap between traditional software evaluation practices and the quality assurance needs of AI-based solutions. This section discusses the current landscape with respect to these standards.

The ISO/IEC 25000 [9] series, also known as SQuaRE (Software product Quality Requirements and Evaluation), is the main set of standards providing a structured approach to defining and assessing the quality of software products and data. It is divided into several divisions (2500n, 2501n, 2502n, 2503n and 2504n) each containing documents pertaining to a specific area, such as quality measurement, requirements, or evaluation. This series offers a comprehensive conceptual framework for software and data quality which is mature and widely adopted, but its applicability to ML-based systems is still evolving. The ISO/IEC 25010 [10], for example, defines product quality in terms of characteristics like functional suitability, performance efficiency and reliability. However, it lacks guidance on evaluating non-deterministic behavior, model drift and learned functionality, which are typical traits of ML components.

The ISO/IEC 25012 [11] standard defines data quality through a set of measures categorized into two types: inherent and system-dependent. Examples of Inherent characteristics include accuracy, completeness, and consistency, while system-dependent characteristics cover aspects such as availability and portability. However, despite its comprehensive extensiveness, the standard does not address data representativeness or bias, both critical considerations in the context of machine learning.

Similarly, the ISO IEC 25023 [12] defines quantitative metrics and measurement methods for the quality metrics defined in the 2501n division but fails to capture critical features of ML pipelines such as model generalization, overfitting and interpretability.

The ISO/IEC 25059 [13] is a recently released extension which seeks to address many of these shortcomings by introducing ML and AI specific quality dimensions to the SQuaRE framework. Such dimensions include Transparency, Explainability, Robustness to uncertain and/or adversarial inputs, Fairness, and Bias mitigation. However, while promising, ISO/IEC 25059 remains very young and has not yet translated into widely recognized actionable evaluation methods or tooling. Its adoption and alignment with other emerging and existing frameworks in the long run is yet to be seen.

Data quality standards for AI are crucial because they ensure the data used to train and operate AI models is accurate, complete, consistent, and reliable. This directly impacts the performance, fairness, and trustworthiness of AI systems. The ISO/IEC 5259 [14] is another relevant standard that is closely related to the 25000 series. ISO/IEC 5259 describes a data quality model for data analytics and artificial intelligence based on ML. Similarly to the ISO/IEC 25012, ISO/IEC 5259 differentiates between two inherent and system-dependent characteristics, but also introduces additional attributes tailored to the specific needs of ML, especially in terms of data quality. Measures such as representativeness, diversity and timeliness all fill this role.

Finally, ISO/IEC TR 24028 [15] and ISO/IEC TR 24029 [16] are also worth mentioning. Although more limited in scope, these technical reports provide an overview of the approaches available for assessing and mitigating risks related to the trustworthiness and the robustness (or lack thereof) of AI systems, respectively. ISO/IEC TR 24028 addresses methods to evaluate and enhance qualities such as availability, resiliency, and reliability, often through transparency and explainability techniques. In contrast, ISO/IEC TR 24029 places particular emphasis on the development of robust neural networks, which, as previously mentioned, are extensively adopted in industry, government, and academia.

3.3 Standards Addressing AI System Life Cycle Processes

Ensuring the quality and reliability of complex software systems requires more than evaluating their final outputs, it also demands systematic oversight across the entire system lifecycle, from initial conception to decommissioning. AI-based software presents some criticalities in this department, due to having a life cycle that is fundamentally different and much more data-centric with respect to more traditional software solutions.

A key document for the AI system life cycle processes is ISO/IEC 5338 [17]. The AI system life cycle model provided by this document describes the evolution of an AI system from inception through retirement. It does not prescribe a specific life cycle. Instead, it concentrates on AI-specific processes that can occur during the system life cycle. AI-specific processes can occur during one or more of the life cycle stages and individual stages of the life cycle can be repeated during the system's existence. The processes defined in the ISO/IEC 5338 are grouped into four categories: Agreement, Organizational, Project-Enabling, and Technical Management processes.

ISO/IEC TR 5469 [18] applies IEC 61508-style [19] functional safety principles to AI systems, outlining the safety lifecycle, risk classification, design strategies, and validation checks needed to ensure dependable AI in safety-critical applications. Its aim is to help developers of safety-related systems apply AI technologies appropriately within safety functions by fostering awareness of AI properties, functional safety risk factors, applicable safety methods, and potential constraints. The document also addresses the challenges of achieving functional safety in AI systems and proposes potential solution concepts. This is achieved by describing methods and techniques for incorporating AI within a safety-related function to deliver its intended functionality, applying non-AI safety-related functions to ensure the safety of AI-controlled equipment, and using AI systems to design and develop safety-related functions.

ISO/IEC TR 24027 [20] is also relevant to the topic, as it addresses the specificities of dealing with bias in AI systems across the whole life cycle. The standard acknowledges that developing bias-free AI is difficult, as bias may stem from structural deficiencies in system design, arise from the cognitive biases of stakeholders, or even be inherent in the datasets used to train models. This document addresses the issue, especially with regards to AI-aided decision-making, by providing measurement techniques and methods for assessing bias and treating the related vulnerabilities.

The ISO/IEC WD 25704 [21] is a standard under development which provides a process assessment model as a basis for the assessment of AI process capability based on the process measurement framework for the processes performed during AI system life cycle stages in ISO/IEC 22989 [3]. The processes performed during AI system life cycle stages are those defined in ISO/IEC 5338 [17]. Based on ISO/IEC 33020 [22], the process measurement framework for AI systems (as defined in the ISO/IEC WD 25704) aims to provide a set of indicators for measuring performance and capability of those processes. These indicators are used as a basis for collecting evidence that enables an organization to determine its process capability level. This document applies to any type of organization that provides, develops, or uses products or services that utilize AI systems.

Finally, ISO/IEC AWI TS 25223 [23] is another document currently in draft that aims to provide general and technical guidance, as well as requirements, for developing and applying methods to quantify uncertainties in AI systems. It defines fundamental terminology for uncertainty quantification, outlines the characteristics of selected approaches, and illustrates these approaches through specific applications across all stages of the AI system life cycle.

The previous standards are general purpose (i.e., they are not addressing a specific application domain). Nevertheless, a few domain-specific standards addressing the assessment of AI system lifecycle processes have been released so far. One of them is Automotive SPICE (ASPICE) 4.0 [24]. Automotive SPICE provides a process framework that disciplines the software development activities at a high level of abstraction and allows their process capability assessment to match predefined sets of numerous process requirements. ASPICE, as a de-facto process standard, is used by car manufacturers to push software process improvement among suppliers of software-intensive systems [25]. Process capability is defined as a characterization of the ability of a process to meet current or projected business goals. ASPICE is compliant with the ISO/IEC 33004 [26] and ISO/IEC 33020 [22]. Many car manufacturers worldwide use this standard to qualify suppliers by requiring them to achieve defined capability levels on specific processes. Given the ever-increasing use of ML-based components in the modern automobiles, the recently released ASPICE 4.0 includes a group of processes (along with related process indicators for being assessed) addressing the ML life cycle. These processes are ML Requirements Analysis, ML Architecture, ML Training, and ML Model Testing.

Domain-specific standards also play a significant role in addressing the safety and assurance of ML-based systems. In the rest of this section, we focus on standards dealing with the automotive domain. Other domain specific standards of interests exist but, due to space limitations, they are not described in this paper.

ISO 21448 [27], also known as SOTIF (Safety Of The Intended Functionality), is the reference standard for functional safety related to random hardware faults. SOTIF was introduced to complement the ISO 26262 [28] standard that provides requirements for the entire safety life cycle of automotive software-intensive systems. ISO 21448 mandates the use of risk assessment and mitigation actions to evaluate and ensure safety in scenarios that are either within the Operational Design Domain (ODD) or outside but likely to occur. The standard also addresses validation and verification procedures, which should be driven by comprehensive testing of both known and unknown unsafe conditions. In particular, the standard suggests development of test plans that cover as many potentially unsafe operational scenarios as possible. In this context, ISO 21448 introduces the concept of "unknown unsafe scenarios", acknowledging that unsafe behaviors can arise even when a system is functioning correctly according to its design and emphasizing the need for scenario-based testing. Overall SOTIF is one of the first formal standards to explicitly incorporate uncertainty and suggest techniques to address it, which is highly relevant to ML-based software.

Moreover, a new standard, ISO/PAS 8800 [29], has been recently released to provide industry-specific guidance on the use of AI in safety-related functions of road vehicles. It defines a framework for managing system safety in AI-based functions that builds upon and remains compatible with existing standards, particularly the already mentioned ISO 26262 and ISO 21448. Functional safety risks arising from AI system malfunctions are addressed by reinterpreting and expanding relevant clauses from ISO 26262, especially Part 6 (product development at the software level) and Part 8 (supporting processes). Risks related to AI performance limitations are treated by extending the concepts and guidance provided in ISO 21448. The standard also introduces a causal model for identifying sources of functional insufficiencies in AI systems, intended to guide the derivation of safety requirements and corresponding risk reduction measures.

Although still new and currently limited in scope to the automotive domain, ISO/PAS 8800 marks a significant step forward towards a safe and structured deployment of AI (and ML) functions and has the potential to become of paramount importance in a wide range of safety-critical applications beyond road vehicles.

3.4 International Regulatory Documents

In parallel with standards development, several initiatives from national governments or international entities to release legislative, regulatory materials, and "soft law" (i.e., opinions, reports, recommendations, etc.) related to the use of AI arose.

The European Union is actively shaping the regulatory environment for AI and ML-based systems. While standards like ISO focus on how to evaluate or engineer quality, regulations define legal obligations to which developers, manufacturers, and deployers must adhere.

The AI Act (released in July 2024) [30] is the EU's proposed legal framework for ensuring trustworthy and safe AI. It adopts a horizontal, risk-based approach, classifying AI systems into four categories: unacceptable, high-risk, limited-risk, and minimal-risk. These are determined based on the system's potential impact on human health, safety, and fundamental rights. The unacceptable risk category includes AI applications that manipulate human behavior, those that use real-time remote biometric identification in public spaces, and those used for social scoring. According to the act, these are prohibited.

High risk systems include those expected to have potential impact on the general safety of persons. For such AI applications, the act mandates stringent requirements related to safety, transparency, and quality. These include logging, technical documentation, robustness guarantees, and ensuring data representativeness. High-risk systems must also undergo conformity assessments, for which the use of "harmonized standards" is encouraged to demonstrate compliance. Finally, AI systems in the limited and minimal-risk categories are primarily subject to transparency obligations, to ensure users are informed that they are interacting with an AI system and allowing them to make informed choices.

The AI Act has a broad scope and represents an ambitious step toward comprehensive AI regulation. Although full adoption is scheduled for August 2026, and its practical effectiveness and uniform implementation across EU member states remains to be seen, it is important to mention that the AI Act will not operate in isolation. Its scope intersects with several cross-domain regulations already in force, such as the GDPR (General Data Protection Regulation) [31], the CRA (Cyber Resilience Act) [32], and the DSA (Digital Services Act) [33]. In addition, domain-specific frameworks will also apply. For example, the MDR (Medical Device Regulation) [34] and IVDR (In Vitro Diagnostic Regulation) [35] govern healthcare applications, while the GSR (General Safety Regulation) [36] and UNECE WP.29 R155 [37] apply to the automotive sector. This overlapping regulatory landscape introduces significant compliance complexity that developers and deployers will have to face.

4 Conclusions and Final Remarks

In this paper we presented a survey of the existing (released and in-progress) standards and regulations dealing with AI. Given the varsity of the topic, we organized the presentation by clustering them into four categories: AI-related Standards for Organizational and Risk Management, Standards Addressing Quality Evaluation of AI-based Products, Standards Addressing AI System Life Cycle Processes, and International Regulatory Documents. The survey does not pretend to be exhaustive. This is because the rush to release AI specific standards both general and domain-specific is in full swing and thus new standard documents and new standardization initiatives arise frequently. Moreover, because of space limitations we decided to focus on those we consider the most representative to provide the readers with an overall idea of state-of-the-art in such a field. The principal purpose of this paper is to enlighten a crucial aspect for the consolidation and further development of the AI-based technologies and for the increase of maturity of organizations producing and using them. We aim at triggering a discussion on the actual needs and current shortcomings in terms of availability of standards dealing with AI-based technologies.

From the survey of standards dealing with AI-based technology, it emerges that the corpus of standards is, at the current time, still insufficient to face the pervasiveness of such technologies in all everyday-life aspects. In particular, the aspect we consider most crucial in the current effort to standardization is the demand for a coordination of the efforts to avoid overlapping and redundancies in standards, to achieve a complete coverage of the AI-related key aspects of development and use of AI-based technologies, and to shorten the time-to-release. Moreover, we believe that standardization bodies should prioritize the release of standards dealing with the safety impact of AI-based systems.

This paper aims to highlight the importance of standards for AI-based systems and to trigger a discussion and stimulate new and more exhaustive contributions on such a topic from academic, industry, and legislative bodies.

References

1. Jiang, Y., Li, X., Luo, H., Yin, S., Kaynak, O.: Quo vadis artificial intelligence? Discov. Artif. Intell. **2**(1), 4 (2022)
2. Ertel, W.: Introduction to Artificial Intelligence. Springer Nature (2024)
3. ISO/IEC 22989 - Information technology - Artificial intelligence - Artificial intelligence concepts and terminology, Geneva, Switzerland (2022)
4. ISO/IEC 23053 - Framework for Artificial Intelligence (AI) Systems Using Machine Learning (ML), Geneva, Switzerland (2022)
5. ISO/IEC 42001 - Information technology - Artificial intelligence - Management system, Geneva, Switzerland (2023)
6. ISO/IEC 42006 - Information technology - Artificial intelligence - Requirements for bodies providing audit and certification of artificial intelligence management systems, Geneva, Switzerland (2025)
7. ISO/IEC 23894 - Information technology - Artificial intelligence - Guidance on risk management, Geneva, Switzerland (2023)

8. ISO 31000 - Risk management - Guidelines, Geneva, Switzerland (2018)

9. ISO/IEC 25000 - Systems and software engineering - Systems and software Quality Requirements and Evaluation (SQuaRE) - Guide to SQuaRE, Geneva, Switzerland (2014)

10. ISO/IEC 25010 - Systems and software engineering - Systems and software Quality Requirements and Evaluation (SQuaRE) - Product quality model, Geneva, Switzerland (2023)

11. ISO/IEC 25012 - Software engineering - Software product Quality Requirements and Evaluation (SQuaRE) - Data quality model, Geneva, Switzerland (2008)

12. ISO/IEC 25023 - Systems and software engineering - Systems and software Quality Requirements and Evaluation (SQuaRE) - Measurement of system and software product quality, Geneva, Switzerland (2016)

13. ISO/IEC 25059 - Software engineering - Systems and software Quality Requirements and Evaluation (SQuaRE) - Quality model for AI systems, Geneva, Switzerland (2023)

14. ISO/IEC 5259 - Artificial intelligence - Data quality for analytics and machine learning (ML), Geneva, Switzerland (2024)

15. ISO/IEC TR 24028 - Information technology - Artificial intelligence - Overview of trustworthiness in artificial intelligence, Geneva, Switzerland (2020)

16. ISO/IEC TR 24029 - Artificial Intelligence (AI) - Assessment of the robustness of neural networks, Geneva, Switzerland (2021)

17. ISO/IEC 5338 - Information technology - Artificial intelligence - AI system life cycle processes, Geneva, Switzerland (2023)

18. ISO/IEC TR 5469 - Artificial intelligence - Functional safety and AI systems, Geneva, Switzerland (2024)

19. IEC 61508 - Functional safety of electrical/electronic/programmable electronic safety-related systems, Geneva, Switzerland (2010)

20. ISO/IEC TR 24027 - Information technology - Artificial intelligence (AI) - Bias in AI systems and AI aided decision making, Geneva, Switzerland (2021)

21. ISO/IEC AWI 25704 - Artificial Intelligence - Process assessment model for AI system life cycle processes (Draft), Geneva, Switzerland (2025)

22. ISO/IEC 33020 - Information technology - Process assessment - Process measurement framework for assessment of process capability, Geneva, Switzerland (2019)

23. ISO/IEC AWI TS 25223 - Information technology - Artificial intelligence - Guidance and requirements for uncertainty quantification in AI systems (Draft), Geneva, Switzerland (2025)

24. Automotive SPICE 4.0 - Process Capability Assessment Model (2023)

25. Fabbrini, F., Fusani, M., Lami, G., Sivera, E.: A SPICE-based software supplier qualification mechanism in automotive industry. Softw. Process: Improve. Pract. **12**(6), 523–528 (2007)

26. ISO/IEC 33004 - Information technology - Process assessment - Requirements for process reference, process assessment and maturity models, Geneva, Switzerland (2025)

27. ISO 21448 - Road vehicles - Safety of the intended functionality, Geneva, Switzerland (2022)

28. ISO 26262 - Road vehicles - Functional safety Part 1: Vocabulary, Geneva, Switzerland (2018)

29. ISO/PAS 8800 - Road vehicles - Safety and artificial intelligence, Geneva, Switzerland (2024)

30. European Parliament and of the Council.: Artificial Intelligence Act - Regulation (EU) 2024/1689. Off. J. Eur. Union **OJ**(L 2024/1689), 12.7.2024 (2024)

31. European Parliament and of the Council.: General data protection Regulation (GDPR) - Regulation (EU) 2016/679. Off. J. Eur. Union **OJ**(L 119), 4.5.2016 (2016)

32. European Parliament and of the Council. Cyber Resilience Act - Regulation (EU) 2024/2847. Off. J. Eur. Union **OJ**(L 2024/2847), 20.11.2024 (2024)

33. European Parliament and of the Council.: Digital Services Act - Regulation (EU) 2022/2065. Off. J. Eur. Union **OJ**(L 277), 27.10.2022 (2022)

34. European Parliament and of the Council. \"Medical devices regulation - Regulation (EU) 2017/745. Off. J. Eur. Union **OJ**(L 117), 5.5.2017 (2017)

35. European Parliament and of the Council. In Vitro Diagnostic Regulation - Regulation (EU) 2017/746. Off. J. Eur. Union **OJ**(L 117), 5.5.2017 (2017)
36. European Parliament and of the Council.: General Safety Regulation (GSR) for motor vehicles - regulation (Eu) 2019/2144. Off. J. Eur. Union **Oj**:(1 325), 16.12.2019 (2019)
37. United Nations Economic Commission for Europe.:, UNECE WP.29 - UN Regulation No. 155 (R155) on Vehicle Cybersecurity. Off. J. Eur. Union **OJ**(L 82), 9.3.2021 (2019)

Chatting About Flaky Tests with Standard LLMs. An Empirical Exploration

Marcin Szwarc and Bartosz Walter[(✉)] [ID]

Poznan University of Technology, Faculty of Computing and Telecommunications, Poznan, Poland
`marcinszwarc@hotmail.com`, `bartosz.walter@cs.put.poznan.pl`

Abstract. Flaky tests yield inconsistent results without code changes, which undermines software reliability and may increase development costs, emphasizing the importance of effective detection methods. Despite various research efforts over the past 15 years, existing techniques often show limited accuracy and adoption. This study explores whether commonly available Large Language Models (LLMs) are suitable for detecting flaky tests in software. Using the International Dataset of Flaky Tests, we asked selected LLMs, including GPT and Gemini, to classify Java test cases as flaky or non-flaky. Results show that LLMs are unable to do so consistently. This research underscores the challenges of using general-purpose LLMs for flaky test detection and highlights the need for more effective solutions.

Keywords: flaky tests · Large Language Models · classification

1 Introduction

Most software is built and maintained incrementally, with code modules being written and integrated into the code base at different times. This process usually requires changes to already existing code, which, in turn, needs to be regularly tested to prevent the introduction of new defects.

A popular technique for verifying software is regression testing, which relies on a suite of automated test cases that, once developed, can be easily and frequently run to discover possible recurring defects that have already been fixed.

For the results of the automatic test cases to be reliable, they have to be stable, meaning that they should alter their outcome if and only if a change has been made to the code executed by a test and the change either introduces or corrects a defect in that code. Otherwise, such a test is called *flaky* and does not reflect the actual correctness of the software module it is supposed to test [13]. As such, flaky tests pose a significant threat to the production code quality.

Flaky tests have been of particular interest in the research literature for over 15 years, and various techniques for their detection have been proposed. Due to the problem's non-trivial nature, most approaches focus only on a single category of flaky tests, leveraging their properties to perform the classification [14].

G. Scanniello et al. (Eds.): PROFES 2025, LNCS 16362, pp. 334–345, 2026.
https://doi.org/10.1007/978-3-032-12092-2_28

The existing algorithms and tools include static, dynamic, and hybrid procedures. Similarly, their complexity varies from a trivial rerunning of the test case to elaborate analyses of the runtime behavior and/or development history. On the other hand, there is a growing interest in using available AI-related tools to support various activities in the software development process. According to the StackOverflow Survey[1], 40% of developers commonly use commercial LLMs or chat-bots to debug their code, and 26% more are interested in doing so; additionally, 41% consider AI tools as a reliable information source.

There have also been promising attempts to detect flaky tests using large language models (LLMs) [5,18]. Still, they require a custom setup, combined with other elaborate classification methods, or fine-tuned for effective source code processing. While the commonly available multi-purpose and out-of-the-box LLMs, frequently used by developers, have been found to provide effective aid in various programming tasks, like code generation and refactoring, their applicability for detecting flaky tests has not been considered yet and is unknown.

This paper empirically explores popular, commercially available LLMs and their fitness for detecting flaky tests in source code. Our work focuses on using the models exactly as they are provided by their vendors, without any additional fine-tuning, to mimic the situation of an ad hoc use of such a system.

1.1   Motivation

The use of software engineering-related tools backed by AI has been growing very rapidly, with 63% of professional developers declaring that they use them in their activities. Of these, 83% claim that these tools increase their productivity, as pointed out in the already mentioned Stack Overflow Survey[1].

This contrasts with the observed low adoption of dedicated tools for detecting flaky tests. Querying Google search engine for the names of a few of them (DTDETECTOR, cited 212 times in Google Scholar [23]; IDFLAKIES, with 197 citations [12]; POLDET, with 112 citations [8]; and NONDEX, having just 41 citations [7]) yields merely hundreds and up to a few thousand results[2]. In contrast, the seminal work for the modern LLMs [20] has been cited 189k+ times.

The gap between the low adoption of existing traditional detectors and the observed success of AI-backed assistants supporting developers in various programming tasks encouraged us to investigate how reliable they could be in that area. This paper presents an exploratory study that empirically verifies if and to what extent the commercially available LLMs could effectively support developers in identifying flaky tests. While LLMs excel in transforming textual inputs, they keep struggling with reasoning about interpreting the texts. Although detecting flaky tests requires understanding the runtime properties

---

[1] https://survey.stackoverflow.co/2024/ai.
[2] https://www.google.com/search?q=%22dtdetector%22+flaky&nfpr=1&hl=en,
  https://www.google.com/search?q=%22idflakies%22+flaky&nfpr=1&hl=en,
  https://www.google.com/search?q=%22poldet%22+flaky&nfpr=1&hl=en,
  https://www.google.com/search?q=%22nondex%22+flaky&nfpr=1&hl=en.

of programs, we conjecture that AI-supported identification of patterns in code could provide some reliable assistance.

Being aware that fine-tuned tools trained on curated datasets will likely deliver better results than generic models, we also know that software developers commonly use the latter for their workflows. Therefore, we want to specifically assess the usefulness of such of tools for detecting flaky tests.

2   Related Work

Various techniques have been proposed to detect flaky tests, including heuristic-based methods, dynamic analysis, machine learning approaches, and test rerun strategies [14]. This section briefly overviews these approaches but focuses on recent advances in applying ML to detecting and fixing flaky tests.

The most straightforward approach relies on rerunning test suites several times in identical conditions, in an attempt to capture differences in results. Unfortunately, it applies only to some categories of tests and is computationally ineffective compared to the number of discovered issues. That paved the way for more robust methods, based on commonly known classifiers. Pinto et al. [15] examined Random Forest, Decision Tree, Support Vector, and others, to find that Random Forest offers the highest performance. Verdecchia et al. developed an FLAST tool [21] that used the kNN algorithm for the test classification. It had a comparable performance, but used fewer system resources.

Studies by Pontillo et al. [16,17] indicated that detecting the flakiness is feasible using only static code properties, with the performance comparable to the baseline approaches.

Classification relies on extracting features that would represent relevant properties of the problem. Alshammari et al. [1] proposed FLAKEFLAGGER, based on eight features representing static and dynamic properties of the subject test case, and eight indicators of test smells. The classifier did not require source code to produce the feature set.

Another approach relying on Machine Learning was suggested by Camara et al. [2] in their work based on FLAKEFLAGGER. For every test case, they computed eight numeric features, representing static and dynamic properties of the test method, and eight boolean properties related to certain test smells, including Conditional Logic, Indirect Testing, and Assertion Roulette. Contrary to some of the works mentioned above, the source code itself was not a part of the feature set for classification (but was still needed to calculate the metrics used by the model).

These works were then extended by Parry et al. [14], who augmented the feature set to sixteen code characteristics. A work by Gruber et al. [6] used a weighted flip rate as a metric of the history of a test execution. Flip rate reflects the number of changes in the test case outcome.

The advent and considerable progress in applying Large Language Models to various tasks also embraced the detection of flaky tests. For example, Fatima et al. [5] proposed FLAKIFY, based on CodeBERT language model. They fine-tuned the model using a set of flaky tests to include the defect. In that work, CodeBERT transformed the input code into a vector, which was later classified by a neural network-based classifier. Additionally, to overcome CodeBERT's narrow context window, the test code was preprocessed to remove all instructions unrelated to test smells. FLAKIFY can be referred to as a black-box technique, as it operates on the test code only, without having access to the production code. FLAKIFY achieved a high F_1 score, surpassing 90%.

Noticeably, previous works that employed LLMs for detecting flaky tests required a custom setup and processing pipeline, including code-oriented fine-tuning. However, the actual developers do not typically have access to such a setup. Instead, they tend to rely on common AI assistants and commercial-grade tooling, the capabilities of which have not yet been studied in detail in the context of detecting test flakiness.

3   Experimental Design

3.1   Dataset

In this study, we used the International Dataset of Flaky Tests (IDoFT) [11], which includes around 10,000 confirmed flaky tests (as of March 2025) coming from various open-source projects. We retrieved the dataset on 9 November 2024, from its GitHub repository (commit `67a1670`).[3]

To minimize the risk of introducing an additional latent variable related to the programming language, we analyzed only flaky tests in Java code from IDoFT's Maven-enabled projects, a total of approximately 7,300 projects. This is the largest part of the dataset, allowing for controlling bias related to programming languages and project configuration schemas.

Since IDoFT contains only confirmed flaky tests, we needed to make it more balanced and augment it with a comparable number of stable (non-flaky) tests to check how well the LLMs recognized them. We did so in two ways: (1) we gathered fixed versions of flaky tests, using the pull requests linked from the IDoFT, and (2) we scanned through the projects referenced by the IDoFT and then randomly chose test cases that had not already been included in the flaky dataset. Notably, the second approach does not guarantee that the tests considered as non-flaky are indeed stable; instead, it relies on the assumption that such test cases are less likely to be flaky. In total, we collected 9,306 tests, of which 4,775 were flaky, which means the dataset is balanced.

Tests may expose flaky behavior for several reasons. In general, it is not possible to identify the root cause of an IDoFT test's flakiness, including whether the root cause is located in the test code or the production code. Therefore, by operating with the full dataset, the LLMs may be unable to discover some flaky tests, not due to their inability to perform the task but rather because the faulty code was not included in a prompt. To mitigate that risk, we identified a subset of flaky tests in our dataset that are known to be defective, i.e., they have been

---

[3] https://github.com/TestingResearchIllinois/idoft/blob/67a1670/pr-data.csv.

confirmed to include the factor that caused their flakiness. Then, the *defective* dataset includes tests that satisfy the following conditions:

- there is a linked pull request for each test that aims to remove its flakiness,
- the pull request includes changes made to the test,
- the pull request has been approved.

We consider test code to be changed if either the test case itself has been changed or at least one of the *setup* or *teardown* methods in the relevant class has been modified. Thus, even a single line difference can cause multiple test cases to be considered changed. Of 4,775 flaky tests, 460 were considered *defective*.

405 of the *defective* tests have stable counterparts ("fixed defective"), obtained from accepted pull requests that aimed to remove the flaky behavior of these tests. We could not collect the corrected versions of some tests because the hash of the pull request's merge commit was absent in the repository.

The internal structure of the *full* set and its *defective* subset is different. Every entry in the IDoFT is tagged with its category, which refers to what factors contribute to the observed flakiness, and a single test can have multiple categories assigned. Although the most common category in both is *implementation dependency*, its share varies across datasets. The frequencies of the groups' three most popular categories of flaky tests are shown in Table 1.

Table 1. The most frequent categories of flaky tests in the dataset

Category	All flaky	Defective only
implementation dependent	58.9%	93.3%
order dependent	20.5%	5.0%
non-deterministic	13.8%	0.2%
other	9.2%	1.5%

3.2   LLM Selection

Our goal in this work is to explore the suitability of widely used and popular LLMs for detecting flaky tests. Therefore, we focused on off-the-shelf, general-purpose models without additional fine-tuning. In this work, we used the following four models provided by two vendors:

- OpenAI (1) GPT-4o mini, and (2) o3-mini,
- Google (3) Gemini 2.0 Flash Lite, and (4) 2.0 Flash Thinking (experimental).

The choice of models was guided by their popularity, immediate availability at no- or very low cost, and the reported broad spectrum of general-purpose applications. The models from both providers have been found to provide high-quality answers to various programming problems. While GPT appears more effective in refining the response iteratively [22], this advantage does not play an important role in our case, as we submit the entire context of a problem in a single prompt. In that case, the performance of the models is comparable.

The models we used come with relatively recent knowledge cut-off dates, so they may have already been trained on many of the entries from our dataset and know the correct answer in advance. We decided not to exclude such tests because, in real-life scenarios, it is possible to stumble upon test cases similar to the ones from public datasets. Therefore, our results are closer to an upper bound for the actual models' performance in the task, though.

The selected models represent two categories: "standard" (GPT-4o and Gemini 2.0 Flash) and "reasoning" (o3 and Gemini 2.0 Flash Thinking). The latter is, according to their vendors,[4] more capable in tasks requiring analytical approach, such as solving math and logic problems. On the other hand, they need more computational power and thus the access to them is more tightly rate-limited and/or their cost is higher. Therefore, we included both models to explore whether a significant cost increase leads to better results.

3.3 Prompt Compilation

For our prompts, we used the Zero-Shot Learning (ZSL) approach [4], which involves a single request sent to the LLM containing a problem description and a question. We decided to follow this approach, as it reduced the number of arbitrary decisions to make about the prompt structure and experimental settings. This was especially significant, given that we were unaware of any previous research that would have adopted a similar procedure. Furthermore, we also took advantage of the Chain-of-Thought (CoT) technique, which requires the model to "think aloud" before providing an answer, by appending "Let's think step by step" to the prompt [10].

We compiled prompts of different lengths, with the longer ones containing more components with detailed description of the problem and examples. The prompts we built consisted of up to five components:

- **Question** – included in every prompt, asking the LLM to determine whether the test (referenced explicitly by its qualified name) is flaky, without providing any additional comments;
- **Explanation** – tells the LLM what the flaky tests are;
- **Causes** – enumerates a few common root causes for test flakiness, but with no reference to how they can manifest in code;
- **Symptoms** – includes examples of source code traits that can make a test flaky;
- **Code example** – a short example of a flaky test case due to incorrect assumptions about item ordering in Java Maps (prompts with this component may be considered as One-Shot Learning [4]).

---

4 https://openai.com/index/introducing-o3-and-o4-mini/,
  https://web.archive.org/web/20250201183704/https://deepmind.google/
  technologies/gemini/flash-thinking/.

As a result, we have prepared eight prompt templates, ranging from very simple (e.g., including a question only) to more elaborate compositions of several components. More details about the prompts are provided in the replication package (Sect. 7).

3.4   Orchestration

This experimental procedure involved the following steps, all automated and implemented as separate runnable scripts:

1. Clone all repositories at all commit hashes referenced in the IDoFT dataset. Skip repositories that cannot be cloned (e.g., due to excessive path length or the missing commit hash in the repository).
2. Make an index of all classes present in each repository. Skip repositories that contain files using an encoding other than UTF-8.
3. Remove tests from the dataset that cannot be found using the index.
4. Use the index to find test methods not identified as flaky and randomly pick a subset, similar in size to the set of flaky tests.
5. Process the attached pull requests to decide if the flaky test should be marked as *defective*. If so, fetch its corrected version.
6. Generate prompts for every one of the test cases. A random sample of eight templates will be taken using a homogeneous distribution for that purpose.
7. Iteratively query the LLMs using the generated prompts.

As a consequence of Step 6, every test case is assigned a dedicated prompt, which is then submitted to all evaluated models.

4   Results

Most related work on this subject uses the F_1 metric to measure the quality of the models. However, in some experimental settings, we observed a significant positive bias, and the corresponding values of F_1 would make the results appear better than they actually are. Therefore, we employ the P_4 metric instead, which extends F_1 to penalize both positive and negative biases of the classifier [19].

The performance of the models varied significantly, as presented in Table 2, with the best results delivered by Gemini Thinking (across all categories of tests: $P_4 = 58\%$ on the *full* dataset and 1 pp. lower for the *defective* tests).

However, most models performed better on the *full* dataset than on defective tests. To be able to rule out the possibility that this divergence results from the different compositions of both sets, in the right part of Table 2 we present P_4 scores calculated solely using ID tests. As reported in Table 1, the *defective* set has a much higher share of the *implementation-dependent* (ID) tests than the *full* one.

In addition to the impact of the model on the quality of the results, another significant factor was the specific prompt being used. However, we found no

Table 2. P_4 values achieved by the models, both across all categories of flakiness and only *implementation-dependent*. The best scores in each column are bolded.

Model	All categories			*ID* only		
	All tests	Defective	Diff.	All tests	Defective	Diff.
GPT-4o mini	56%	49%	–7 pp	33%	48%	+15 pp
o3-mini	28%	47%	+19 pp	21%	48%	+27 pp
Gemini 2.0 F. Lite	15%	9%	–6 pp	7%	9%	+2 pp
Gemini 2.0 F. Thinking	**58%**	**57%**	–1 pp	**34%**	**57%**	+23 pp

clear relationship between the presence of specific prompt components and the P_4 score.

Due to the complexity of the table that presents the P_4 scores versus the prompt, it is included in the replication package (see Sect. 7).

To check how grounded the answers are, we calculated inter-rater agreement using Cohen's kappa. Figures for selected model pairs for the whole dataset are presented in Table 3. The full collection of kappa values (including ones for the defective dataset) is included in the replication package.

Table 3. Cohen's kappa scores between surveyed models, whole dataset.

	GPT-4o mini	o3-mini	Gemini Lite
Gemini Thinking	0.411	0.120	0.012
Gemini Lite	0.029	0.005	
o3-mini	0.082		

The highest agreement score between models for the full dataset was between Gemini 2.0 F. Thinking and GPT-4o mini ($\kappa = 0.411$). In contrast, the lowest $\kappa = 0.005$ was between Gemini 2.0 F. Lite and o3-mini. Regardless of the models, the score is low or very low, suggesting a (very) poor agreement.

5   Discussion

The accuracy of the provided answers substantially varied among the tested models. None of them was trained specifically for detecting flaky tests, so the observed results could be attributed to differences in training datasets or the size of context window in the model. It is also possible that some models have been trained on IDoFT, which was used then as a test set. Leakage od data between the sets could challenge reliability of the results.

It is also unclear which elements of the prompts make them more effective. There are cases in which including elements that individually improve the accuracy, make it worse when combined.

Regardless of the impact of the specific prompt and the model choice on the accuracy achieved, the results suggest that all subject LLMs struggle with detecting flaky tests. Our results consistently remain much worse than those reported in earlier works, based on their tailored tools and approaches, which use models trained on curated datasets, finetuned and optimized for code analysis. It is even more evident when we consider the poor agreement between answers provided by models for each prompt, which could mean that their responses are much more of a guess than a reliable verdict. This could support observations by Chen et al. [3], who concluded that LLMs do not perform well in tasks related to predicting dynamic software behavior, like in this case. Effective reasoning about runtime properties of source code based solely on static code analysis appears not feasible.

The approach we used gives significantly worse results than other ML-based techniques (e.g., [15, 21]), even in comparison to the most closely related tool, FLAKIFY by Fatima et al. [5]. This and other previous papers reported F_1 scores exceeding 90%, while the highest F_1 value in our study varies between 53% and 60%.

Other differences between our approach and the earlier ones include the classifier complexity. These used earlier were significantly smaller, e.g., FLAKIFY was based on the CODEBERT model, which accepts only 512 tokens as input. Other previous techniques also take into account a limited set of features. Therefore, some pre-processing steps were required, which could have amplified the features strongly connected to flakiness and omitted irrelevant ones. In our scenario, the models were given no opportunity to learn what aspects of the input lead to test instability, other than during the original training, which their vendor did.

6   Threats to Validity

The observed differences between our results and existing work prompts us to identify issues that could challenge validity of our study and its findings. We focus on two categories that are most applicable in this case.

External threats embrace problems with generalizability and applying the results beyond the scope of the study. In this work, we used off-the-shelf LLMs, just as they are provided by vendors. Little is known about their training sets; the number of parameters and architecture are unknown and could not be verified independently. As we noted previously, we limited our analysis to Java code only, and results for other languages could be different.

Internal threats concern the factors that could challenge the causal inference of between the input and output. In our study it is unknown if the models know the concept of flakiness, and if the definitions are consistent. We can also conjecture that the models were already trained on examples of flaky tests, but this assumption cannot be reliably verified. Another important factor is the intrinsic indeterminism of the LLMs, which could provide different or even contradictory answers to the same prompt.

7   Conclusions

While various tools have been developed to detect and fix flaky tests, their popularity and adoption by developers remain relatively low. Existing tools typically rely on manipulating the test execution, combined with analysis of metadata, commit history, or previous test runs, to provoke changes in behavior. Several detectors based on Machine Learning have also been proposed, but none used an *off-the-shelf* language model [14]. Our exploration and experiments with such Large Language Models suggest that their accuracy is still far inferior to the capabilities of other available tools. The quality of the results provided by LLMs depends heavily on the specific model used and the input composition. The low consistency and stability of the results currently render them inapplicable in the practical setting. Our results with constructing prompts of different structures give no useful hints on how the prompts could be effectively improved to ensure more accurate detection of such tests, and we conjecture that such a universal recipe could not exist. Furthermore, our findings align with the conclusions of existing works on code understanding by LLMs [3] or, more generally, on their analytical capabilities [9], stating that LLMs perform poorly in these tasks.

We conjecture that the significant discrepancy between our results and the earlier results can be attributed to our usage of the general-purpose models exactly as they are provided by their vendors, specifically with no fine-tuning steps. This was done to ensure that the experiment scenario matches the environment in which software developers work most closely. However, the results suggest that the already popular tools, used alone, do not excel in detecting flaky tests.

Possible directions for further research include conducting a similar study on a broader and more diverse set of LLMs (e.g., from other providers) and/or using additional techniques to construct prompts, such as Few-Shot Learning [4]. Moreover, AI agents or fine-tuned LLMs may also be an interesting way forward.

Replication Package

All Python scripts and input data that we used in this study, as well as almost 170,000 responses received from LLMs, and detailed aggregate results are included in a replication package in Zenodo.[5]

---

[5] https://doi.org/10.5281/zenodo.15496618.

References

1. Alshammari, A., Morris, C., Hilton, M., Bell, J.: FlakeFlagger: predicting flakiness without rerunning tests. In: Proceedings - International Conference on Software Engineering, pp. 1572–1584. IEEE Computer Society (5 2021). https://doi.org/10.1109/ICSE43902.2021.00140

2. Camara, B., Silva, M., Endo, A., Vergilio, S.: On the use of test smells for prediction of flaky tests. In: ACM International Conference Proceeding Series (2021). https://doi.org/10.1145/3482909.3482916

3. Chen, J., Pan, Z., Hu, X., Li, Z., Li, G., Xia, X.: Reasoning runtime behavior of a program with LLM: How far are we? (2024). https://arxiv.org/abs/2403.16437

4. Dang, H., Mecke, L., Lehmann, F., Goller, S., Buschek, D.: How to prompt? opportunities and challenges of zero- and few-shot learning for human-AI interaction in creative applications of generative models (2022). https://arxiv.org/abs/2209.01390

5. Fatima, S., Ghaleb, T.A., Briand, L.: Flakify: a black-box, language model-based predictor for flaky tests. IEEE Trans. Softw. Eng. **49** (2023). https://doi.org/10.1109/TSE.2022.3201209

6. Gruber, M., Heine, M., Oster, N., Philippsen, M., Fraser, G.: Practical flaky test prediction using common code evolution and test history data. In: Proceedings - 2023 IEEE 16th International Conference on Software Testing, Verification and Validation, ICST 2023, pp. 210–221. Institute of Electrical and Electronics Engineers Inc. (2023). https://doi.org/10.1109/ICST57152.2023.00028

7. Gyori, A., Lambeth, B., Shi, A., Legunsen, O., Marinov, D.: NonDex: a tool for detecting and debugging wrong assumptions on Java API specifications. Proceedings of the ACM SIGSOFT Symposium on the Foundations of Software Engineering 13-18-November-2016, pp. 993–997 (11 2016). https://doi.org/10.1145/2950290.2983932

8. Gyori, A., Shi, A., Hariri, F., Marinov, D.: Reliable testing: Detecting state-polluting tests to prevent test dependency. In: 2015 International Symposium on Software Testing and Analysis, ISSTA 2015 - Proceedings, pp. 223–233 (7 2015). https://doi.org/10.1145/2771783.2771793

9. Hu, Y., Song, K., Cho, S., Wang, X., Foroosh, H., Yu, D., Liu, F.: Can large language models do analytical reasoning? (2024). https://arxiv.org/abs/2403.04031

10. Kojima, T., Gu, S.S., Reid, M., Matsuo, Y., Iwasawa, Y.: Large language models are zero-shot reasoners. In: Advances in Neural Information Processing Systems, vol. 35 (2022)

11. Lam, W.: International Dataset of Flaky Tests (IDoFT) (2020). http://mir.cs.illinois.edu/flakytests

12. Lam, W., Oei, R., Shi, A., Marinov, D., Xie, T.: iDFlakies: A framework for detecting and partially classifying flaky tests. In: Proceedings - 2019 IEEE 12th International Conference on Software Testing, Verification and Validation, ICST 2019, pp. 312–322. Institute of Electrical and Electronics Engineers Inc. (4 2019). https://doi.org/10.1109/ICST.2019.00038

13. Luo, Q., Hariri, F., Eloussi, L., Marinov, D.: An empirical analysis of flaky tests. In: FSE 2014: Proceedings of the 22nd ACM SIGSOFT International Symposium on Foundations of Software Engineering (2014)

14. Parry, O., Kapfhammer, G.M., Hilton, M., McMinn, P.: A survey of flaky tests. ACM Trans. Softw. Eng. Methodol. **31** (10 2021). https://doi.org/10.1145/3476105

15. Pinto, G., Miranda, B., Dissanayake, S., D'Amorim, M., Treude, C., Bertolino, A.: What is the vocabulary of flaky tests? Proceedings - 2020 IEEE/ACM 17th International Conference on Mining Software Repositories, MSR 2020 11, pp. 492–502 (6 2020). https://doi.org/10.1145/3379597.3387482
16. Pontillo, V.: Static test flakiness prediction. In: Proceedings of the ACM/IEEE 44th International Conference on Software Engineering: Companion Proceedings, ICSE '22, pp. 325–327. Association for Computing Machinery, New York (2022). https://doi.org/10.1145/3510454.3522680
17. Pontillo, V., Palomba, F., Ferrucci, F.: Toward static test flakiness prediction: a feasibility study. In: Proceedings of the 5th International Workshop on Machine Learning Techniques for Software Quality Evolution, pp. 19–24. MaLTESQuE 2021. Association for Computing Machinery, New York (2021). https://doi.org/10.1145/3472674.3473981
18. Rahman, S., Baz, A., Misailovic, S., Shi, A.: Quantizing large-language models for predicting flaky tests. In: 2024 IEEE Conference on Software Testing, Verification and Validation (ICST), pp. 93–104. IEEE (2024)
19. Sitarz, M.: Extending F1 metric, probabilistic approach. Advances in Artificial Intelligence and Machine Learning **3** (2023). https://doi.org/10.54364/AAIML.2023.1161
20. Vaswani, A., et al.: Attention is all you need. Advances in neural information processing systems **30** (2017)
21. Verdecchia, R., Cruciani, E., Miranda, B., Bertolino, A.: Know you neighbor: Fast static prediction of test flakiness. IEEE Access **9**, 76119–76134 (2021). https://doi.org/10.1109/ACCESS.2021.3082424
22. Vishnu, S., Sahil, Garg, N.: Unveiling the role of GPT-4 in solving LeetCode programming problems. Comput. Appl. Eng. Educ. **33**(1), e22815 (2025). https://doi.org/10.1002/cae.22815, https://onlinelibrary.wiley.com/doi/abs/10.1002/cae.22815
23. Zhang, S., Jalali, D., Wuttke, J., Mulu, K., Lam, W., Ernst, M.D., Notkin, D.: Empirically revisiting the test independence assumption. In: 2014 International Symposium on Software Testing and Analysis, ISSTA 2014 - Proceedings, pp. 385–396. Association for Computing Machinery, Inc (7 2014). https://doi.org/10.1145/2610384.2610404

Critical Analysis of ASPICE® 4.0 Machine Learning Engineering Process Requirements

Fabio Falcini[1] and Giuseppe Lami[2(✉)]

[1] INTACS automotive SPICE® Assessor, Pisa, Italia
[2] Istituto di Scienza e Tecnologie dell'Informazione "A.Faedo", Consiglio Nazionale delle Ricerche, Pisa, Italia
giuseppe.lami@sti.cnr.it

Abstract. The introduction of machine learning development paradigm into the automotive software industry has made necessary to update the applicable quality evaluation standards such as Automotive SPICE®. As a result the Automotive SPICE® community timely tackled this challenge with the introduction of the version 4.0 containing a first baseline of process requirements for machine learning engineering. The paper provides a succinct critical analysis of related ASPICE® new content with particular reference to the current state of the art of machine learning development practices. The outcome of this paper aims at being an input for the forthcoming improvement initiatives within the Automotive SPICE working groups.

Keywords: Critical Analysis · Machine Learning · Automotive SPICE® · Quality Evaluation

1 Introduction

The integration of machine learning within the automotive sector and in particular within the development of on board vehicle functions such as, for example, automatic emergency breaking (AEB), required that the relevant quality evaluation frameworks such as Automotive SPICE® [1] (also commonly abbreviated as ASPICE®) to also consider this innovative paradigm of automotive Electronic Control Unit (ECU) development. In fact, companies, especially in the Advanced Driver Assistance Systems (ADAS) market, are actively investing in machine learning to build platforms that closely mimic human driving intelligence.

The application of new content of ASPICE® related to machine learning engineering poses a challenge to assessors and industrial players. Accordingly, it is authors intention to contribute the growth and improvement of this part of the standard with a critical analysis paper.

This paper is structured as follows: Sect. 2 provides a brief background on Automotive SPICE® and its latest evolution. Section 3 presents an overview of machine learning in the context of automotive software development. Section 4 provides the outcome of the critical analysis which has no intention to represent an in-depth review of the ASPICE standard. Finally, Sect. 5 offers some concluding remarks.

G. Scanniello et al. (Eds.): PROFES 2025, LNCS 16362, pp. 346–352, 2026.
https://doi.org/10.1007/978-3-032-12092-2_29

2 Background on Automotive SPICE®

Automotive SPICE®, introduced in early 2000s by some major car manufacturers, is the reference process standard for assessing quality of development processes for electronic and software-based systems. Its key features can be summarized as follows:

- Process-centric
- Identification of expected outcomes and work products content
- Controlled planning and control of project activities
- Systematic quality checks and reviews.

Automotive SPICE® has been developed by Working Group 13 of the Quality Management Center (QMC) in the German Association of the Automotive Industry and is a registered trademark of the Verband der Automobilindustrie e.V. (VDA).

The abbreviation SPICE® stands for Software Process Improvement and Capability Determination. Automotive SPICE® combines a process reference model and a process assessment model in one standard. And conforms to the regulations of the ISO/IEC 33xxx family (process assessment), e.g., ISO/IEC 33001, ISO/IEC 33002, ISO/IEC 3304 [2].

Since its deployment. Automotive SPICE® has reshaped the face of the software automotive software industry throughout the overall OEM's supply chain by means of obligation of execution of assessments. Automotive SPICE® assessments evaluate the quality or more precisely the process capability of the development processes for a defined organization. The following picture shows the architecture of the ASPICE® standard.

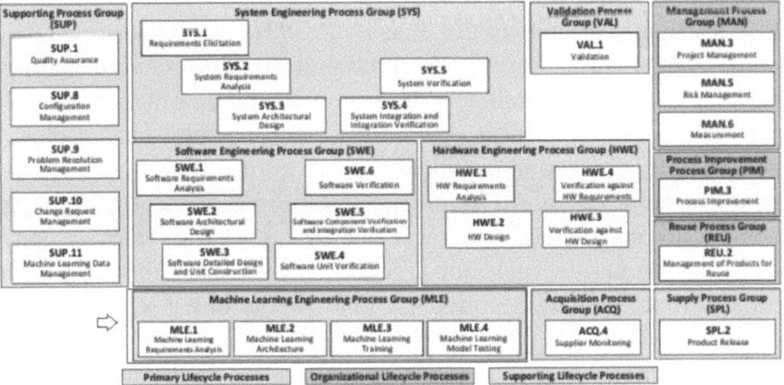

Fig. 1. Automotive SPICE process reference model - Overview []

The framework enables so benchmarking and comparing process capabilities across different suppliers, helping automotive OEMs evaluate and select suppliers based on their process maturity and capability. In the planning for an assessment, the client of the assessment (also called "sponsor") defines the processes to be assessed.

2.1 Notes on Automotive SPICE® 4.0

ASPICE® 4.0 has introduced a set of updates to improve quality and efficiency of the standard. These new features enhance process capability, integrate advanced engineering practices, and ensure higher levels of safety and compliance.

Inclusion of processes to address Machine Learning Engineering (MLE.1 – MLE.4) and hardware engineering (HWE.1 – HWE.4), as well as adding a validation process for the overall system (VAL.1) and a support process for data management in machine learning (SUP.11).

At the same time, ten process areas have been removed. They belong to the categories of acquisition (six processes), support (three processes) and supply (one process). Theses process areas were seldom used so these changes that at first appear to be large, in reality is rather small.

In version 3.1 all verification processes and the support processes expect that a strategy drives the process implementation. This aspect was overloaded with expectations at Capability Level 1 (CL1). Thus, the base practice with "strategy" has been removed and moved to capability level 2 (CL2).

3 Machine Learning in Automotive Software Industry

Machine learning [8] is a subcategory of Artificial Intelligence (AI) that allows computerized system to learn and use new information without specific human input. Machine Learning (ML) uses statistical methods to understand patterns in data, allowing it to perform complex tasks and solve problems often more efficiently than traditional methods.

Machine learning in the automotive industry [5, 9, 10] refers to the use of algorithms and statistical models that enable vehicles and manufacturing systems to learn from data, recognize patterns, and make intelligent decisions with minimal human intervention. By analyzing the big amounts of sensor, operational, and behavioral data, machine learning makes cars smarter, safer, and more efficient.

In automotive applications, ML is integrated across a wide range of domains, including autonomous driving, predictive maintenance, driver behavior analysis, and real-time decision-making. It forms the backbone of advanced vehicle systems, helping cars adapt to dynamic environments and continuously improve performance through continuous learning.

Machine learning involves a series of steps to develop, train and deploy models that can learn from data and make predictions or decisions. These processes are essential for creating intelligent systems that can adapt and improve over time.

3.1 Machine Learning and Automotive SPICE® 4.0

The actual definition of the standard for Machine Learning states: "In Automotive SPICE Machine Learning (ML) describes the ability of software to learn from specific training data and to apply this knowledge to other similar tasks."

As stated before, "Machine Learning" and "Automotive SPICE®" are now integrated because Automotive SPICE® v4.0 has incorporated a new process group for Machine

Learning Engineering (MLE) to address the complexities and challenges of developing machine learning-based systems, which are vital for applications related, for instance, to autonomous driving.

The MLE process group, supported by standards such as ISO/IEC 23053:2022, guides organizations on how to systematically develop, manage, and validate machine learning applications to ensure safety, reliability, and compliance within the stringent automotive framework.

3.2 ASPICE® 4.0 MLE – Machine Learning Engineering Process Group

ASPICE® 4.0 includes four specific processes (MLE.1 – MLE.4) dedicated to machine learning engineering. These processes focus on developing and integrating AI and data-driven technologies into automotive systems. MLE involves a series of steps to develop, train and deploy models that can learn from data and make predictions or decisions. These processes are essential for creating intelligent systems that can adapt and improve over time.

- MLE.1: Machine Learning Requirements Analysis
  Defines and analyzes machine learning requirements, ensuring they are clear, complete and aligned with system-level requirements.
- MLE.2: Machine Learning Architecture
  Focuses on the collection, preparation and management of data used for training and testing machine learning models, emphasizing data quality and relevance.
- MLE.3: Machine Learning Model Training
  Covers the design, training and validation of machine learning models, ensuring they meet specified performance and reliability criteria.
- MLE.4: Machine Learning Testing Model
  Deals with testing machine learning models into production environments.

Additional ASPICE features associated with these processes are:

- MLE.1: Machine Learning Requirements Analysis
  It has 7 base practices (or process requirements) and 5 expected output
- MLE.2: Machine Learning Architecture
  It has 7 base practices and 5 expected output
- MLE.3: Machine Learning Model Training
  It has 7 base practices and 6 expected output
- MLE.4: Machine Learning Test Model
  It has 5 base practices and 6 expected output.

4 Critical Analysis of ASPICE® 4.0 Machine Learning Process Requirements

The following sections contain the authors' critical analysis [11] of machine learning engineering process group of ASPICE®.

The following critical analysis does at aims at providing a systematic and in-depth review of ASPICE® content related to machine learning, but rather an initial qualitative effort conducted by an ASPICE® professional to promote the discussion and growth within the ASPICE® community and automotive industry.

It is important to emphasize that ASPICE® is process model that is widely and world-wide applied by OEMs and suppliers - this implies that even a minimal improvement in terms of its understandability, suitability and applicability results in a huge benefit for the software automotive industry.

4.1 Analysis Method

Critical analysis is a method of examining, evaluating, and interpreting information or ideas to understand their meaning, strengths, and weaknesses [6]. Key features of a critical analysis are:

- Interpretation: Understanding the deeper meaning or message behind the content.
- Evaluation: Assessing the quality, effectiveness, and implications of the work.
- Evidence-Based Judgment: Formulating conclusions supported by data, examples, or logical reasoning.

In the context of this analysis, the process SUP.11 Machine Learning Data Management is out of scope as it is not pivotal in the quality evaluation of machine learning engineering process group.

The method applied by the authors is meant to be a trade-off between the application of expert judgment and of a structured approach guided by the analysis of specific features or quality attributes selected by the authors. The quality attributes (listed in alphabetic order) used by the authors to identify observations for an enlarged public debate are:

1. Adequacy of each MLE process output expectations in terms of nature and content
2. Compatibility with other relevant standards
3. Completeness vs. state of the art of machine learning engineering
4. Integration within the overall ASPICE® framework
5. Relevancy of process requirements vs. state of the art of machine learning engineering
6. Suitability for industrial implementation by OEMs and Suppliers
7. Technology independence
8. Understandability.

Accordingly, the analysis is structured with a general section to collect observations across the MLE process group, dedicated sections listing specific observations to end with additional considerations, if any.

It is intentional avoiding the introduction of articulated proposals for improvement as this is meant to be addressed by a more coral effort in a second stage of this initiative.

4.2 General Findings

Observation 0 MLE process group appears to be structured in a basic way, especially in terms of the limited number of base practices which tends to lead to oversimplification. It inevitably needs further development for a more fruitful adoption in industrial practice.

Observation 1 MLE process group is not depicted explicitly according to a V model which is instead fully applicable in this context [12].

Observation 2 The overall MLE process group leans in unbalanced way towards the software engineering side of machine learning engineering and avoids its strict links with system and HW engineering.

Observation 3 The overall MLE process group leans in implicit way towards deep learning that is actually a sub-set of machine learning (which is a subset of AI).

4.3 MLE.1: Machine Learning Requirements Analysis

The purpose is to refine the machine learning-related software requirements into a set of ML requirements.

4.3.1 MLE.1 Process Improvement Opportunities

Observation 4 MLE.1 BP.1 does not involve system requirements (only SW requirements) which are fully relevant to machine learning engineering.

Observation 5 The guidance to structure machine learning requirements in BP.2 by means of "Note" statements content is too generic.

4.4 MLE.2: Machine Learning Architecture

The purpose is to establish an ML architecture supporting training and deployment, consistent with the ML requirements, and to evaluate the ML architecture against defined criteria.

4.4.1 MLE.2 Process Improvement Opportunities

Observation 6: MLE.2 BP.5 appears to be propagated as is from SWE.3 without taking into adequate consideration the specifics of machine learning engineering.

Observation 7: MLE.2 BP.6 does not address traceability to SYS.2 (system architecture level).

4.5 MLE.3: Machine Learning Training

The purpose is to optimize the ML model to meet the defined ML requirements.

4.5.1 MLE.3 Process Improvement Opportunities

Observation 8: MLE.3 BP.3 is excessively dense in terms of process content as it addresses too succinctly a set of highly complex process steps that are the core of machine learning engineering.

Observation 9: MLE.3 BP.4 does not address traceability between training data set and test data set.

Observation 10: MLE.3 process does not address explicitly "Record and evaluate the ML training and validation results" as it is required for MLE.4 process (for test data).

4.6 MLE.4: Machine Learning Model Testing

The purpose is to ensure compliance of the trained ML model and the deployed ML model with the ML requirements.

4.6.1 MLE.4 Process Improvement Opportunities

Observation 11: MLE.4 BP.4 is not fully clear and as result it may lead to confusion and overhead. It might require re-wording and more guidance in shape of "Note" statements.

4.7 Additional Considerations

Observation 12: The introduction of Machine Learning into Automotive SPICE® 4.0 while providing a structured approach to the discipline lacks an explicit integration with key automotive standards such as ISO 26262 [4], ISO 21448 [3], ISO 21434 [7] and others.

5 Conclusions and Final Remarks

As machine learning is now part of the state of the art for the development of automotive electronic, ASPICE® 4.0 has introduced a new process group for Machine Learning, Engineering to assess the process quality of the related project implementations.

The critical analysis conducted in this paper by the authors has identified about ten observations that could be instrumental to an improvement initiative of this segment of the standard.

In conclusion this paper reflects the fact that the MLE process group specification added in Automotive SPICE® 4.0 is a usable process quality evaluation tool for the automotive industry and, in the opinion of the authors it suffers, unsurprisingly, of limited maturity in terms of content and process guidance.

References

1. Automotive SPICE® 4.0 - Process Capability Assessment Model (2023)
2. ISO/IEC 33004 - Information technology - Process assessment - Requirements for process reference, process assessment and maturity models (2015)
3. ISO 21448 - Road vehicles - Safety of the intended functionalit (2022)
4. ISO 26262 - Road vehicles - Functional safety (2018)
5. https://visuresolutions.com/automotive/machine-learning/
6. https://researchmethod.net/critical-analysis/
7. ISO/SAE 21434 - Road vehicles - Cybersecurity Engineering (2021)
8. https://poisson.phc.dm.unipi.it/~quattrocchi/ML.pdf
9. Mondal, S., Goswami, S.: Machine learning applications in automotive engineering: Enhancing vehicle safety and performance. J. Process Manage. New Technol. **12**, 61–71 (2024)
10. AI in Automotive Market Size - By Component, By Technology, By Process, By Application, Growth Forecast (2025–2034)
11. Singh, A. Critical analysis and writing the critique. SSRN Elect. J. (2021)
12. Falcini, F., Lami, G. and Costanza, A. M. Deep learning in automotive software. IEEE Softw. **34**(3 (May 2017)), 56–63 (2017)

Software Product Quality: Some Thoughts About Its Evolution and Perspectives in the AI years

Luigi Buglione[1]([✉]) and Francesco Merola[2]

[1] GUFPI-ISMA (Gruppo Utenti Function Point Italia – Italian Software Metrics Association),
Roma, Italia
`luigi.buglione@gufpi-isma.org`
[2] ISTI-CNR, PISA , Italy
`francesco.merola@isti.cnr.it`

Abstract. "Quality is free" was the title of a famous 1979 book by Philip Crosby, one of the Total Quality Management (TQM) gurus that for many people could have been misleading. "Quality" is part of what currently are the so-called NFRs (Non- Functional Requirements), complementing FURs (Functional User Requirements) from a product-view perspective. Any requirement generates tasks/activities (thus efforts and costs, it's not free at all…) and must be properly sized for improving project estimates from the early stages. Quality Models (QMs) constantly evolved from the mid '70s, from the FCM (Factor-Criteria-Model) until the current ISO models included in the SQuARe family (25000 series). The last model published in 2023 was the ISO/IEC 25059 about a revision of the 25010quality model in the light of these AI years. This paper will discuss from an evolutionary perspective what software quality has been, is and should/could be perceived and defined during next years, by a measurement perspective.

Keywords: Software Quality · Quality Models · Non · functional Requirements · FPA · SNAP · ISO 25010 · ISO 25012 · ISO 25059 · GQM · SQuARe

1 Introduction

'Quality' is a risky and misleading term because including so many meanings and attributes – even if often seen simply as 'defectability' - within a single word that often in assessments and evaluations it besides in the 'qualitative' side more than be extended also in the 'quantitative' one, finding proper measures for quantifying it. Thus, questions such as 'which is the value for quality? How to measure quality?' are typical also in the Software Engineering community. It can be quite easy to count something but less to evaluate its quality side, because difficult to express the core question ("what does it mean quality"?). Philip Crosby, one of the Total Quality Management (TQM) gurus, in one of his most known books discussed that "quality (part of what now are called non-functional aspects) is NOT for free" [1]. Each activity included in a project scope needs effort and thus costs. Another well-known quote from Tom Demarco said

G. Scanniello et al. (Eds.): PROFES 2025, LNCS 16362, pp. 353–365, 2026.
https://doi.org/10.1007/978-3-032-12092-2_30

that "you cannot control what you cannot measure". But coming one step back, it's also true that "you cannot measure what you cannot define". Coming again one step back, "you cannot define what you don't know". Thus, it's a knowledge problem and the priority is to move from a common, shared definition. Reading these three statements in the opposite order, (1) if you know something, you're able to properly describe it and share such definition with others; (2) if you're able to share definitions, it'll be easier to quantify such 'thing' in the same way (looking at metrology, two measurers should vary very few counting/evaluating the same 'thing' → repeatability); (3) if you're able to measure something in a proper way, understanding what attribute(s) you're measuring, you can have information and should be sufficiently aware for taking decisions. Just a short example for better expressing the need and value when having (or not) a clear and not ambiguous definition: asking what is a LOC (Line of Code), possible answers could be: (a) a physical statement; (b) a logical statement; and both could be complemented (c) with or (d) without commented lines. Thus, counting LOCs for a software system, numbers could vary a lot just applying slightly different definitions.[1] Another short example with Function Points (FP): the IFPUG method till v4.2 formally included the so-called VAF (Value Adjustment Factor), expressing 14 non-functional attributes 'adjusting' the initial functional size value. Thus, AFP (Adjusted FP) formula included also VAF, while UFP (Unadjusted FP) not. But what should the FP acronym mean? Which should be the right number of Function Points to count and declare for such activity? As in Fig. 1, since any 'thing' to be evaluated is a mix of quantity and quality and each side has different parameters for being evaluated (in terms of productivity, costs and so on), it's fundamental to deeply analyze the 'quality' side – that has been right now the less explored (also because more complex) part of the 'yin-yang' representation.

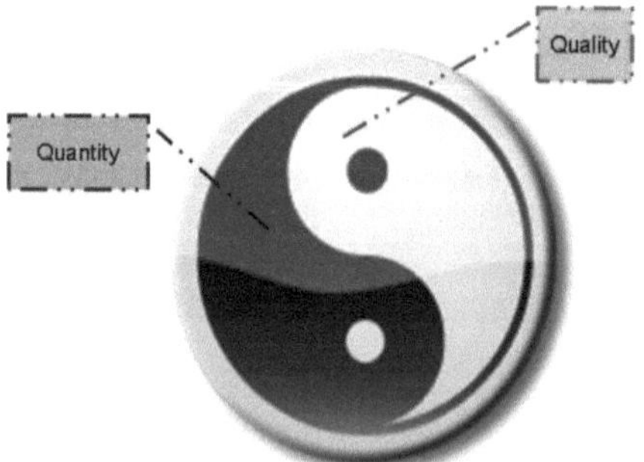

Fig. 1. Quantity and Quality – a 'Yin-Yang' representation[2]

This paper - that expands and updates a 2014 text [3] - is organized as follows: Sect. 2 will propose a short history of software quality models (QM) from mid '70s on. Section 3 will discuss the stakeholders' issue: the inclusion (or not) of an attribute in a

---

[1] According to Jones [2], there could be variability till 500% between extremes.

[2] Another way to express the same concept is using a coin: quality and quantity are the two faces of a coin. It's not possible to obtain a comprehensive evaluation not dealing with both faces. But each one has its own properties (attributes) and measures.

QM could be also due to the viewpoint faced and the stakeholders included (or not) in the analysis. Moving from the historical perspective shown, Sect. 4 will propose insights about how QM are evolving and should still evolve for properly catching the value for software quality during next AI years.

2 A Short History of Quality Models (QM)

Our core question is: what is quality? 'Quality' is a multi-facet term because it's an aggregator for multiple attributes. If you should express why, you've appreciated a certain food, you would start to list a series of 'attributes' such as flavor, taste, way to be presented, freshness of ingredients, the quality/price ratio, etc. Next step would be their quantification, trying to find a shared way to 'count' them. That's the application of the well-known Goal-Question-Metric (GQM) paradigm [4]. The same happened (and still happens) in Software Engineering with Quality Models (QM). If the 'quantity' side expresses the functionalities (what the software product – not the software project! - is asked to do), the 'quality' side should express the non-functionalities (how those functions should work for satisfying its users-clients). Thus, a QM can be defined as a shared list of attributes/characteristics that an entity of interest (EoI) can own, expressing its non-functional side (how'). A QM can be articulated in one or more tiers: in the second case, there will be a hierarchy of attributes with high-level and low- level attributes. For 'completing' a QM, typically a further tier is added with measures that help in quantifying a certain attribute. Now, a list of well-known QMs will be presented, highlighting their distinctive features to identify useful elements for improving the next generation of QMs.

2.1 FCM (Factor-Criteria-Model)

This is the first QM, produced in the mid '70s within the Air Navy [5].

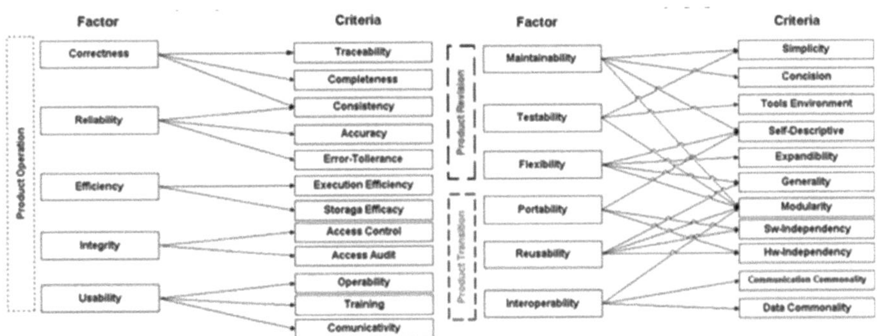

Fig. 2. Factor-Criteria-Model

It contained 11 factors (the first layer-tier) and 23 criteria (the second layer). Each factor was linked to 2+ criteria, as shown in Fig. 2. Of course, as in any QM, each element needs to have a clear definition with unambiguous statements. Factors were classified into three moments in time along the software life cycle (SLC): product operation, product revision, product transition.

2.2 Boehm Quality Model

One year later, Boehm proposed his own QM [6], with 7 high-level characteristics (1st level) and 12 primitive characteristics (2nd level), as shown in Fig. 3. Also here, a high-level characteristic could be linked to 2+ primitive characteristics. This model introduced the 'utility' concept, splitting the 'as-is utility' and the 'maintainability' for software products.

2.3 ISO 9126:1991

Moving from such early QMs, ISO decided – after the realising of the first 9001 version in 1986 – to release its own QM [7]. The model included 6 characteristics and 18 sub-characteristics (shown in Fig. 4). Here each high-level characteristic is subdivided in a more refined list, with no-crossed links.

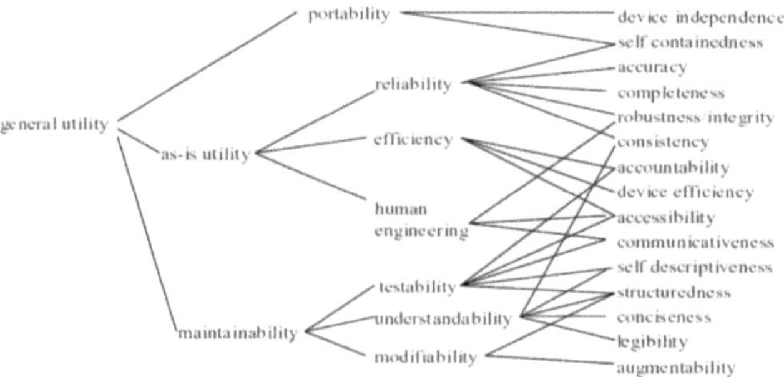

Fig. 3. Boehm's Quality Model

IEEE 1061-1992 replied the content of ISO 9126:1991, including such list of 'attributes' in the Appendix A. In 1998, IEEE 1061-1998 deleted such list, considering an open list of values and not a closed list of attributes.

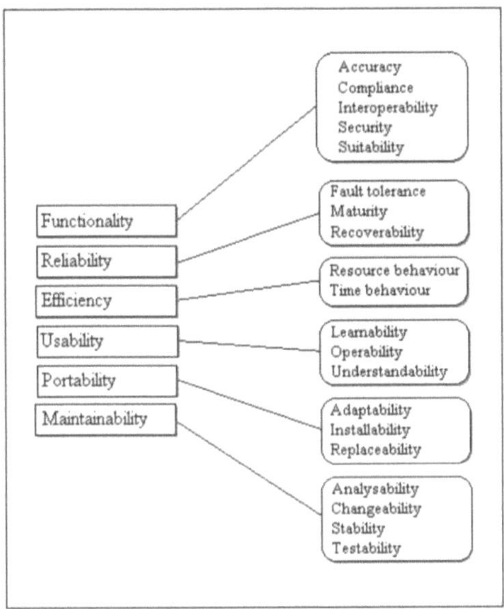

Fig. 4. ISO 9126:1991

2.4 ISO 9126-1:2001

After 10 years, ISO refined its view on quality and proposed the new version for the 9126 QM [8]. This introduced the concept of different viewpoints by different stakeholders: internal, external (Fig. 5) and quality in use viewpoints (Fig. 6). The first two contain 6 characteristics and 26 sub-characteristics. Each low-level characteristic was linked with 1+ process(es) from the ISO/IEC 12207 process model for any related process improvement activity. The quality in-use viewpoint added four additional characteristics.

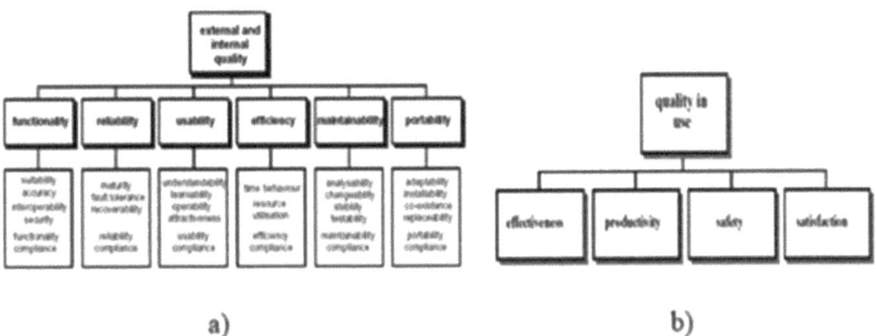

Fig. 5. ISO 9126-1:2001 – External/Internal Quality views (a) and Quality in-use view (b)

2.5 ISO 25010:2011

After 10 more years, ISO revised again its view on quality and evolved 9126 into the SQuaRE (Software product Quality Requirements and Evaluation) 25000 series with the new 2501x block of standards [9].

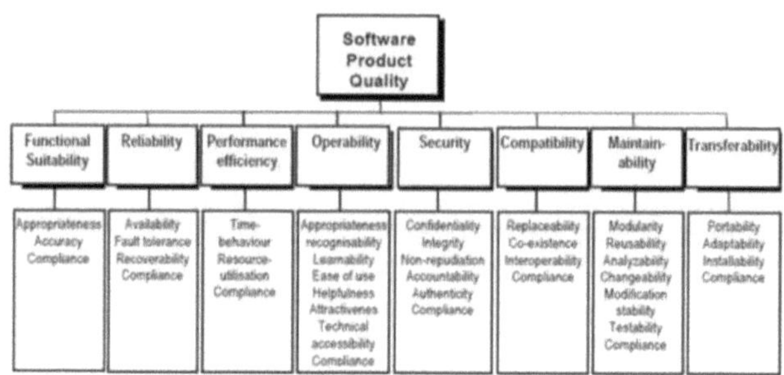

Fig. 7. ISO 25010:2011

ISO 25010:2011 included 8 characteristics and 38 sub-characteristics, depicted in Fig. 7. It refined some characteristics (e.g. Usability evolved into Operability, stressing more the Accessibility issue than before) and introduced others as Security.

2.6 ISO 25010:2023

The current version of this ISO standard – revised after 12 years - now includes 9 characteristics and 40 sub-characteristics (see Fig. 8). The term 'Usability' evolved in 'Interaction Capability', 'Safety' was a new characteristic added and now 'Replaceability' became 'Flexibility', adding some interesting sub-characteristics like 'Scalability'. The 'quality' concept is evolving, and a growing number of attributes shows an increasing impact of non-functional attributes when managing a software projects. At the same time, this revision of the ISO 25010 standard kept out the 'quality- in-use' attributes, creating a separate document, coded 25019 [10] (Fig. 9).

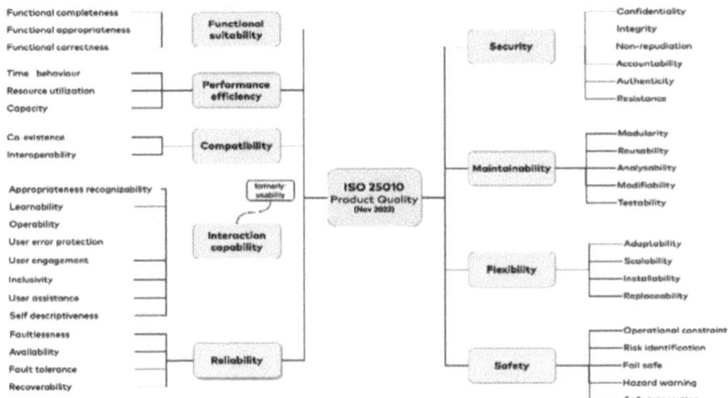

Fig. 8. ISO 25010:2023

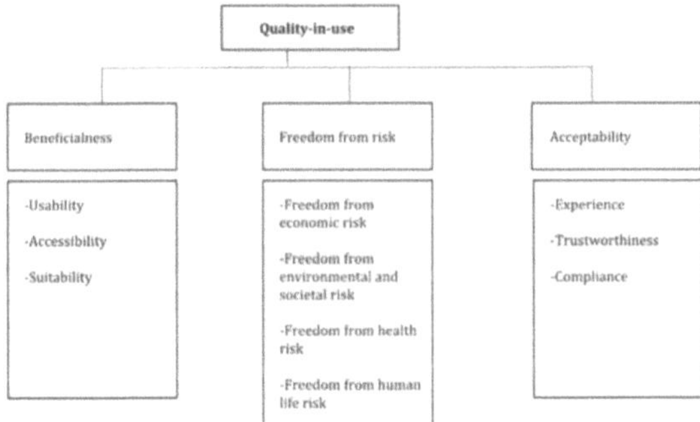

Fig. 9. ISO 25019:2023

2.7   ISO 25059:2023

After many years, now it's the "AI (Artificial Intelligence) age" and specific QMs are (and will be) in place. The ISO 25059 QM is designed to cover this role, and is shown in Fig. 10.

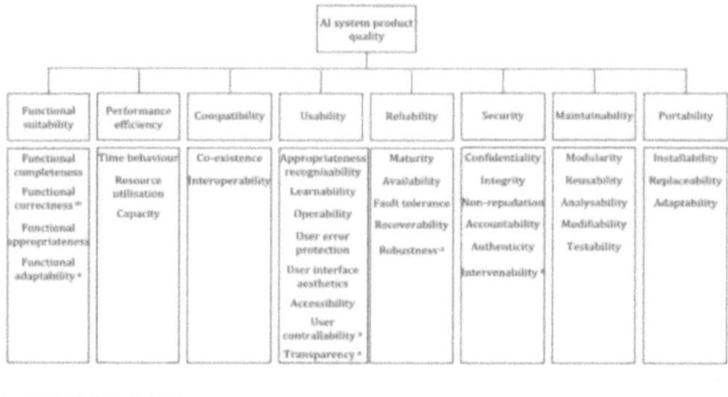

Fig. 10. ISO 25059:2023 [11]

Five (5) new sub-characteristics and one (1) modified against the original 25010:2011 version (not the 2023 one previously discussed), working on "Functional Suitability", "Usability", "Reliability" and "Security". Notably, the standard introduces attributes such as "Robustness" and "Transparency", which do not typically apply to traditional software, but are of paramount importance for AI software.

Due to its novelty, the 20509 doesn't currently have its 'metric companion' document, as ISO 25023:2016 is for ISO 25010:2011. Since AI software are 'hungry' for (good) data in order to improve their reliability, the ideal companion is more and more likely to be ISO 25012, the Data Quality Model [12]. Created in 2008, it represents a fundamental standard. Incorrect data might not generate a software incident but rather a service incident. For example, a driver's license may have expired. From a service management perspective, this should lead to actions concerning the driver and their driving activity, even though the software continues to function correctly when updating such data. Additional or improved controls could be implemented, but from a technical perspective, the software would still be working properly, while the data itself would fail to meet the 'Currentness' characteristic.

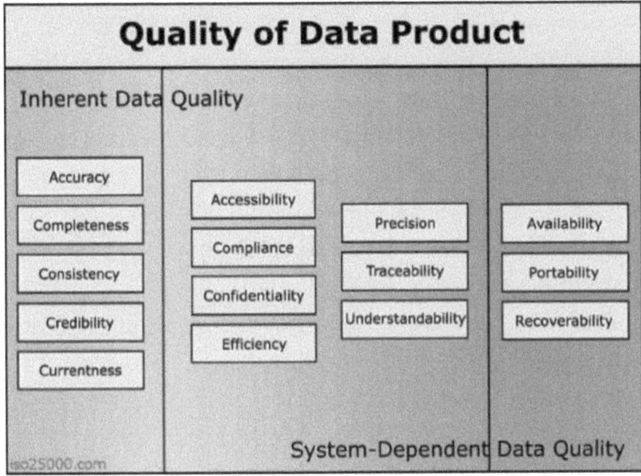

Fig. 11. ISO 25012:2008 [12]

In these AI years (and what we'll see in the short while) it's sufficient to consider how much time LLMs (Large Language Models) need for being trained and ask to be excused if a people correct them…In particular, the 'inherent data quality' attributes (see Fig. 11) will take more attention from the project teams.

2.8 Other QMs and NFR-related approaches

Other possible QMs are:

- <u>FURPS(+)</u>: FURPS is the acronym for a software product quality taxonomy – as well as ISO 9126 - by Grady & Caswell [13] and refined with more attributes into FURPS + [14]. FURPS stands for Functionality (to be split into: Feature Set, Capabilities, Generality, Security), Usability (Human Factors, Aesthetics, Consistency, Documentation), Reliability (Frequency/severity of failure, Recoverability, Predictability, Accuracy, Mean time to failure), Performance (Speed, Efficiency, Resource consumption, Throughput, Response time), Supportability (Testability, Extensibility, Adaptability, Maintainability, Compatibility, Configurability, Serviceability, Installability, Localizability, Portability). The " +" addition represents an aid for remembering concerns such as: Design requirements, Implementation requirements, Interface requirements and Physical requirements.
- <u>ECSS-E-10A + ISO 21351:2005</u>: ECSS (European Cooperation for Space Standardization) is an initiative established to develop a coherent, single set of user- friendly standards for use in all European space activities. Among the several standards produced, 'technical requirements' are diffusely treated. ECSS-E-10A [15] was used for creating ISO 21351:2005 [16].
- <u>IFPUG VAF</u>: from Albrecht's initial study till IFPUG CPM v4.2, the FPA method proposed a 'value adjustment factor' (VAF) based on 14 non-functional attributes (GSC – General System Characteristics), mostly referred to the software product, some others to the software project entity. The 14 GSC are: Data Communication, Distributed Data Processing; Performance; Heavily Used Configuration; Transaction Rate; Online Data Entry; End-User Efficiency; Online Update; Complex Processing;

Reusability; Installation Ease; Operational Ease; Multiple sites; Facilitate change. The aim of VAF was to 'adjust' the product functional size by a series of quality attributes for 'optimizing' the statistical relationship in historical series of adjusted product functional size vs project effort. In 1998 ISO decided to keep of such element from any FSM (Functional Size Measurement) method, because not proportional to the product functional side, stating that non-functional requirements (NFR) must be evaluated apart from FUR in a different way. In the current IFPUG CPM v4.3 such list has been maintained in Appendix C [17].

- IFPUG SNAP: IFPUG proposed in 2011 a new separate methodology from FPA named SNAP (Software Non-functional Assessment Process). From the analysis of product NFR, the method calculates the number of SNAP Points (SP). The current v2.4 [18, 19] includes 14 sub-categories grouped into 4 categories. As in FPA, each sub- category has 2 + complexity parameters for deriving for each SCU (SNAP Counting Unit) the associated number of SP. Here the list of categories and sub-categories that could be used also as a QM, not considering the SP calculation algorithm: **Data Operations** (Data Entry Validation; Logical & Mathematical Operations; Data Formatting; Internal Data Movements; Delivering Added Value to Users by Data Configuration); **Interface Design** (UI Changes; Help Methods; Multiple Input Methods; Multiple Output Methods); **Technical Environment** (Multiple Platform; Database Technology; Batch Processing System); **Architecture** (Component Based Software (CBS); Multiple Input/Output Interface).

3 Possible Criteria for a QM

Analyzing the proposed QM it is possible to derive the following considerations in order to understand the value to be provided by a QM:

- Stakeholders – as stressed in well-recognized management guides such as PMBOK [20] or ITIL [21], it is fundamental to understand from the beginning which are the right stakeholders to involve for creating a good QM. For instance, users are fundamental but often have been considered only for providing final feedback (customer/user satisfaction), not for driving assessment criteria. Remember that a customer (the business) is not necessarily the user but could be separate people. Remember also to involve those secondary stakeholders (e.g. foreign tourists could be useful for describing how to improve a mobile touristic app for a certain city providing a different viewpoint than a citizen from that city).
- Grouping criteria – quality represents the 'how' a product should be realized according to initial requirements. Thus, several criteria should be considered. For instance (a) Time: a lifecycle view should be included and/or linked to a QM (e.g. ISO 9126–1:2001 inserted the related process(es) from ISO 12207 and target audience for any sub-characteristic). It could be useful for improving the product during its lifetime for maintainability purposes. (b) Viewpoint/Stakeholder positioning: internal, external and quality in-use viewpoints, as proposed by ISO from 2001 with 9126–1 and now with the 25010 standards; (c) Viewpoint/Context-Content: the wider the list of attributes and sub-attributes, the more comprehensive the analysis of a product by its QM. As in the Balanced Scorecard (BSC) approach, it'd be desirable to have at least

4–5 perspectives (e.g. time, cost, risk, quality, ethics, etc.) against which grouping quality attributes.

4 Quality Models and the Next AI Years

Looking at the content of the presented QM against the period they were produced, it is possible to list a series of thoughts, possibly useful for designing QM for the next AI years:

- Content: having several product attributes in a QM is useful for better describing and evaluating a product, but as usual – the right number of attributes is in the middle (not too many, not too few). Product observation is fundamental for listing what is needed, and it could change with time. For instance, smartphones have created a different way to describe and define 'operability' and/or 'usability' against mobile software produced just 3–4 years ago because of the 'touching' interaction on the screen. Again, sustainability can be a new product quality attribute to consider for new systems/software [22] because of a 'greener' perspective on software. In the AI years, the 'interaction capability' of AI-based software and a reduced number of interactions for receiving a trustable information will be the 'black-oil'.
- Usage: QM can be used not only for a 'retrospective' evaluation but also in early SLC phases as simple checklists for understanding the level of completeness for a product design, moving from a 'wishing list'. Another way to use QM is for estimation purposes: since QM express NFR, estimators can use needed NFR-related (quality) measures to be included (at least $2+$ ones) as independent proxies in estimation models, allowing the reduction of MRE (Mean Relative Error) figures as much as possible, saving project resources and improving the overall project value for its stakeholders (e.g. ISO 9126 parts 2-3-4 define a plenty of measures to be read and applied). The increasing number of NFR-issues in QMs confirm such trend: 'value' is asking more and more the accomplishment of non-functional requirements. AI tools can help to better pre-classify requirements using the "ABC schema" [28], or help creating mind maps as the input for a root-cause analysis (RCA) [29] (e.g. with Google NotebookLM).
- Perspectives/Viewpoint: a stakeholder's analysis is needed for understanding if the proper number of viewpoints is included (or not) in a QM. If too few perspectives have been included when designing a QM, feedback could be lower than expected at the delivery stage. A more comprehensive design can reduce maintenance costs along with the product expected lifetime. New AI-based competencies are also emerging, and need to be considered for producing better software. Some examples could come from this recent UNESCO initiative [23] or in Italy the UNINFO working group on roles and skills in the new AI world [27] that will impact on the new versions of e-CF, the European Competency Framework).
- Measurement: last but not least, the measurement issue, that's the lower level in a multi-tier model as a QM is. People less skilled in measurement typically affirm that anything can be measured. But, as stated in the introduction, if you are able to describe an entity of interest, you'll also be able to measure it (e.g. using the GQM

approach). ISO 15939 [24] refined the GQM paradigm proposing MIM (Measurement Information Model) template that could be a good way to start defining how to monitor & control a non-functional (quality) attribute for a product. The suggestion is to follow a revised version of the well-known 5W + H approach (who, why, what, when, where, how), adding a second 'H' (how much), that could represent 'targets – thresholds' for checking the process-in levels for that measure. AI can speed up and reduce working times, but the accuracy for results against historical data is and will remain an essential goal.

5 Conclusions and Final Remarks

Quality Models (QM) represent a good way in Software Engineering for evaluating software products from their initial concept till their realization and in-use stage. Non-functional requirements (NFR) are composed of quality and technical requirements; thus, quality is one the two sides, maybe the more complex to analyze. Since quality is a multifaceted concept, it's very difficult to find a complete and stable definition for it: quality definition can evolve over time related to newer ways users could request, of course influenced by technology (e.g. smartphones, cloud computing, etc.). QM can help sharing the view on products and be used both in a qualitative (checklists) and quantitative way (measuring low-level attributes with 1+ related measures). The new upcoming AI years will consolidate some new technology paradigm and will propose new ones: the important thing will be to observe more interesting trends for proposing evolutions and integrations of new, emerging facets for quality more than creating new models at all. Again, even if trivial, we need to clearly define which is the entity to be analyzed (product, process, project, organization, resources) in order to avoid effort/cost estimation issues [25]. Evolution, not revolution, can be the right way to understand more about the 'how' realize better software systems.

References

1. Crosby, P.: Quality is Free: The Art of Making Quality Certain, Mc Graw-Hill, 1979, ISBN 9780070145122
2. Jones, C.: Applied Software Measurement: Assuring Productivity and Quality, 2/e. McGraw-Hill (1996). ISBN 978-0070328266
3. Buglione, L.: Software product quality: some thoughts about its evolution and perspectives. In: 20th IMEKO TC4 International Symposium and 18th International Workshop on ADC Modelling and Testing Research on Electric and Electronic Measurement for the Economic Upturn, Benevento, Italy, Sept 15–17, , pp. 737–742 (2014). ISBN-14: 978-92-990073-2-7
4. Basili, V.B., Caldiera, G., Rombach, H.D.: The Goal Question Metric Approach, Encyclopedia of Software Engineering. Wiley (1994). www.cs.umd.edu/projects/SoftEng/ESEG/papers/gqm.pdf
5. McCall, J.A., Richards, P.K., Walters, G.F.: Factors in Software Quality, Voll. I, II, III: Final Tech. Report, RADC-TR-77-369. Rome Air Development Center, Air Force System Command, Griffiss Air Force Base, NY (1977)
6. Boehm, B.W., Brown, J.R., Kaspar, H., Lipow, H., MacLeod, G.J., Merritt, M.: Characteristics of Software Quality. Elsevier North-Holland (1978)

7. ISO/IEC.: IS 9126:1991 - Information Technology - Software Product Evaluation – Quality Characteristics and Guidelines for Their Use
8. ISO/IEC.: IS 9126-1:2001 - Software Engineering -- Product Quality -- Part 1: Quality Model
9. ISO/IEC.: IS 25010:2023, Systems and Software Engineering -- Systems and Software Quality Requirements and Evaluation (SQuaRE) -- System and Software Quality Models
10. ISO/IEC 25019:2023 – Quality-in-use Models (Nov 2023)
11. ISO/IEC 25059:2023 – Quality Models for AI Systems (June 2023)
12. ISO/IEC 25012:2008 (R2025) – Data Quality Models (Dec 2008)
13. Grady, R., Caswell, D.: Software Metrics: Establishing a Company-Wide Program. Prentice Hall (1987). ISBN 0138218447
14. EELES, P.: Capturing Architectural Requirements. IEEE DeveloperWorks (2005). www-128.ibm.com/developerworks/rational/library/4706.html
15. ECSS.: Space Engineering – System Engineering: Part 6. Functional and Technical Specifications. European Cooperation for Space Standardization, ECSS-E-10 Part 6A rev.1 (October 31 2005). www.ecss.nl
16. ISO.: IS 21351:2005, Space Systems – Functional and Technical Specifications (May 19, 2005). www.iso.ch
17. IFPUG.: Function Points Counting Practices Manual (release 4.3.1). International Function Point User Group, Westerville, Ohio (January 2010). www.ifpug.org
18. IFPUG.: SNAP (Software Non-Functional Assessment Process) APM v2.4. (Sept 2017). www.ifpug.org
19. ISO/IEC/IEEE 32430:2025, Software Engineering – Software Non-functional Size Measurement (Feb 2025)
20. PMI.: A Guide to the Project Management Body of Knowledge (PMBOK), 7th ed. (2021). www.pmi.org
21. AXELOS. ITIL Foundation, 4th ed. (2019). www.axelos.com
22. Lami, G., Buglione, L.: Measuring Software Sustainability from a Process-Centric Perspective, Proceedings of IWSM-MENSURA 2012, 22th Int.Workshop on Software Measurement and 7th Int. Conference on Software Process and Product Measurement, Assisi (Italy), October 17–19, pp.53–39 (2012)
23. UNESCO.: What you need to know about UNESCO's new AI competency frameworks for students and teachers (Feb 20 2025). https://shorturl.at/4HfrB
24. ISO/IEC/IEEE 15939:2017 (R2022) - Systems and Software Engineering -- Measurement Process (May 2017)
25. Buglione, L., Ebert, C.: Estimation, Encyclopedia of Software Engineering, Taylor & Francis Publisher (June 2012). ISBN: 978-1-4200-5977-9
26. Kaplan, R., Norton, D.: The Balanced Scorecard: Translating Strategy Into Action, Harvard Business School Press (1996). ISBN 0875846513
27. UNI/CT 526/GL 08 "Profili di ruolo professionale operanti nel settore AI". www.uninfo.it
28. Buglione L., The next frontier: measuring and evaluating the nonfunctional productivity, metricviews. IFPUG Newslett. **6**(2), 11–14 (August 2012). http://goo.gl/Bznof
29. Buglione, L.: Strengthening CMMI maturity levels with a quantitative approach to root-cause analysis. Proceedings of the 5th Software Measurement European Forum (SMEF 2008), Milan (Italy)

Correction to: Development of a Model-Driven DevOps Solution Based on Context-Engineered LLM Code Generation: PROFES Doctoral Symposium

Uldis Karlovs-Karlovskis

Correction to:
Chapter 10 in: G. Scanniello et al. (Eds.): *Product-Focused Software Process Improvement. Industry, Doctoral-Symposium, Tutorial, and Workshop Papers*, LNCS 16362, https://doi.org/10.1007/978-3-032-12092-2_10

In the originally published version of the chapter, the acknowledgments section was inadvertently missed. The acknowledgments section has been added as below.

The research leading to these results was supported by the EU Recovery and Resilience Facility within the Project No. 5.2.1.1.i.0/2/24/I/CFLA/003 "Implementation of consolidation and management changes at Riga Technical University, Liepaja University, Rezekne Academy of Technology, Latvian Maritime Academy and Liepaja Maritime College for the progress towards excellence in higher education, science and innovation" academic career PhD grant (ID 1017).

I would like to express my sincere gratitude to my thesis supervisor, Prof. Oksana Ņikiforova, and to Prof. Óscar Pastor and Prof. Jordi Cabot for their valuable guidance and support.

The updated version of this chapter can be found at
https://doi.org/10.1007/978-3-032-12092-2_10

Author Index

G. Scanniello et al. (Eds.): PROFES 2025, LNCS 16362, pp. 367–368, 2026.
https://doi.org/10.1007/978-3-032-12092-2

MIX
Papier aus verantwortungsvollen Quellen
Paper from responsible sources
FSC® C105338

If you have any concerns about our products,
you can contact us on
ProductSafety@springernature.com

In case Publisher is established outside the EU,
the EU authorized representative is:
**Springer Nature Customer Service Center GmbH
Europaplatz 3, 69115 Heidelberg, Germany**

Printed by Libri Plureos GmbH
in Hamburg, Germany